# Bland County
# Virginia

# MARRIAGES

# 1861–1929

## Jo Ann Tickle Scott

**Heritage Books**
**2024**

# HERITAGE BOOKS

*AN IMPRINT OF HERITAGE BOOKS, INC.*

## Books, CDs, and more—Worldwide

For our listing of thousands of titles see our website
at
www.HeritageBooks.com

Published 2024 by
HERITAGE BOOKS, INC.
Publishing Division
5810 Ruatan Street
Berwyn Heights, MD 20740

International Standard Book Number
Paperbound: 978-0-7884-7776-8

# FORWORD

I want to dedicate this book to my husband Emery and to my
daughter Jennifer, who have helped me make the time and to
my parents John Daniel & Ruby Morehead Tickle, who are missed.
My thanks to my cousins Parke Bogle and Donna Distel
for giving me the interest. Thanks to Ronnie Hall and all the
other Courthouse Folks for letting me have a place to work.

Having worked with Genealogy for about 3 years I'm very new to it.
However, this is something I feel that needs to be done. I want Bland
County to be among the others having their history in print.
I am proud of my county, and of the many families who have
lived here in the past and who live here now. I believe they
should be remembered.

The writing in the original book is very hard to read, at times
impossible. The spelling isn't the best and the pens they used,
at this time, were messy and hard to make the letters. If you
look at the original, you can see the changes taking place in
the way people write. If there are mistakes, they are not intentional.
They are just typos, or the case of the original being unreadable.

Many thanks to a very special lady, **Mildred Wilson Richardson,**
for the many hours she has given to help check the original
marriage certificates to make this book as correct as possible.
Information, gleaned from the certificates, has been added, causing
some jamming of words. Due to the work and index' being nearly
finished, before this was thought of, more room could not be made
unless the whole project was scrapped and completely redone.

If anyone knows the names of the people whose names are only
initials, please contact me. I would be most interested in the information.

Jo Ann Tickle Scott
Route 3 Box 55
Bland, VA 24315
Ph: 540-688-4458
E-mail: jotickle@aol.com

# Example
# How to read information in Book!

Date: =Month Day Year    of Marriage
Name: John Doe = 1 part of the couple
A. = Age
S.= Single, D. = Divorce, W.= Widowed/Widower
Bland, Wythe, etc are all VA counties
Counties outside this state are so noted.
P. = Parents' names
Oc. = Occupation of the Husband
M. = Minister who performed the marriage

** out of order due to mistakes in the original book
underlined surnames are maiden names of Women
*** one that was left out by mistake

First names of some of the males are abbreviated:
Wm. = William, Jno = John, Jas = James, Jos = Joseph, Rob't = Robert,
 Dan'l = Daniel, etc.

There have been several names added to the parents from the files I have
searched and of those that have been searched, and given to me,
by relatives and friends. Many thanks to all who have helped me to gather
the information that is in my files.  If everyone was as interested as you,
the genealogists' wouldn't have as much trouble gathering important data
as they sometimes do.

Begin Page 1 of Original Book

Date: 8-18-1861
Wm. J. Morehead — Minnie A. Neel
A. 26 S. Pulaski — A. 23 S. Giles
P. — P. Hiram & Nancy
Oc. Farmer — M. Wm. E. Neel

Date: 9-3-1861
Peter Litz — Mary E. Cline
A. 29 W. Wythe — A. 24 W. Wythe
P. Samuel & July A. — P. Franklin Akers
Oc. Farmer — M. A.M. Young

Date: 10-1-1861
A.J. Stowers — Mary Lampert
A. 25 S. Tazewell — A. 19 S. Wythe
P. Wm. & Christina — P. Joseph & Elizabeth
Oc. Farmer — M. A.M. Young

Date: Nov 10, 1861
Wilbern Robinett — Clarissa Steele
A.28 S. Bland — A. 31 S. Tazewell
P.Dan'l & Elizabeth — P. David & Martha
Oc. Farmer — M. J.J. Greever

Date: 11-20-1861
Franklin Leonard — Jane Guillion
A.22 S. — A. 20 A.
P.John & Polly — P. Frank & Nancy
Oc. Farmer — M. J.J. Green

Date: 12-15-1861
James Andrew Wilson — Barbara A. Maxwell
A. 24 S. Smyth — A. 18 S. Bland
P. Wm. A. & Margaret — P. Isaac & Eva M.
Oc. Farmer — M. J.J. Green

Date: 12-26-1861
Henry W. Steel — Matilda Jane Kitts
A.37 S. Wythe — A. 24 S. Wythe
P.Christina Burris — P. Henry & Polly
Oc. Wheelwright — M. A.A. Ashworth

Date: 3-13-1862
William Andrews — Mary E. Neel
A. 28 S. Wythe — A. 19 S. Wythe
P. Hardy & Sarah — P. Fielding & Sophia
Oc. Farmer — M. Wm. E. Neel

Date: 4-16-1862
Daniel T. Aaron — Martha C. Edwards
A. 26 S. Tazewell — A. 17 S. Carroll
P.Robt. & Catherine — P. Wm. & Martha C.
Oc. Farmer — M. Wm. E. Neel

Date: 10-16-1862
James A. Dillow — Frances A. Grady
A. 23 S. Bland — A. 18 S. Bland
P. Addison & Louvisa — P. John & Amanda
Oc. Farmer — M. G.W.K. Green

Date: 10-30-1862
Ephriam Waddle — Emalouise Devor
A. 44 s. Wythe — A. 27 S. Wythe
P. Robinett & Polly — P. Wm. & Julia
Oc. Farmer — M.Geo. Wash. Kellinger Green

Date: 7-29-1862
John Henry Pegram — Almira A. Bogle
A. 30 W. NC — A. 23 S. Bland
P. Geo. & Willie — P. Jas. & Susan Kennison
Oc. Farmer — M. Martin Bibb

Date: 8-3-1862
Benjamin F. Clark — Mary S. E. Muncy
A.22 S.Washington, TN — A. 21 S. Giles
P. Hiram & Elizabeth — P. David & Parmelia
Oc. Farmer — M. Wm. E. Neel

Date: 11-5-1862
Thompson E. Gregory — Martha J. Steel
A.21 S. Pittsylvania Co. — A. 21 S. Wythe
P.Jon K. & Elizabeth — P. Geo. Steel
Oc. Farmer — M. Wm. E. Neel

Date: 11-19-1862
Nathaniel M. Farley — Mary A. Wilkinson
A. 45 W. Lee Co. — A. 24 W. Wythe
P. Francis & Mahala — P. Baltzer & Rhoda Helvey
Oc. Farmer — M. Joshua Bruce

Date: 12-4-1862
Hiram A. Neel — Margaret M. Steel
A.21 S. Tazewell — A. 19 S. Wythe
P. Rob't & Nancy — P. Geo. & Emma
Oc. Farmer — M. Samuel A. Wheeler

Date: 1-15-1863
Giles A. King | Mary E. Austin
A.21 S. Pulaski | A.18 S. Franklin
P. Allen & Sarah | P. John & Adaline
Oc. Farmer | M. John H. Hoge

Date: 12-4-1862
William Stowers | Elender Robinett
A. 50 W. Tazewell | A. 31 S. Wythe
P.Mordicia & Polly | P. Hiram & Rebecca
Oc. Farmer | M. G.W.K. Green

Date: 4-6-1863
George Thompson | Mary Ann Puckett
A.48 W. Wythe | A. 23 S. Tazewell
P.John & Rhoda | P. Polly Puckett
Oc. Farmer | M. W.E. Neel

Date: 5-5-1865
Harvey C. Hearn | Nancy E. Lukins
A.40 W. Wythe | A. 23 S. Montgomery
P. Wm. T. & Susannah | P.Abram & Emily
Hicks/ Hix |
Oc. Farmer | M. L.J. Miller

Date: 5-26-1863
A.J. Gearing | C.J. Hicks
A. 37 W. Augusta | A. 26 S. Tazewell
P. John & Elizabeth | P. Joseph S. Hicks
Oc. Saddler | M. G.W.K. Green

Date: 6-14-1863
John H. Duncan | Cinthia Caldwell
A. 31 S. Pulaski | A. 21 S. Mercer
P. Jas & Julia D. | P. Andrew Caldwell
Oc. Farmer | M. W.E. Neel

Date: 7-3-1863
Alex F. Miller | Nancy J. Hamilton
A.22 S. Giles | A. 20 S. Wythe
P. Charles & Ann M. | P. Timothy & Margaret
Oc. Farmer | M. L.J. Miller

Date: 8-25-1863
Thomas Jones | Lucinda Hopkins
A. 22 S. Wilson, NC | A. 21 S. Bland
P. Wm. & Nancy J. | P. Polly Hopkins
Oc. Farmer | M. W.E. Neel

Date: 10-20-1863
John W. McNeil | Cintha E. Miller
A. 31 S. Pochontas | A. 16 S. Bland
P. John & Rebecca | P. Abraham Woodson & Rachel Hearn
Oc. School teacher | M. L. J. Miller

Date: 11-25-1863
H.P. Thompson | Rebecca M. Pauley
A. 22 S. Wythe | A. 23 S. KY
P. Geo. & Polly | P.
Oc. Farmer | M. A. A. Ashworth

Date : 12-30-1863
George Steel | Louvicia Waddle
A. 56 W. Wythe | A. 34 S. Wythe
P. Rob't & Rebecca | P. Robinett & Polly
Oc. Farmer | M. Geo. Wash. Kellinger Green

Date : 1-5-1864
William Wooldrige | Eliza Melvin
A. 24 S. Appomatox | A. 19 S. Giles
P.Rob't & Elizabeth | P. Catherine Melvin
Oc. Farmer | M. John H. Hoge

Date: 1-5-1864
Daniel L. Harman | Frances E. Hamilton
A.23 S. Giles | A. 21 S. Wythe
P. Wesley & Phebe Fielder | P. Lochard & Mary
Oc. Farmer | M. L. J. Miller

Date 1-16-1864
Wm. C. Honaker | Polly Ann Ratliff
A.23 S. Pulaski | A. 21 S. Wythe
P. Henry & Elizabeth | P. Lewis B. & Polly Ann
Oc. Farmer | M. W. E. Neel

Date: 2-25-1864
Samuel G. Crockett | Barbara E. Thompson
A.23 S. Tazewell | A. 26 S. Wythe
P. John & Mary P. | P. Patten & Elizabeth
Oc. Blacksmith | M. Geo. Wash. Kellinger Green

Date: 2-19- 1864
Joseph B. Stump | Martha A. Stowers
A. 22 S. Tazewell | A. 18 S. Tazewell
P. Jacob & Polly | P. John & Dica
Oc. Farmer | M. W. E. Neel

Date: 3-15-1864
F. M. Alderman     Virginia O. Comerford
A. 23 S. Floyd     A. 21 S. Bland
P. Phillip & Polly     P. Jas & Isabelle

Oc. Farmer     M. G. W. Penley

Date: 3-17-1864
Lorenzo Dow Bogle     Charlotte Waddle
A. 39 W. Wythe     A. 27 S. Wythe
P. Geo Wm &     P. James & Nancy
Margaret Jane Ray Scott
Oc. Farmer     M.G.W.K. Green

Date : 7-1-1864
George Wash. Stowers     Mary A. Stowers
A. 20 S. Tazewell     A. 21 S. Wythe
P. Hickman & Polly     P. Wm. & Christina
Oc. Farmer     M. G.W.K. Green

Begin Page 2 of Original Book
Date: 8-15-1864
Joseph Thompson     Elizabeth Carr
A. 72 W. Wythe     A. 36 S. Giles
P. Andrew & Anna     P. Polly Carr
Oc. Farmer     M. G.W.K. Green

Date: 12-27-1864
B.D. Graves     Nancy Kegley
A.22 S. Augusta     A. 22 S. Wythe
P.Augustus & E.R.     P. Isaac & Prudence
Oc. Farmer     M. G.W.K. Green

Date: 1-25- 1864
John Johnson     Lydia Waddle
A. 28 S. Montreal, Can.     A. 33 W. Wythe
P. Geo & Susan     P. Dan'l & Eliz. Robinett
Oc. Farmer     M. G.W.K. Green

Date: 10-17-1865
Harvey Bennett Tickle     Nancy M. Smith
A.25 S. NC     A. 20 S. Wythe
P. Dan'l &     P. John D. & Sarah
Sarah Elizabeth Lineberry Blessing
Oc. Farmer     M. L. J. Miller

Date: 10-16-1865
A.J. Neel     Mary A. Noel
A.26 S. Tazewell     A. 24 W. Tazewell
P.Thos & Sarah     P. Mary Fox
Oc. Farmer     M. Geo. W. K. Green

Date: 3-17-1864
Jacob Franklin Kitts     Lutheria Bruce
A. 26 S. Wythe     A. 21 S. Wythe
P. Andrew J.&     P. Isaiah Bruce
Mary "Polly" Leedy     Naomi McNeil Evans
Oc. Farmer     M. G.W.K. Green

Date: 4-7-1864
James Milton Pruett     Elizabeth Armenta Fanning
A. 22 S. Giles     A. 19 S.Giles
P.Wm. & Elizabeth     P. Joseph & Jane

Oc. Farmer     M. G. W. Penley

Date: 8-2-1864
James A. S. Ratliff     Elizabeth Hagar
A. 26 S. Tazewell     A. 22 S. Tazewell
P. Lewis B. & Polly     P. Esq. Hagar & Elizabeth
Oc. Farmer     M. G.W. Martin

Date: 10-27-1864
William A. Purkey     Darthula Thompson
A. 23 S. Wythe     A. 24 S.Wythe
P. Dan'l & Letitcia     P. Archer & Polly
Oc. Farmer     M. G.W.K. Green

Date : 1-25-1864
Newton Waddle     Mary E. Finley
A. 22 S. Wythe     A. 19 S. Wythe
P. James & Nancy     P. Jas & Rebecca
Oc. Farmer     M. G.W.K. Green

Date: 10-26-1865
Eli Steel     Polly Angeline Havens
A. 24 S. Wythe     A. 23 S.Wythe
P. Rob't & Rhoda     P. A. & E.
Oc. Farmer     M. Geo. W. K.Green

Date: 10-17-1865
C. J. Hudson     Eliza Groseclose
A. 28 S. Wythe     A. 26 S. Wythe
P. Geo. & Hannah     P. Francis & Mary

Oc. Farmer     M. G.W.K. Green

Date: 11-16-1865
J.B. Henderson     Sarah A. Pauley
A. 30 S. Giles     A. 23 S. Wythe
P. J. A. & E.     P. Hiram & Barbara
Oc. Farmer     M. Geo. W. Penley

Date: 11-20-1865
Richard F. Sexton          Delilah S. Stafford
A.21 S. Morgan, KY         A. 21 S. Giles
P. Stephen & Martha        P. Wm & Jane
Oc. Farmer                 M. A. Q. Harman

Date: 11-5-1865
William F. Kimberling      Rebe' J. Kimberling
A. 24 S. Wythe             A. 26 S. Wythe
P. Sol. & Elizabeth        P. Jos. & Elizabeth
Oc. Farmer                 M.Geo. W.K. Green

Date: 10-25-1865
R.K. Kelly                 Mary Garyson
A. 23 A. Richmond, KY      A. 21 S. Smyth
P. Rob't E.& R.F.          P. F. & Nancy
Oc. Farmer                 M. Robert C. Graham

Date: 11-2-1865
W. C. Williams             Sallie Gillespie
A. 22 S. Giles             A. 24 S. Wythe
P. J. & N.                 P.
Oc. Farmer                 M. Geo. W. Penley

Date: 11-23-1865
David Wright               Martha Jane Morehead
A. 22 S. Giles             A. 20 S. Pulaski
P. John & S.               P. Dan'l F. &
                           Isabella Eliz. Saunders
Oc. Farmer                 M. B.F. White

Date: 11-17-1865
James Crabtree             A.J. Kinsel
A.22 S. Tazewell           A. 22 S. Wythe
P. J. &. P                 P. J. & M.
Oc. Farmer                 M. G.W.K. Green

Date: 12-13-1865
George Wohlford            Louv' J. Mustard
A. 23 S. Giles             A. 22 S. Giles
P.Sam'l & Eliz.            P. J. & L.
Nicewander
Oc. Farmer                 M. John H. Hoge

Date: 12-24-1865
Isaac F. Pruett            Lucinda S. Fanning
A. 24 S. Giles             A. 17 S. Giles
P. Wm & Elizabeth          P. Jos & Jane
Oc. Farmer                 M. L. J. Miller

Date: 10-26-1865
John D. Dillman            Barbara A. Kimberling
A. 24 S. Indiana           A. 19 S. Wythe
P. Geo & Mary A.           P. Jos & Elizabeth
Oc. Farmer                 M. Geo. W. K. Green

Date: 10-24-1865
Jno W. Lambert             Alpha Lambert
A. 21 S. Tazewell          A. 25 S. Giles
P. Thos. K. & Charl'       P. Jn. T. & Emily
Oc. Farmer                 M. G.W.K. Green

Date: 11-2-1865
Joseph Moore               Elizabeth Nestor
A. 21 S. Craig Co.         A. 26 W. Wythe
P.John & Isabel            P. Elizabeth Jones
Oc. Farmer                 M. J. P. Curtis

Date: 11-1-1865
Joseph Gills               Elizabeth Lury
A. 36 W. Franklin          A.34 S. Orange Co., NC
P. Gideon & Mary           P.
Oc. Farmer                 M. G.W.K. Green

Date: 11-8-1865
Johile Thompson            Mary Dudley
A.22 S. Wythe              A. 21 S. Giles
P. J. & Sally              P. Jas & Lucy
Oc. Farmer                 M. John H. Hoge

Date: 11-31-1865
W. W. Gullion              E. M. Dillman
A. 21 S. Smyth             A. 23 S. Indiana
P. F. & N. A. Gullion      P. G. & M.
Oc. Farmer                 M. G.W.K. Green

Date: 12-7-1865
F. J. Jones                M. A. Blankenship
A. 25 S. Franklin          A. 18 S. Giles
P. Wm & A.                 P. E. & S. A.

Oc. Farmer                 M. L. J. Miller

Date: 12-19-1865
A. S. Wilson               Joanna Hedrick
A. 24 S. Wythe             A. 16 S. Wythe
P. J.M. & E.               P. Rufus &
Oc. Mechanic               M. D. F. Palmer

4

Date : 12-12-1865  
Jno Thompson. Sr.    S. Bruce  
A. 40 W. Wythe    A. 38 W. Tazewell  
P. John Thompson    P. John Lewis  
Oc. Famer    M. G.W.K. Green  

Date: 1-28-1866  
Silo Adkins    M.V. Maxwell  
A. 28 S. Wayne    A. 22 W. Smyth  
P. P. & C. A.    P. M. J. & A. Wilson  

Oc. Farmer    M. J. J. Greever  

Date: 1-9-1866  
B. L. Nunn    M.E. Blankenship  
A. 19 S. Franklin    A. 18 S. Giles  
P. T. & N.    P. E. & S. A.  
Oc. Farmer    M. L. J. Miller  

Date: 1-18-1866  
Tom B. Wygal    Sarah Mustard  
A. 36 S. Pulaski    A. 21 S. Giles  
P. J. & M. A.    P. Joshua & Eliz. Davis  
Oc. Farmer    M. A.Q. Harman  

Date: 2-8-1866  
W.C. Thompson    S. L. Crawford  
A. 22 S. Wythe    A. 16 S. Mercer  
P. Geo & Polly    P. John & C.  
Oc. Farmer    M. W.E. Neel  

Date: 2-6-1866  
S. H. Hall    M. S. Hall  
A. 24 S. Franklin    A. 17 S. Franklin  
P. H. & K.    P. S. & M.  
Oc. Farmer    M. A.A. Ashworth  

Date: 2-15-1866  
Johule M. Bruce    M. J. Foglesong  
A.27 S. Wythe    A. 26 S. Wythe  
P. Josiah & Minerva    P. Henry & Julia  
Justice  
Oc. Farmer    M. G.W.K. Green  

Date: 2-26-1866  
Thos J. Wohlford    Edna O. Nye  
A. 27 S. Wythe    A. 23 S. Wythe  
P. Jno Jacob & Frances    P. A. J. & Elizabeth  
Smith  
Oc. Merchandising    M. James P. Curtis  

Date: 12-14-1865  
H. T. Tibbs    S. E. Tibbs  
A. 24 S. Goochland    A. 28 S. Goochland  
P. A. & E.    P. Isam'? & E.  
Oc. Farmer    M. D.F.Palmer  

Date: 1-4-1866  
Absolum Ray Bogle    Elizabeth Susan Repass  
A. 24 S. Tazewell    A. 20 S. Wythe  
P. Mark Reed & Jane    P. Isaac & Phebe Clara  
Newberry    Hedrick  
Oc. Farmer    M. John A. Smith  

Date: 1-16-1866  
R. N. Wheeler    N. A. Nunn  
A. 22 S. Carroll    A. 20 S. Franklin  
P. A. M. & N.    P. T. & N.  
Oc. Farmer    M. L. J. Miller  

Date: 1-18-1866  
E. S. Carpenter    M. J. Wilson  
A. 24 S. North Hampton    A. 22 S. Giles  
P. J. E. & Eliza    P. E. & Reb'  
Oc. Farmer    M. B. F. White  

Date: 2-1-1866  
Jos. C. Hutsell    Anne Thompson  
A. 48 W. Wythe    A. 42 S. Wythe  
P. Michael & Julia Ann Cooley    P. Amos & Mary Bruce  
Oc. Farmer    M. A. A. Ashworth  

Date: 2-20-1866  
Henry Burton    N. C. Fanning  
A. 22 S. Giles    A. 21 S. Giles  
P. T. & J.    P. J. & S.  
Oc. Farmer    M.  

Begin Page 3 of Original Book  
Date: 2-15-1866  
M. S. Baumgardner    M. E. Doak  
A. 21 S. Wythe    A. 18 S. Wythe  
P. John & M.    P. Robert & M.  

Oc. Farmer    M. G.W.K. Green  

Date: 2-20-1866  
Henry Burton    N. C. Fanning  
A. 22 S. Giles    A. 21 S. Giles  
P. T. & J.    P. J. & S.  

Oc. Farmer    M. L. J.. Miller

Date: 2-27-1866
John J. Hunter          Elizabeth Wilkinson
A. 26 S. Tazewell       A. 30 S. Wythe
P. Wm & M.              P. John & Rhoda
Oc. Farmer             M.

Date: 2-27-1866
J. M. Kinder            M. A. Baumgardner
A. 27 S. Wythe          A. 25 S. Wythe
P. S. & A.              P. J. M. Baumgardner
Oc. Farmer             M. D. F. Palmer

Date: 3-1-1866
Andrew Jas. Kitts       Nancy M. Wyrick
A. 41 W. Wythe          A. 31 S. Wythe
P. Jacob & Mary         P. Asa & Miranda Bogle
Oc. Farmer             M. J. H. Hoge

Date: 3-7-1866
Solomon King            Sarah Jones
A. 43 W. Warren, NC     A. 20 S. Wythe
P. Bennett & B.         P. Charlotte Hancock
Oc. Farmer             M. A. Q. Harman

Date: 3-3-1866
J. M. Cooley            C. V. Baumgardner
A. 28 S, Wythe          A. 25 S. Wythe
P. J. T. & C.           P. J. & M.
Oc. Farmer             M. D.F. Palmer

Date: 3-21-1866
James Taylor            S. E. Taylor
A. 20 S. Tazewell       A. 18 S. Giles
P. Polly Taylor         P. W. & R.
Oc. Farmer             M. Isaac S. Harman

Date: 3-28-1866
Rufus French            S. M. Day
A. 26 S. Giles          A. 18 S. Tazewell
P. J. & R               P. William & R.
Oc. Farmer             M. L. J.. Miller

Date: 3-20-1866
William H. Muncy        H. V. Thomas
A. 24 S. Wythe          A. 24 S. Wythe
P. James & J.           P. J. & W. C.
Oc. Farmer             M. L. J. Miller

Date: 3-20-1866
William J. Pauley       M. B. Muncy
A. 28 S. Russell        A. 26 S. Wythe
P. J. & S.              P. J. & J.
Oc. Farmer             M. L. J. Miller

Date 3- ? -1866
A. L. Hannah            Harriett H. Allen
A. 34 S. Botetourt      A. 20 S. Giles
P. J & H.               P. Madison & Maria Bane
Oc. Farmer             M. J. H. Hoge

Date: 5-2-1866
William F. Tolbert      J. A. Melvin
A. 22 S. Pulaski        A. 21 S. Giles
P. J. & C.              P. E. & C.
Oc. Blacksmith         M. James P. Curtis

Date: 5-23-1866
James Burton            S. A. Fanning
A. 27 S. Giles          A. 19 S. Giles
P. Lewis & Julia        P. Joseph & Jane
Oc. Farmer             M. L. J. Miller

Date: 5-22-1866
William Waddle          M. C. Waddle
A. 22 S. Wythe          A. 15 S. Wythe
P. Wm. Wash. & Ann      P. Mil. & M.
Oc. Farmer             M. James A. Brown

Date: 5-29-1866
R. H. Bailey            L. J. Honaker
A. 23 S. Mercer         A. 18 S. Tazewell
P. Elijah & S. F.       P. F. C. & M.
Oc. Farmer             M. James Calfee?

Date: 6-13-1866
J. H. Fletcher          M. J. Stowers
A. 18 S. Giles          A. 17 S. Giles
P. Mary A. Terry        P. Warden & Polly
Oc. Farmer             M. James Calfee

Date: 6-21-1866
Marion Boling           L. M. Neel
A. 21 S. Giles          A. 17 S. Tazewell
P. Jos & Frances        P. D. A. & E.
Oc. Farmer             M. L. J. Miller

Date: 1-18-1866
J. W. Finley         Nannie Neel
A. 28 S. Wythe     A. 21 S. Giles
P. Jas & Rebecca    P. H. & N.
Oc. Farmer       M. L. J. Miller

Date: 7-24-1866
Elias Stowers      Sarah Stowers
A. 19 S. Tazewell   A. 17 S. Tazewell
P. Warden & Mary   P. John & Dicy
Oc. Farmer       M. W. E. Neel

Date: 7-26-1866
David Flemming    Catherine Young
Thompson         Munsey Wagner
A. 24 S. Tazewell   A. 25 W. Giles
P. Jas F.& Sarah Hearn  P. Jacob & Mary Fanon
Oc. Farmer       M. D. F. White

Date: 8-27-1866
Thomas B. Hamilton  M. E. Melvin
A. 22 S. Wythe     A. 14 S. Giles
P. Lochard & Mary   P. Elizabeth Thompson (Mother)
Oc. Farmer       M. I. S. Harman

Date: 9-20-1866
M. J. Robinett     R. E. Shannon
A. 25 S. Wythe     A. 21 S. Tazewell
P. H. & R.         P. Jo. A. C. Shannon
Oc. Farmer       M. Wm. E. Neel

Date: 9-25-1866
Pleasant T. Hancock  Thursa V. Wyrick
A. 23 S. Wythe     A. 22 S. Wythe
P. Obediah & Jane   P. Asa & Mariana
Oc. Farmer       M. L. J. Miller

Date: 10-18-1866
John Groseclose    Ern' Kirby
A. 27 S. Wythe     A. 21 S. Wythe
P. J. & B.         P. S. & M.
Oc. Farmer       M. G.W.K. Green

Date: 11-15-1866
Augustus M. Farlow  E. M. Myers
A. 21 S. Wythe     A. 20 S. Tazewell
P. Jas. B. & Christina M. P. Nancy Myers
Oc. Farmer       M. John A. Smith

Date: 7-10-1866
John Devor       S. E. Stowers
A. 27 S. Wythe     A. 16 S. Wythe
P. Wm & Julia     P. Jas & Dicia
Oc. Farmer       M. G.W.K. Green

Date: 7-15-1866
William S. Herron  Eliz. Jane "Mollie" Waggoner
A. 40 W. Carrel, TN  A. 34 W. Wythe
P. Chas & Mary    P. Wm & Susan Hearn
Oc. Farmer       P. L J. Miller

Date: 8-16-1866
M. A. Fletcher     M. E. Davis

A. 23 S. Giles      A. 27 W. Botetourt
P. Rolen & Rhoda   P. Stephen Sands
Oc. Farmer       M. Isaac S. Harman

Date: 9-5-1866
Henry T. Doak     Barbara J. Wilson
A. 18 S. Wythe     A. 23 S. Wythe
P. Rob't & Amanda   P. Rob't & Catherine
Oc. Farmer       M. J. J. Greever

Date 9-13-1866
Jackson Chandler   M. C. Cameron
A. 33 S. Wythe     A. 20 S. Smyth
P. Geo & Virginia    P. Agnes Cameron
Oc. Farmer       M. J. P. Curtis

Date 10-4-1866
N. M. Havens      Rebecca Harman
A. 21 S. Giles      A. 28 W. Wythe
P. John & Joanna    P. Asa & Marinda Wyrick
Oc. Farmer       M. G.W.K. Green

Date: 10-16-1866
Iasiah Bruce       Naomia McNeil Evans
A. 60 W. Wythe     A. 44 W. Franklin
P. Rev. Joshua & Sarah Hearn P. Daniel McNeil
Oc. Farmer       M. L. J. Miller

Date: 11-22-1866
John W. Havens    Lettie Waddle
A. 31 S. Wythe     A. 29 S. Wythe
P. Andrew & Elizabeth  P. Rob't & Polly
Oc. Farmer       M. G.W.K. Green

Date: 12-4-1866  
William H. Farley | Bidsey Roling  
A. 33 S. Giles | A.25 S. Floyd  
P. Frank & Mahala | P. Jas & Frances  
Oc. Farmer | M. L. J.. Miller

Date: 1-10-1866  
H. C. French | Susannah A. Miller  
A. 20 S. Giles | A. 18 S. Giles  
P. Jerm & M.A. | P. Abraham Woodson &  
| Rachel Hearn  
Oc. Farmer | M. L. J. Miller

Date 12-12-1866  
J. W. Srader | Emily C. Lambert  
A. 23 S. Wythe | A. 22 S. Giles  
P. Jn & Christina | P. Jas. & Emily  
Oc. Farmer | M. L. J. . Miller

Date 1-4-1866  
S. G. Heldridge? | M. J. Thompson  
A. 17 S. Wythe | A. 19 S. Wythe  
P. Jn. C. & Elizabeth | P. Josiah & Anna  
Oc. Farmer | M. G.W.K. Green

Begin Page 4 of Original Book  
Date: 1-9-1867  
A. R. Kidd | Charlotte Repass  
A. 23 S. Tazewell | A. 19 S. Tazewell  
P. H. C. & Matilda | P. Isaac & Phebe  
Oc. Farming | M. John A. Smith

Date: 1-15-1867  
A. H. Wyrick | S. M. Helvey  
A. 26 S. Wythe | A. 21 S. Giles  
P. Asa & Marinda Bogle | P. John K. & Nancy Hutsel  
Oc. Farmer | M. L. J. Miller

Date: 1-30-1867  
William Lambert | M. J. Painter  
A. 30 S. Wythe | A. 20 S. Wythe  
P. Henry & Emily | P. James C. & E. J.  
Oc. Farmer | M. G.W. K. Green

Date: 2-21-1867  
E. S. Kidd | Clarissa Muncy  
A. 29 S. Tazewell | A. 30 W. Wythe  
P. Geo & Evaline | P. William Muncy  
Oc. Farmer | M. L. J. Miller

Date: 2-21-1867  
John W. Conley | Mira J. Suiter  
A. 24 S. Giles | A. 22 S. Tazewell  
P. Skidmore & Alice | P. Alex & Catherine

Oc. Farmer | M. L. J. Miller

Date: 3-20-1867  
Charles Martin Rudder | Jane Raines  
A. 32 S. Halifax | A. 27 W. Giles  
P. Edward M. & Eliz. | P. Sam'l & Eliz. Wohlford  
Oc. Farmer | M. Geo. W. Penley

Date: 1-16-1867  
W. W. Hamilton | Darthulia Moore  
A. 25 S. Wythe | A. 18 S. Giles  
P. Timothy & Margaret | P. Rich' & Elizabeth  
Oc. Shoemaker | M. Geo. W. Penley

Date: 1-15-1867  
William Gratton Mustard | Martha Ella McDonald  
A. 28 S. Wythe | A. S. Logan  
P. Wm & Annah Patton | P. Wm. & Maria Bane  
Oc. Merchandising | M. G.W.K. Green

Date: 2-5-1867  
Obadiah Smith | D. S. Helvey  
A. 27 S. Serra Co. NC | A. 30 S. Wythe  
P. John & Liddie | P. Baltzer & Rhoda  
Oc. Farmer | M. John H. Hoge

Date: 2-14-1867  
William A. Robinett | Agnes Adkins  
A. 24 S. Tazewell | A. 18 S. Tazewell  
P.Hiram & Dicey | P. P. & Rhoda Adkins  
Oc. Farmer | M. W. E. Neel

Date: 3-7-1867  
Jas Thos Burton | Mary Eliz. Muncy  
A. 22 S. Pulaski | A. 21 S. Wythe  
P. Jas Harvey & | P. Jacob & Martha  
Virginia Jane Detimore  
Oc. Farmer | M. L. J. Miller

Date: 3-21-1867  
Jno. C. Stowers | N. A. Groseclose  
A. 27 S. Tazewell | A. 22 S. Wythe  
P. Wm & C. | P. Jacob & S.  
Oc. Farmer | M. G.W. K. Green

Date: 3-26-1867  
Rayburn P. Akers     Lizzabeth Bird  
A. 38 W. Montgomery     A. 34 S. Floyd  
P. D. & C.     P. Jno. & Elizabeth  
Oc. Farmer     M. A.A. Ashworth

Date: 5-9-1867  
John Starling     Sarah Hagar  
A. 21 S. Tazewell     A. 22 S. Tazewell  
P. J. & T.     P. E. & E.  
Oc. Farmer     M. G.W.K. Green

Date: 6-6-1867  
Jno. Wyrick     A. S. Spangler  
A. 28 S. Wythe     A. 25 S. Wythe  
P. Jeff & Polly     P. Peter & Betsy  
Oc. Farmer     M. A.A. Ashworth

Date: 7-3-1867  
John J. Carr     Elizabeth Nisewander  
A. 22 S. Giles     A. 26 S. Giles  
P. Jas & Fannie     P. Harvey & Malinda  
Oc. Farmer     M. Isaac S. Harman

Date: 8-8-1867  
Joel H. Spangler     Elizabeth S. Hudson  
A. 32 W. Wythe     A. 26 W. Tazewell  
P. Peter & Nancy     P. Jas J. & Griever?  
Oc. Farmer     M. J. W. Dickey

Date: 8-15-1867  
S. S. Robinett     Lucinda Neel  
A. 21 S. Tazewell     A. 18 S. Tazewell  
P. H. & D.     P. A. & F.  
Oc. Farmer     M. Wm. E. Neel

Date: 8-24-1867  
Wm. P. Bruce     Mary J. Compton  
A. 30 S. Wythe     A. 18 S. Tazewell  
P. Josiah & Virginia T.     P. W. W. & Nancy  
Oc. Farmer     M. L. J. Miller

Date: 9-17-1867  
Rufus Nisewander     Nancy Christina Harman  
A. 23 S. Giles     A. 18 S. Giles  
P. Harvey & Malinda     P. Rob't W. & Cynthia  
Oc. Farmer     M. Isaac S. Harman

Date: 5-1-1867  
Ephiram Waddle     Amanda Robinett  
A. 46 W. Wythe     A. 37 S. Wythe  
P. R. & M     P. H. & R.  
Oc. Farmer     M. G.W.K. Green

Date: 5-14-1867  
C. F. Sneed     M. C. Bird  
A. 22 S. Chesterfield     A. 18 S. Giles  
P. J. H. & S.     P. Jane Bird  
Oc. Carpenter     M. A.A. Ashworth

Date 6-7-1867  
W. H. Ramsey     Polly A. Blankenship  
A. 25 S. Franklin     A. 17 S. Wythe  
P. Thos & W.     P. Elias & Lettie A.  
Oc. Farmer     M. L. J. Miller

Date 7-23-1867  
J. A. T. Groseclose     E. J. Groseclose  
A. 23 S. Wythe     A. 19 S. Wythe  
P. Wm & Adaline     P. Joseph & Betsy  
Oc. Farmer     M. Isaac S. Harman

Date: 8-8-1867  
Henry Foglesong     Mary A. Rose  
A. 34 S. Wythe     A. 21 S. Bedford  
P. Simon & C.     P. Wm. H. & E.  
Oc. Farmer     M. J. W. Dickey

Date: 8-21-1867  
G.W. Bryant     Elizabeth Gills  
A. 31 S. Fairfield, Conn     A. 31 W. Tazewell  
P. S.W. & M. J.     P. Jno. & Polly Lewis  
Oc. Farmer     M. G.W.K. Green

Date: 8-29-1867  
Marshall Smith     M. F. Wilkinson  
A. 35 S. Orange     A. 26 S. Wythe  
P. Jno. & Susan     P. Jim & Rhoda  
Oc. Mechanic     M. G.W.K. Green

Date: 9-12-1867  
John R. Crawford     Ellen Derkin  
A. 28 S. Giles     A. 24 W. Giles  
P. Wm. S. & Eliza     P. Elisha & Etta Burton?  
Oc. Farmer     M. G.W.K. Green

Date: 9-18-1867
Jas R. Lampert          Nancy J. Hancock
A. 22 S. Wythe          A. 19 S. Patrick Co.
P. Henry & Emaline      P. Chas & Mary A.
Oc. Farmer              M. G.W.K. Green

Date: 9-24 -1867
Alex. Umbarger          Susan C. Crutchfield
A. 19 S. Wythe          A. 19 S. Wythe
P. Jacob & Elizabeth    P. W. J. & Elizabeth
Oc. Farmer              M. G.W.K. Green

Date: 10-10-1867
Ballard Preston Brown   Lucinda Robinett
A. 36 S. Giles          A. S. Wythe
P. Col. Geo. Wash. &    P. Jas Jezeerel
Emma Crump              Jerusha Newberry
Oc. Farmer              M. L. J. Miller

Date: 10-30-1867
William F. Cecil        Mary J. Hughes
A. 26 S. Tazewell       A. 20 S. Tazewell
P. Jas & Sarah          P. Jas. C. & Jane
Oc. Farmer              M. H. Honaker

Date: 11-13-1867
Gordon Wohlford         Matilda Ann Byrnes
A. 21 S. Giles          A. 21 S. Wise
P. Sam'l & Elizabeth    P. Dr. Jno. Wesley &
                        Sarah Mustard
Oc. Farmer              M. J. H. Hoge

Date: 11-13-1867
Lewis Hagar             Ellen J. Bridges
A. 28 S. Tazewell       A. 20 S. Augusta
P. Squire & Elizabeth   P. Wm. M. Bridges
Oc. Farmer              M. H. Honaker

Begin Page 5 of Original Book
Date: 11-26-1867
George W. Stowers       Sarah J. Shannon
A. 22 S. Tazewell       A. 20 S. Tazewell
P. Colby & Lockey       P. Jas & Nancy
Oc. Farmer              M. John A. Smith

Date: 1-15-1868
J. E. French            Judy R. Day
A. 26 S. Giles          A. 16 S. Tazewell
P. Isaac & Rhoda        P. Wm & Rachel
Oc. Farmer              M. W. E. Neel

Date: 9-19-1867
James A. Tibbs          Mary Wilson
A. 20 S. Wythe          A. S. Wythe
P. Geo M. & Mary        P. Rob't Wilson
Oc. Farmer              M. G.W.K. Green

Date 10-1-1867
Wm H. Keffer            H. J. Grayson
A. 33 S. Pulaski        A. 25 S. Smyth
P. Sam'l & Mary         P. Franklin & Nancy
Oc. Physician           M. Joseph H. Martin

Date: 10-17-1867
Sam'l Dillman           M. E. Wyrick
A. 29 S. Indiana        A. 20 S.Wythe
P. Geo & Mary           P. Jefferson & Polly

Oc. Mechanic            M. G.W. K. Green

Date: 10-31-1867
Jno Kinder              L. J. Groseclose
A. 36 W. Wythe          A. 27 S. Wythe
P. Ruben & Sarah        P. Jacob & Susan
Oc. Farmer              M. G.W.K. Green

Date: 11-13-1867
Joseph Foglesong        H. M. Wilson
A. 30 S. Wythe          A. 24 S. Wythe
P.Simon & Christina     P. Jas. & Elizabeth

Oc. Farmer              M. G.W. Green

Date: 11-24-1867
Rob't S.Thompson        L. E. Thompson
A. 24 S. Wythe          A. 25 S. Wythe
P. Josiah M. & Anna     P. Jos R. & Easter
Oc. Farmer              M. G.W.K. Green

Date: 12-26-1867
Jas. P. Bottomly        Minerva Hanshew
A. 25 S. Wythe          A. 24 S. Wythe
P. Jos. & Luci          P. An' & Elizabeth
Oc. Farmer              M. A. M. Young

Date: 1-29-1868
J. M. Repass            Ibbie Groseclose
A. 31 S. Tazewell       A. 22 S. Wythe
P. Reuben & Esther      P. Jezreel & Margaret
Oc. Physician           M. A.A. Ashworth

Date: 2-11-1868
J. B. Thompson | M. E. McCoy
A. 55 W. Wythe | A. 31 W. Montgomery
P. A. & M. | P. Jas & Jane Burton
Oc. Farmer | M. L. J. Miller

Date: 2-20-1868
Jackson Stowers | Mollie Wyley
A. 21 S. Tazewell | A. 27 S. Tazewell
P. Ho' & Sallie | P. Jno & Ellen
Oc. Farmer | M. Wm. E. Neel

Date: 2-26-1868
Jno W. Kirby | Cyntha E. Repass
A. S. Wythe | A. S. Wythe
P. Stephen & M.A. | P. Jos & E.J.
Oc. Farmer | M. G.W.K.Green

Date: 2-26-1868
A.W. Wynn | A. E. Repass
A. 22 S. Tazewell | A. 18 S. Tazewell
P. Josiah M. & Margaret | P. Isaac & Phebe
Oc. Farmer | M. John A. Smith

Date: 3-17-1868
J. M. Crow | Christina Groseclose
A. 19 S. Wythe | A. 32 S. Wythe
P. Jno & Catherine | P. A. & M.
Oc. Farming | M. A.A. Ashworth

Date: 3-24-1868
N.D. Webster | R.M. Havens
A. 34 S. Carroll | A. 36 S. Wythe
P. Elbert & Sallie | P. And'. & Elizabeth

Oc. Farmer | M. G.W.K. Green

Date: 5-13-1868
Jackson Nye Tickle | Mary Ann Waggoner
A. 21 S. Giles | A. 16 S. Wythe
P. Hezekiah C. & | P. Geo. Eli &
Caroline Matilda Farmer | Eliz. Jane Hearn
Oc. Farmer | M. J.H. Hoge

Date: 5-25-1868
J. C. Crockett | S. J. Crump
A. 58 W. Wythe | A. 40 W. Pittsylvania
P. Jno & Agnes | P. Jer' T. & Catherine
Oc. Farmer | M. W.K. Williams

Date 2-26-1868
G. W. Hurt | S. B. Wyley
A. 26 S. Wythe | A. 25 S. Giles
P. S. & M. | P. Jas & Ellen
Oc. Farmer | M. Wm. E. Neel

Date: 2-20-1868
Wm E. Lampert | R. E. Umbarger
A. 22 S. Wythe | A. 17 S. Wythe
P. Jas & E. | P. Wm & M. M.
Oc. Farmer | M. G.W.K. Green

Date: 3-5-1868
J. H. Pearson | M.E. Hutchinson
A. 32 S. Prince Edward | A. 24 S. Carig
P. Jno & Sarah | P. Rob't & E.
Oc. Merchant | M. Wm. E. Neel

Date: 3-10-1868
John W. McGinnis | Elizabeth W. Grayson
A. 30 S. Carroll | A. 17 S. Wythe
P. Allen A. & Eliza | P. Ran' & Cynthia
Oc. Merchandising | M. D. Sullins

Date: 3-19-1868
J. M. Neece | S. A. Criger
A. 36 W. Montgomery | A. 30 S. Wythe
P. Valentine & Margaret | P. Reuben & Mollie
Oc. Carpenter | M. G.W. K. Green

Date 4-2-1868
Hyman Mathew Kitts | Crosby D. Kitts
A. 21 S. Wythe | A. 16 S. Wythe
P. Jacob & Matilda | P. Peter & Amanda M.
 | Hounshell
Oc. Farmer | M.

Date: 5-17-1868
E. Leonard | E.M. Cameron
A. 21 S. Wythe | A. 16 S. Wythe
P. Jno & Polly | P. Jas & Esther

Oc. Farmer | M.

Date: 6-30-1868
H. J. Havens | Susannah Havens
A. 21 S. Giles | A. 18 S. Wythe
P. Jon & Joanna | P. An.' & Elizabeth
Oc. Farmer | M. A.A. Ashworth

Date: 7-9-1868  
Samuel Steel | Polly Ann Waddle  
A. 44 S. Wythe | A. 34 S. Wythe  
P. Rob't & Rhoda | P. Robinett & Polly  
Oc. Farmer | M. A.A. Ashworth  

Date: 8-5-1868  
E. W. Eagle | M. J. Deavor  
A. 34 S. Wythe | A. 27 S. Wythe  
P. Jno & Abigail | P. Wm. & Julia  
Oc. Minister | M. A.A. Ashworth  

Date: 8-9-1868  
Jno Kyle | Rebecca Finley  
A. 58 S. Ireland | A. 43 W. Wythe  
P. Wm & Margaret | P. Thos. & Catherine Deavor  

Oc. Merchant | M. R.C. Graham  

Date: 10-22-1868  
Hiram Lambert | Lettie Hopkins  
A. 19 S. Wythe | A. 24 S. Tazewell  
P. Jno & Mahala | P. Rebecca Hopkins  
Oc. Farmer | M. G.W.K. Green  

Date: 11-19-1868  
Henry Groseclose | Mary Deavor  
A. 40 S. Wythe | A. 19 S. Wythe  
P. J. & E. | P. J.W. & E.  
Oc. Farmer | M.  

Date: 11-26-1868  
E. S. Stowers | Ludema Thompson  
A. 22 S. Wythe | A. 22 S. Wythe  
P. Wm & Christine | P. A. & Polly  
Oc. Farmer | M. G.W.K. Green  

Date: 11-23-1868  
Edward Neel | Eva Victoria Lambert  
A. 22 S. Tazewell | A. 21 S. Wythe  
P. Jas & Mahala | P. Jno & M.  
Oc. Farmer | M. John A. Smith  

Date: 12-20-1868  
G. D. Havens | S. A. Groseclose  
A. 23 S. Wythe | A. 25 S. Wythe  
P. Andy & Elizabeth | P. Francis & Molly  
Oc. Farmer | M. G.W.K. Green  

Date 7-23-1868  
William Wilson | Mary Stuart  
A. 72 W. Rockbridge | A. 30 W. Russell  
P. Jno & Elizabeth | P. Jas & Mary Burket  
Oc. Farmer | M. A. M. Towney?  

Date: 9-3-1868  
J. W. Thompson | M. Kirby  
A. 25 S.Wythe | A. 26 S. Wythe  
P. Arch & Polly | P. Stephen & Molly  
Oc. Farmer | M. G.W.K. Green  

Date: 10-15-1868  
Chas Russell Burton | Va. Caroline Kitts  
A. 21 S. Pulaski | A. S. Wythe  
P. Jas Harvey & | P. Andrew J. &  
Va. Jane Detimore | Mary "Polly" Leedy  
Oc. Farmer | M. L. J. Miller  

Date 11-7-1868  
Jas R. Wheeler | Susan Coldwell  
A. 29 S. Carroll | A. 29 S. Montgomery  
P. A. & N. | P. Roland & Elizabeth  
Oc. Teacher | M. L. J. Miller  

Date 11-16-1868  
P. P. E. Neel | Eliza S. Haneger  
A. 25 W. Tazewell | A. 25 S. Tazewell  
P. Thos & Sarah | P. Wm. & B. E.  
Oc. Farmer | M. A.A. Ashworth  

Date 11-29-1868  
W. F. French | C. E. Lambert  
A. 25 S. Tazewell | A. 22 S. Giles  
P. A. & L. | P. Jas F. & Emily  
Oc. Farmer | M.  

Date: 12-1-1868  
Robert Patton | Nancy Nisewander  
A. 26 S. Wythe | A. 22 S. Giles  
P. Hiram & Sena | P. Harvey & Malinda  
Oc. Farmer | M. L. J. Miller  

Date: 12-22-1868  
S. C. Overstreet | M. E. Woodyard  
A. 24 S. Bedford | A. 21 S. Giles  
P. T. J. & H. | P. E. & C.  
Oc. Farmer | M. L. J. Miller

Date: 12 24-1868
G.A. Williams                     M. S. Thorn
A. 31 S. Rockingham         A. 21 S. Tazewell
P. J. & M.                            P. G.C. Thorn

Oc. Farmer                         M. William Hicks

Date: 1-7-1869
Jas Thompson                     E.S. Thompson
A. 20 S. Wythe                   A. 22 S. Wythe
P. J. M. & Ann                    P. J.B. & C.
Oc. Farmer                         M. G.W.K. Green

Begin Page 6 of Original Book
Date: 1-7-1869
R. A. Walters                      Nancy Stowers
A. 20 S. Giles                     A. 22 S. Tazewell
P. Geo & Margaret            P. Gordon & Sallie

Oc. Farmer                         M. Peter A. Suiter

Date: 1-21-1969
H.P. Wheeler                      M.L. Cooper
A. 22 S. Carroll                  A. 21 S. Franklin
P. A. M. & Nancy              P. Alex. & Mary
Oc. Farmer                         M. L. J. Miller

Date: 2-13-1869
R. A. French                      F. J. Clark
A. 17 S. Tazewell             A. 16 S. Tazewell
P. Austin & S.                    P. R. & S.

Oc. Farmer                         M. Peter R. Suiter

Date: 3-29-1969
James S. Robinett              Eleanor R. Hoge
A. 23 S. Wythe                  A. 17 S. Giles
P. Jas & Jerusha               P. G.D. & Rebecca
Oc. Farmer                         M. J. H. Hoge

Date: 2-8-1869
S. S. Kimberling               M.A. Bails
A. 19 S. Wythe                  A. 18 S. Smyth
P. Jos & Elizabeth            P. Jas R. & Elizabeth
Oc. Farmer                         M. Wm Hicks

Date: 4-15-1869
S. B. Stephens                   J. M. Meadows
A.22 S. Giles                     A. 23 S. NC
P. S.&.A. Underwood        P.
Oc. Farmer                         M. J. M. Umphrie

Date: 12-31-1868
William Baltzer Helvey, Jr.    Elizabeth J. Wheeler
A. 25 S. Giles                     A. 18 S. Wythe
P. John Kennerly &           P. H.P. & B.
Nancy Hutsell
Oc. Farmer                         M. L.J. Miller

Date 1-7-1869
William A. Muncy             R.E. Workman
A. 35 S. Giles                     A. 25 S. Wythe
P. Zach. & Ann Oney        P. Jas T. Workman
Oc. Farmer                         M. Wm Hicks

Date: 1-14-1869
Jno P. Roach                      Louisa V. Pauley
A. 31 S. Monroe                A. 17 S. Giles
P. Isaac & Delilah            P. Hiram Addison &
                                            Anna Barbara Helvey
Oc. Merchandising            M. William Hicks

Date: 2-11-1869
A.L. Lambert                     July A. Cecil
A. 19 S. Tazewell             A. 17 S. Tazewell
P. H. H. & P. C.                 P. Josh' & Sallie
Oc. Farmer                         M. Peter R. Suiter

Date: 3-18-1869
Wm Paris Bogle               Frances Jane King
A. 23 S. Wythe                  A. 19 S. Giles
P. Lorenza Dow &            P. J.B. & M. M.
Mary Dunn
Oc. Farmer                         M.

Date 2-1-1869
A.T. Kidd                          Rhoda J. Repass
A. 22 S. Tazewell             A. 16 S. Tazewell
P. Wm S. & Malinda         P. Isaac & Phebe
Oc. Farmer                         M. John A. Smith

Date: 4-1-1869
William B. Ashworth        M. E.Compton
A. 25 S. Pulaski                A. 24 S. Tazewell
P. A. A. & Nancy              P. W. W. & Nancy
Oc. Farmer                         M. L. J. Miller

Date: 4-6-1869
Jacob F. Kitts                    Cynthia J. Wyrick
A. 30 W. Wythe                A. 19 S. Wythe
P. Andrew J. & Polly Leedy  P. Asa & Marinda Bogle
Oc. Farmer                         M. A.A. Ashworth

Date: 5-11-1869
P.W. Davis
A. 39 S. Tazewell
P. Jas & Louisa
Oc. Farmer

Elvira Suiter
A. 29 S. Tazewell
P. Alex. & Polly
M. P.P. Greever

Date: 5-18-1869
J.R. Kidd
A. 22 S. Tazewell
P. H.C. & Matilda
Oc. Farmer

Elizabeth J. Neel
A. 22 S. Tazewell
P. J. M. & Malinda
M. John A. Smith

Date: 5-19-1869
D. O. McNeil
A.38 S. Floyd
P. Dan'l & Elizabeth
Oc. Merchant

Sarah E. Wohlford
A. 25 S. Wythe
P. Sam'l & Sarah
M. L. J. Miller

Date: 6-1-1869
J.P. Pauley, Jr
A. 22 S. Giles
P. J. S. & Mary
Oc. Farmer

Rebecca Pauley
A. 32 W. Giles
P. Josh' Day
M. Isaac S. Harman

Date: 6-13-1869
William G. Stowers
A. 20 S. Wythe
P. Wm & Christina
Oc. Farmer

L. E. Terry
A. 21 S. Wythe
P. Wm & Margaret
M. Peter R. Suiter

Date 6-24-1869
Rufus W. Clark
A. 21 S. Giles
P. Jas & Mahala
Oc. Farmer

Nancy L. Workman
A. 19 S. Wythe
P. Tiffany & M.A.
M. L. J. Miller

Date: 7-7-1869
Newton Montgomery
Kitts
A. 20 S. Wythe
P. Jacob & Matilda
Oc. Farmer

Ellen Brown Baumgardner

A. 20 S. Wythe
P. Jas & Malinda
M. J. J. Greever

Date: 7-15-1896
T. H. Shrader

A. 30 S. Wythe
P. Wm & Betsy
Oc. Merchanic

C. M. Nye

A. 22 S. Giles
P. A.J. & Elizabeth
M. J.H. Hoge

Date: 7-28-1869
James H. Bird
A. 21 S. Wythe
P. Jno R. & Susan
Oc. Farmer

Mary J. Corder
A. 19 S. Giles
P. B. F. Corder
M. A.A. Ashworth

Date: 8-7-1869
D. C. Warner
A. 22 S. Wythe
P. Mary Warner
Oc. Farmer

Margaret Stafford
A. 26 W. Giles
P. Willis & Sary Jones
M. W. H. Stevens

Date: 8-19-1869
A.T. Suiter
A. 27 S. Tazewell
P. A.F. & Catherine
Oc. Farmer

S. J. Pruett
A. 17 S. Giles
P. Joshua & N.J.
M. Peter R. Suiter

Date: 8-24-1869
S. P. Smith
A. 24 S. Carroll
P. G. & Nancy
Oc. Farmer

E. S. Williams
A. 21 S. Grayson
P. Wm & M.S.
M. Wm Hicks

Date: 9-30-1869
Hiram Hounshell
A. 33 S.Wythe
P. Henry & Elizabeth
Oc. Farmer

Nancy A. Kitts
A. 32 W. Wythe
P. Jno. & Eliz. Heldreth
M. A.A. Ashworth

Date 9-22-1869
Wm W. Fanning
A. 32 S. Giles
P. Jas & Jane
Oc. Farmer

Cintha A. Beard
A. 28 S. Pulaski
P. J.H. & V.J. Burton
M. L. J. Miller

Date: 10-6-1869
P. W. Harman
A. 21 S. Wythe
P. F. M. & Nancy
Oc. Farmer

A.V. Purkey
A. 20 S. Wythe
P. Dan'l & Letitia
M. G.W.K. Green

Date: 10-27-1869
H. Joe.? Kitts
A. 26 S. Wythe
P. And' & Polly
Oc. Farmer

Emma Loutricia Lambert
A. 20 S. Giles
P. I?. P. & S. R.
M. L. J. Miller

Date: 11-25 -1869  
S. B. Hall                 E. J. Cassell  
A. 23 S. Giles        A. 21 S. Wythe  
P. Hiram & Kitty     P. Jno W. & F.A.  
Oc. Mechanic        M.A.A. Ashworth  

Date: 12 9-1869  
Sam'l D. Bales      Elizabeth V. Harner  
A. 22 S. Wythe       A. 18 S. Wythe  
P. John R. & Mary M.   P. J.J. & Mary M.  
Oc. Farmer          M. A.A. Ashworth  

Date: 1-1-1870  
John J. Mustard     Minnie M. Stuart  
A. 27 S. Giles        A. 23 S. Pulaski  
P. Wm & Ann       P. Wm & Margaret  
Oc. Farmer          M. J. H. Hoge  

Date: 1-2-1870  
Giles W. Lamb      Susan Ann Ramsey  
A. 21 S. Giles        A. 16 S. Henry  
P. Gabriel & Martha   P. W. S. & Elizabeth  
Oc. Farmer          M. J.H. Hoge  

Date: 2-2-1870  
Floyd A. Ashworth  Susan M. Eaton  
A. 22 S. Pulaski      A. 23 S. Giles  
P. W.W. & Juliana    P. John & E.H.  
Oc. Music Teacher   M. J. H. Hoge  

Date: 2-18-1870  
Matthew Boyd      Mary Johnston  
A. 22 S. Wythe       A. 37 W. Monroe  
P. A.& M.            P. S.A. & Nancy Bridges  
Oc. Farmer          M.G.W.K. Green  

Date: 3-9-1870  
Thomas A. Green    Annie E. Wright  
A.22 S. Harper's Ferry  A. 19 S. Lexington  
P.Thos W. & Emma   P. J. R. & E.A.  
Oc. Merchant       M. J. H. Hoge  

Date: 3-24-1870  
J. T. Preston        Matilda Carr  
A. 32 S. Franklin     A. 33 S. Giles  
P. C. & M. M.        P. Mary Carr  
Oc. Farmer          M. Phillip S. Sutton  

Date: 11-30-1869  
J.K. Jones           S.A.E. Surratt  
A. 40 W. Giles      A. 19 S. Wythe  
P. John & Nancy    P. Jas & Susan  
Oc. Farmer          M. J.H. Hoge  

Date: 12-22-1869  
Francis E. Stowers  Arminta A. Wimmer  
A. 18 S. Giles        A. 17 S. Mercer  
P. Warden & Polly   P. Harry S. & Sally  
Oc. Farmer          M. P. R. Suiter  

Date: 1-15-1870  
Thos J. Neel        Naomia J. Nye  
A. 29 S. Giles        A. 20 S. Giles  
P. Elias & Nancy    P. A. J. & Elizabeth  
Oc. Farmer          M. P. S. Sutton  

Date: 2-2-1870  
Samuel Stimpson   Mary E. Ashworth  
A. 21 S. Floyd       A.19 S. Pulaski  
P. N. B. & Lydia     P. W.W. & Juliana  
Oc. Farmer          M. A.A. Ashworth  

Date: 2-16-1870  
Henry Stowers     Angeline Groseclose  
A. 20 S. Tazewell    A. 23 S. Wythe  
P. Colby & Lockey   P. Jacob & Susan  
Oc. Farmer          M. P. R. Suiter  

Begin Page 7 of Original Book  
Date: 2-23-1870  
John Moore         Eliza Jane Niece  
A. 29 S. England    A. 17 S. Kentucky  
P. Thos & Isabella   P. Marshall & Susan  
Oc. Miner           M. J. H. Hoge  

Date: 3-13-1870  
W.A. Mahaffey     S.E. French  
A. 26 S. Washington  A. 23 S. Tazewell  
P. Hugh & Mary     P. A. & S.  
Oc. Farmer          M. Peter R. Suiter  

Date: 4-21-1870  
J. F. Locke         Mary J. Thompson  
A. W.               A. S. Giles  
P.                  P. J. B. & Esther  
Oc. Mechanic       M. A. A. Ashworth  

15

Date: 5-4-1870  
Edward A. Mills     Maggie J. Hicks  
A. 22 S. Charlotte CH    A. 19 S. Buncomb, NC  
P. Jas B. & Louisa    P. Wm & Elizabeth  
Oc. Farmer    M. J. H. Hoge  

Date: 6-18-1870  
Samuel L. Kitts    Augusta M. Deavor  
A. 23 S. Wythe    A. 17 S. Wythe  
P. S. Steel & E.Kitts    P. Wm & Juliet  
Oc. Farmer    M. B.F.? White  

Date: 8-71870  
John T. Bandy    Eliza A. Albert  
A. 21 S. McDowell    A. 22 S. Wythe  
P. Jas C. & Betsy    P. Wm & Letitia  
Oc. Farmer    M. Phillip S. Sutton  

Date: 8-11-1870  
William Taylor    Permelia Mustard  
A. 52 W. Grayson    A. 41 W. Halifax  
P. Wm & Harda?    P. Jas & Permelia Tynes  
Oc. Farmer    M. J. H. Hoge  

Date: 9-5-1870  
A. J. Muncy    S. A. Bolton  
A. 21 S. Tazewell    A. 19 S. Giles  
P. Jno R. & Jemima    P. David Bolton  
Oc. Farmer    M. G.W.K.Green  

Date: 10-5-1870  
A.W. Kidd    Rebecca E. Kidd  
A. 34 S. Tazewell    A. 37 W. Tazewell  
P. Geo & Evaline    P. Alex. & Kathrina Suiter  
Oc. Farmer    M. J. H. Hoge  

Date: 10-13-1870  
E. M. Melvin    S.A. Crawford  
A. 21 S. Giles    A. 21 S. Giles  
P. E. & C.    P. Wm & E.  
Oc. Farmer    M. A.A. Ashworth  

Date: 10- -1870  
Samuel M. Stimson    Martha A. T. Crawford  
A. 23 S. Giles    A. 25 S. Giles  
P. Chas & Elizabeth    P. Wm & Catherine  
Oc. Farmer    M. J.H. Hoge  

Date: 6-2-1870  
John J. Hunter    Lucinda J. Wyrick  
A. 31 W. Tazewell    A. 33 S. Wythe  
P. Wm & Maria    P. Asa & Marinda  
Oc. Farmer    M. L. J. Miller  

Date: 7-14-1870  
James F. Cassell    Christina Groseclose  
A. 20 S. Smyth    A. 19 S. Wythe  
P. John M. & Frances    P. Jos & Elizabeth  
Oc. Mechanic    M. P.P. Green, E.S. Church  

Date: 8-15-1870  
John W. Murcer    Unia L. Tibbs  
A. 21 S. Wythe    A. 21 S. Wythe  
P. David & Mary    P. Geo & Mary  
Oc. Farmer    M. Edw. Vertigase  

Date: 9-1-1870  
Rob't Carr    Lucie A. King  
A. 19 S. Giles    A. 20 S. Giles  
P. Matilda Preston    P. J.B. & Mary  
Oc. Farmer    M. J.H.Hoge  

Date: 9-19-1870  
George Nisewander    Cyntha Harman  
A. 22 S. Giles    A. 20 S. Giles  
P. Harvey & Matilda    P. R. W. & Agatha  
Oc.Farmer    M. Isaac S. Harman  

Date: 10-12-1870  
John Tibbs    Katherine Williams  
A. 47 S. Bland    A. 45 S. Bland  
P. Jas & Agnes    P. Jacob & Mary  
Oc. Farmer    M. John A. Bell?  

Date: 10-6-1870  
H. W. Thompson    Mary R.? Jones  
A. 21 S. Wythe    A. 21 S. Wythe  
P. John & Betsy    P. Betsy Jones  
Oc. Farmer    M. J. H. Hoge  

Date: 11-28-1870  
C.H.C. Fulkenson    E.G. Grayson  
A. 25 S. Sw    A. 20 S. Smyth  
P. A.H. & N.B.    P. Frank & Nancy  
Oc. Merchant    M. R.C. Graham

Date: 12-5-1870
J. S. Woodall
A. 22 S. Patrick
P. Fayette & Nancy
Oc. Farmer

Mary J. Thompson
A. 21 S. NC
P. Jas & Florence
M. William Hicks

Date: 12-18-1870
Jno P. Hicks
A. 18 S. Tazewell
P. Jos & Maria

Oc. Farmer

Unie V. Edwards
A. 16 S. Tazewell
P. Wm & Martha

M. P. J. Lockhart

Date: 12-29-1870
J. D. Wynn
A. 23 S. Tazewell
P. Wm & Ann
Oc. Farmer

M. E. Edwards
A. 22 S. Grayson
P. Wm & Mahala
M. John A. Smith

Date: 1-7-1871
H. C. Fanning
A. 27 S. Bland
P. Jos & Jane

Oc. Farmer

Mary J. Robinett
A. 16 S. Bland
P. Jezreel & Mary

M. L. J. Miller

Date: 1-24-1871
John T. Rider
A. 29 S. Giles
P. Hiram & Sophronia
Oc. Farmer

Louvenia V. Wyrick
A. 21 S. Giles
P. Ephriam & Isabel
M. A. A. Ashworth

Date: 2-24-1871
James D. Honaker
A. 24 S. Tazewell
P. Henry & Elizabeth
Oc. Farmer

Helen Pool
A. 28 S. Giles
P. Simkins & Malinda
M. J. T. Frazier

Date: 3-29-1871
Robert H. Bane
A. 34 S. Giles
P. Jessie & Anna
Oc. Farmer

Frances M. McDonald
A. 23 S. Wyoming Co., WV
P. Wm & Maria
M. J.H. Hoge

Date: 5-13-1871
T. G. Hudson
A. 24 S. Wythe
P. Isaac & Elizabeth

Oc. Farmer

Lou. V. Repass
A. 24 S. Wythe
P. John & Mary E.

M. James H. Brown

Date: 12-22-1870
J.P. King
A. 22 S. Giles
P. Allen & Sarah
Oc. Farmer

Jane Carver
A. 25 S. Tazewell
P. Rob't & Catherine
M. J. T. Frazier

Date: 12-21-1870
Joshua H. Bruce
A. 45 W. Wythe
P. Jas & Elizabeth
Justice
Oc. Farmer

Julia K. Eaton
A. 33 S. Giles
P. John & Elizabeth

M. J. H. Hoge

Date: 1-4-1871
John A. Hemger
A. 18 S. Tazewell
P. Wm & Barbary
Oc. Farmer

Amanda V. Kidd
A. 17 S. Tazewell
P. Henry C. & Matilda
M. John A. Smith

Date 1-9-1871
John Wesley Harman
A. 32 W. Giles
P. Henry Wesley &
Phebe Fielder
Oc. Farmer

Martha Jane Burton
A. 27 S. Pulaski
P. Jas. Harvey &
Va. Jane Detimore
M. L. J. Miller

Date: 1-26-1871
William R. Repass
A. 18 S. Tazewell
P. Joel & Elander
Oc. Farmer

Martha Jane Waddle
A. 24 S. Wythe
P. Jos & Rhoda
M. John A. Smith

Date 3-24-1871
David E. Neel
A. 21 S. Tazewell
P. James R. & Mahala
Oc. Farmer

Mollie E. Brown
A. 19 S. Tazewell
P. Jas B. Brown
M. John A. Smith

Date 4-3-1871
William Rider
A. 27 S. Bland
P. Hiram & Sophia?
Oc. Farmer

Ellen Harman
A. 23 S. Tazewell
P. Henry & Julia
M. Isaac S. Harman

Date: 6-30-1871
Andrew Jackson Kitts
A. 24 S. Wythe
P. Andrew J. &
Polly Leedy
Oc. Farmer

Hester Ann Tickle
A. 19 S. Wythe
P. Hezekiah C. &
Caroline Matilda Farmer
M. J. C. Smith

Date: 7-19-1871  
George Floyd Kitts — Martha Ann Dilman  
A. 21 S. Wythe — A. 21 S. Wythe  
P. Jos & — P. Geo & Mary  
Sarah Elizabeth Bales  
Oc. Farmer — M. J.A. Smith

Date 8-25-1871  
Wm. N. Bruce — Lucinda Franklin  
A. 28 S. Giles — A. 34 S. Giles  
P. Amos & Ellen — P. John & Nancy  
Oc. Farmer — M. L. J. Miller

Date: 10-12-1871  
Jno F. Strock — Sarah A. Bird  
A. 32 S. Orangeburg, SC — A. 25 S. Franklin  
P. David & Sarah — P. John R. & Susan Ann  
Oc. Farmer & Mechanic — M. L. J. Miller

Date: 10-30-1871  
Harvey J. Waddle — Rhoda A. Devor  
A. 27 S. Wythe — A. 26 S. Wythe  
P. Jos Waddle &  
Minerva Lampert — P. Wm & Juliet  
Oc. Farmer — M. John C. Smith

Date: 11-21-1871  
Joseph Kimberling — Rachel Crow  
A. 19 S. Lancaster, WIS — A. 24 S. Wythe  
P. Solomon & Elizabeth — P. John & Catherine  
Oc. Farmer — M.

Date: 12-8-1871  
Robert P. Hancock — Sarah J. Collins  
A. 19 S. Bland — A. 23 S. Bland  
P. Eliza A. Hancock — P. Jas & Mary Ann  
Oc. Farmer — M. William Hicks

Date: 1-4-1872  
William Ray Kitts — Nannie Edith Burton  
A. 18 S. Wythe — A. 18 S. Pulaski  
P. Andrew Jas & — P. Jas H. & Jane  
Nancy Bower Bogle  
Oc. Farmer — M.

Date: 1-17-1872  
Daniel Robinett — Ellen Stowers  
A. 23 S. Wythe — A. 23 W. Tazewell  
P. Hiram & Dicy — P. Colby & Locky  
Oc. Farmer — M. Peter R. Suiter

Date: 8-25-1871  
Freeling Clay Bogle — Martha Jane Bogle  
A. 25 S. Wythe — A. 32 S. Tazewell  
P. Jas Buchanan & — P. Mark R. &  
Eliza Jane Munsey — Jane Newberry  
Oc. Farmer — M. John A. Smith

Begin Page 8 of Original Book  
Date 9-14-1871  
Thomas G. Coburn — Cynthia M. Britts  
A. 23 S. Mercer — A. 19 S. Craig  
P. David & Tabitha — P. Wm & Sally  
Oc. Farmer — M. L. J. Miller

Date 10-17-1871  
Francis M. Robinett — Lavlet Lampert  
A. 38 S. Wythe — A. 24 S. Wythe  
P. Hiram & Rebecca — P. Jas & Elizabeth  
Oc. Farmer — M. J. C. Smith

Date 11-8-1871  
James W. Doke — Elizabeth C. Neel  
A. 20 S. Wythe — A. 17 S. Tazewell  

P. Rob't & Margaret — P. Matthew & Louisa  
Oc. Farmer — M. J. C. Smith

Date 12-13-1871  
Giles M. Waddle — Hannah B. Price  
A. 24 S. Giles — A. 25 S. Mercer, WV  
P. Nancy N. Waddle — P. Geo P. & Mary  
Oc. Mechanic — M. John Williams

Date: 1-4-1872  
John Havens — Laura J. Hancock  
A. 22 S. Wythe — A. 18 S. Wythe  
P. Jas & Mary J. — P. G. M. & Julia A  
Oc. Farmer — M. P. J. Lochart

Date: 1-7-1872  
Isaac Carper — Mary Ann Shelton  
A. 21 S. Craig — A. 22 S. Patrick  
P. Isaac & Rebecca — P. Frederick & Esther  

Oc. Farmer — M. Peter R. Suiter

Date: 12-19-1871  
Jacob Waggoner — Fanie J. Kirby  
A. 44 W. Tazewell — A. 22 S. Wythe  
P. Elias & Arminta — P. Stephen & Margaret  
Oc. Farmer — M. J.J. Greaever

Date: 2-5-1872
Franklin G. Robinett    Sarah S. Cundiff
A. 18 S. Tazewell    A. 26 W. Tazewell
P. Prudence Robinett    P. Jos & Elizabeth Lambert
Oc. Farmer    M.   P.R.Suiter

Date: 3-14-1872
James F. Collins    Mary Ann Holt
A. 21 S. Montgomery    A. 22 S. Rockingham
P. Floyd & Mary    P. Wm & Elizabeth
Oc. Farmer    M. Isaac S. Harman

Date:3-28-1872
Robert M. Ashworth    Ellie Honaker
A. 24 S. Pulaski    A. 22 S. Tazewell
P. Armistead A. & Nancy P. A. J. & Ellen
Oc. Farmer    M. J.H. Hoge

Date: 4-4-1872
E.B. Collins    Mary E. Wright
A. 21 S. Wisconsin    A. 25 S. Pulaski
P. Edward & Elizabeth    P. Thos & Luvina
Oc. Farmer    M. A.A. Ashworth

Date: 4-25-1872
Adam D. Groseclose    Partha Ann Wall
A. 25 S. Wythe    A. 23 S. Wythe
P. Wm & Adaline    P. Stephen & Sarah
Oc. Farmer    M. J. Calvin Smith

Date: 6-18-1872
George W. Dillman    Lucinda J. Hearn
A. 26 S. Franklin, Ind.    A. 16 S. Wythe
P. Geo & Mary    P. Harvey & Christina Wyrick
Oc. Mechanic    M. George K. Green

Date: 6-26-1872
A. A. Tibbs    S. A. Hanshew
A. 28 S. Wythe    A. 26 S. Wythe
P. Geo M. & Mary    P. And' & Elizabeth
Oc. Farmer    M. D.A. Snow

Date: 8-1-1872
Levi Groseclose    Sarah K. Foglesong
A. 28 W. Wythe    A. 19 S. Wythe
P. Abraham & Polly    P. Henry & Julia
Od. Farmer    M. G.W.K. Green

Date: 2-5-1872
Jas H. Ball    Matilda Hewitt
A. 17 S. Wythe    A. 16 S. Tazewell
P. Dan'l & R. A.    P. M. & Rebecca
Oc. Farmer    M. William Hicks

Date 3-14-1872
J. W. Compton    Maria J. Bird
A. 24 S. Tazewell    A. 20 S.
P. W.W. & Nancy    P. Benj.V. Bird
Oc. Farmer    M. A.A. Ashworth

Date: 3-26-1872
Isaac N. Shrader    Alpha Lambert
A. 22 S. Tazewell    A. 25 W. Giles
P. John & Christina    P. John & Emily
Oc. Farmer    M. L. J. Miller

Date: 4-11-1872
James T.Taylor    Cyntha Wohlford
A. 29 S. Pulaski    A. 21 S. Giles
P. Rob't E. & Matilda    P. Sam'l & Elizabeth
Oc. Mechanic    M. A.A. Ashworth

Date: 5-20-1872
Wythe G. Dunn    Sarah Jane Edwards
A. 23 S. Wythe    A. 19 S. Wythe
P. Joseph & Sarah    P. Wm & Mahala
Oc. Mechanic    M. George K. Green

Date: 6-26-1872
Joseph Ewald    Elizabeth Brynes
A. 26 S. Wythe    A. 19 S. Wise
P. Anthony & Lucinda    P. J.W. & Sarah
Oc. Merchant    M. J.A. Meurer

Date: 7-1-1872
Charles C. Kitts    Lauretta Neel
A. 20 S. Wythe    A. 16 S. Tazewell
P. Joseph & Elizabeth    P. Matthew & Elizabeth
Oc. Farmer    M. G.W.K. Green

Date 8-13-1872
C. B. P. Price    Sarah M. Mustard
A. 22 S. Mercer    A. 23 S. Giles
P. Geo P. & Mary    P. John & Vicy
Oc. Farmer    M. J.H. Hoge

Date: 8-16-1872
John W. Chandler    R. C. Hall
A. 24 S. Carroll    A. 21 S. Giles
P. H. A. & N.J.    P. H. & C.
Oc. Farmer    M. A.A. Ashworth

Date: 9-4-1872
James M. Brown    Annie S. Bishop
A. 19 S. Giles    A. 23 S. Giles
P. Geo W. & Maria    P. Wm M. Bishop
Oc. Farmer    M. J.? T. Frazier

Date.9-8-1872
Franklin R. Crigger    Regina V. Robinett
A. 26 S. Wythe    A. 31 S. Wythe
P. Reuben & Mary    P. Hiram & Rebecca

Oc. Farmer    M. G.W.K. Green

Date 9-23-1872
John W. Blessing    Elizabeth Jerusha Bogle
A. 22 S. Wythe    A. 26 S. Tazewell
P. Harvey & Eliza Jane    P. Mark Reed & Jane Newberry
Oc. Farmer    M. John A. Smith

Date: 10-10-1872
Henry Foglesong    Nancy M. Bails
A. 28 S. Wythe    A. 16 S. Smyth
P. Henry & Julia    P. Jas R. & Mary M.
Oc. Farmer    M. W. Hicks

Date 10-17-1872
William T. McNutt    Mary M. Hudson
A. 25 S. Sevier, TN    A. 24 S. Wythe
P. Jn S. & Elizabeth    P. Isaac & Elizabeth
Oc. Farmer    M. ? B.?

Date 11-14-1872
William A. Bennett    Bettie E. Woodyard
A. 19 S. Wythe    A. 19 S. Giles
P. John A. & Jane V.    P. Almarine & Jane
Oc. Mechanic    M. A.A. Ashworth

Date: 11-20-1872
Jonas H. Groseclose    Mary M. Baumgardner
A. 21 S. Wythe    A. 20 S. Wythe
P. Jacob & Susan    P. John & Malinda
Oc. Farmer    M. A.A. Ashworth

Date: 11-28-1872
John Greason Perry    Mary Jane Groseclose
A. 22 S.Tazewell    A. 20 S. Wythe
P. Jesse & Angeline    P. Wm & Adaline
Oc. Farmer    M. J. B. Greaen?

Date: 12-6-1872
Preston W. Rice    Julia Frances Wilson
A. 31 S. Pittsylvania    A. 20 S. Giles
P. Thos & Nancy    P. Edward & Rebecca
Oc. Teacher    M. A.A. Ashworth

Begin Page 9 of Original Book
Date: 12-15-1872
John W. S.Townley    Mary Catherine Harman
A. 37 S. Greenbrier    A. 25 S. Wythe
P. M. J. & E. D.    P. Adam Q. & Susanna Eaton
Oc. Mechanic    M. Wm Hicks

Date: 12-31-1872
Noah B. Wolf    Rebecca A. Fanning
A. 25 S. Smyth    A. 22 S. Giles
P. Jas & Mary Ann    P. John & Levina
Oc. Mechanic    M. L. J. Miller

Date: 12-24-1872
Henry Thompson    Sarah E. Kitts
A. 23 S. Wythe    A. 23 S. Wythe
P. Arch & Polly    P. Lee A. & Malinda
Oc. Farmer    M. William Hicks

Date: 12-26-1872
William H. Lambert    Ellen Linkous
A. 22 S. Giles    A. 25 S. Montgomery
P. John & Emily    P. H. & Mary E.
Oc. Farmer    M. Peter R. Suiter

Date 1-2-1873
Calvin G. Crockett    Kate C. Crump
29 S. Smyth    A. 20 S. Pittsylvania Co.
P. John C & Mary J.    P. Geo W. & Sallie J.
Oc. Farmer    M. J. Calvin Smith

Date: 1-8-1873
Joseph W. Carter    Paulina J. Chandler
A. 21 S. Mercer    A. 20 S. Patrick
P. Randolph & Mary    P. Hiram A. & Nancy
Oc. Farmer    M. William Hicks

Date: 1-16-1873
John T. Lampert
A. 30 S. Wythe
P. Henry & Emeline

Oc. Farmer

Jane Havens
A. 29 S. Giles
P. Rebecca F. Havens

M.  William Hicks

Date: 1-29-1873
Andrew J. Wimmer
A. 34 W. Montgomery
P. Sam'l & Massie

Oc. Carpenter

Mary Jane Terry
A. 25 S. Tazewell
P. Wm Terry &
  Margaret Lampert
M. Peter R. Suiter

Date: 1-30-1873
Theodore J. B. Spangler
A. 20 S. Wythe
P. John & Mary E.
Oc. Farmer

Corrola Devor
A. 25 S. Wythe
P. Wm & Juliet
M. William Hicks

Date: 2-3-1873
Noah B. Williams
A. 21 S. Smyth
P. Wm & Christina
Oc. Farmer

Eunice L. Groseclose
A. 24 S. Wythe
P. Jacob & Susannah
M.

Date: 2-13-1873
John G. Dilman
A. 32 W. Johnston, TN
P. Geo & Mary
Oc. Farmer

Amanda E. Kimberling
A. 21 S. Wythe
P. Jos & Elizabeth
M. William Hicks

Date: 2-6-1873
William H. Benton
A. 21 S. Giles
P. Elias & Sarah
Oc. Farmer

Alvira Stowers
A. 19 S. Tazewell
P. Colby & Lockey
M.  Wm. E. Neel

Date: 2-23-1873
Wythe G. Painter
A. 21 S. Wythe
P. Jas C. & Eliza

Oc. Bricklayer

Virginia Caroline Tickle
A. 18 S. Wythe
P. Hezekiah C. &
Caroline Matilda Farmer
M.  J. C. Smith

Date: 3-13-1873
James M. Hamilton
A. 21 S. Giles
P. Timothy & Margaret

Oc. Physician

Annie E. Mustard
A. 17 S. Giles
P. Harvey R. & Maria

M.  I. S. Harman

Date: 3-26-1873
James Tabor
A. 30 W. Tazewell
P. Elender Tabor
Oc. Farmer

Luvina V. Cameron
A. 26 S. Tazewell
P. Duncan & Margaret
M. A.A. Ashworth

Date: 4-10-1873
J. Taylor Gollehon
A. 24 S. Smyth
P. Jas & Margaret
Oc. Teacher

Mary V. Tilson
A. 16 S. Wythe
P. H. H. & Jane
M. C.W. Cooper

Date: 5-10-1873
William T. Woods
A. 22 S. Wythe
P. Moses & Julia
Oc. Farmer

Erveline Cooley
A. 23 D. Wythe
P. Benj. & Mary Jane
M. C. W. Cooper

Date: 5-28-1873
Ephriam W. Eagle
A.
P.
Oc.

Elizabeth C. Neel
A.
P.
M.

Date: 6-12-1873
Joseph M. Alley
A. 23 S. Tazewell
P. Wm. A. & Angeline
Oc. Farmer

Fannie Umpswiller
A. 25 S. Tazewell
P. John & Matilda
M. J. A. Smith

Date. 7-1-1873
Henry T. Lampert
A. 23 S. Wythe
P. Henry & Emaline
Oc. Farmer

Mary E. Bailes
A. 19 S. Smyth
P. Jas R. & Mary M.
M. William Hicks

Date: 7-3-1873
Allen C. Burris
A. 21 S. Jackson, OH
P. C. H. & Polly
Oc. Farmer

Mary J. Kimberling
A. 25 S. Wythe
P. Soloman & Elizabeth
M. J. C. Smith

Date: 7-17-1873
Arista Gratton Harman
A. 24 S. Wythe
P. Adam Q. & Susanna
Oc. Farmer

Rebecca J. Honaker
A. 21 S. Tazewell
P. A. J. & Ellen
M. Robert A. Hutsell

Date: 8-17-1873
Ephriam W. King     Margaret S. Williams
A. 26 S. Wythe     A. 17 S. Smyth
P. Geo & Mary     P. Wm & Christina
Oc. Farmer     M. J. Mahood

Date: 8-19-1873
William J. Spangler     Darthula A. Wilson
A. 29 S. Wythe     A. 28 W. Wythe
P. Peter & Betsy     P. Elias & Annie Foglesong
Oc. Farmer     M. J. J. Greaver

Date: 8-27-1873
James M. Stafford     Vicey Melvin
A. 37 S. Giles     A. 23 S. Giles
P. Ralph A. & Peggy     P. Edmond & Catherine
Oc. Farmer     M. J. H. Hoge

Date: 8-28-1873
Samuel H. Harden     Frances V. Umbarger
A. 22 S. NC     A. 16 S. Wythe
P. John G. & Maria     P. Jas & Margaret
Oc. Farmer     M. Robert A. Hutsell

Date: 9-4-1873
Abraham B. Honaker     Helen M. Forbes
A. 25 S. Tazewell     A. 21 S. Scott, KY
P. Andrew J. & Elener     P. John W. & Louisa J.
Oc. Farmer     M. William Hicks

Date: 9-18-1873
James G. Kegley     Elizabeth F. Bird
A. 35 W. Wythe     A. 26 S. Floyd
P. Isaac & Prudence     P. B.V. & Catherine
Oc. Farmer     M. A.A. Ashworth

Date: 10-2-1873
Thomas H. Groseclose     Alice M. Havens
A. 20 S. Wythe     A. 19 S. Wythe
P. Jane Groseclose     P. And. & Elizabeth
Oc. Farmer     M. John A. Smith

Date: 10-2-1873
Henry W. Steel     Virginia J. Brown
A. 23 S. Tazewell     A. 21 S. Wythe
P. John & Catherine     P. John & Catherine
Oc. Farmer     M. John A. Smith

Date: 2-5-1873
N. Chrisman Neel     Rhoda J. French
A. 21 S. Tazewell     A. 28 W. Tazewell
P. Henry & Lydia     P. Austin & Lucinda
Oc. Farmer     M. L. J. Miller

Date: 10-29-1873
William H. Suthers     Sarah H. C. Hudson
A. 25 S. Tazewell     A. 23 S. Wythe
P. John H. & Jane R.     P. Isaac & Elizabeth
Oc. Cabinet Maker     M. J. J. Greaver?

Date: 11-11-1873
Gregory H. Ewald     Thursa A. McOlgan
A. 24 S. Wythe     A. 21 S. Botetourt
P. Anthony & Lucinda     P. Jas & Ann E.
Oc. Merchant     M. James Meurer?

Date: 12-3-1873
Samuel P. Terry     Margaret L. Gibson
A. 23 S. Tazewell     A. 17 S. Tazewell
P. Wm & Margaret     P. Sam'l T. & Jane
Oc. Farmer     M. Peter R. Suiter

Date: 12-22-1873
David E. Brown     Malinda B. Cameron
25 S. Tazewell     A. 23 S. Tazewell
P. Jas B. & Sarah     P. Duncan & Margaret F.
Oc. Farmer     M. S. Rhudy

Date: 12-22-1873
Seton A. Stimson     Louisa V. Adkins
A. 22 S. Floyd     A. 19? S. Tazewell
P. Nelson B. & Lydia     P. Peter & Rhoda
Oc. Farmer     M. Peter R. Suiter

Date: 2-12-1874
Lorenza Dow Helvey     Sarah Ann Eliz. Miller
A. 20 S. Giles     A. 18 S. Giles
P. John Kennerly &
Sarah Dora Munsey     P. Dr. L. J. & Martha L.
Oc. Farmer     M. J. M. Crisman

Date: 2-28-1874
Robert G. Cecil     Susan H. Burgess
A. 23 S. Tazewell     A. 18 S. Mercer

P. Joshua & Sarah     P. David & Elizabeth
Oc. Farmer     M. Peter R. Suiter

Date: 2-19-1874  
Walter Shewey / Laura E. Fry  
A. 21 S. Grant. WI / A. 22 S. Wythe  
P. A. W. & Ann / P. Abraham & Julia  
Oc. Farmer / M. S. Rhudy

Date: 3-5-1874  
James M. Bailey / Julia H. Honaker  
A. 20 S. Mercer / A. 20 S. Tazewell  
P. John M. & Sally / P. Peter C. & Mary A.  

Oc. Farmer / M. James Cafee

Date: 3-4-1874  
John Stinson / Hester Ann Bussey  
A. 25 S. Giles / A. 15 S. Monroe, WV  
P. Hiram & Ruth / P. Thompson & Elizabeth  
Oc. Farmer? / M. A. A. Ashworth

Date: 3-19-1874  
George W. Kinzer / Annie E. Bruce  
A. 29 S. Wythe / A. 19 S. Wise  
P. Christian & Mary / P. J. Henderson & Margaret A.  
Oc. County Surveyor / M. J. H. Hoge

Date: 4-8-1874  
George W. Kidd / Cosby Repass  
A. 20 S. Tazewell / A. 19 S. Tazewell  
P. H. C. & Mima / P. Isaac H. & Phebe  
Oc. Farmer / M. J. A. Smith

Date: 5-17-1874  
Eldred L. Scott / Mary Stowers  
A. 19 S. Wythe / A. 19 S. Wythe  
P. John M & Barbara / P. Jas M. & Dicey  
Oc. Farmer / M. James A. Brown

Date: 7-16-1874  
Columbus A. Brown / Victoria C. Repass  
A. 21 S. Alleghaney / A. 17 S. Tazewell  
P. John & Elizabeth / P. Isaac & Phebe  
Oc. Farmer / M. J. A. Smith

Date: 8-22-1874  
William S. Collins / Mildred A. Akers  
A. 22 S. Giles / Age 23 S. Pulaski  
P. Jas & Mary Ann / P. Moses & Catherine  
Oc. Farmer / M. William Hicks

Date 3-4-1874  
Frederick M Wheeler / Rebecca J. Coburn  
A. 24 S. Carroll / A. 25 S. Mercer, WV  
P. Andrew M. & Nancy / P. David & Ursley  
Oc. Farmer / M. L. J. Miller

Date: 3-12-1874  
William E. Miller / Mary L. Ramsey  
A. 20 S. Giles / A. 17 S. Henry  
P. Abram Woodson & / P. Wm & Elizabeth  
Rachel Hearn  
Oc. Farmer / M. L. J. Miller

Date: 3-18-1874  
Rowlett W. Snead / Mary V. Cundiff  
A. 21 S. Chesterfield / A. 17 S. Tazewell  
P. John H. & Rachel / P. Elizabeth Cundiff  
Oc. Carpenter / M. A. A. Ashworth

Date: 3-30-1874  
Franklin G. Huddle / Alpha C. Doak  
A. 21 S. Wythe / A. 18 S. Wythe  
P. David & Lausahamy? / P. Rob't & Amanda  
Oc. Farmer / M. J. C. Repass

Date: 3-16-1874  
William Sam'l Hutchins / Rhoda Lou Harman  
A. 23 S. Botetourt / A. 23 S. Giles  
P. Arch & Martha J. / P. Jno W. & Hester A.  
Oc. Carpenter / M. L. J. Miller

Date: 6-16-1874  
James Larkin Corder / Minerva J. Pauley  
A. 19 S. Giles / A. 16 S. Tazewell  
P. B. F. & Julia A. / P. Madison & Rebecca B.  
Oc. Carpenter / M. L. J. Miller

Date: 7-29-1874  
William A. Perkey / Martha S. Ingraham  
A. 32 W. Wythe / A. 24 S. Wythe  
P. Dan'l & Letitia / P. Wm & Prudence  
Oc. Farmer / M. J. C. Smith

Date: 9-2-1874  
Joseph M. Kinder / Sophia King  
A. 35 W. Wythe / A. 28 S. Wythe  
P. Solomon & Amanda / P. Jacob & Julia  
Oc. Farmer / M. J. C. Smith

Date: 8-20-1874
Charles Monroe Wright    Cecilia Susan Bussey
A. 24 S. Giles    A. 18 S. Tazewell
P. Francis & Vicey    P. Thompson & Elizabeth
Oc. Farmer    M. J. H. Hoge

Date: 9-9-1874
Joseph S. Fisher    Lucinda A. Repass
A. 35 W. Wythe    A. 27 S. Wythe
P. Jos & Sarah    P. Stephen & Rosanna
Oc. Farmer    M. James A. Brown

Date: 9-16-1874
George W. Groseclose    Tena E. Tobler
A. 20 S. Wythe    A. 16 S. Tazewell
P. Jos & Elizabeth    P. James & Mary
Oc. Farmer    M. J. J. Greaver?

Date: 9-24-1874
Charles E. Walker    Louise M. Walker
A. 22 S. Tazewell    A. 22 S. Tazewell
P. David A. & Harriett    P. Benj. S. & Elizabeth
Oc. Farmer    M. W.E. Neel

Date: 9-23-1874
Rufus F. Nisewander    Julia Ann Gills
A. 30 W. Giles    A. 15 S. Tazewell
P. Harvey & Malinda    P. Benj. T. & Mary
Oc. Farmer    M. L. J. Miller

Date: 9-23-1874
Samuel W. Williams    Maggie A. Grayson
A. 26 S. Henry    A. 17 S. Wythe
P. Robt W. & Elizabeth P.    P. A. J. & R. V.
Oc. Attorney    M. William Hicks

Date: 11-3-1874
William Ira Vest    Mary E. Dillon
A. 20 S. Franklin    A. 23 S. Montgomery
P. Flemming & Sarah    P. John W. and Docia
Oc. Farmer    M. L. J. Miller

11-12-1874
Christopher Collins    Margaret M. Akers
A. 22 S. Wisonsin    A. 24 S. Pulaski
P. Edmon & Elizabeth    P. Moses & Catherine
Oc. Farmer    M. William Hicks

Date: 11-16-1874
Wythe C. Newberry    Elizabeth L. Mustard
A. 23 S. Wythe    A. 24 S. Giles
P. Henry & Elizabeth    P. John & Louvisa
Robinett    Patterson
Oc. Farmer    M. J. H. Hoge

Date: 11-17-1874
Doctor Wm M. Wright    Sarah Ann Bruce
A. 20 S. Giles    A. 22 S. Wyoming
P. Francis M. & Bicy    P. John Grayson &
Stafford    Elizabeth Jane Robinson
Oc. Teacher    M. William Hicks

Date: 11-21-1874
Armestead A. Bird    Frances M. A. Gills
A. 23 S. Wythe    A. 19 S. Tazewell
P. Stephen W. & Malinda    P. Benj F. & Mary Ann
Oc. Farmer    M. Armstead A. Ashworth

Date: 11-23-1874
John F. Strock    Julia A. G. Price
A. 35 W. Orangeburg, SC    A. 22 S. Mercer
P. David & Sarah    P. Geo P. & Mary
Oc. Carpenter    M. A. A. Ashworth

Date 11-24-1874
John D. Rummion    Frances A. Hammons
A. 19 S. Pulaski    A. 17 S. Giles
P. John & Caroline    P. Gordon & Sarah
Oc. Farmer    M. J. H. Hoge

Date: 12-2-1874
Jesse G. Linkous    Mary M. Nunn
A. 19 Tazewell    A. 20 S. Franklin
P. Abraham & Emily    P. Thos & Nancy
Oc. Farmer    M. L. J. Miller

Date: 12-2?-1874
Thomas J. Neil    Dolphia J. Tickle
A. 38 W. Tazewell    A. 29 W. Montgomery
P. Thos & Sarah    P. Esther Oliver
Oc. Farmer    M. Isaac S. Harman

Date: 12-9-1874
Louis A.? Leffel    Julia A. Thornton
A. 22 S. Craig    A. 19 S. Mercer
P. Wm & Mary A.    P. K. C. & Virginia
Oc. Fermer    M. Samuel W. Austin

Date: 12-17-1874
John Marcus                     Susan J. Dunnigan
A. 21 S. Caldwell, NC           A. 18 S. Wythe
P. Wilburn M. & Dunavine        P. Ruel M. & Mary
Oc. Farmer                      M. J. C. Smith

Date: 12-24-1874
James M. Surratt                Elizabeth Tickle
A. 51 D. Laurens Dist, SC       A. 21 S.
P. Osborne & Mary               P. Wm Tickle
Oc. Laborer                     M. William Hicks

Begin Page 11 of Original Book
Date: 1-5-1875
James F. Muncy                  Fannie J. King
A. 23 S. Giles                  A. 24 S. Giles
P. Jas A. & Jemima              P. J. B. & M. M.
Oc. Farmer                      M. J. A. Smith

Date 1-9-1875
Milton Farrington               Ludema McHaffey
A. 52 W. Guilford, NC           A. 28 W. Tazewell
P. Sam'l & Sally                P. Austin & Lucy French
Oc. Farmer                      M. Peter R. Suiter

Date: 2-9-1875
George W. Robinett              Eliza Foglesong
A. 48 S. Wythe                  A. 39 W. Wythe
P. Hiram & Rebecca              P. John T. Crabtree
Oc. Farmer                      M. G.W.K. Green

Date 2-19-1875
Samuel M. Stuart                Mary E. Bird
A. 24 S. Pulaski                A. 18 S. Wythe
P. Wm & Peggy                   P. Wm. M. & Eliza J.
Oc. Carpenter                   M. A.A. Ashworth

Date: 2-19-1875
Thomas J. Collins               Caroline C. Shrader
A. 19 S. Wythe                  A. 14 S. Wythe
P. Edward & Elizabeth           P. Joseph & Nora
Oc. Farmer                      M. B.R. Wilburn

Date: 2-18-1875
James R. Hager                  Mary C. Cameron
A. 33 W. Tazewell               A. 34 S. Tazewell
P. Squire & Elizabeth           P. Duncan & Margaret
Oc. Farmer                      M. John A. Smith

Date: 3-1-1875
James P. Crutchfield            Cornelia A. Fortner
A. 21 S. Smyth                  A. 19 S. Tazewell
P. Wm & Elizabeth               P. Luemma J. Fortner
Oc. Farmer                      M. B. R. Wilburn

Date: 3-4-1875
Joesph M. Ashworth              Catherine H. Stuart
A. 20 S. Wythe                  A. 19 S. Pulaski
P. Armestead A. & Parthena      P. Wm & Peggy
Oc. Farmer                      M. A.A. Ashworth

Date: 3-10-1875
Nathaniel M. Farley             Levis M. Willis
A. 20 S. Giles                  A. 17 S. McDowell
P. N. M. & Mary                 P. Sam'l & Sarah A.

Oc. Farmer                      M. L. J. Miller

Date: 5-13-1875
William Dunnagan                Mary M. Bogle
A. 28 S. Surry, NC              A. 17 S. Wythe
P. Lewis & Nancy                P. Andrew T.&
                                Maria Cubine
Oc. Farmer                      M. J. H. Hoge

Date: 5-25-1875
Jas L. Lampert                  Angeline Kitts
A. 21 S. Wythe                  A. 19 S. Wythe
P. David & Margaret             P. Peter & Amanda M.
                                Hounshell
Oc. Laborer                     M. G.W.K. Green

Date: 5-27-1875
Richard K. Clark                Mary J. V. Hager
A. 22 S. Wythe                  A. 17 S. Tazewell
P. Richard & Susan              P. Jacob J. & M. J.

Oc. Farmer                      M. L. J. Miller

Date: 5-26?-1875
James D. Honaker                Susan H. Linkous
A. 28 W. Tazewell               A. 21 S. Tazewell
P. Henry & Elizabeth            P. Abram & Emaline
Oc. Farmer                      M. L. J. Miller

Date: 5-31-1875
William Dillow                  Mary E. Waddle
A. 24 S. Wythe                  A. 23 S. Wythe
P. Addison & Vicy               P. Calvin & Isabella
Oc. Farmer                      M. Isaac S. Harman

Date: 7-1-1875
George S. Huddle Martha E. Turley
A. 20 S. Wythe A. 16 S. Tazewell
P. Daniel & Margaret P. Thos & M. T.
Oc. Farmer M. William E. Neel

Date: 7-1-1875
Rufus Peery Martha S. Hatch
A. 19 S. Tazewell A. 18 S. Tazewell
P. Giles & Mary P. Thos & Massilla
Oc. Farmer M. Wm. E. Neel

Date: 7-13-1875
George S. Thompson Mary Ann Davis
A. 19 S. Wythe A. 21 S. Giles
P. Jas & Sarah P. Isaac J. & Mahala
Oc. Farmer M. J. H. Hoge

Date: 7-27-1875
Erastus G. Stowers Mary I. Lambert
A. A. 20 S. Tazewell A. 24 S. Wythe
P. Hickman & Sarah P. Stephen & Malinda

Oc. Farmer M. G.W. K. Green

Date: 8-26-1875
Isaiah Stuart Bruce Maria T. Myers
A. 22 S. Wyoming A. 22 S. Wythe
P. Jas Harvey & Mary P. J. B. & Margaret
Margaret Russell (Shipp)
Oc. Farmer M. G.W.K. Green

Date: 9-5-1875
Cliaborn Green Viney Calender
A. 24 S. Wythe A. 18 S. Mercer
P. Jacob & Joanna P. Calander
Oc. Laborer M. G.W.K. Green

Date: 9-21-1875
Charles M. Sarver Martha Adkins
A. 23 S. Tazewell A. 15 S. Tazewell
P. John & Marsha P. Peter & Rhoda

Oc. Farmer M.

Date: 9-23-1875
Henry D. Price Melvina J. Price
A. 38 S. Mongtomery A. 27 S. Mercer
P. Jno P. & Phebe P. Geo P. & M.A.
Oc. Farmer M. B. R. Wilburn

Date: 7-1-1875
Enos Davidson Victoria Clay
A. 26 S. Tazewell A. 21 S. Giles
P. Jas & Peggy P. Anderson & Viney Clark
Oc. Blacksmith M. L. J. Miller

Date: 7-2-1875
Jackson Green Elizabeth Ann Page
A. 26 W. Wythe A. 17 S. Wyoming
P. Milton & Mary P. Griffen & Sally
Oc. Laborer M. J. C. Smith

Date: 7-18-1875
Rush F. Lampert Marsha E. Havens
A. 23 S. Wythe A. 17 S. Giles
P. Henry & Emaline P. Jane Havens
Oc. Farmer M. G.W.K. Green

Date: 8-18-1875
Francis M. Compton Rhoda A. Muncy
A. 25 S. Tazewell A. 23 S. Wythe
P. W. W. & Nancy P. Andrew Jackson &
 Sarah Jane Peery
Oc. Farmer M. William Hicks

Date: 9-5-1875
Eli Leady Mary Muncy
A. 66 W. Wythe A. 33 W. Monroe
P. John & Polly P. James & Mahala Clark
Oc. Farmer M. G.W.K. Green

Date: 9-21-1875
D.W. Dunn Cynthia Stowers
A. 28 S. Wythe A. 23 S. Wythe
P. Jos & Sarah P. Jas M. & Dicy
Oc. Co. Treasurer M. B.R. Wilburn

Date: 9-23-1875
Francis Wright Mattie Ann Bruce
A. 63 W. Ireland A. 23 S. Wythe
P. Francis Wright P. Jas. Harvey &
 Margaret Russell (Shipp)
Oc. Farmer M. B. R. Wilburn

Date: 10-5-1875
Emory A. Sharitz Charlotte S. Bruce
A. 28 S. Wythe A. 18 S. Wise
P. Jos & Patsy P. J. Henderson & Margaret
Oc. Farmer M. B. R. Wilburn

Date: 10-21-1875
James H. Stowers | Sophia E. Robinett
a. 26 S. Tazewell | A. 16 S. Wythe
P. Gordon & Sarah | P. Hiram & Dicy
Oc. Farmer | M. Peter R. Suiter

Date: 11-1-1875
James Houdashell | Louisa C. Hanshew
A. 19 S. Wythe | A. 21 S. Wythe
P. Henry & Delila J. | P. Andrew & E.
Oc. Farmer | M. C.W. Cooper

Date: 11-3-1875
Joseph W. Cameron | Elizabeth C. Kidd
A. 30 S. Tazewell | A. 25 S. Tazewell
P. Duncan & Margaret | P. Wm. S. & Malinda

Oc. Farmer | M. J. A. Smith

Date: 11-5-1875
George Dabney Painter | Elizabeth Nancy Tickle
A. 21 S. Wythe | A. 23 S. Wythe
P. Jos Cowan & | P. Hezekiah C. &
Eliza Chandler | Caroline Matilda Farmer
Oc. Bricklayer | M. J. C. Smith

Date: 11-11-1875
Hiram A. Pauley | Elizabeth Wyrick
A. 57 W. Wythe | A. 30 S. Wythe
P. John & Polly | P. Asa & Marinda Bogle
Oc. Farmer | M. L. J. Miller

Date: 11-25-1875
G. F. Rider | Julia A. Tolbert
A. 28 D. Giles | A. 30 W. Giles
P. Hiram & S. | P. Edward & Catherine Indian?
Oc. Farmer | M. L. J. Miller

Date: 12-6-1875
John R. Linkous | Lizzie V. Nunn
A. 24 S. Giles | A. 15 S. Franklin
P. Abraham & Emaline | P. Thos & Nancy
Oc. Farmer | M. Peter R. Suiter

Date: 12-9-1875
James K. Jones | Mary Colbret
A. 49 D. Giles | A. 33 S. NC
P. John & Nancy | P. Rob't & Ann
Oc. Farmer | M. G.W. K. Green

Begin Page 12 of Original Book
Date: 12-24-1875
Paris H. Chandler | Sallie Ann Hall
A. 18 S. Carroll | A. 21 S. Wythe
P. Pauline Chandler | P. Hiram & C.V.
Oc. Farmer | M. J.C. Smith

Date: 12-26-1875
Clifton H. Britts | Mary E. Warden
A. 21 S. Craig | A. 18 S. Wythe
P. Wm & Sarah | P. Thos. & Malinda
Oc. Farmer | M. L. J. Miller

Date: 12-28-1875
Charles Edwards | Margaret A. Wilson
A. 48 W, Rockingham | A. 39 S. Wythe
P. Chas & Polly | P. Jos & Elizabeth?
Oc. Farmer | M. J. C. Smith

Date: 12-28-1875
James Harvey Mustard | Harriet E. Price
A. 24 S. Pulaski | A. 17 S. Giles
P. Wm. D. & Paulina Tynes | P. Geo. P. & Mary E.
Oc. Farmer | M. A.A. Ashworth

Date 12-30-1875
Giles M. Linkous | Susan D. Woodyard
A. 18 S. KY | A. 26 S. Giles
P. W.A. & Polly | P. Levi S. & Dranah
Oc. Farmer | M. Peter R. Suiter

Date 12-29-1875
Isaac L. Johnston | Sarah E. Bowles
A. 25 S. Pulaski | A. 26 S. Carroll
P. Lewis & Patsey | P.
Oc. Farmer | M. A. A. Ashworth

Date: 12-30-1875
William K. French | Virginia E. Miller
A. 24 S. Giles | A. 20 S. Giles
P. J. P & M. A. | P. Abraham Woodson &
| Rachel Hearn
Oc. Farmer | M. L. J. Miller

Date: 12-30-1875
Enoch S. Alley | Mary E. Sublett
A. 23 S. Davidson Co, NC | A. 28 S.
P. Jos & Mary | P. Sam'l D. & Petra
Oc. Carpenter | M. J. A. Smith

Date: 12-22-1875
B. L. Bird | M. A. Thornton
A. 24 S. Wythe | A. 21 S. Mercer
P. John R. & Susan | P. K. C. & Virginia
Oc. Farmer | M. A. A. Ashworth

Date: 12-25-1875
John Johnston | Maria Hobbs
A. 23 S. Madison | A. 17 S. Giles
P. David & Sophia | P. Thos & Julia
Oc. Farmer | M. John Trigg

Date: 2-3-1876
Charlie Martin Rudder | Louisa Jerusha Mustard
A.38 W. Halifax | A. 21 S. Giles
P. Ed. M & Elizabeth | P. Wm P. & Louisa Robinett
Oc. Farmer | M. J. H. Hoge

Date: 2-25-1876
Henley F. Nicewander | Rhoda Nisewander
A. 21 S. Giles | A. 18 S. Giles
P. Alex. & Mary | P. Harvey R. & Malinda
Oc. Farmer | M. J. H. Hoge

Date: 3-22-1876
Charles Thomas | Nannie V. Thompson
A. 25 S. Wythe | A. 23 S. Giles
P. John & Katy | P. F. M. Thompson

Oc. Carpenter | M. A.A. Ashworth

Date: 3-23-1875
John Gordon Muncy | Julia Missouri Havens
A. 19 S. Wythe | A. 20 S. Wythe
P. Jacob & Martha | P. John & Jemima
Detimore
Oc. Farmer | M. J. C. Smith

Date: 3-29-1876
Jasper N.Kinzer | Emma V. Hicks
A. 33 S. Carroll | A. 20 S. Henderson Co, NC
P. Michael & Elizabeth | P. Wm & Elizabeth M.
Oc. Farmer | M. G.W.K. Green

Date: 3-30-1876
William H. Hale | Elizabeth Carpenter
A. 53 W. Giles | A. 38 S. Northampton
P. Chas & Catherine | P. John C. & Eliza
Oc. Farmer | M. William Hicks

Date: 3-30-1876
Lelon Thomas Stimson | Julia Suiter
A. 24 S. Floyd | A. 20 S. Tazewell
P. Nelson B. & Lydia | P. A. T. & Lydia
Oc. Farmer | M.

Date: 4-4-1876
Howard Shewey | Louisa Seagle
A. 21 S. Grant Co, Wis | A. 20 S. Wythe
P. A. W. & Ann | P. C. A. & Rebecca
Oc. Farmer | M.

Date: 4-5-1876
John T. Farmer | Virginia B. Hancock
A. 21 S. Pulaski | A. 25 S. Wythe
P. Richard B. & Rachel | P. Obadiah & Jane

Oc. Farmer | M. Alex Phillippi

Date: 4-13-1876
William Sam'l. Mustard | Hester Adaline Newberry
A. 22 S. Giles | A. 20 S. Wythe
P. Harvey R.& Mariah | P. Henry & Elizabeth
Wohlford | Robinett
Oc. Farmer | M.

Date: 1-5-1876
Edmond Wilson | Cynthia Hatch
A. 45 W. Mechlenburg | A. 34 W. Mercer
P. Geo & Rachel | P. Frank Brown &
| Mary Perry
Oc. Farmer | M. Peter R. Suiter

Date: 1-6-1876
John David Davis | Margaret Eliz. Bogle
A. 20 S. Giles | A. 19 S. Giles
P. David Davis & | P. Andrew T. &
Jane Thompson | Maria Cubine
Oc. Farmer | M. J. H. Hoge

Begin Page 13 of Original Book

Date: 1-13-1876
Franklin J. Suiter | Mary Grey Updike
A. 40 S. Tazewell | A. 20 S. Greenbrier
P. Alex & Mary | P. Albert G. & Mary A. Smith
Oc. Farmer | M. J. C. Smith

Date: 5-20-1876
Henry Short | Nannie Nisewander
A. 18 S. Russell | A. 21 S. Giles
P. Jas & Elizabeth | P. H. R. & Malinda
Oc. Laborer | M. J. H. Hoge

28

Date: 6-21-1876
James M. Sheppard    Cosby Wohlford
A. 25 S. Wythe    A. 27 S. Giles
P. E.A. & R. N.    P. Sam'l & Elizabeth
Oc. Carpenter    M. Isaac S. Harman

Date: 8-9-1876
Boyd Thompson    Sarah M. Spangler
A. 22 S. Wythe    A. 25 S. Wythe
P. J. M. & Annie    P. John & Mary
Oc. Farmer    M. George K. Green

Date: 8-23-1876
Edward C. Wyley    Mary M. Stinson
A. 21 S. Giles    A. 21 S. Giles
P. Jno & Priscilla    P. Hiram & Rutha
Oc. Farmer    M. A. A. Ashworth

Date: 7-23-1876
Watson P. Fox    Sarah L. Stimson
A. 23 S. Tazewell    A. 19 S. Floyd
P. Stephen & Elizabeth    P. N. B. & Mary J.

Oc. Farmer    M. William H. Kelley

Date: 9-17-1876
Charles M. Sarver    Martha J. Adkins
A. 24 S. Tazewell    A. 16 S. Tazewell
P. John & Martha    P. Peter & Rhoda
Oc. Farmer    M. Peter R. Suiter

Date: 9-27-1876
George S. Crabtree    Susan E. Crabtree
A. 29 S. Tazewell    A. 19 S. Wythe
P. Reece & Jemima    P. Reece & Polly A.
Oc. Farmer    M. J. C. Smith

Date: 9-28-1876
George W. Hubble    Matilda A. Williams
A. 18 S. Smyth    A. 18 S. Smyth
P. W. H. & Elizabeth    P. Wm & Christina
Oc. Farmer    M. C. W. Cooper

Date: 10-5-1876
Thomas J. Starling    Victoria D. Carver
A. 20 S. Tazewell    A. 22 S. Tazewell
P. Jno C. & Tabetha    P. James & Mary

Oc. Farmer    M. Peter R. Suiter

Date: 8-3-1876
Rice G. Thomas    Susan V. Woodyard
A. 25 S. Wythe    A. 18 S. Giles
P. John & Katie    P. A. R. & Jane
Oc. Bricklayer    M. J. C. Smith

Date: 8-17-1876
Levi S. Woodyard    Rachel Stowers
A. 51 W. Guilford, NC    A. 44 W. Giles
P. Walter & Ann    P. Roland & Sally Fletcher
Oc. Farmer    M. Peter R. Suiter

Date 8-29-1876
John C. Stowers    Jane Repass
A. 37 W. Tazewell    A. 28 S. Wythe
P. Wm & Christina    P. Eli & Elizabeth
Oc. Farmer    M. G.W.K. Green

Date: 9-14-1876
Samuel Reed Bogle    Cynthia E. Smith
A. 24 S. Tazewell    A. 16 S. Tazewell
P. Mark Reed & Jane    P. Jno A. & Julia
Newberry    Waggoner
Oc. Farmer    M. L. J. Miller

Date: 9-21-1876
Stephen H. Kidd    Lyddia A. Repass
A. 25 S. Tazewell    A. 18 S. Tazewell
P. Wm S. & Malinda    P. Isaac & Phebe
Oc. Farmer    M. J. A. Smith

Date: 9-24-1876
H. S. C. Pauley    Sarilda A. Pauley
A. 21 S. Giles    A. 16 S. Tazewell
P. Jacob S. & Mary A.    P. Wm. M. & Rebecca B.B.
Oc. Laborer    M. J. C. Smith

Date: 10-4-1876
John J. Lucas    Molly M. Woodyard
A. 24 S. Giles    A. 20 S. Giles
P. John & Julia Ann    P. A. R. & Jane
Oc. Shoemaker    M. A. A. Ashworth

Date: 10-24-1876
James Wm. Banes    Margaret Ann Tickle
A. 24 S. Pulaski    A. 20 S. Pulaski
P. Jermiah &    P. Peter & Mary Ann
Sarah Davis    Journell
Oc. Farmer    M. J. C. Smith

Date: 10-24-1876
A. J. Whalen
A. 38 D. Wythe
P. Pauline Whalen
Oc. Farmer

Isabella V. Thompson
A. 18 S. Mercer
P. Wm H. & Sarah J.
M. A.A.Ashworth

Date: 10-29-1876
James F. Williams
A. 27 S. Smyth
P. Wm. B. & Christina
Oc. Farmer

Eva J. Kinder
A. 16 S. Wythe
P. John & Catherine
M. C.W. Cooper

Date: 11-28-1876
Robert S. Thompson
A. 34 W. Wythe
P. Josiah M. & Annie
Oc. Farmer

Amayitty Henderson
A. 19 S. Wythe
P. Elias & Rhoda
M. G.W.K. Green

Date: 11-30-1876
Samuel V. Morris
A. 21 S. Wythe
P. Sam'l H. & Rachel
Oc. Farmer

Octavia J. Miller
A. 15 S. Giles
P. AbrahamW. & Rachel
M. L. J. Miller

Date: 12-14-1876
William G. Thomasson
A. 24 S. Roanoke
P. Jos H. & Mary
Oc. Farmer

Louisa M. Suiter
A. 24 S. Tazewell
P. A. L. & Lyddia
M. John C. Smith

Date: 12-20-1876
John F. Myers
A. 25 S. Wythe
P. J. B. & Margaret
Oc. Farmer

Louisa P. Kitts
A. 18 S. Wythe
P. H. G. & Virginia E.
M. J. H. Hoge

Begin Page 14 of Original Book

Date:12-26-1876
Madison A. Fletcher
A. 38 W. Giles
P. Roland & Jane
Oc. Farmer

Etta V. Stowers
A. 20 S. Tazewell
P. John W. & Rachel C.
M. G.W.K. Green

Date: 1-3-1877
James Hedrick
A. 32 S. Wythe
P. Rufus & Jane
Oc. Carpenter

Missouri J. Waddle
A. 21 S. Wythe
P. Michael & Margaret
M.

Date: 1-10-1877
James D. Crawford
A. 34 S. Giles
P. John & Elizabeth
Oc. Farmer

Mary E. Price
A. 24 S. Mercer
P. Geo P. & Mary E.
M. A. A. Ashworth

Date: 1-24-1877
James H. Overstreet
A. 22 S. Bedford
P.Tilmon J. & Nancy
Oc. Farmer

Mary S. Meadows
A. 16 S. Giles
P. John H. & Mary Pegram
M. A.Q. Harman

Date: 1-25-1877
Daniel M. Bailey
A. 29 S. Mercer
P. Jas M. & Julia T.

Oc. Farmer

Mary E. Bishop
A. 21 S. Craig
P. Wm M. & Lucy

M. William H. Kelley

Date: 2-1-1877
Leonard Franklin Morehead
A. 28 S. Pulaski
P. Dan'l F. &
Isabelle Elizabeth Saunders
Oc. Farmer

Emma Louise Robinett
A. 20 S. Giles
P. Jezreel & Mary Ann
Ward
M. L. J. Miller

Date: 2-5-1877
Henry P. Lambert
A. 22 S. Wythe
P. Jas & Mandana
Oc. Farmer

Rhoda A. Repass
A. 18 S. Wythe
P. Eli & Elizabeth
M. G.W.K. Green

Date: 2-14-1877
George W. Gibson
A. 21 S. Tazewell
P. S.T. & Jane
Oc. Farmer

Nancy E. Terry
A. 19 S. Tazewell
P. Wm & Margaret
M. Peter R. Suiter

Date: 2-15-1877
James T. Kinser
A. 22 S. Montgomery
P. Thos. H. & Elizabeth
Oc. Farmer

Emma S. Wilson
A. 23 S. Tazewell
P. Edward & Rebecca
M. L. F. Miller

Date: 2-22-1877
Reece Winston
A. 22 S. Miss.
P. Rob't & Mary
Oc. Farmer

Victoria Lambert
A. 21 S. Giles
P. John F. & Emily
M. Peter R. Suiter

Date: 2-22-1877
William Rice Miller        Emily Jane Muirhead
A. 21 S. Giles             A. 17 S. Giles
P.Dr. Lorenzo John &       P. Andrew Ausborn &
Martha Lois Bird           Elizabeth J. Miller
Oc. Farmer                 M.   J. H. Hoge

Date: 3-8-1877
William H. Stowers         Rebecca J. Robinett
A. 22Tazewell              A. 21 S. Tazewell
P. Gordon & Sarah          P. Hiram & Dicy

Oc. Farmer                 M.

Date: 2-27-1877
Charles H. Wilson          Eliza A. Shrader
A. 20 S. Tazewell          A. 22 S. Tazewell
P. Edward & Rebecca        P. John & Christina
Oc. Farmer                 M. J. A. Smith

Date: 4-5-1877
William M. Adkins          Cynthia A. Ashworth
A. 25 S. Tazewell          A. 17 S. Tennessee
P. Peter & Rhoda           P. Wm W. & Julia
Oc. Merchant               M. A.A. Ashworth

Date: 4-10-1877
Jacob  Trinkle             Lucy Noble
A. 54 W. Pulaski           A. 40 S. Monroe
P. Stephen & Sarah         P. Wm & Nancy
Oc. Farmer                 M. John H. Hoge

Date: 5-29-1877
George W. Eagle            Olivia P. Bogle
A. 22 S. Wythe             A. 23 S. Tennessee
P. Sam'l M. & Martha J.    P. Jas Buchanan &
                           Eliza Jane Munsey
Oc. Farmer                 M.  G.W. K. Green

Date: 6-7-1877
Jessie W. Hicks            Mollie W. Cormer?
A. 26 S. Tazewell          A. 24 S. Pulaski
P. Jos T. & Maria          P. Rob't & Elizabeth
Oc. Farmer                 M. L. J. Miller

Date: 6-18-1877
George S. Tibbs            Mary A. Patterson
A. 24 S. Wythe             A. 15 S. Bland
P. Geo M. & Mary           P. I. N. & Virginia
Oc. Farmer                 M. G.W.K. Green

Date: 3-22-1877
Lynsey T. Lambert          Sarah E. Tickle
A. 24 S. Wythe             A. 22 S. Smyth
P. John & Mahala           P. Peter & Mary A.

Oc. Farmer                 M.

Date: 3-29-1877
William Garland  Harman    Arminta Victoria Harman
A. 21 S. Giles             A. 17 S. Giles
P. Addison &               P. John Wesley
Sarah Elizabeth Ellis      & Sarah Virginia Moore
Oc. Mechanic               M. Isaac S. Harman

Date: 2-26-1877
James W.  Davis            Nancy J. King
A. 24 S. Pulaski           A. 17 S. Wythe
P. Sam'l C. & Eliza A.     P. David & Eliza
Oc. Farmer                 M. A. Q. Harman

Date: 4-5-1877
Ralph B.Wyrick             Victoria L. Deavor
A. 41 S. Wythe             A. 25 S. Wythe
P. Asa & Marinda           P. H. H. & Louisa
Oc. Farmer                 M. L. J. Miller

Date: 4-26-1877
Marcus L. Hancock          Margaret V. Wyrick
A. 20 S. Wythe             A. 21 S. Wythe
P. Mary J. Hancock         P. Jas S. & Nancy
Oc. Farmer                 M. L. J. Miller

Date: 6-5-1877
Charles A. Waddle          Angeline Waddle
A. 20 S. Wythe             A. 24 S. Wythe
P. Jos & Rhoda             P. Dan'l & Peggy

Oc. Farmer                 M. P. P. Hayes

Date: 6-12-1877
Samuel Franklin            Nancy J. Neel
A. 21 S. Tazewell          A. 21 S. Tazewell
P. John & Polly            P. H. P. & Lyddia
Oc. Farmer                 M. Peter R.Suiter

Date: 6-25-1877
Charles Y. Anderson        Adeline Waddle
A. 18 S. Smyth             A. 23? S. Wythe
P. Chas H. & Lucy          P. David & Lyddia
Oc. Farmer                 M. G.W.K. Green

31

Date: 6-30-1877
James W. Green              Rachel C. Kitts
A. 23 S. Pittsylvania     A. 19 S. Wythe
P. J. T. & M. C.           P. Peter & Amanda
Oc. Farmer               M. G.W.K. Green

Date: 7-3-1877
George W. Starling      Rebecca Hager
A. 23 S. Tazewell       A. 31 S. Tazewell
P. John C. & Tabitha    P. Polly Hager
Oc. Farmer              M. Peter R. Suiter

Date: 7-23-1877
Floyd Winfield Kitts     Susan Bell Bogle Kitts
A. 20 S. Wythe         A. 18 S. Wythe
P. Jas. Wash. &          P. Andrew Jas. &
Mary "Polly"Prunty     Nancy Bower Bogle
Oc. Farmer              M. John H. Hoge

Date: 7-28-1877
Samuel D. Collins      Margaret E. Patterson
A. 21 S. Wythe         A. 18 S. Wythe
P. Edward & Elizabeth  P. J. N. & Virginia Bogle

Oc. Farmer              M. William Hicks

Date: 8-9-1877
Gordon H. Tickle       Ellen M. Dilman
A. 26 S. Wythe         A. 18 S. Wythe
P. Hezekiah C. &       P. Geo & Mary
Caroline Matilda Farmer
Oc. Farmer              M. J. C. Smith

Date: 8-30-1877
John R. Peak           Sophia E. Kitts
A. 21 S. Carroll         A. 16 S. Wythe
P. Aaron & Sally       P. Peter & Amanda
Oc. Farmer              M. P. P. Hays

Date: 9-20-1877
Giles B. Thomas       Rosa Surrett
A. 39 S. Wythe         A. 17 S. Wythe
P. John & Catherine    P. Jas M. & Susan
Oc. Farmer              M.

Date: 9-13-1877
James Harman        Urbana Robinett
A. 43 S. Smyth         A. 39 S. Wythe
P. Jezreel & Elizabeth  P. Hiram & Rebecca
Oc. Farmer              M. G.W.K. Green

Date: 9-26-1877
Ballard S. White       Sarah V. Dillow
A. 22 S. Giles          A. 21 S. Giles
P. Jas & Mahala       P. John W. & Docia B.
Oc. Farmer              M. L. J. Miller

Date: 10-4-1877
Erastus G. Neel        Isabell V. Kidd
A. 24 S. Tazewell       A. 20 S. Tazewell
P. M. A. & Barbara S.   P. Wm S. & Almira
Oc. Farmer              M. John A. Smith

Date: 10-9-1877
J. W. B. Wright       Sarah E. Bogle
A. 28 S. Giles          A. 18 S. Giles
P. John & Lettitia      P. John & Julia A.
Oc. Farmer              M. John W. Bowman

Date: 10-4-1877
James M. Gross       Sarah A. Miller
A. 21 S. Tazewell       A. 19 S. Tazewell
P. Harvey & Mary E.   P. Jacob E. & Jane
Oc. Minister            M. P. J. Lockhart

Date: 10-25-1877
Ephram Leonard       Mary Cox
A. 26 W. Wythe        A. 28 W. Carroll
P. John W. & Polly     P. Alex & Peggy Greggory

Oc. Farmer              M. F. F. Repass

Date: 11-7-1877
John Grimes Pauley    Barbara Eliz. Havens
A. 20 S. Wythe         A. 22 S. Wythe
P. Hiram A. &          P. Jas & Jane
Nancy Havens
Oc. Farmer              M. G.W.K. Green

Date: 4-7-1877
Albert McDonald       Margaret Carter
A. 21 S. Wyoming     A. 20 S. Wythe
P. Roland & Agnes     P. Julia A. Carter
Oc. Laborer             M. G.W.K. Green

Date : 11-15-1877
Henderson G. Thompson Victoria Shannon
A. 23 S. Wythe         A. 23 S. Tazewell
P. A. G. & Sarah       P. Nancy Shannon
Oc. Farmer              M. Wm. E. Neel

Date: 11-29-1877  
Peter A. Tibbs     Catherine Wilson  
A. 21 S. Wythe     A. 19 S. Wythe  
P. Geo & Mary     P. John L. & Elizabeth  
Oc. Farmer     M. James Mahood  

Date: 12- 13-1888  
Henry Umbarger     Mary J. Henderson  
A. 40 S. Wythe     A. 23 S. Washington  
P. Jonas & Julia     P. Elias & Rhoda  
Oc. Farmer     M. G.W.K. Green  

Date: 2-4-1878  
Henry J. Woods     Sophia Cameron  
A. 34 S. Wythe     A. 36 W. Wythe  
P. Moses & Sarah     P. John Tobler  
Oc. Farmer     M. P.P. Hayes  

Date: 2-28-1878  
Stephen V. Frey     Margaret E. Davis  
A. 23 S. Wythe     A. 24 S. Giles  
P. Abram & Judith     P. Hiram G. & Cosby  
Oc. Farmer     M. W. S. Jordan  

Date: 3-7-1878  
Henderson G. Adkins     Victoria G. Suiter  
A. A. 22 S. Tazewell     A. 20 S. Tazewell  
P. Peter & Rhoda     P. Alex. & Lyddia  
Oc. Farmer     M. Peter R. Suiter  

Date: 3-20-1878  
Thomas J. Hanshew     Martha J. Walker  
A. 23 S. Tazewell     A. 20 S. Tazewell  
P. John & Elsie     P. Benj. S. & Elizabeth  
Oc. Farmer     M. Peter R. Suiter  

Date: 4-7-1878  
Charles T. Robinett     Arminta N. V. French  
A. 26 S. Tazewell     A. 19 S. Tazewell  
P. Hiram & Dicy     P. Austin & Lucinda  
Oc. Farmer     M. Peter R. Suiter  

Date: 5-23-1878  
Randolph J. Harman     Zelda Brown  
A. 32 S. Wythe     A. 23 S. Tazewell  
P. F. M. & Nancy     P. John  

Oc. Farmer     M. G.W.K. Green  

Date: 12-6-1877  
James A. Woodyard     Lucinda A. Linkous  
A. 18 S. Giles     A. 16 S. Giles  
P. Levi & Diannah?     P. W.A. & Mary  
Oc. Farmer     Peter R. Suiter  

Date: 1-31-1878  
Alfred F. Haynes     Martha O. Kitts  
A. 21 S. Bumount, WV     A. 23 S. Wythe  
P. Henry & Ally     P. Jas W. Kitts  
Oc. Farmer     M. W.S. Jordon  

Date: 2-19-1878  
Jessie Barnett     Julia Gibson  
A. 21 S. Patrick     A. 21 S.Russell  
P. Eliza Barnett     P.  
Oc. Laborer     M. A. Q. Harman  

Date: 3-4-1878  
Phlegar Harley     Jane Dillow  
A. 35 W. Montgomery     A. 28 S. Giles  
P. Allen     P. Wesley & Docia  
Oc. Farmer     M. L. J. Miller  

Date: 3-13-1878  
Joesph W. Ramsey     Judy C. Blankenship  
A. 23 S. Franklin     A. 24 S. Giles  
P.Wm. L. & Elizabeth     P. Elias & Letitia  
Oc. Farmer     M. L. J. Miller  

Date: 3-28-1878  
Grayson S. Compton     Harriet J. Kinser  
A. 26 S. Tazewell     A. 23 S. Tazewell  
P. Jas M. & Lucinda     P. Thos. H. & Elizabeth  
Oc. Farmer     M. L. J. Miller  

Date: 4-16-1878  
Charles C. Wilson     Nancy J. Cameron  
A. 25 S. Smyth     A. 19 S. Tazewell  
P. Wm. D. & Susan     P. David & Eliza A.  
Oc. Farmer     M. F.F. Repass  

Date: 5-28-1878  
Stephen S. Kitts     Mary M. Tibbs  
A. 33 S. Wythe     A. 26 S. Wythe  
P. Peter & Amanda     P. Sallie Tibbs  
M. Hounshell  
Oc. Farmer     M.

Date: 6-9-1878  
Haney Wynesett     Oregan V. Umbarger  
A. 20 S. Hawkins, TN    A. 20 S. Wythe  
P. Noah & Darthula     P. Wm & Christina  
Oc. Farmer           M. P.P. Hayes  

Date: 6-27-1878  
William L. Hamilton    Elizabeth A. C. Nye  
A. 38 W. Giles        A. 21 S. Giles  
P. Timothy & Margaret   P. A. J. & Elizabeth  
Oc. County Clerk      M. William Hicks  

Date: 7-11-1878  
E. M. Fortner        Sarah J. Starks  
A. 25 S. Giles         A. 23 S. Tazewell  
P. Hardy & Mary      P. J. M. & Emeline  
Oc. Farmer          M. J. H. Wingo  

Date: 7-11-1878  
Charles C. Spangler    Sarah J. Umbarger  
A. 22 S. Wythe        A. 27 S. Wythe  
P. Wm. & Christina     P. Peter J. & Elizabeth  
Oc. Farmer          M. F. Repass  

Date: 7-11-1878  
Randolph Dunn Bogle   Nannie Bower Kitts  
A. 19 S. Wythe        A. 16 S. Wythe  
P. Lorenza Dow      P. Andrew J. &  
& Mary "Polly" Dunn    Nancy Bower Bogle  
Oc. Farmer          M. J. H. Hoge  

Date: 7-29-1878  
Josiah M. Thompson    Phebe Repass  
A. 67 W. Wythe       A. 57 W. Tazewell  
P. Amos & Mary    P. John & Elizabeth Hedrick  

Oc. Farmer          M. John A. Smith  

Date: 8-21-1878  
Saunders M. Hamilton   Sallie Ann Mustard  
A. 34 S. Giles         A. 21 S. Giles  
P. Tim. & Margaret E.    P. James Harvey &  
                  Marshall Marcia Robinett  
Oc. Farmer          M. J. H. Hoge  

Date: 8-19-1878  
Ramsey Bullard      Cosby J. M. Gordon  
A. 28 S. Hanover, SC    A. 21 S. Wythe  
P. Abram & Tena      P. Mathias & Ella  

Oc. Laborer         M. G.W.K. Green  

Date: 9-3-1878  
Creed M. Flick       Mary Etta Bolton  
A. 20 S. Giles         A. 19 S. Giles  
P. Madison & Ellen J.    P. David & Margaret  
Oc. Farmer          M. W. S. Jordon  

Date: 9-17-1878  
James H. Surratt      Cynthia H. Pauley  
A. 24 S. Wythe        A. 14 S. Giles  
P. Jas & Susannah     P. Rebba B.  
Oc. Laborer         M. W. S. Jordon  

Date: 9-19-1878  
James Stimson       Vistia A. Thompson  
A. 29 S. Giles         A. 17 S. Bland  
P. John & Elizabeth     P. A. G. & Sarah  
Oc. Farmer          M. P. J. Lockhart  

Date: 9-21-1878  
Robert J. Pugh       Sarah J. Umberger  
A. 24 S. Giles         A. 17 S. Wythe  
P. Geo. W. & Elizabeth   P. Wm. & Amanda W.  
Oc. Carpenter        M. F. F. Repass  

Date: 9-23-1878  
William W. Carver     Letitia L. Bridges  
A. 27 S. Tazewell      A. 25 S. Wythe  
P. Rob't & Catherine    P. Wm. & Harriett  
Oc. Farmer          M. Peter R. Suiter  

Date: 10-1-1878  
David O. Wright      Melvina M. Shrader  
A. 35 W. Giles        A. 31 S. Wythe  
P. John & Letitia      P. John & Christina  
Oc. Farmer          M. W. S. Jordon  

Date: 11-20-1878  
Jessie N. Neel        Manerva A. Empswiller  
A. 23 S. Tazewell      A. 18 S. Tazewell  
P. John & Malinda     P. John & Matilda  
Oc. Farmer          M. A. F. Cumbow  

Date: 11-21-1878  
William H. Flick      Sarah E. Bussey  
A. 23 S. Giles         A. 19 S. Giles  
P. Wm. Mad. & Ellen J.   P. Thompson & Elizabeth  
Oc. Farmer          M. J. H. Hoge

Date: 11-26-1878
Jno W. Bruce
A. 57 W. Giles
P. Wm & Susan
Oc. Mechanic

Sallie Jones
A. 33 S. Wythe
P. Elizabeth Jones
M. Isaac S. Harman

Date: 11-28-1878
Willard I. King
A. 24 S. Giles
P. John B. & Mary
Oc. Laborer

Angeline J. Franklin
A. 18 S. Tazewell
P. Paula & John
M. Isaac S. Harman

Date: 12-12-1878
Newton Montgomery
Kitts
A. 27 W. Wythe
P. Jacob & Matilda

Oc. Farmer

Eliza. Angeline Williams

A. 18 S. Smyth
P. Wm. Bonham &
Christina Hanshew
M. F.F. Repass

Date: 12-31-1878
John H. King

A. 36 S. Rockingham, NC
P. S. Bins & Zilpa?

Oc. Laborer

Nannie Burks

A.30 D. Wythe
P. Victoria Burks

M. W. D. Mitchell

Date: 12-18-1878
J. Hoge Thompson
A. 28 S. Wythe
P. A. G. & Sarah M.
Oc. Farmer

Rhoda L. Fannon
A. 26 S. Wythe
P. Acles & Sarah
M. Wm. D. Mitchell

Date: 1-24-1879
Oley G. Stimson
A. 23 S. Floyd
P. N. B. & Mary
Oc. Farmer

Isabella V. Walker
A. 23 S. Tazewell
P. Thos. F. & A. A.
M. Wm. E. Neel

Date: 1-9-1879
Adam R. Burgess
A. 20 S. Tazewell
P. Thos J. & M. A.
Oc. Farmer

Susan V. Neel
A. 21 S. Tazewell
P. John M. & Malinda
M. A. F. Cumbow

Date: 1-11-1879
James S. McFarland
A. 22 S. Tazewell
P. Jacob & Eliza. E.
Oc.

Sarah B. Hanshew
A. 17 S. Bland
P. Sam'l & Nancy E.
M.

Date: 1-23-1879
John A. Compton
A. 25 S. Tazewell
P. Wm. W. & Nancy

Oc. Farmer

Mollie B. Gregory
A. 20 S. Tazewell
P. Richard S.

M. W.D. Mitchell

Date: 1-30-1879
Reece Monroe Kitts
A. 23 S. Wythe
P. Rufus Morgan &
Nancy Ann Heldreth
Oc. Farmer

Ellen Mariah Bales
A. 17 S. Bland
P. Jas. R. & Mollie

M.

Date:2-5-1879
Henderson Pruett
A. 23 S. Giles
P. Wm & Elizabeth
Oc. Farmer

Luvenea Fanning
A. 19 S. Giles
P. John & Elizabeth
M. A. F. Cumbow

Date: 2-27-1879
A. G. Hall
A. 22 S. Tazewell
P. Thos. & Elizabeth
Oc. Farmer

Josie M. Maxwell
A. 24 S. Tazewell
P. Jas & Rachel A.
M. John A. Smith

Date: 3-5-1879
Stephen A. Repass
A. 27 S. Wythe
P. Jas.. A. & Lucinda
Oc. Farmer

Mary C. Groseclose
A. 20 S. Wythe
P. Jos. & Elizabeth
M. J. B. Greever

Date-3-6-1879
Silvey H. Tibbs
A. 23 S. Wythe
P. Geo M. & Mary ·
Oc. Farmer

Margaret A. Kitts
A. 15 S. Wythe
P. Jos & Elizabeth
M. J. C. Smith

Date: 3-26-1879
John A. Burgess
A. 17 S. Bland
P. Raiburn & Rosanna
Oc. Laborer

Alice Noel
A. 18 S. Bland
P. Lafayette & Mary
M. J. A. Smith

Date: 3-27-1879
A. J. Dillman
A. 25 S. Wythe
P. Geo & Mary
Oc. Farmer

America L. Hayton
A. 18 S. Wythe
P. Peter &
M. F.F. Repass

Date: 4-3-1879
Charles Franklin        Mary Ellen Gills
A. 24 S. Tazewell       A. 18 S. Bland
P. John & Paula         P. B. F. & Polly
Oc. Farmer              M. Isaac S. Harman

Date: 4-18-1879
George Brown            Mary S. Neel
A. 24 S. Tazewell       A. 22 S. Tazewell
P. Jas B. & Sarah       P. Thomas & Sarah
Oc. Farmer              M. John A. Smith

Date: 5-2-1879
Thomas Neel             Nancy Repass
A. 66 W. Tazewell       A. 46 W.
P. Wm & Nancy           P. David
Oc. Farmer              M. John A. Smith

Date: 5-29-1879
Charles W. Sharitz      Mary L. Sheppard
A. 27 S. Wythe          A. 25 S. Giles
P. Jos. & Patsey        P. E. A. & Rhoda N.

Oc. Farmer              M. George W. Penley

Date: 5-29-1879
Mathias Lampert         Hester A. Stowers
A. 22 S. Wythe          A. 22 S. Tazewell
P. Jas & Mandanna       P. Hickman & Sarah
Oc. Farmer              M. Wm. E. Neel

Date: 7-24-1879
Samuel G. Shrader       Rebecca J. Harman
A. 23 S. Tazewell       A. 25 W. Tazewell
P. John & Christina     P. A. J. & Nellie
Oc. Farmer              M.

Date: 9-4-1879
Giles W. Lamb           Mary A. Farley
A. 29 W. Giles          A. 28 S. Giles
P. Gabriel & Martha     P. Nathaniel & Polly
Oc. Farmer              M. L. J. Miller

Date: 10-16-1879
John C. Johnston        Mary C. Carr
A. 24 S. Pulaski        A. 23 S. Giles
P. Henry & Nancy        P. Matilda Carr
Oc. Farm Hand           M. George W. Penley

Date: 4-16-1879
Wm. K. Dillow           Edmonia M. Dillow
A. 24 S. Wythe          A. 18 S. Wythe
P. Betsey Dillow        P. Wm. & Nicketie
Oc. Laborer             M. W. D. Mitchell

Date: 5-1-1879
Charles H. Taylor       Philis O. Williams
A. 23 S. Columbus, OH   A. 17 S. Floyd
P. Wm. Taylor & Lena Hogue   P. Sam'l & Harriett
Oc. Teacher             M. Peter R. Suiter

Date: 5-14-1879
George R. Hufford       Mollie E. McNutt
A. 30 S. Wythe          A. 28 S. TN
P. A. J. & Alice L      P. Jno. S. & Eliz. E.
Oc. Teacher             M. J. J. Scherer

Date: 5-27-1879
Paris B. Harman         Martha J. Rinehart
A. 21 S. Bland          A. 18 S. Bland
P. Henry Wesley &       P. Andy & Lena
Phebe Fielder
Oc. Farmer              M. A. A. Ashworth

Date: 6-19-1879
Samuel R. Williams      Harriett L. Neel
A. 25 S. Smyth          A. 20 S. Tazewell
P. Wm. B. & Christina   P. Mathias & Mary L.
Oc. Farmer              M. F.F. Repass

Date: 8-26-1879
Wm. Neal Harman         Orlena Farmer Whalen
A. 54 S. Giles          A. 29 D. Carroll
P. Elias & Polly        P. John Shockley
Oc. Farmer & Lawyer     M. L. J. Miller

Date: 9-23-1879
James V. Gibson         Caroline Honaker
A. 21 S. Tazewell       A. 17 S. Tazewell
P. Sam'l I. & Jasse     P. Henry & Betsey
Oc. Farmer              M. R. M. Ashworth

Date: 10-21-1879
William G. Stafford     Mary F. Shewey
A. 34 S. Giles          A. 21 S. Grant, Wis.
P. Ralph & Margaret     P. A. W. & Anna
Oc. Farmer              M. A.F. Cumbow

Date: 10-22-1879
Samuel E. Sarver          Dela V. Blankenship
A. 18 S. Giles            A. 22 S. Mercer
P. J. G. & Francis        P. W. W. & Julia
Oc. Farmer                M. L. J. Miller

Date: 11-26-1879
Erastus W. Steel          Caroline Adkins
A. 26 S. Tazewell         A. 22 S. Smyth
P. Graniar? & Clarissa    P.
Oc. Farmer                M. P. P. Hays

Date: 11-6-1879
Gordon B. Muirhead        Mary Iasbell Miller
A. 30 Pulaski             A. 22 S. Giles
P. Dan'l F. & Isabelle    P. L. J. & Sarah
Elizabeth H. Saunders
Oc. Farmer                M. J. H. Hoge

Date: 12-24-1879
David B. Umbarger         Christina Umbarger
A. 23 S. Wythe            A. 23 S. Bland
P. Wm & Amanda            P. Peter & Maria
Oc. Farmer                M. J. Mahood

Date: 12-18-1879
Thomas A. Williams        Mary L. King
A. 19 S. Giles            A. 19 S. Giles
P. B. P. & Francis E.     P. John B. & Mary
Oc. Farmer                M. G. W. Penley

Date: 12-25-1879
John Hatch                Malissa Hatch
A. 23 S. Craig            A. 17 S. Craig
P. Clabourn & Lucinda     P. John & Jane

Oc. Laborer               M.

Date: 1-13-1880
John W. F. Logan          Matilda J. Bruce
A. 23 S. Scott            A. 27 S. Wythe
P. Cephas H. & Letitia    P. Geo & Sallie

Oc. Farmer                M. W. D. Mitchell

Date: 1-1-1880
Maxwell Hill              Nancy Collins
A. 20 S. Wyoming          A. 22 S. Bland
P. M. S. & Elizabeth      P. Jas & Mary
Oc. Farmer                M. A. Q. Harman

Date: 10-30-1879
Henderson P. Eagle        Missouri L. Maxwell
A. 22 S.Wythe             A. 20 S. Tazewell
P. Sam'l & Martha         P. Jas E. & Rachel
Oc. Farmer                M. John A. Smith

Date: 11-27-1879
Beryle B. Harman          Virginia C. Havens
A. 27 S. Tazewell         A. 25 S. Wythe
P. Daniel & Lucinda       P. John & Joanna
Oc. Farmer                M. W.D. Mitchell

Begin Page 17 of Original Book
Date: 12-11-1879
Robert S. Wyrick          Elizabeth B. Hancock
A. 22 S. Wythe            A. 17 S. Bland
P. Asa & Marinda          P. George & Julia
Bogle
Oc. Farmer                M. Isaac S. Harman

Date: 12-24-1879
William F. McColgin        Mary A. Grayson
A. 25 S. Botetourt        A. 21 S. Wythe
P. Jas & A.E              P. Jas W. & Emily
Oc. Clerk in Store        M. J. D. Thomas

Date: 12-24-1879
James A. Lampert          Rebecca C. Kimberling
A. 29 S. Wythe            A. 22 S. Wythe
P. Stephen & Malinda      P. Stephen & Elizabeth
Oc. Farmer                M. J. Mahood

Date: 1-22-1879
B. W. Johnston            M. E. Waggoner
A. 21 S. Giles            A. 16 S. Bland
P. Edward & Sarah         P. Franklin P. &
                          Catherine Young Munsey
Oc. Farmer                M. L. J. Miller

Date: 1-1-1880
John Dunagan              Julia Annie Harman
A. 30 S. Surry, NC        A. 20 S. Giles
P. Lewis & Nancy          P. Addison F. &
                          Sarah Elizabeth Ellis
Oc. Farmer                M. G. W. Penley

Date: 1-21-1880
William Elgin Neel        Charlotte Kidd
A. 22 S. Bland            A. 17 S. Bland
P. Augustus & Fannie      P. Wm. S. & Almiria
Oc. Farmer                M. Peter R. Suiter

Date: 1-4-1880
Charles M. Burton    Matilda Stowers
A. 21 S. Tazewell    A. 21 S. Tazewell
P. Elias & Sally    P. Hickman & Sally
Oc. Farmer    M. Peter R. Suiter

Date: 2-12-1880
Jacob B. Moore    Fannie N. Sublett
A. 24 S. Giles    A. 28 S. Giles
P. Richard & Elizabeth    P. Samuel D. & Petro?
Oc. Farmer    M. J. T. Taylor

Date: 2-11-1880
Elijah H. Kimberling    Louisa C. Harner
A. 21 S. Wythe    A. 22 S. Wythe
P. Henry & Barbary    P. J. J. & Mary M.
Oc. Farmer    M. Geo R. Maiden

Date: 3-4-1880
Geo W. Linkous    Attelia Ann Wylie
A. 31 S. Montgomery    A. 19 S. Tazewell
P. Abraham & Emaline    P. James E. & Susan
Oc. Farmer    M. R. M. Ashworth

Date: 4-22-1880
Ballard P. Perkins    Sallie A. Clark
A. 19 S. Giles    A. 20 S. Tazewell
P. Francis    P. Richard & Susan
Oc. Laborer    M. A.F. Cumbow

Date: 4-22-1880
Sims F. Stowers    Elizabeth M. Cundiff
A. 28 S. Tazewell    A. 18 S. Bland
P. Gordon & Sallie    P. John W. & Sarah L.
Oc. Farmer    M. Peter R. Suiter

Date: 4-14-1880
Gordon P. Pauley    Sarah S. Thompson
A. 25 S. Wythe    A. 18 S. Wythe
P. Hiram & Nancy    P. Joseph & Nancy
Oc. Farmer    M. A. Q. Harman

Date: 5-26-1880
J. M. Tuggle    Matilda J. Honaker
A. 21 S. Mercer, WV    A. 19 S. Tazewell
P. John & Lucindia    P. Peter C. & Mary A.
Oc. Farmer    M. R. M. Ashworth

Date: 1-1-1880
Martin Jefferson Stowers    Emaline Stowers
A. 19 S. Tazewell    A. 23 S. Tazewell
P. Hickman & Sally    P. Sims. Stowers
Oc. Blacksmith    M. Peter R. Suiter

Date: 2-12-1880
Robert Davidson    Louisa Clay
A. 28 S. Tazewell    A. 22 S. Giles
P. James & Peggy    P. Anderson & Malinda
Oc. Laborer    M. A. Q. Harman

Date: 4-1-1880
Andrew F. Cumton    Caroline C. Honaker
A. 25 S. Bland    A. 24 S. Tazewell
P. William & Eliza    P. Andrew J. & Nellie
Oc. Minister of Gospel    M. L. J. Miller

Date: 3-5-1880
Griffin Page    Eliza J. Barnett
A. 61 W. Botetourt    A. 50 W. NC
P. Thomas & Percilla    P.
Oc. Blacksmith    M. J. T. Taylor

Date: 4-22-1880
David W. Hanshew    Sarah M. McFarland
A. 23 S. Smyth    A. 19 S. Wythe
P. Jacob & Christina    P. Saunders & Catherine
Oc. Farmer    M. Geo A. Maiden

Date: 4-15-1880
James A. Lampert    Martha E. Hancock
A. 35 W. Wythe    A. 37 S. Patrick
P. Henry & Ellen    P. Charles & Nancy
Oc. Farmer    M. F.F. Repass

Date: 5-9-1880
Charles F. Collins    Virginia L. Bruce?
A. 33 W. Bomen?, KY    A. 23 S. Wythe
P. Wm. & Victoria    P. James & Mary
Oc. Painter    M. L. J. Miller

Date: 5-10-1880
Robert H. Davis    Isabelle E. Carr
A. 21 S. Giles    A. 18 S. Bland
P. Isaac J. & Mahala    P. Matilda Carr
Oc. Laborer    M. J. T. Taylor

Date: 5-20-1880
Dr. Daniel Alex. Miller   Mary Eliz. Newberry
A. 25 S. Giles   A. 18 S. Laurence, MD
P. Lorenzo John &   P. Robb't Lemuel &
Martha Lois Bird   Margarte Hoge Hunter
Oc. Physician   M. Geo W. Penley

Date: 5-20-1880
Clinton B. Harman   M. C. Compton
A. 26 S. Bland   A. 25 S. Tazewell
P. Isaac S. & Rachel   P. W.W. & N. C.
Oc. Farmer   M. W. D. Mitchell

Date: 5-17-1880
Robert Nelson   Mary E. Clark
A. 21 S. Stokes, NC   A. 16 S. Bland
P. Richard & Susan   P. Hasten & Martha
Oc. Farmer   M. A. F. Cumbow

Date: 7-8-1880
Winton Carr   Elvisia J. Jones
A. 22 S. Giles   A. 22 S. Wythe
P. James & Fannie   P. James J. & Charlotte
Oc. Laborer   M. J. T. Taylor

Date: 8-26-1880
D. E. Neel   S. B. Kidd
A. 29 W. Tazewell   A. 25 S. Tazewell
P. James R. & Rebecca   P. Henry C. & Matilda

Oc. Farmer   M. John A. Smith

Date: 8-20-1880
Charles W. Cassell   Louisia J. Umbarger
A. 25 S. Wythe   A. 18 S. Bland
P. John M. & Francis   P. Thos P. & Eliz. A.
Oc. Farmer   M. F.F. Repass

Date: 8-4-1880
Samuel H. Tolbert   Eliz. P. Whalen
A 23 S. Giles   A. 19 S. Giles
P. Betsy Tolbert   P. Hiram & Mary
Oc. Farmer   M. James T. Taylor

Date: 9-1-1880
Washing. G. Dehart   Rebecca E. Moore
A.22 S. Giles   A. 19 S. Giles
P. Isaac N. & Polly   P. Richard & Elizabeth
Oc. Farmer   M. Armstead A. Ashworth

Date: 5-23-1880
Wm Jackson Blankenship Lutheria Dillow
A. 19 S. Mercer, WV   A. 22 S. Wythe
P. Daniel & Mary E.   P. Addison & Vicy

Oc. Laborer   M. W.D. Mitchell

Date: 5-4-1880
John Patten Hall   Leititia V. Hughs
A. 20 S. Wythe   A. 19 S. Mercer, WV
P. Mary J. Hall   P.
Oc. Laborer   M. W. D. Mitchell

Date: 7-28-1880
John Poage Allen   Fannie R. Bullman
A. 40 S. Giles   A. 25 S. King & Queen
P. Madison & Mariah Bane   P. John W. & Lucy E.
Oc. Merchant   M. W. D. Mitchell

Date: 7-20-1880
George Niswander   Precilla Pool
A. 32 W. Giles   A. 30 S. Giles
P. Harvey & Matilda   P. Thompkins & Malinda
Oc. Farmer   M. L. J. Miller

Date: 8-5-1880
Jesse W. Bruce   Elizabeth S. Munsey
A. 27 S. Wythe   A. 23 S. Wythe
P. Josiah &   P. Andrew Jackson &
Manervia S. Justice   Sarah J. Peery
Oc. Farmer   M. H. E. Bailey

Begin Page 18 of Original Book
Date: 8-10-1880
Franklin Wall   Edmeny? Danegan
A. 22 S. Surry, NC   A. 17 S. Bland
P. Henry & Lucinda   P. Ruel M. & Mary
Oc. Farmer   M. L. J. Miller

Date: 9-1-1880
James P. King   Matilda J. Gills
A. 22 W. Pulaski   A. 18 S. Bland
P. Allen & Sarah   P. Benj. F. & Mary
Oc. Farmer   M. Wm. E. Neel

Date: 9-29-1880
Jessy N. Bailey   Fannie Snapp
A. 24 S. Mercer   A. 17 S. WV
P. William & Matilda   P. William & Jane
Oc. U.S. Mail Carrier   M. J. H. Hoge

Date: 10-26-1880  
Neely Helmendollar     Mary A. Kidd  
A. 32 W. Tazewell     A. 25 S. Bland  
P. Granger & Matilda     P. Elizabeth Kidd  
Oc. Farmer     M. John A. Smith  

Date: 10-26-1880  
Charles L. Parsel     Martha J. Davis  
A. 23 S. Franklin     A. 21 S. Wythe  
P. John & Mary     P. Sam'l C. & Eliza  
Oc. Mining     M. Isaac S. Harman  

Date: 11-3-1880  
George Olesey?     Elizabeth Harden  
A. 27 S. Wythe     A. 23 S. Wythe  
P. Stephen & Delilah     P.  

Oc. Farmer     M. G.W.K. Green  

Date: 12-1-1880  
Haywood A. Groseclose     Mary A. Thompson  
A. 23 S. Wythe     A. 21 S. Wythe  
P. Andrew     P. James & Sallie  
Oc. House Plaster     M. W. D. Mitchell  

Date: 12-24-1880  
William J. Lambert     Sarah E. Meadows  
A. 22 S. Bland     A. 22 S. Bland  
P. Isaac P. & Susan     P. Francis Meadows  
Oc. Teacher     M. A. Q. Harman  

Date: 12-2-1880  
Allen C. Stowers     Amanda V. French  
A. 21 S. Bland     A. 19 S. Giles  
P. Hickman & Sallie     P. J. G. & Mary  
Oc. Farmer     M. Peter R. Suiter  

Date: 12-15-1880  
James M. Lefew     Priscilla E. Fletcher  
A. 27 S. Floyd     A. 18 S. Bland  
P. Wm B. & Eliza     P. John F. & Mary  

Oc. Farmer     M. James T. Taylor  

Begin Page 19 of Original Book  
Date 7-2-1881  
John P. Cubine     Amanda A. Whalen  
A. 21 S. Tennessee     A. 16 S. Bland  
P. Patrick M. & Elvina     P. Hiram & Mary A.  
Oc. Farmer     M. James T. Taylor  

Date: 10-24-1880  
David O. Wright     Matilda K. Wilson  
A. 37 W. Giles     A. 38 S. Wythe  
P. John & Letitia     P.  
Oc. Farmer     M. F.F. Repass  

Date: 11-16-1880  
Gordon Sifford     Lucy C. McCoy  
A. 24 S. Pulaski     A. 16 S. Bland  
P. John & Rachel     P. James N. & Margaret  
Oc. Farmer     M. George W. Penley  

Date: 11-18-1880  
William Foster Waggoner     Octavia Victoria Munsey  
A. 20 S. Wythe     A. 20 S. Wythe  
P. Geo. Eli &     P. James H. &  
Eliz. Jane Hearn     Margaret L. Hutsell  
Oc. Farmer     M. W. D. Mitchell  

Date: 12-2-1880  
Newton A. Irvin     Martha M. Cundiff  
A. 22 S. Giles     A. 17 S. Bland  
P. Isaac N. & Lucinda     P. John W. & Sarah  
Oc. Farmer     M. Peter R. Suiter  

Date: 12-30-1880  
J.H. Richardson     Emma M. Robinett  
A. 28 S. Wythe     A. 22 S. Wythe  
P. Cullen & Eliza     P. Hiram & Dicy  
Oc. Farmer     M. A.A. Ashworth  

Date: 12-22-1880  
William Humphrey Hanshew     Rebecca Jane Fields  
A. 22 S. Bland     A. 22 S. Smyth  
P. Samuel & Nancy     P. Solomon & Malinda  
Oc. Farmer     M. F.F. Repass  

Date: 12-30-1880  
Giles Henderson Burton     Callie Dixie Kitts  
A. 21 S. Pulaski     A. 20 S. Bland  
P. James Harvey &     P. Andrew James &  
Virginia Jane Detimore     Nancy Bower Bogle  
Oc. Farmer     M. L. J. Miller  

Date: 6-27-1881  
William D. King     Ollie V. Thompson  
A. 24 S. Pulaski     A. 17 S. Bland  
P. Solomon B. & Catherine     P. Wm. H & S. Jane  
Oc. Farmer     M. James T. Taylor

Date: 1-13-1881
Mark R. Deavor            Rachel S. Havens
A. 19 S. Bland            A. 18 S. Bland
P. Henry & Louisa         P. James & Jane

Oc. Blacksmith            M.  J. H. Hoge

Date: 2-2-1881
Creed F. Pauley           Marteley Kitts
A. 24 S. Wythe            A. 22 S. Tazewell
P. Thomas G. & Ann        P. John D. & Jane

Oc. Farmer                M.  Adam Quinn Harman

Date: 2-24-1881
James B. Compton          Virginia A. Gregory
25 S. Tazewell            A. 19 S. Bland
P. W.W. & Nancy           P. Richard S. & Julia
Oc. Farmer                M. W. D. Mitchell

Date: 3-25-1881
Robert Kitts              Mary A. Lampert
A. 27 S. Wythe            A. 37 S. Wythe
P. Peter & Manda          P. Henry & Emaline
Oc. Farmer                M. James Mahood

Date: 4-24-1881
James G. Higgenbotham     Laura Stimpson
A. 33 S. Smyth            A. 22 S. Floyd
P. James G. & Isabella    P. N. B. & Mary J.
Oc. Farmer                M. O.R. Smith

Date: 5-22-1881
Charles Goff              Carrie Edwards
A. 34 S. Bedford          A. 27 S. NC
P. Lorenzo & Elizabeth    P. William & Martha
Oc. Mechanic              M. W. D. Mitchell

Date: 5-30-1881
Carson? A. Grubb          Rebecca J. Rakes
A. 32 S. Wythe            A. 24 S. Wythe
P. Nicholas & Catherine   P. Johnson & Rhoda J.
Oc. Laborer               M. F.F. Repass

Date: 7-17-1881
Chas W. Harman            M. A. M. Sheppard
A. 27 S. Bland            A. 22 S. Bland
P. Edward & Rhoda         P. John & E.J.
Oc. Farmer                M. L. J. Miller

Date: 2-3-1881
John Wm. Shufflebarger    Henrietta Muncy
A. 27 S. Pulaski          A. 18 S. Bland
P.  Newton S. & Anne      P. Tunis A. &
Anne P.  Wygal            Mary E.Clark
Oc. Mechanic              M. L. J. Miller

Date 2-10-1881
Jacob Adam Wagoner, M.D.  Martha Josephine Miller
A. 20 S. Bland            A. 20 S. Bland
P. James E. &             P. Dr. Lorenzo John &
Ailsey Munsey             Martha Lois Bird
Oc. Farmer                M. Wm. D. Mitchell

Date: 3-14-1881
Robert N. Marcus          Flora A. Penley
A. 25 S. Coldwell, NC     A. 16 S. Bland
P. Wilburn & America      P. Braxton H. & Adaline
Oc. Farmer                M. Geo W. Penley

Date: 4-20-1881
Wm. N. Linticum?          Lucy Ann Brown
A. 53 S. Pittsylvania     A. 28 W. Tazewell
P. Thomas & Delila        P. Wm. M. & Susan
Oc. Farmer                M.  A. J. Frazier

Date: 5-6-1881
Edward E. Epperson        Mary A. Hancock
A. 18 S. Wythe            A. 23 S. Wythe
P. E.E. & Drucilla F.     P. G. W. & Julia
Oc. Farmer                M. W. D. Mitchell

Date: 5-25-1881
William R. Cubine         Mary Rider
A. 23 S. Giles            A. 27 S. Giles
P. Patrick & Melvina      P. Hiram & Matilda
Oc. Farmer                M. J. T. Taylor

Date: 6-5-1881
William A. Wilson         Louisa L. Fanning
A. 29 S. Washington       A. 25 S. Giles
P. John M. & Mary E.      P. John & Louvenia
Oc. Minister M.E. Ch.     M.  G. P. Hareless?

Date: 7-14-1881
Samuel S. Davis           Sallie Repass
A. 32 S Bland             A. 21 S. Bland
P. H. G. & Cosby          P. Joseph & E. J
Oc. Farmer                M. Rev. W. D. Mitchell

Date: 7-28-1881
Robert A. Robinett
A. 24 S. Bland
P. P. G. & Malinda
Oc. Farmer

Lucy J. Pruett
A. 16 S. Bland
P. Henry P. & Mary E.
M. Peter R. Suiter

Date: 8-16-1881
James W. Hicks
A. 28 S. Buncombe, NC
P. Wm & Elizabeth
Oc. Teacher

Lula J. Grayson
A. 22 S. Wythe
P. A. J. Rose
M. J.J. Scherer

Date 7-28-1881
Hiram Stinson
A. 66 W. Giles
P. Jacob & Polly
Oc. Farmer

Sarah M. Thompson
A. 48 W. Wythe
P. Joseph & Mariah
M. J. H. Hoge

Date: 8-25-1881
James T. Gills
A. 23 S. Bland
P. Benjamin F. & M. E.
Oc. Farmer

Eliza Corner
A. 21 A. Bland
P. Robert & Catherine
M. W. E. Neel

Date: 8-30-1881
Thomas Colbert
A. 19 S.
P.
Oc. Farmer

Lucretia J. Collins
A. 21 S. Pulaski
P. Elizabeth
M. F. F. Repass

Date: 8-31-1881
Wm. F. Mullins
A. 25 S. Tazewell
P. Austin & Sarah
Oc. Farmer

V. E. Shrader
A. 23 S. Bland
P. John & Christina
M. R. M. Ashworth

Date: 9-7-1881
T. L. Copenhaver
A. 29 S. Smyth
P. Thomas & Rachel
Oc. Teaching

L. A. Tilson
A. 19 S. Bland
P. H. H. & Mary
M. F. F. Repass

Date: 9-15-1881
John W. Pruett
A. 20 S. Bland
P. H. P. & Mary E.
Oc. Farmer

Sarah L. French
A. 22 S. Bland
P. J. G. & Polly
M. Peter R. Suiter

Date: 10-13-1881
Gratton R. Muncy
A. 23 S. Bland
P. Gemima
Oc. Farmer

Mary L. Thomas
A. 15 S. Bland
P. Vice Ann
M. R. M. Ashworth

Date: 9-22-1881
Wm. T. Pruett
A. 23 S. Bland
P. Henry & Martha J.
Oc. Farmer

Nancy Robinett
A. 19 S. Bland
P. Patten G. & Malinda
M. Peter R. Suiter

Date: 10-22-1881
John Clark
A. 23 S. Henry Co, NC
P. Richard & Sue

Oc. Farmer

Martha A. French
A. 19 S. Bland
P. G. P. & Sarah

M. R. M. Ashworth

Date: 11-16-1881
Lafayette M. Newberry
A. 25 S. Bland
P. Harman & Mary
Ann McDonald
Oc. Farmer

Mary Louise Bird
A. 22 S. Bland
P. Benj. Valentine &
Catherine
M. Armstead A. Ashworth

Date: 11-16-1881
Wm. E. Peery
A. 20 S. Tazewell
P. W. E. & C. M.
Oc. Farmer

Josephine Auustus Newberry
A. 20 S. Bland
P. Harman & Mary A. McD.
M. G. W. Penley

Date: 11-17-1881
Robert J. Waddle
A. 29 S. Bland
P. Michael & M.
Oc. Farmer

Lenora C. Stowers
A. 21 S. Bland
P. James & Dicy
M. G. W. Penley

Date: 11-22-1881
Christian S. Douthat
A. 27 S. Giles
P. Jacob & Barbara
Oc. Machinist

Virginia Z. Shultz
A. 18 S. Henry
P. Zephani? & Sarah V.
M. J. H. Hoge

Date 11-22-1881
Harmon Sheppard
A. 24 S. Bland
P. E. A. & Rhoda
Oc. Farmer

Bessie Neel
A. 18 S. Bland
P. Nannie J.
M. J. H. Hoge

Date: 11-29-1881
Gratton Crockett Pauley    Mary Geneva Kitts
A. 27 S. Bland            A. 21 S. Bland
P. Hiram A. &            P. David N. &
Nancy Havens             Mollie Adaline Tickle
Oc. Farmer               M. L. J. Miller

Date: 12-18-1881
E. H. Waggoner           Jennie Berge
A. 27 S. Smyth           A. 23 S. Smyth
P. Jacob & Ann           P. Margaret & Martin
Oc. Farmer               M. F. F. Repass

Date: 12-28-1881
Jesse A. Perkins         Nancy J. Conley
A. 21 S. Giles           A. 21 S. Giles
P. James & Lucy J.       P. John & Eliza

Oc. Farmer               M. C. E. Weggins

Date: 12-29-1881
J. G. Cassell            Sallie A. Corder
A. 26 S. Bland           A. 17 S. Bland
P. Wm & Mary F.          P. B. F. & Julia A.
Oc. Mechanic             M. J. H. Hoge

Date: 11-22-1881
John Hancock             Barbara Pauley
A. 24 S. Bland           A. 24 S. Bland
P. George & Julia        P. Jacob & Mary
Oc. Farmer               M. A.A. Ashworth

Date:        1881
George Hancock           Sed. Pawley
A.  W                    A.  S.
P.                       P. Jacob & Mary
Oc. Farmer               M.
(Put in original book from memory)

Date: 1-5-1882
William Dillow           Virginia B. Pawley
A. 59 W. Bland           A. 36 S. Bland
P. Abram & Elizabeth     P. John & Ellen
Oc. Farmer               M. J. H. Hoge

Date: 1-17-1882
James A. Clark           Elizabeth J. Lambert
A. 28 S. Greenbrier, WV  A. 29 S. Bland
P.                       P. Isaac P. & Susan
Oc. Farmer               M. L. J. Miller

Date: 12-18-1881
James R. Neel            Virginia D. Edwards
A. 24 S. Tazewell        A. 21 S. Wythe
P. Mathias & Mary L.     P. Charles & Martha

Oc. Farmer               M. F.F. Repass

Date: 12-21-1881
John W. Woodyard         Genettie V. Stowers
A. 26 S. Giles           A. 25 S. Bland
P. L. L. Woodyard        P. John & Rachel
Oc. Farmer               M. R. M. Ashworth

Begin Page 20 of Original Book
Date: 12-22-1881
Ralph Mont. Stafford     Mary Elizabeth Crawford
A. 38 S. Bland           A. 26 S. Bland
P. Ralph A. &            P. Wm. & Catherine
Mary Margaret Orr        Webb
Oc. Farmer               M. J. H. Hoge

Date: 11-10-1881
J. W. Hoback             Nicatie Thompson
A. 22 S. Wythe           A. 21 S. Bland
P. Charles & Rhoda       P. George & Polly
Oc. Farmer               M. A. A.Ashworth

Date: 11-24-1881
J. M. Ashworth           Orlena C. Roach
A. 27 S. Bland           A. 22 S. F.C., W.VA
P. A. A. & Parthena      P. Isaac & Delilah
Oc. Farmer               M. J. T. Taylor

Date 1-5-1882
Charles L. Davidson (B)  Elizabeth Allen (B)
A. 22 S. Bland           A. 21 S.
P. Hugh & A.             P.
Oc. Farmer               M. George W. Penley

Date: 1-12-1882
Martin Dunagan           Cynthia M. Harman
A. 24 S. N C             A. 17 S. Giles
P. Lewis & Nancy         P. Addison & Sarah E.
Oc. Farmer               M. J. H. Hoge

Date: 2-2-1882
George H. Fanning        Martha E. Chapman
A. 19 S. Bland           A. 16 S. Giles
P. John & Elizabeth      P. Jas Wm. & Mary Octavia
Oc. Farmer               M. L. J. Miller

Date: 3-1-1882
Marion A. Thompson          Mollie J. Wiley
A. 22 S. Bland              A. 21 S.
P. Elisha G. & E. A.        P. James E. & Susan
Oc. Farmer                  M.  R. M. Ashworth

Date: 3-8-1882
Jacob F. Kerr               E. Mildred Price
A. 29 S. Giles              A. 20 S. Bland
P. Henry & Francis          P. I. K. & Elvira  J.
Oc. Farmer                  M.  F. F. Repass

Date: 3-16-1882
Harvey J.  Muncy            Catherine E. Kitts
A. 19 S. Bland              A. 20 S. Bland
P. James H. &               P. Jas. Wash. &
Margaret L. Hutsell         Julia Ann Havens
Oc. Farmer                  M.  J. H. Hoge

Date: 3-30-1882
Andrew M. Kitts             Lidia Louisa Ony
A. 40 W. Bland              A. 34 W. Smyth
P. Peter & Amanda           P. James & Nancy
Oc. Farmer                  M.  J. Mahood

Date: 4-20-1882
Harvey W. Shannon           Rebecca Allen
A. 24 S. Bland              A. 22 S. Bland
P. John C. & Mary           P. Madison  & Emily Susan
                            Carpenter
Oc. Farmer                  M. J. M. Humphreys

Date: 5-3-1882
Marcus Lafayette Bowles  Mary Etta Tickle
A. 21 S. Wythe              A. 16 S. Bland
P. William R. & Polly       P. Hezekiah C. & Matilda
                            Caroline Matilda Farmer
Oc. Farmer                  M.  G.W.K. Green

Date: 6-8-1882
Harvey W. Adkins            Emma E. Walker
A. 22 S. Bland              A. 21 S. Bland
P. Peter & Rhoda J.         P. Thomas F. & Julia A.
Oc.  Farmer                 M. Wm. E. Neel

Date: 6-16-1882
George Coburn               Elizabeth Kidd
A. 23 S. Bland              A. 23 S. Bland
P. David & Catherine        P. Margaret Ann
Oc. Farmer                  M.  G.W.K. Green

Date: 3-1-1882
John P. Burns?              Mary J. Havens
A. 24 W. Carroll            A. 20 S. Bland
P. Thomas T. & Anna         P. Alexander & Elizabeth
Oc. Farmer                  M.  J. T. Taylor

Date: 3-15-1882
Elisha Blankenship          Nancy  Holland
A. 23 S. Giles              A. 14 S. Franklin
P. Andrew J. & Sarah J.     P. John & Birtha
Oc. Farmer                  M.  R. M. Ashworth

Date: 3-23-1882
William P. King             Mima E. Umbarger
A. 29 S. Wythe              A. 24 S. Bland
P. George & Mary            P. William & Mandy

Oc. Farmer                  M.  F. F. Repass

Date: 4-5-1882
Joseph Hounshell            Margaret A. Kimberling
A 23 S. Bland               A. 26 S. Bland
P. Henry & Martha           P. Stephen & Eliza
Oc. Farmer                  M.  J. Mahood

Date: 4-27-1882
John Wolf                   Susan M. Saunders
A. 52 W. Alleghany          A. 40 S. Pulaski
P. Isaac & Martha           P. McCajoh?

Oc. Mechanic                M.  J. T. Taylor

Date: 6-8- 1882
John C.  Waddle             R. A. Waddle
A. 22 S. Bland              A. 22 S. Bland
P. David & Margaret         P. Michael & M.

Oc. Farmer                  M.  G.W.K. Green

Date 6-15-1882
Francis M. Starling         Kittie M. Bridges
A. 24 S. Tazewell           A. 16 S. Bland
P. John C. & Lobisa?        P. Ellen J. Hager
Oc. Farmer                  M.  John A. Smith

Date 6-22-1882
William H.  Kidd            Margaret J. Hager
A. 21 S. Tazewell           A. 21 S. Bland
P. Henry  C. & Matilda      P. Elizabeth
Oc. Farmer                  M. John A. Smith

Date: 6-27-1882
Benjamin R. Sutton     Sarah C. Hardy
A. 31 S. W. Pulaski     A. 21 S. Mercer, WV
P. John & Eliza     P. John & Sarah
Oc. Farmer     M. J. H. Hoge

Date: 6-29-1882
Augustus Coburn     Nannie A. Robinett
A. 22 S. Mercer, WV     A. 20 S. Bland
P. David & Catherine     P. Dicie

Oc. Farmer     M. R. M. Ashworth

Date: 7-20-1882
James Havens     Nancy C. Bowles
A. 18 S. Bland     A. 14 S. Bland
P. James & Mary J.     P. William & Polly Jane

Oc. Farmer     M. A. A. Ashworth

Date: 8-28-1882
Jno Kennerly Helvey     Louvena M. Pruett
A. 65 W. Montgomery     A. 29 S. Giles
P. Palser & Rhoda     P. H. M. & Isabelle
Oc. Farmer     M. R. M. Ashworth

Date: 7-27-1882
George L. Bane     Sallie V. Allen
A. 27 S. Giles     A. 25 S. Bland
P. Samuel & Lucy     P. Madison & Emily
Oc. Farmer     M. J. H. Humphreys

Date: 8-13-1882
Franklin A. Meadows     Elizabeth J. Rinheart
A. 37 S. Giles     A. 27 S. Bland
P. George & Hannah     P. Henderson & Lucinda
Oc. Farmer     M. John A. Smith

Date 8-31-1882
W. L. Hancock     Mary E. Epperson
A. 22 S. Bland     A. 22 S. Wythe
P. George W. & Julia     P. E. E. & D. P.
Oc. Farmer     M. C. E. Wiggins

Date: 9-3-1882
R.? L. Tibbs     L. J. Lampert
A. 23 S. Bland     A. 22 S. Bland
P. Ashby & Elizabeth     P. James & N. M.

Oc. Farmer     M. G.W.K. Green

Date: 6-27-1882
William A. Corner     Matilda Myers
A. 22 S. Bland     A. 23 S. Bland
P. James & Jane     P. John & Sophia
Oc. Farmer     M. L. J. Miller

Date: 7-20-1882
Charles M. Neel     Isabella A. Tickle
A. 21 S. Bland     A. 18 S. Bland
P. George W. & Mollie     P. Hezekiah C. &
    Caroline Matilda Farmer
Oc. Farmer     M. A.A. Ashworth

Date: 7-20-1882
Ballard Graham Kitts     Elizabeth J. Va. Kitts
A. 24 S. Bland     A. 18 S. Bland
P. James Wash. &     P. Harvey G. & Eliz.Va.
Mary Prunty     Bogle
Oc. Farmer     M. J. H. Hoge

Date: 7-27-1882
Marion C. Farmer     Louisa E. Harman
A. 22 S. Carroll     A. 18 S. Smyth
P. Noah     P. James W. & Margaret C.
Oc. Farmer     M. J. T. Taylor

Date: 8-9-1882
J. H. Nisewander     C. M. Patton
A. 21 S. Bland     A. 14 S. Bland
P. Alexander & Mary     P. Robert & Mary
Oc. Farmer     M. J. T. Taylor

Begin Page 21 of Original Book
Date: 8-15-1882
J. W. Fletcher     Matilda Sublett
A. 23 S. Bland     A. 18 S. Bland
P. Floyd & Elizabeth     P. Samuel D. & P.
Oc. Farmer     M. James T. Taylor

Date: 8-31-1882
Gordon H. Tickle     Christine Geneva Pauley
A. 31 S. Wythe     A. 18 S. Bland
P. Hezekiah & C. Matilda F.     P. Hiram A. & Nancy Havens
Oc. Farmer     M. C. E. Wiggins

Date 9-14-1882
Breckinridge Harvey Kitts     Emma Caroline Bowles
A. 18 S. Bland     A. 17 S. Wythe
P. David N.     P. William & Mary
& Molly Adaline Tickle     "Polly" Jane Austin
Oc. Farmer     M. C. E. Wiggins

45

Date: 10-19-1882
James B. Walker          Mary J. Ferrell
A. 20 S. Tazewell        A. 25 S. Carroll
P. Samuel & Sallie       P. William & Nancy
Oc. Farmer               M. John A. Smith

Date: 11-15-1882
Lindsey T. Walker        Jane Umbarger
A. 24 S. Tazewell        A. 21 S. Bland
P. Wm. T. & Catherine    P. Peter & Mima
Oc. Farmer               M. James Mahood

Date: 10-30-1882
John R. Birge            Ellen M. Kitts
A. 23 S. Smyth           A. 17 S. Bland
P. Martin & Margaret     P. Joseph & Elizabeth
Oc. Farmer               M. J. C. Smith

Date: 12-7-1882
James F. Kitts           Belle Havens
A. 32 S. Bland           A. 25 S. Bland
P. Peter & Mandy         P. Marguriette
Oc. Farmer               M. Armestead A. Ashworth

Date: 12-13-1882
Amos W. Tieche           Alice L Updike
A. 27 S. W.C.O.          A. 19 S. Bland
P. F. L. & Elizabeth     P. Albert Gallatin &
                         Hannah Jane Paxton
Oc. Merchant             M. J. C. Smith

Date: 12-21-1882
Isaac G. Pawley          Elizabeth Lampert
A. 56 W. Wythe           A. 32 S. Wythe
P. John & Polly          P. James & Elizabeth
Oc. Farmer               M. H. G. Davis

Date: 2-28-1883
William G. Birge         Mary F. Walker
A. 23 S. Smyth           A. 17 S. Bland
P. Martin & Margaret     P. A. L. & Susan
Oc. Farmer               M. F.F. Repass

Date: 3-22-1883
Whitney E. Willes        Nancy A. Thompson
A. 23 S. Giles           A. 19 S. Montgomery
P. Wm. E. & Margaret     P. Hezekiah B. & S. A.
Oc. Farmer               M. Peter R. Suiter

Date: 10-26-1882
Robert R. Burress        Martha Neel
A. 23 S. Smyth           A. 25 S. Bland
P. Raymond R. & Rose A.  P. Guss & Fannie
Oc. Farmer               M. John A. Smith

Date: 11-23-1882
Jesse W. Brown           Mary J. Wineset
A. 23 S. Wythe           A. 19 S. Carroll
P. John A. & Mary C.     P. Noah & Darthula
Oc. Farmer               M. G.W.K. Green

Date: 12-6-1882?
Peter G. Gearing         Ardelia I. Waggoner
A. 22 S. Bland           A. 18 S. Bland
P. A. Jackson & Amelia   P. Jaco & A. F.
Oc. Farmer               M. R. A. Kelley

Date: 12-7-1882
James H. Lindamood       Laura A. Kitts
A. 36 W. Wythe           A. 21 S. Bland
P. Joseph & Anne         P. Ganam & A. E.
Oc. Carpenter            M. Francis N. Panley

Date: 12-14-1882
Larkin Thompson          Virginia A. Guy
A. 24 S. Montgomery      A. 24 S. Bland
P. Hezekiah & Sarah      P. Lydia

Oc. Farmer               M. Peter R. Suiter

Begin Page 22 of Original Book
Date: 1-24-1883
Robert W. Tuggle         Mary C. Honaker
A. 34 S. Mercer, WV      A. 18 S. Bland
P. John & Lucinda        P. Peter C. & Mary A.
Oc. Farmer               M. R. M. Ashworth

Date: 3-4-1883
Winton J. Linkous        Hester A. Robinett
A. 21 S. Bland           A. 18 S. Bland
P. Martha                P. P. G. & Malinda
Oc. Farmer               M. Peter R. Suiter

Date: 4-5-1883
Benton W. Miller         Annabelle G. Dunagan
A. 24 S. Bland           A. 17 S. Bland
P. Abram & Rachel        P. R. M. & Mary
Oc. Farmer               M. L. J. Miller

Date: 4-24-1883
Harvey E. Crawford          Rhoda C. Myers
A. 25 S. Mercer, WV         A. 21 S. Bland
P. Thos B. & Elizabeth      P. John & Sophia
Oc. Farmer                  M. L. J. Miller

Date: 5-24-1883
James W. Meadows            Ila B. Parsel
A. 20 S. Giles              A. 22 S. Franklin
P. H. & Francis Pegram      P. John & Mary
Henry was J. W. M.'s step father.
Oc. Farmer                  M. F. F. Repass

Date: 6-21-1883
James H. Corner             Nannie S. Straley
A. 23 S. Bland              A. 25 S. Giles
P. Nancy Corner             P. James & Jane
Oc. Farmer                  M. Jno. E. Naff

Date: 6-27-1883
Martin Williams             Nannie B. Mustard
A. 25 S. Pittsylvania       A. 19 S. Bland
P. R. W. & E. P.            P. Wm N. & Caroline
Oc. Lawyer                  M. Jno E. Naff

Date: 7-26-1883
James T. Whitaker           Ellen Grubb
A. 21 S. Smyth              A. 21 S. Wythe
P. Jermiah & Emaline        P. Geo. W. & Mary
Oc. Farmer                  M. F. F. Repass

Date: 8-3-1883
C. P. Compton               Agnes L. Stowers
A. 28 S. Tazewell           A. 21 S. Bland
P. James N. & Lucinda       P. Peter R. & Araminta
Oc. Farmer                  M. J. A. Smith

Date: 8-23-1883
William E. Carr             Nannie Eliz. Harman
A. 24 S. Bland              A. 18 S. Bland
P. Matilda Carr             P. John Wesley &
                            Sarah Virginia Moore
Oc. Farmer                  M. J. H. Hoge

Date: 9-27-1883
John J. Powers              Jennie Baker
A. 29 S. Bland              A. 20 S. Bland
P. John & Julia Ann         P. Louisa Baker
Oc. Shoemaker               M. J. T. Taylor

Date: 4-25-1883
Wm. M. Furgusson            Mary S. Bogle
A. 25 S. Franklin           A. 25 S. Bland
P. Ocly & Ruth A.           P. John & Julia Ann
Oc. Merchant                M. Jno E. Naff

Date: 5-31-1883
Wm. H. H. Corner            Maggie Sublett
A. 21 S. Bland              A. 25 S. Bland
P. Geo & Nancy M.           P. Sam'l D. & Peters?

Oc. Farmer                  M. J. T. Taylor

Date: 6-26-1883
B. F. Parker                Maggie H. Barnett
A. 36 W. England            A. 20 S. Virginia
P. Peter & Mary             P. Louvia Barnett
Oc. Mechanic                M. J. C. Smith

Date: 7-25-1883
William C. Hedrick          Ninnie A. Bird
A. 22 S. Tazewell           A. 19 S. Bland
P. Wm. & Z. C.              P. Wm M. & Eliza J
Oc. Editor                  M. A. A. Ashworth

Date: 7-27-1883
Roland Neel                 A. M. McNeel
A. 25 S. Mercer, WV.        A. 27 S. Bland
P. Henry M. & Sarah A.      P. Jacob V. & Delilah
Oc. Farmer                  M. L. J. Miller

Date: 8-16-1883
Rufus M. Umbarger           Eliza J. Neel
A. 28 S. Bland              A. 17 S. Bland
P. James & Margaret         P. Alex. & Mary
Oc. Farmer                  M. C. G. Davis

Date: 9-11-1883
Austin L. Bird              Genevia J. Miller
A. 22 S. Bland              A. 16 S. Bland
P. John R. & Susan          P. Geo W. & Sallie A.

Oc. Farmer                  M. John P. Roach

Date: 9-27-1883
Franklin E. Muncy           Mary J. McCoy
A. 24 S. Bland              A. 25 S. Montgomery
P. Skidmore & Julia A.      P. James N. & Margaret E.
Oc. Carpenter               M. Geo. W. Penley

Date: 10-3-1883
John F. Kimberling     Nancy C. Hounshell
A. 21 S. Bland     A. 24 S. Bland
P. Stephen & Eliza     P. Henry B. & Martha J.
Oc. Farmer     M.  C. G. Davis

Date: 10-9-1883
Samuel Patton     Josephine Waddle
A. 21 S. Smyth     A. 18 S. Bland
P. Sam'l & Catherine     P. Calvin & Margaret
Oc. Farmer     M. Francis H. Farley

Date: 10-11-1883
John D. Smith     Mary G. A. Shrader
A. 23 S. Bland     A. 21 S. Bland
P. Paul C. & Mary E.     P. John L. & Christina
Oc. Farmer     M. Thomas C. Pattison

Date: 10-25-1883
Joseph T. Sublett     Minnie Jones
A. 29 S. Bland     A. 17 S. Bland
P. Sam'l D. & Petero?     P. Ellen M. Jones
Oc. Farmer     M. J. T. Taylor

Date: 12-12-1883
George W. Crawford     Agnes S. Myers
A. 23 S. Mercer, WV     A. 19 S. Bland
P. Hiram & Elizabeth     P. John & Sophia
Oc. Farmer     M. Levi K. McNeil

Date: 12-26-1883
James F. Grayson     Lucy Ann McNutt
A. 22 S. Bland     A. 20 S. Bland
P. James W. & Emma     P. Jno S. & Elizabeth
Oc. Farmer     M. G.W.K. Green

Date: 9-11-1884
Alexander Fortner     Lucretia M. Crow
A. 26 S. Wythe     A. 20 S. Smyth
P. John & Nancy     P.
Oc. Farmer     M. James Mahood

Date: 1-17-1884
John Myers     Julia Blankenship
A. 60 W. Craig     A. 44 W. Bland
P. William & Charity     P. Joseph & Susan
Oc. Farmer     M. L. J. Miller

Date: 10-2-1883
Robert Wylie     E.R.C. Hamilton
A. 43 S. Owingsville, Ky     A. 26 W. Giles
P. Wm. O. & Jane     P. A. J. & Elizabeth
Oc. Lawyer     M. J. T. Taylor

Date: 10-23-1883
Isaac A. Biby     Virginia L. French
A. 21 S. Giles     A. 16 S. Bland
P.Nicholas & Martha     P. Isaac E. & Catherine
Oc. Farmer     M. R. M. Ashworth

Date: 10-22-1883
John P Talbert     Marie Adkins
A. 22 S. Stokes Co. NC     A. 20 S. Bland
P.James N. & Mollie     P. Peter & Rhoda
Oc. Farmer     M. J. A. Smith

Date: 11-22-1883
John F. Gylpin     Austin D. Repass
A. 24 S. Bland     A. 20 S. Bland
P. John Gylpin & Nancy Dillow     P. Austin D. & Genieve
Oc. Farmer     M.  J. A. Smith

Date: 12-19-1883
Harvey M. Burton     Octavia P. Wheeler
A. 21 S. Bland     A. 16 S. Bland
P. Francis & Julia     P. Rob't M. & Mary
Oc. Farmer     M.  L. J. Miller

Date: 12-24-1883
Andrew J. Wynn     Julia A. Hughes
A. 20 S. Bland     A. 22 S. Bland
P. William & Millie     P.
Oc. Farmer     M. Jno E. Naff

Begin Page 23 of Original Book
Date: 1-3-1884
John C. Gregory     Sarah A. Fox
A. 22 S. Tazewell     A. 16 S. Tazewell
P. S. C. & S. Virginia     P. G. C. & Jane
Oc. Farmer     M. John A. Smith

Date: 1-23-1884
Floradore A. Crabtree     Sarah J. Lampert
A. 17 S. Bland     A. 27 S. Bland
P. James & Agnes     P. John & Mahala
Oc. Farmer     M. Frank H. Farley

Date: 10-29-1883 James Akers A. 22 S. Pulaski  Nancy Woodyard  A. 26 S. Giles  (Left out)**
P. Dandridge & Parthena  P. Levi S. & Dianne  Oc. Farmer  M. R. M. Ashworth

Date: 1-30-1884
Samuel L. Kitts  Amanda E. Wilson
A. 36 W. Bland  A. 21 S. Bland
P. Elizabeth  P. Jno. L. & Elizabeth
Oc. Farmer  M. H. G. Davis

Date: 3-8-1884
John C. Farley  Eliza E. Ratcliff
A. 24 S. Giles  A. 14 S. Washington
P. H. M. & Mary A.  P. John H. & Louisa J.
Oc. Farmer  M. John E. Naff

Date: 4-9-1884
William A. Warner  Mary L. Wheeler
A. 20 S. Bland  A. 18 S. Bland
P. Wm. T. & Catherine  P. Rob't N. & Nancy A.
Oc. Farmer  M. Thomas C. Pulliam

Date: 4-10-1884
Paris D. Pruett  Rhoda A. French
A. 25 S. Bland  A. 16 S. Bland
P. Henry P. & Mary E.  P. J. G. & Mary
Oc. Farmer  M. R. M. Ashworth

Date: 4-16-1884
Gabriel Helmandollar  Elvira Kidd
A. 20 S. Tazewell  A. 19 S. Bland
P. Granger & Matilda  P. Chapman & Matilda
Oc. Farmer  M. Jno. A. Smith

Date: 4-24-1884
Phillip Dunagan  Martha A. B. Overstreet
A. 28 S. Surrey, NC  A. 25 S. Bedford
P. Louis & Nancy  P. Tilman J. & Nancy A.
Oc. Farmer  M. Jno P. Roach

Date: 5-7-1884
Thos. Jefferson Halsey  Sylvia Caldonia Tickle
A. 27 S. Wythe  A. 18 S. Giles
P. Sephen & Sally  P. Peter C. & Mary Ann Journell
Oc. Farmer  M. Jno. E. Naff

Date: 5-28-1884
Thos. G. Dangerfield  Mittie D. Keeling
A. 21 S. Tazewell  A. 18 S. Tazewell
P. H. E. French  P. A. J. & Francis
Oc. Farmer  M. R. M. Ashworth

Date: 6-2-1884
James A. Sarver  Viola M. Walker
A.  Tazewell  A.  Bland
P. John & Susan  P. Benj. L.? & Elizabeth
Oc. Farmer  License not returned

Date: 6-5-1884
E. J. Kidd  V. J. Price
A. 22 S. Bland  A. 21 S. Giles
P. Jas M. & Margaret A.  P. Geo P.
Oc. Farmer  M. James T. Taylor

Date: 6-17-1884
J. B. Updyke  N. G. Compton
A. 44 W. Amhurst  A. 34 S. Bland
P.  P. Jas R. & Rhoda

Oc. Farmer  M. John E. Naff

Date: 6-24-1884
Allen Taylor Newberry  Nannie E. Gross
A. 80 W. Wythe  A. 28 S. Bland
P. Rev. Samuel &  P. Harvey G. &
Eunice Powers  Mary E. Irving
Oc. Farmer  M. John E. Naff

Date: 6-25-1884
Peter Adkins  Ellen V. Hern
A. 49 W. Bland  A. 20 S. Bland
P. Isaac & Elizabeth  P. Harvey & Nancy C.
Oc. Farmer  M. R. M. Ashworth

Date: 7-16-1884
John E. Croy  Adnia Harman
A. 22 S. Giles  A. 16 S. Bland
P. Isaac & Sarah F.  P. Wm Neal & Orlena Farmer
Oc. Teacher  M. Jno P. Roach

Date: 8-14-1884
Henry Hughes  Minta A. Wimmer
A. 23 S. Bland  A. 28 W. Bland
P. Crock & Betsey  P. Harvey & Sarah
Oc. Farmer  M. Peter R. Suiter

Date: 8-20-1883
T. K. Lindamood  Laura T. Repass
A. 28 S. Wythe  A. 22 S. Bland
P. Jno H. & Martha J.  P. James A. & Lucinda
Oc. Farmer  M. L. J. Miller

49

Date: 8-30-1883
D. B. Groseclose | Mary J. Buck
A. 27 S. Bland | A. 22 S. Wythe
P. Joseph & Elizabeth | P. Felix & Margaret A.

Oc. Teacher | M. J. B. Greever

Date: 9-16-1884
E. F. Ferrell | Missouri B. French
A. 21 S. Giles | A. 19 S. Bland
P. Mike & Louisa | P. Preston & Sarah
Oc. Farmer | M. James H. Wingo?

Date: 9-21-1884
Dallas Lee Tickle | Alice V. Morris
A. 20 S. Giles | A. 17 S. Giles
P. John & Adolpha | P. Samuel H. & Rachel
Oliver; A.J. Neil, step father
Oc. Mechanic | M. L. J. Miller

Date: 9-25-1884
Chas Switzer | Georgia Woodyard
A. 25 S. Montgomery | A. 15 S. Bland
P. J. W. & H. A. | P. A. R. & Jennie
Oc. Mechanic | M. J. C. Smith

Date: 10-16-1884
Jno. Allen Bogle | Lillie V. Penley
A. 36 S. Bland | A. 16 S. Bland
P. Dunn & Julia Newbery | P. Braxton & Adaline Suiter

Oc. Teacher | M. Jno E. Naff

Date: 10-16-1884
Richard Waddle | Dilla C. Kegley
A. 21 S. Bland | A. 17 S. Bland
P. Ephriam & Emaline | P. J. G. & Hester A.
Oc. Farmer | M. G.W.K. Green

Date: 10-28-1884
Jonas Umbarger | Barbara E. Neel
A. 23 S. Bland | A. 17 S. Bland
P. Jonas & Margaret | P. Alex & Mary M.
Oc. Farmer | M. H. G. Davis

Date: 11-1-1884
D.P.R. Hoback | Telia A. Hancock
A. 21 S. Wythe | A. 17 S. Bland
P. Joseph & Elizabeth | P. Geo. W. & Julia Ann
Oc. Farmer | M. Geo W. Penley

Date: 9-10-1884
Peter H. Tickle | Rosa Collins
A. 21 S. Giles | A. 21 S. Giles
P. Peter & Mary Ann | P. James C. & Margaret
Journell
Oc. Farmer | M. Jno E. Naff

Date: 9-18-1884
Jno W. Jones | Eliza B. Corner
A. 24 S. Bland | A. 15 S. Bland
P. Jas M. & Charlotte | P. Nancy Corner
Oc. Farmer | M. A. Q. Harman

Date: 9-25-1884
Green D. Bruce | Nannie E. Stafford
A. 27 S. Bland | A. 20 S. Bland
P. John & Louisa | P. Ballard P. & M.J.E.

Oc. Famer | M. Jno. E. Naff

Date: 10-4-1883
James W. Robinett | Susan J. Hoge
A. 21 S. Bland | A. 20 S. Wise
P. Jezreel & Mary A. | P. Dan'l S. & E. Jane
Oc. Farmer | M. J. H. Hoge

Date: 10-16-1884
Gordon Andrew Muirhead | Tacy Adaline Pruett
A. 31 W. Bland | A. 17 S. Bland
P. Daniel & Isabelle | P. Jas Milton & Elizabeth
Elizabeth H. Saunders | Araminta Fanning
Oc. Farmer | M. Jno P. Roach

Date: 10-28-1884
Rob't L. Neel | Sarah E. Umbarger
A. 19 S. Bland | A. 21 S. Bland
P. Alex & Mary M. | P. Jonas & Margaret
Oc. Farmer | M. H. G. Davis

Date: 10-30-1884
Wm R. Tolbert | Zarilda C. Adkins
A. 24 S. Stokes, NC | A. 18 S. Bland
P. James & Mary | P. Peter
Oc. Farmer | M. Peter R. Suiter

Date: 11-5-1884
Jefferson D. Wilson | Victory D. Miller
A. 22 S. Montgomery | A. 22 S. Bland
P. Harvey P. & Theodora | P. L. J. & Martha L.
Oc. Farmer | M. Armstead A. Ashworth

Date: 11-6-1884
Samuel H. Helvey             Nickatie K. Miller
A. 23 S. Bland              A. 20 S. Bland
P.Kennerly & Sallie         P. L. J. & Martha L.
Oc. Farmer                  M. A. A. Ashworth

Date: 12-24-1884
George M. Guy               Nancy A. E. Thompson
A. 20 S. Montgomery         A. 22 S. Wythe
P. Wm L. & Lydia            P. David & Nancy
Oc. Farmer                  M. R. M. Ashworth

Date: 12-31-1884
Wm. Buchanan Stuart         Sarah Mariah Mustard
A. 27 S. Bland              A. 21 S. Bland
P. William & Margaret       P. Harvey R. & Mariah
Myers                       Wohlford
Oc. Carpenter               M. J. T. Taylor

Date: 2-5-1885
Jasper N. Fannon            Sarah A. Lampert
A. 31 S. Bland             A. 24 S. Bland
P. Acles & Sarah            P. Henry & Emma
Oc. Farmer                  M. A. A. Ashworth

Date: 2-9-1885
John F. Sarver              Laura C. Hager
A. 30 S. Craig              A. 25 S. Bland
P. James & Etta             P. Jacob & Margaret
Oc. Farmer                  M. R. M. Ashworth

Date: 2-17-1885
Wm Howe Hoge                Ollie V. Mahood
A. 32 S. Pulaski            A. 23 S. Tazewell
P. Wm E. & Jane             P. James & Amanda
Oc. Farmer                  M. James A. Brown

Date: 3-4-1885
Robert C. Adkins            Mary J. Tilson
A. 28 S. Wythe              A. 40 W. Wythe
P. James M. & Lydia         P. Jacob & Ann
Oc. Farmer                  M. C. W. Cooper

Date: 3-25-1885
John H. Thorn               Lelia O. Updyke
A. 28 S. Bland              A. 22 S. Bland
P. Gordon C. & Agnes        P. Albert Gallatin &
                            Mary Agnes Smith
Oc. Merchant                M. John E. Naff

Date: 12-17-1884
Chas W. Terry               Ida Z. Penley
A. 29 S. Bland              A. 18 S. Bland
P. Wm & Margaret            P. Braxton & Adaline
Oc. Farmer                  M. P.P. Hayes

Date: 12-25-1884
Jno W. Daugherty            Angline Walker
A. 18 S. Tazewell          A. 26 S. Bland
P. David A. & Nannia L.     P. Chas F. & Julia A.
Oc. Carpenter               M. Wm. E. Neel

Begin Page 24 of Original Book
Date: 1-13-1885
Thomas N. Biby              Harriet Pennington
A. 19 S. Indianna          A. 21 S. WV
P. Nicholas & Martha        P. William & Kate

Oc. Farmer                  M. R. M. Ashworth

Date: 2-7-1885
Daniel Haden (B)            Cally Adams (B)
A. 24 S. Bland              A. 16 S. Bland
P. Victoria & Ephriam       P. Cyrus
Oc. Blacksmith              M. P.P. Hayes

Date: 2-12-1885
Wm. C. Allen                Lucy J. Morris
A. 40 W. Carroll            A. 24 S. Giles
P. John & Sarah             P. Samuel & Rachel
Oc. Farmer                  M. L. J. Miller

Date: 3-3-1885
Jefferson Brown (B)         Martha Brown (B)
A. 22 S. Giles              A. 26 S. Giles
P. Samson & Clementine      P. Ross & Hannah
Oc. Farmer                  M. Simon L Mann

Date: 3-17-1885
Chanavha ?T. Hanks          Fannie S. Compton
A. 24 S. Carroll            A. 24 S. Bland
P. Edward & Eliza           P. John R. & Rhoda
Oc. Farmer                  M. John E. Naff

Date; 3-25-1885
Squire B. Hager             Lizzie Wirt
A. 19 S. Bland              A. 17 S. Giles
P. Sena B.                  P. Russell & Delilah

Oc. Farmer                  M. R. M. Ashworth

Date: 3-25-1885
Charles Roberson (B)          Susan Colander(B)
A. 21 S. Giles                A. 17 S. Bland
P. Emaline                    P. George & Letitia
Oc. Farmer                    M. Simon L. Mann

Date: 4-9-1885
John S. Bird                  Victoria A. Bennett
A. 27 S. Bland                A. 19 S. Pittsylvania
P. John R. & Susan            P. George W. & Mary
Oc. Farmer                    M. John H. Hoge

Date: 4-14-1885
John H. Collins               Gillie B. Akers
A. 22 S. Bland                A. 19 S. Pulaski
P. James & Mary A.            P. Moses & Sarah

Oc. Farmer                    M. A. Q. Harman

Date: 4-23-1885
James Magruder Morehead   Melinda Jane Shrader
A. 29 S. Bland                A. 30 S. Bland
P. Dan'l F. & Isabelle        P. John & Christina
Elizabeth H. Saunders         Day
Oc. Farmer                    M. R. M. Ashworth

Date: 4-23-1885
Pleasant T. Hancock          Mary E. Wyrick
A. 42 W. Wythe               A. 33 S. Bland
P. Obediah & Nannie          P. Sanders & Nancy
Oc. Farmer                    M. John H. Hoge

Date: 4-23-1885
Henry Hiram Kitts            Lucinda C. McFarland
A. 26 S. Bland               A. 28 S. Bland
P. Jacob & Matilda           P. L. D. & Matilda
Oc. Farmer                    M. F. F. Repass

Date: 4-29-1885
William H. Tilson            Mary R. Kegley
A. 31 S. Bland               A. 22 S. Bland
P. Harman & Mary             P. Mitchell & Matilda

Oc. Farmer                    M. J. T. Taylor

Date: 5-13-1885
Wm. Ribble Patterson         Harriett Emily Tickle
A. 24 S. Wythe               A. 18 S. Bland
P. James H. & Nancy          P. Peter C. & Mary
                             Ann Journell
Oc. Farmer                    M. P. P. Hayes

Date: 6-24-1885
Wythe G. Kitts               Alice Niswander
A. 26 S. Bland               A. 19 S. Bland
P. Gannam &                   P. Jacob H. & Susan
Abagail Ann
Oc. Farmer                    M. B. F. White?

Date: 7-2-1885
Geo. W. Hancock              Isabella  Shrader
A. 25 S. Bland               A. 17 S. Bland
P. Mary Hancock              P. Joseph & Sarah C.

Oc. Farmer                    M. P. P. Hayes

Date: 7-16-1885
Wm R. Heart                  Maria V. Brown
A. 25 S. Wythe               A. 28 S. Bland
P.Benjamin & Betsy           P. Alex. & Mary
Oc. Farmer                    M. John E. Naff

Date: 7-23-1885
Henry H. Pruett              Ann E. Terry
A. 21 S. Bland               A. 17 S. Henry
P. Henry P & Mary E.         P. J. Milton & Martha
Oc. Farmer                    M. R. M. Ashworth

Date: 8-19-1885
J. H. H. Gravely             Mary J. Hedrick
A. 43 W. Henry               A. 25 S. Tazewell
P. Willis & Ann              P. William & Zillah
Oc. Farmer                    M.   John E. Naff

Date: 8-23-1885
Rob't S. Doak                Nannie Love
A. 21 S. Bland               A. 19 S. NC
P. Robert & Manda            P. J. S. & H. A.
Oc. Farmer                    M. F. F. Repass

Date: 9-8-1885
Austin French                Jennie Guy
A. 73 W. Giles               A. 22 S. Montgomery
P. John & Obedience          P.
Oc. Farmer                    M. Peter R. Suiter

Date: 9-10-1885
Harvey M. Woodyard           Harriet Nisewander
A. 24 S. Bland               A. 23 S. Bland
P. A. R. & Jane              P. W. H. & Ann
Oc. Farmer                    M. John E. Naff

Date: 9-16-1885
Joseph Tibbs — Keziah Wilson
A. 23 S. Bland — A. 20 S. Logan, WV
P. Asbury & Eliza — P. Wm & Jemimah
Oc. Farmer — M. F. F.Repass

Date: 9-22-1885
Wm. E. Patterson — Amanda Pawley
A. 21 S. Bland — A. 19 S. Bland
P. Newton & Virginia — P. Jacob & Mary
Oc. Farmer — M. P. P. Hayes

Date: 10-13-1885
James M. Stowers — Elizabeth Cregar
A. 56 W. Tazewell — A. 48 S. Wythe
P. Mordecai & Polly — P. George & Nancy
Oc. Farmer — M. J. A. Mahood

Date: 10-21-1885
Anderson Glendy (B) — Susan R. Davidson (B)
A. 25 S. Pulaski — A. 17 S. Bland
P. David & Letitia — P. Hugh & Elsie
Oc. Farmer — M. Simon L. Mann

Date: 10-22-1885
R. E. Lee Ashworth — Geneva A. Bird
A. 21 S. Bland — A. 17 S. Bland
P. A. A. & Parthena — P. Price & Francis
Oc. Farmer — M. R. M. Ashworth

Date: 10-29-1885
Thos. L. Sanger — Geneva Linkous
A. 24 S. Pulaski — A. 28 S. Bland
P. George & Elizabeth — P.
Oc. Farmer — M. R. M. Ashworth

Date: 10-29-1885
Wm P. Thompson — Amanda M. Chapman
A. 19 S. Bland — A. 16 S. Giles
P. H. P. & Rebecca — P. James & Mary O.
Oc. Farmer — M. A. A. Ashworth

Date: 11-5-1885
C. M. Scott — Odris? D. Repass
A. 27 S. Bland — A. 22 S. Bland
P. John M. & Barbara — P. John & Minerva
Oc. Merchant — M. James A. Brown

Date: 9-16-1885
Ballard P. Leffel — Virginia P. Thornton
A. 25 S. Tazewell — A. 16 S. Bland
P. Wm A. & Sarah A. — P. K. C. & Virginia
Oc. Farmer — M. J. T. Taylor

Date: 11-9-1885
James Thompson — Mary J. Tickle
A. 25 S. Wythe — A. 14 S. Bland
P. David & Nancy — P. John & Adolpha Oliver
Oc. Farmer — M. Peter R. Suiter

Date: 11-12-1885
Sam L. Wall — Nannie S. Dunagan
A. 23 Surrey, NC — A. 17 S. Bland
P. Henry & Lucinda — P. Lewis & Nancy
Oc. Farmer — M. George W. Penley

Date: 11-12-1885
John W. Stowers — Susan E. Smith
A. 22 S. Bland — A. 23 S. Bland
P. Colby & Lockie — P. John A. & Julia
Oc. Farmer — M. Wm E. Neel

Begin Page 25 of Original Book
Date: 11-13-1885
Henry J. Belcher — Nancy S. Stowers
A. 17 S. Mercer, WV — A. 19 S. Bland
P. A. G. & Martha — Colby & Lockie
Oc. Farmer — M. John A. Smith

Date: 11-19-1885
C. C. Thompson — Nannie B. Wynn
A. 24 S. Bland — A. 17 S. Tazewell
P. Harvey G. & Sophia — P. Andrew & Abagail
Oc. Farmer — M. John A. Smith

Date: 12-2-1885
John F. Jessup (B) — Jennie R. Armstrong (B)
A. 25 S. NC — A. 16 S. Bland
P. — P. Jackson & Susan
Oc. Farmer — M. Peter R. Suiter

Date: 12-3-1885
James A. Morris — Mary C. Robinett
A. 22 S. Wythe — A. 30 S. Bland
P. Jesse & Caroline — P. Patton G. & Malinda
Oc. Farmer — M. R. M. Ashworth

Date: 12-17-1885
H. P. Pruett                  Annie E. Gibson
A. 47 W. Giles                A. 40 W. Mongtomery
P. Wm. & Elizabeth            P. N. M. & Lucy
Oc. Farmer                    M. J. C. Smith

Date: 12-23-1885
H. W. Nisewander              Beulah E. Hall
A. 23 S. Bland                A. 18 S. Bland
P. Alex & Mary A.             P. Sam'l & Susan
Oc. Printer?                  M. Isaac Baker

Date: 12-24-1885
Pearis D. Lampert             Mary J. Shrader
A. 19 S. Bland                A. 18 S. Bland
P. Betsy Lampert              P. Joseph & Sarah
Oc. Farmer                    M. J. W. Bowman

Date: 12-31-1885
Wm. J. Bruce                  Elvira A. Starks
A. 23 S. Bland                A. 19 S. Bland
P. John & Louisa              P. James & Caroline
Oc. Far,er                    M. James T. Taylor

Begin Page 26 of Original Book
Date: 1-5-1886
Newton E. Harman              Nannie Jane Beard
A. 20 S. Bland                A. 23 S. Pulaski
P. Abraham Fielder &          P. James & Cynthia
Margaret Cubine
Oc. Farmer                    M. J. H. Hoge

Date: 1-7-1886
Gary Clark                    Arminta French
A. 26 S. Bland                A. 16 S. Bland
P. Richard & Susan            P. Wm P. & Elizabeth

Oc. Farmer                    M. R. M. Ashworth

Date: 1-18-1886?
John H. Eagle                 Etta U. Maxwell
A. 26 S. Bland                A. 22 S. Bland
P. S. M. & Martha J.          P. J. E. & Rachel A.

Oc. Farmer                    M. John A. Smith

Date: 1-23-1886
Joseph A. Burrass             Cordelia V. Waddle
A. 20 S. Tazewell             A. 17 S. Smyth
P. Thos. & Mary A.            P. Calvin & Margaret
Oc. Farmer                    M. Jno A. Smith

Date: 11-21-1885
John E. Thompson              Rachel C. Pawley
A. 19 S. Bland                A. 24 S. Bland
P. Elizabeth                  P. Thomas & Telia A.
Oc. Farmer                    M. A. Q. Harman

Date: 12-24-1885
W. Luther Brown               Callie Newberry
A. 27 S. Bland                A. 19 S. Bland
P. A. B. & Mary A.    P. Henry & Elizabeth Robinett
Oc. Farmer                    M. Geo. W. Penley

Date: 12-30-1885
Miller Bane Allen             Hannah J. Hudson
A. 40 S. Giles                A. 27 S. Bland
P. Madison & Maria Bane       P. Isaac & Elizabeth
Oc. Farmer                    M. James A. Brown

Date: 10-? -1885
Lewis Henderson (B)           Matilda Harman (B)
A. 25 S. Pulaski              A. 37 W. Bland
P.                            P. License Not returned
Oc.                           M. G. W. K. Green

Date: 1-7-1886
N. E. Winesett                Susan B. Brown
A. 25 S. Carroll              A. 19 S. Wythe
P. Noah & Darthula            P. Jno & Mary C.

Oc. Farmer                    M. J. Mahood

Date: 1-14-1886
Harvey John Kitts             Sarah Eliz. Williams
A. 29 S. Bland                A. 22 S. Smyth
P. Joseph &                   P. Wm. Bonham &
Sarah Elizabeth Bales         Christina Hanshew
Oc. Farmer                    M. F. F. Repass

Date: 1-21-1886
Andrew J. Shufflebarger       Mary J. Stowers
A. 29 S. Pulaski              A. 22 S. Bland
P. Newton S. &                P. Isaac F. &
Ann Wygal                     Virginia Robinett
Oc. Farmer                    M. P. P. Hayes

Date: 2-2-1886
J. W. Gullian                 Susan R. Rakes
A. 22 S. Smyth                A. 18 S. Bland
P. John & Elizabeth           P. Johnson & Rhoda
Oc. Farmer                    M. C. W. Cooper

Date: 2-17-1886
Jno. H. Sublett
A. 28 S. Bland
P. Saml D. & Petra
Oc. Farmer

Ollie C. Talbott
A. 16 S. Bland
P. Wm & Julia
M. J. T. Taylor

Date: 3-7-1886
D. Hoge Bird
A. 27 S. Bland
P. Stephen W. & Malinda
Oc. Farmer

Amanda R. Ruble
A. 17 S. Tazewell
P. M. A. & Christina
M. Peter R. Suiter

Date: 4-8-1886
Chas. L. Mustard
A. 20 S. Bland
P. Henry P. & Franzenia
Crawford
Oc. Farmer

Henrietta Mustard
A. 25 S. Bland
P. Wm P. & Louisa
Robinett
M. G. W. Penley

Date: 4-14-1886
Elias Foglesong
A. 44 W. Wythe
P. Henry & Julia

Oc. Farmer

Mary C. Umbarger
A. 22 S. Bland
P. Peter & Jemima

M. J. B. Greever

Date: 4-17-1886
Aldens M. Cox
A. 40 W. Augusta
P. Henry & Nancy
Oc. Farmer

Emaline Tibbs
A. 38 S. Bland
P. James & Sarah
M. F. F. Repass

Date 4-26-1886
Charles E. Miller
A. 29 S. Rockingham
P. Geo W. & Sally
Oc. Carpenter

Sarah E. Ramsey
A. 21 S. Franklin
P. Wm. L. & Elizabeth
M. J. W. Bowman

Date: 4-28-1886
Wm. L. Robinson (B)
A. 21 S. Carroll
P. Jas. H. & Elizabeth
Oc. Farmer

Sarah J. Caldwell (B)
A. 22 S. Carroll
P.
M. J. T. Taylor

Date: 5-6-1886?
N. B. Hancock
A. 33 S. Smyth
P. Elizabeth & Gordon
Oc. Farmer

Margaret Waddle
A. 21 S. Bland
P. Ephriam & Emaline
M. P.P. Hayes

Date: 5-12-1886
Rob't G. Davis
A. 65 W. Giles
P. Isaac & Jane
Oc. Farmer

Mary Foglesong
A. 55 W. Wythe
P. Simon & Christina
M. H. G. Davis

Date: 4-25-1886
Albert B. French
A. 25 S. Mercer, WV
P. Gordon & Mary A.
Oc. Farmer

Mary S. Dunagan
A. 16 S. Bland
P. Rural & Mary
M. A. A. Ashworth

Date: 4-26-1886
Wm R. Woodyard
A. 25 S. Giles
P. Wm. S. & Nancy J.
Oc. Farmer

Nancy Robinett
A. 23 S. Bland
P. Dicy Robinett
M. P. R. Suiter

Date: 4-27-1886
Jas E. Davis
A. 22 S. Carroll
P. Henry & Margaret
Oc. Miller

Ollie E. Bird
A. 20 S. Bland
P. John R. & Susan
M. A. A. Ashworth

Date: 5-30-1886
Jno D. Yonce
A. 26 S. Smyth
P. Jefferson & Jemima
Oc. Farmer

Angeline L. Bails
A. 22 S. Bland
P. James R. & Mary
M. H. G. Davis

Date: 6-3-1886
Chas. M. Sarver
A. 34 W. Tazewell
P. John & Martha
Oc. Farmer

Nancy J. Adkins
A. 28 S. Bland
P. Peter & Rhoda
M. Wm. E. Neel

Date: 6-3-1886
Harvey Crow Powers
A. 22 S. Bland
P. John & Julia A.
Oc. Farmer

Rose Nisewander
A. 25 S. Bland
P. Harvey & Susan
M. J. T. Taylor

Date: 6-9-1886
Charles Edwards
A. 59 W. Rockingham
P. Charles & Polly
Oc. Farmer

Rhoda J. Groseclose
A. 26 S. Bland
P. Jacob & Nancy
M. F. F. Repass

Date: 8-26-1886
E. B. Folden
A. 23 S. Bland
P. Caroline Folden

Oc. Farmer

Ollie V. Harvey
A. 17 S. Montgomery
P. Lyda Harvey

M. Peter R. Suiter

Date: 8-26-1886
Sam'l Price Newberry
A. 22 S. Bland
P. Robt' Lemuel &
Margaret Hoge Hunter
Oc. Farmer

Malissa Rose Miller
A. 17 S. Bland
P. Alex. Flemming &
Nancy Jane Hamilton
M. Geo W. Penley

Date: 9-30-1886
Chas F. Stowers
A. 21 S. Bland
P. Isaac F. & Virginia
Oc. Farmer

Rebeaka Steel
A. 20 S. Bland
P. George & Lavicy
M. John A. Smith

Date: 10-7-1886
Wm. A. Woodyard
A. 21 S. Giles
P. John & Rebeaka
Oc. Farmer

E. Angeline Clark
A. 25 S. Bland
P. James & Mahala
M. P. R. Suiter

Date: 10-21-1886
John E. Shrader
A. 27 S. Bland
P. John & Christina
Oc. Farmer

Nora E. Gleason
A. 15 S. Giles
P. Patrick & Margaret E.
M. Chas C. Pulliam

Date: 10-28-1886
David R. Dooley
A. 28 W. Pittsylvania
P. Jesse & Louisa
Oc. Farmer

Naomia K. Kidd
A. 17 S. Bland
P. Wm. S. & Almira
M. P. R. Suiter

Date: 10-28-1886
Jerome Mitchell
A. 26 S. Floyd
P. Timothy E. &
Ardelia Wohlford
Oc. Carpenter

Mary Ellen Mustard
A. 24 S. Bland
P. Wm. P. &
Louisa Robinett
M. James T.Taylor

Date: 11-10-1886
I. Wesley Kidd
A. 21 S. Bland
P. H. C. & Jemima

Oc. Farmer

Rhoda A. Devor
A. 19 S. Bland
P. H. H. & Louisa

M. John A. Smith

Date: 11-10-1886
C. W. Keister
A. 30 S. Giles
P. Wm & Nancy
Oc. Blacksmith

Lucinda R. Cubine
A. 22 S. Bland
P. Patrick & Melvina
M. J. W. Bowman

Date: 11-15-1886
Jno E. Stowers
A. 47 W. Bland
P. Wm & Christina
Oc. Farmer

Jane G. Kegley
A. 41 D. Bland
P. Isaac & Prudence
M. P. P. Hayes

Date: 11-17-1886
Geo. E. Miller
A. 22 S. Bland
P. Alex Flemming &
Nancy Jane Hamilon
Oc. Farmer

Ella Hoge Newberry
A. 18 S. Bland
P. Rob't Lemuel &
Margaret Hoge Hunter
M. B. F. White

Date: 11-28-1886
Andrew J. Williams
A. 37 S. Smyth
P. Andrew & Rebeaka

Oc. Farmer

Matilda L. McClellend
A. 28 S. Smyth
P. Wm & Margaret

M. F. F. Repass

Date: 11-29-1886
James J. Brown
A. 19 S. Bland
P. Americus Brown
Oc. Farmer

Anglina M. Austin
A. 21 S. Floyd
P. Wm G. & Elizabeth
M. J. W. Bowman

Date: 12-8-1886
John M. Hudson
A. 34 S. Bland
P. Isaac & Elizabeth
Oc. Farmer

Florence O. Repass
A. 27 S. Bland
P. John & Minerva
M. F. F. Repass

Date: 12-23-1886
Sam'l Burke (B)
A. 21 S. Bland
P. Victoria Burks
Oc. Farmer

Sarah A. Harman (B)
A. 18 S. Mercer, WV
P. Rob't & Matilda
M. Simon L. Mann

Date: 12-23-1886
Jas F. Bridges
A. 22 S. Bland
P. Jane Bridges
Oc. Farmer

Nancy R. Walker
A. 19 S. Bland
P. Benjamin & Elizabeth
M. License Not Returned

Date: 1-13-1887
Samuel W. Guy | Genettie V. Woodyard
A. 25 S. Montgomery | A. 27 W. Bland
P. Geo. & Lydia Harvey | P. John & Roshell

Oc. Farmer | M. Peter R. Suiter

Date: 3-3-1887
Geo. A. Bussey | Nannie E. Price
A. 25 S. Mercer, WV | A. 25 S. Montgomery
P. Thompson E. & | P. Geo. P. & Mary
Elizabeth Bralley
Oc. Farmer | M. J. W. Bowman

Date 3-3-1887
Jas. W. H. Brown | Maggie F. Waddle
A. 25 S. Wythe | A. 21 S. Bland
P. Alex & Mary C. | Newton & Mary E.
Oc. Farmer | M. G. W. Green

Date: 4-20-1887
Sam'l L. Repass | Lucinda M. Umbarger
A. 22 S. Bland | A. 20 S. Bland
P. James A. & Lucinda | P. Peter & Jemima
Oc. Farmer | M. H. G. Davos

Date: 5-19-1877
Joseph S. King | Emily V. Pegram
A. 30 S. Bland | A. 16 S. Giles
P. David & Eliza | P. John H. & Fannie L.
Oc. Farmer | M. A.Q. Harman

Date: 8-4-1887
James Albert Tickle | Cynthia Lee Price
A. 20 S. Pulaski | A. 22 S. Bland
P. Wm Green & Laura | P. Geo P. & Mary
Ann Underwood Wilson | Ann Roberts
Oc. Farmer | M. J. H. Hoge

Date: 8-11-1887
A. Paris Thompson | Alice V. Lindamood
A. 31 S. Bland | A. 24 S. Bland
P. Harvey & Sophia | P. John Henry & Martha Jane
Oc. Farmer | M. H. G. Davis

Date: 9-22-1887
Sam'l E. Sarver | Maggie B. Morris
A. 26 W. Giles | A. 22 S. Giles
P. Jeramiah G. & Frances | P. Sam'l H. & Rachel
Oc. Farmer | M. A. A. Ashworth

Date: 2-6-1887
Jasper Robinett Carr | Nannie Dickenson Harman
A. 24 S. Bland | A. 19 S. Giles
P. James & Fannie | P. Addison &
 | Sarah Elizabeth Ellis
Oc. Farmer | M. George W. Penley

Date: 3-3-1887
Lafayette Dillow | Machie M. Burrass
A. 23 S. Bland | A. 19 S. Tazewell
P. Addison & Vicy | P. Thomas & Mary

Oc. Farmer | M. License not returned

Date: 3-17-1887
Joseph Kitts | Mary A. Farley
A. 65 W. Wytne | A. 49 W. Wythe
P. Henry & Polly | P. Baltzer & Rhoda Helvey
Oc. Farmer | M. F. F. Repass

Date: 5-12-1887
Wm. G. Myers | Laura V. Blankenship
A. 26 S. Bland | A. 18 S. Bland
P. John & Sophia | P. Benj. & Juda
Oc. Farmer | M. J. H. Surface

Date: 6-9-1887
Josiah Tibbs | Matilda F. Brown
A. 30 S. Goochland | A. 36 D. Wythe
P. Asbury & Eliza | P. John A. & Margaret.
Oc. Farmer | M. F.F. Repass

Date: 8-4-1887
Henderson G. Thompson | Sarah L. Chapman
A. 19 S. Tazewell | A. 16 S. Bland
P. Hiram P. & Reheaka | P. James Wm. & Mary D.

Oc. Farmer | M. A. A. Ashworth

Date: 9-7-1887
Gus C. Coburn | Alice V. Coldwell
A. 25 D. Mercer, WV | A. 21 S. Craig
P. David & Catherine | P. Noah & Sarah Ann
Oc. Farmer | M. Peter R. Suiter

Date: 10-20-1887
Andrew P. G. Fox | Mary E. Fox
A. 27 S. Tazewell | A. 18 S. Tazewell
P. Mathias & Sarah A. | P. G. C. & R. J.
Oc. Farmer | M. John A. Smith

Date: 10-20-1887
Wm. Kitts                   Victoria Neel
A. 68 W. Wythe              A. 31 S. Tazewell
P. Jacob & Mary            P. Thomas & Sarah
Oc. Farmer                 M. P. P. Hayes

Date: 10-22-1887
Joseph Hellems             Louisa J. Williams
A. 58 W. Botetourt         A. 32 S. Yadkin, NC
P. John & Rebecka          P.
Oc. Blacksmith             M. Peter R Suiter

Date: 11-2-1887
James Ward                 Joannah Peak
A. 39 W. Wythe             A. 26 S. Pulaski
P. John & Polly            P. Aaron & Sally
Oc. Brickmason             M. F. F. Repass

Date: 11-17-1887
Nathaniel E. Hager         Margaret A.Wheeler
A. 22 S. Kanawah,WV        A. 14 S. Giles
P. James & Nancy C.        P. Creed F. & Sarah
Oc. Farmer                 M. R. M. Ashworth

Date: 11-23-1887
E. C. Parsell              Cynthia M. Pegram
A. 23 S. Franklin          A. 18 S. Giles
P. John & Mary Ann         P. John D. & Frances

Oc. Farmer                 M. A. A. Ashworth

Date: 12-9-1887
Charles Corner             Ardelia Nisewander
A. 21 S. Bland             A. 28 S. Bland
P. Nancy Corner            P. Alex & Mary

Oc. Farmer                 M. J. T. Taylor

Date: 12-21-1887
A. E. Peery                Margaret A. Foglesong
A. 30 S. Tazewell          A. 21 S. Bland
P. Stephen & Elizabeth     P. Elias & Sophia
Oc. Farmer                 M. H. E. Bailey

Date: 12-29-1887
Thos. F. Scott             Martha Elliott
A. 25 S. Bland             A. 21 S. Tazewell
P. John & Barbara          P. Wm. A.
Oc. Farmer                 M. J. Mahood

Date: 10-20-1887
Frank Burks (B)            Patsey A. Hobbs (B)
A. 20 S. Wythe             A. 18 S. Bland
P. Victoria Burke          P. Thomas & Lettie
Oc. Farmer                 No Certificate

Date: 10-27-1887
Rufus B. Robinett          Eliza Stowers
A. 32 S. Bland             A. 23 S. Bland
P. Hiram & Dicy            P. Russell & Minta
Oc. Farmer                 No Certificate

Date: 11-3-1887
Godfrey Charlton (B)       Mary Johnson (B)
A. 23 D. Tazewell          A. 18 S. Bland
P. Sam'l & Minerva J.      P. Eli & Hannah
Oc. Farmer                 M. Thos Mawbray

Date: 11-17-1887
Jesse Barnett (B)          Belle E. Hobbs (B)
A. 28 W. Patrick           A. 32 S. Bland
P. Eliza Barnett           P. Thomas & Lettie
Oc. Farmer                 M. S. L. Mann

Date: 11-30-1887
Wm. O. Barnes              Ida M. Newberry
A. 27 S. Tazewell          A. 23 S. Bland
P. Clinton &               P. Harman &
Sarah Gillespie            Mary Ann McDonald
Oc. Farmer                 M. M. W. Doggett

Date: 12-11-1887
Thos G. Lambert            Clara G. Helvey
A. 23 S. Mercer, WV        A. 24 S. Bland
P. John F. & Emily         P. Jno K. & Sarah
                           Dora Munsey
Oc. Farmer                 M. J. H. Surface

Date: 12-21-1887
Coma E. Thompson           Margaret Hutsell Munsey
A. 20 S. Bland             A. 16 S. Bland
P. B. Preston & Jennie     P. Wm H. & Hellen
Oc. Farmer                 License not returned

Date: 1-7-1888
Kent Akers                 Elizabeth French
A.    S. Bland             A..   S. Bland
P.                         P. J. G. & Mary
Oc. Farmer                 M. R. M. Ashworth
Recorded from memory after Court House burned

58

Date: 8-21 1888
Latona Bird              Bettie Boone
A. 18 S. Bland        A. 21 S. Bland
P. J. H. & Mary       P. Rhoda Jane French

Oc. Farmer           M. R. M. Ashworth

Date: 12-6-1888
James Wall           Jennie Thomas
A. 22 S. Surry. NC   A. 18 S. Mercer, WV
P. Henry J & Lydia   P. Wayne & Sarah
Oc. Farmer           M. J. H. Hoge

Date: 7- -1888
Rob't L. Hager      Matilda Clark
A. 23 S. Bland       A. 21 S. Bland
P. J. J. & Margaret  P. Richard & Susan
Oc. Farmer           M. R. M. Ashworth

Date: 1-25-1889
Stanford Anderson Melvin Mary L. Price
A. 50 W. Orange, NC  A. 25 S. Bland
P. Edward & Catherine P. Isaiah K. & E. J.
Oc. Farmer           M. P. P. Kinzer

Date: 2-25-1889
H. F. C. Hanshew   Nancy Riggsby
A. 21 S. Bland       A. 19 S. KY
P. J. F. & M. L.       P. W. M. & Mary

Oc. Farmer    License destroyed before Marriage

Date: 3-6-1889
Rob't H. W. Boling   Amanda V. Stowers
A. 26 S. Tazewell    A. 28 S. Bland
P.A. T. & Barbara.   P. Isaac F. & Virginia
Oc. Farmer           M. G.W.K. Green

Date: 3-28-1889
James Larkin Corder  Sarah Elizabeth Davis
A. 33 W. Bland      A. 19 S. Bland
P. Benjamin & Julia  P. Sam'l C. & Eliza A.
Oc. Carpenter        M. P. P. Kinzer

Date: 4-28-1889
Walter L. Henderson  Alberty Tibbs
A. 22 S. Bland       A. 20 S. Bland
P. Elias & Rhoda    P. James & Mary

Oc. Farmer           M. F.F. Repass

Date: 8-29-1888
Archie Hughes Williams Nannie Lee Grayson
A. 26 S. Pittsylvania  A. 17 S. Bland
P. R. W. & E. P.     P. Andrew Jackson &
                    Rosalie V. Johnson
Oc. Farmer           M. P. P.Kinzer

Date: 2-24-1888
James D. French    Martha E. Hager
A. 18 S. Bland       A. 21 S. Bland
P. O. E. & Christina  P. James & Nancy
Oc. Farmer           M. R. M. Ashworth

Begin Page 28 of Original Book
Date: 1-3-1889
Pearis W. Purkey   Eliza M. E. Lampert
A. 23 S. Bland       A. 18 S. Bland
P. Wm. & Darthula  P. Wm. W. & Rhoda Elizabeth
Oc. Farmer           M. H. G. Davis

Date: 2-6-1889
R. Green Ramsey (B)  Clara Ann Damrel (B)
A. 23 S. Bland       A. 21 S. Bland
P. Richard & Matilda P. Sam'l & Lila
Oc. Farmer           M. Simon L. Mann

Date: 2-26-1889
John Henry Harman  Ida Angeline Kitts
A. 21 S. Bland       A. 21 S. Bland
P. Abraham Fielder  P. Jas. Washington &
& Margaret Cubine   Julia Ann Havens
Oc. Farmer           M. John H. Hoge

Date: 3-27-1889
Erastus J. Bailey    Nannie A. Davis
A. 23 S. Mercer, WV  A. 19 S. Tazewell
P. Alex J. & Hannah L. P. Edward A. & Zarilda
Oc. Carpenter        M. R. M. Ashworth

Date: 3-29-1889
Henry Thos Wall    Luemma Elvira Chapman
A. 22 S. Surry, NC   A. 16 S. Bland
P. Henry J. & Lucinda P. James & Mary
Oc. Farmer           M. Thos C. Pulliam

Date: 5-9-1889
Ira LozierTickle    Mary Elizabeth Florence Hutsell
A. 22 S. Bland       A. 22 S. Bland
P. Dan'l Lineberry &   P. Joseph C. & Anne
Mary Melissa "Polly" Bogle  Thompson
Oc. Farmer           M. J. H. Hoge

59

Date: 5-10-1889
George Clark
A. 24 S. Bland
P. Richard & Susan
Oc. Farmer

Maggie M. French
A. 17 S. Bland
P. Rhoda Jane French
M. R. M. Ashworth (LNR)

Date: 5-12-1889
Millard Clark
A. 21 S. Bland
P. Richard & Susan
Oc. Farmer

Julia Ellison Lambert
A. 13 S. Bland
P. Victoria Lampert
M. Thos C. Pulliam

Date: 5-15-1889
Wm. Washington Bird
A. 36 S. Bland
P. Benj. Valentine &
Catherine C. Saunders
Oc. Farmer

Nannie Lee Va. Burton
A. 15 S. Bland
P. Chas Russell & Virginia
Caroline Kitts
M. P. P. Kinzer

Date: 6-6-1889
Sam'l Mailand Damewood
A. 40 W. Union/Knox, TN
P. Isaac & Milsey

Oc. Farmer

Elizabeth Bodkin
A. 28 S. Kanawha, WV
P. Mary & Josiah

M. Thos Mawbrey

Date: 6-12-1889
Jos Stuart Gross
A. 23 S. Bland
P. Harvey G. & Mary E.
Oc. Farmer

Bettie Bullard Thompson
A. 19 S. Tazewell
P. James & Florauer
M. P. P. Kinzer

Date: 6-24-1889
Geo. F. Daugherty
A. 20 S. Tazewell
P. David Allen & Nannie Lois
Oc. Carpenter

Melissa May Walker
A. 21 S. Bland
P. Thos F. & Julia Ann
M. D. A. S. Loeffel

Date: 6-27-1889
Wm B. McHaffa
A. 19 S. Bland
P. Ludema E.
Oc. Farmer

Eunice Zilla Hager
A. 17 S. Bland
P. Jas R. & Nancy Caroline
M. R. M. Ashworth

Date: 7-9-1889
Gregory Edward Hall
A. 20 S. Bland
P. Sam'l H. & Mary Susan
Oc. Farmer

Octava V. Snead
A. 18 S. Bland
P. Chas F. & Mary Catherine
M. G.W. K. Green

Date: 7-16-1889
Columbus Franklin Tolbert
A. 25 S. Surry, NC
P. J. N. & Mary
Oc. Farmer

Nancy Gibson
A. 27 W. Bland
P. Wm & Peggy Terry
M. Peter R. Suiter

Date: 7-17-1889
W. W. Yost
A. 29 S. Tazewell
P. Wm O. & Elizabeth
Oc. Farmer

Eunice Horton
A. 22 S. Bland
P. Wm. M. & Arabelle
M. John A. Smith

Date: 7-10-1889
Cephus Lawrence
A. 22 S. Montgomery
P. Geo W. &
Rebecca Ellen
Oc. Farmer

Minnie J. Thompson
A. 14 S. Montgomery
P. Hezekiah B. & Elizabeth

M. Peter R. Suiter

Date: 8-8-1889
Martin Luther Rosenbaum
A. 37 S. Wythe
P. Alexander & Ada

Oc. Farmer

Frances Agnes Morehead
A. 23 S. Bland
P. Dan'l & Isabelle
Elizabeth H Saunders
M. P. P. Kinzer

Date: 8-22-1889
Wm. Gordon Steel
A. 23 S. Bland
P. Henry W. & Matilda J.
Oc Farmer

Betie Mona Lindamood
A. 16 S. Wythe
P. James H. & Emily J.
M. H. G. Davis

Date: 8-26-1889
Henry Saddler
A. 59 W. Botetourt
P. Jacob & Polly
Oc. Farmer

Christina French Lampert
A. 40 W. Bland
P. Hiram & Dicy Robinett
M. P. P. Kinzer

Date: 9-4-1889
Geo Wash. Blankenship
A. 24 S. Giles
P. Charlton & Parthena
Oc. Farmer

Margaret Crawford
A. 35 S. Giles
P. Travis & Juda
M. P. R. Suiter

Date: 9-5-1889
Wm. Austin French
A. 23 S. Bland
P. Rhoda Jane French
Oc. Farmer

Laura A. Bird
A. 17 S. Bland
P. J. Henry & Mary J.
M. Peter R. Suiter

Date: 9-8-1889
James Lee Warner          Victoria Amanda Button
A. 22 S. Bland            A. 19 S. Bland
P. W. T. & Catherine      P. Travis & Mary H.
Oc. Farmer                M. Thos C. Pulliam

Date: 10-3-1889
James Robinson            Luemma Crawford
A. 26 S. Giles            A. 16 S. Bland
P. Henry & Phoebe         P. James & Mary
Oc. Farmer                M. R. M. Ashworth

Date: 10-30-1889
Wm. Thos Davis            Parmelia Ann Davis
A. 24 S. Carroll          A. 18 S. Bland
P. Henry & Margaret       P. Sam'l C. & Elizabeth
Oc. Farmer                M. M. C. Graham

Date: 11-1-1889
Geo Washington Perkins    Octavia Bibee
A. 22 S. Giles            A. 17 S. Bland
P. James & Lucy           P. Alex & Nancy
Oc. Farmer                M. R. M. Ashworth

Date: 11-5-1889
Cloyd Winton Casper       Martha Francis Wirt
A. 22 S. Bland            A. 17 S. Giles
P. Matilda Casper         P. Russell R. & Delila Jane
Oc. Farmer                M. D. A. Leffel

Date: 11-6-1889
Jas Chapman Woodyard      Sarah Eliz. Mustard
A. 27 S. Bland            A. 25 S. Bland
P. A. R. & Jennie         P. Wm. D. & Paulina Tynes
Oc. Farmer                M. Jno M. Romans

Date: 11-7-1889
Rona Jno Miller           Mary Estille Williams
A. 19 S. Bland            A. 22 S. Bland
P. Alex F. & Jane         P. Wm C. & Sallie G.
Oc. Farmer                M. Jno H. Hoge

Date: 11-7-1889
Geo A. Vipperman          Mary A. Bennett
A. 19 S. Russell          A. 19 S. Pittsylvania
A. Geo W. & Martha J.     P. Geo W. & Mary
Oc. Rail Roading          M. Jno. M. Romans

Date: 11-10-1889
James M. Kirby            Jane Lambert
A. 22 S. Montgomery       A. 20 S. Bland
P. Peter & Lucinda        P. John & Alpha
Oc. Farmer                M. T.C. Pulliam

Date: 11-10-1889
J. Newton Johnston        Martha Elizabeth Brown
A. 41 W. Giles            A. 16 S. Bland
P. Russell & Jane         P. J. Milton & Anna
Oc. Farmer                M. Jno A. Smith

Date: 11-13-1889
Chas Peery Muncy          Mary Ella Mustard
A. 35 S. Bland            A. 21 S. Bland
P. And. Jack. &           P. W. Newton & Caroline E.
Sarah Jane
Oc. Clerk of Courts       M. Jno E. Naff

Date: 11-21-1889
Rob't Bruce Macon         Minnie Weaver Newberry
A. 30 S. TN               A. 27 S. Bland
P.                        P. Henley Chapman &
                          Mollie E. Steel
Oc. Farmer                M. Jno E. Naff

Begin Page 29 of Original Book
Date: 9-5-1889                              Date: 12-12-1889
Wm. Isam? Cundiff         Cora Alice Bishop    Godfrey Charlton (B)       Marcia Dameron(B)
A. 23 S. Bland            A. 17 S. Montgomery  A. 24 S. Tazewell          A. 21 S. Bland
P. John & Sarah           P. Jacob & Elizabeth P. Sam'l Cazar & Minerva Jane  P. Sam'l & Delila
Oc. Farmer                M. Peter R. Suiter.  Oc. Farmer                 M. E. Studebaker

Date: 12-18-1889
Elmo Depp Hancock         Emily May Allen
A. 25 S. Chesterfield     A. 23 S. Bland
P. D. B. & M. H.          P. Madison & E. S.
Oc. Farmer                M. C. T. Kirtner?

Date: 12-18-1889
Jas. Jackson Groseclose   Susan Alberta Kimberling
A. 26 S. Bland            A. 20 S. Bland
P. Joseph & Elizabeth N.  P. Stephen & Eliza
Oc. Farmer                M. F. F. Repass

Date: 12-18-1889
Newton Crockett Mustard Mollie Salome Whalen
A. 33 S. Bland                 A. 27 S. Bland
P. Wm. P. &                    P. Hiram &
Louisa Robinett                Mary A. Dunlap
Oc. Farmer                     M. J. T. Taylor

Date: 12-24-1889
Thos B. Thompson               Madeline Thompson
A. 23 S. Tazewell              A. 21 S. Bland
P. James & Florauer            P. David F. & Catherine G.
Oc. Farmer                     M. John A. Smith

Date: 12-25-1889
Lafayette Digby Repass         Adeline B. Baumgardner
A. 27 S. Bland                 A. 22 S. Bland
P.Elias & Adaline E.           P. M. L. & M. E.

Oc. Farmer                     M. F. F. Repass

Date: 12-26-1889
James W. Burton                Lola Orga Painter
A. 20 S. Bland                 A. 16 S. Bland
P. C. R. & V. C.               P. W. G. & V. C.
Oc. Farmer                     M. C. W. Kelley

Date: 1-1-1890
Wm Bascomb Allen               Maggie T. Hudson
A. 32 S. Giles                 A. 28 S. Bland
P. Wm B. & Hannah              P. Thos & Elizabeth
Oc. Farmer                     M. J. B. Greever

Date: 1-8-1890
Newton Jackson Wiley           Ollie Columbia Thompson
A. 20 S. Tazewell              A. 21 S. Tazewell
P. James E. & Susan A.         P. Elisha G. & Susan E.

Oc. Farmer                     M. R. M. Ashworth

Date: 1-16-1890
Geo. Lee Tickle                Ella Smith Pegram
A. 20 S. Bland                 A. 16 S. Bland
P. Jackson Nye &               P. John Henry &
Mary Ann Waggoner              Frances Lou Martin
Oc. Farmer                     M. C. W. Kelley

Date: 1-21-1890
James Jonas Umbarger           Julia Ann Crabtree
A. 28 S. Bland                 A. 25 S. Bland
P. Wm. & Christina             P. Rus. & Polly A.
Oc. Farmer                     M. H. G. Davis

Date: 12-23-1889
Romeo Verdie Hall              Ida LuellaHall
A. 16 S. Bland                 A. 19 S. Bland
P. S. A. (now Chandler)        P. L. B. & Emily

Oc. Printer                    M. C. W. Kelley

Date: 12-25-1889
Chas. A. Dutton                Mary Catherine Crow
A. 23 S. Wythe                 A. 20 S. Bland
P. Franklin & Eva              P. Jonas M. & Christina
Oc. Farmer                     M. H. G. Davis

Date: 12-25-1889
Fabias Iterbide Updyke         Roxie Ella Bernard
A. 23 S. Bland                 A. 19 S. Franklin
P. Albert Gallatin &           P. Sam'l H. &
Mary Agnes Smith               Elizabeth H. Pelter
Oc. Farmer                     M. J. T. Taylor

Date 1-1-1890
Hezekiah Franklin C. Hanshew   Nancy Riggsby
A. 21 S. Bland                 A. 20 S. KY
P. J. F. & M. L.               P. W. M. & Mary
Oc. Farmer                     M. F. F. Repass

Date: 1-5-1890
Hiram McClehen(B)              Jane Belle Harman (B)
A. 37 S. Pulaski               A. 18 S. Bland
P. Ben & Cynthia               P.
Oc. Farmer                     M. John M. Romans

Date: 1-15-1890
Chas. L. Stowers               Sarah Margaret Walters
A. 18 S. Bland                 A. 21 S. Bland
P. Travis & Minta              P. Russell & Nancy
Ann Hughs
Oc. Farmer                     M. Peter R. Suiter

Date: 1-16-1890
Chas Wallace McNeil            Alice Ermini Fanning
A. 24 S. Bland                 A. 21 S. Bland
P. Jacob & Delila              P. John & Elizabeth

Oc. Farmer                     M. Jno M. Romans

Date: 1-22-1890
Alexander Stuart(B)            Sallie A.nn Calender(B)
A. 21 S. Giles                 A. 21 S. Bland
P.Isaac & Esther               P. George & Letitia
Oc. Farmer                     M. J. W. Woods

Date: 2-3-1890  
Green Taylor  
A. 35 W. Bland  
P. Parthy Taylor  
Oc. Farmer  

Lucy Rider  
A. 28 S. Bland  
P. Hiram & Matilda  
M. J. T. Taylor  

Date: 2-9-1890  
Harvey H. Bird  
A. 23 S. Bland  
P. Stephen W. & Malinda  
Oc. Plasterer  

Lora E. Harvey  
A. 17 S. Montgomery  
P. Lydia Harvey  
M. Peter R. Suiter  

Date: 2-12-1890  
Jno Wm Burton  
A. 28 W. Giles  
P. Jno F. & Dicy J.  
Oc. Farmer  

Viney R. Henderson  
A. 21 S. Washington  
P. James Henderson & Rebecca L.  
M. J. T. Taylor  

Date: 2-19-1890  
Jos. Wm Whitaker  
A. 30 W. Giles  
P. Geo W. & Eliza Ann  
Oc. Farmer  

Rosa Arlena Dunagan  
A. 22 S. Bland  
P. Rural M. & Mary  
M. Jno P. Roach  

Date: 2-25-1890  
James Collins  
A. 32 W. Wisconsin  
P. Ed & Betsy  
Oc. Farmer  

Elizabeth Collins  
A. 30 S. Bland  
P. James & Mary Ann  
M. Jacob Smith  

Date: 2-27-1890  
Jno. F. Suiter  
A. 23 S. Bland  
P. Peter R. & Margaret  
Oc. Farmer  

Mary Miranda Howard  
A. 23 S. Montgomery  
P. Henry C. & Jennie  
M. Peter R. Suiter  

Date: 3-24-1890  
Rob't Lee Hall  
A. 23 S. Burkes Garden  
P. Thos & Betsy  
Oc. Farmer  

Martha Rebecca McFarland  
A. 23 S. Bland  
P. L. D. & Matilda J.  
M. James Mahoney  

Date: 3-27-1890  
Wiley Winton Burress  
A. 25 S. Bland  
P. Rabourn & Rosana  
Oc. Farmer  

Julia Kidd  
A. 25 S. Bland  
P. H. C. & Jemima  
M. Jno A. Smith  

Date: 3-27-1890  
Henley Taylor Repass  
A. 36 S. Bland  
P. Jas A. & Lucinda J.  
Oc. Farmer & Carpenter  

Eugenia Florence Scott  
A. 27 S. Bland  
P. John & Barbara  
M. James Mahood  

Date: 4-2-1890  
Jas Lynch Hedrick  
A. 36 S. Bland  
P. Wm. & Zilla  
Oc. Farmer & Harness Maker  

Hannah Thomas  
A. 26 S. Bland  
P. Gordon C. & Agnus  
M. G.W.K. Green  

Date: 4-2-1890  
Geo B. Akers  
A. 21 S. Pulaski  
P. Dandridge & Parthena  

Oc. Farmer  

Rachel M. Suiter  
A. 17 S. Bland  
P. Peter & Margaret E.  

License not returned  

Date: 4-10-1890  
Jacob Creed Bogle Kitts  
A. 28 S. Bland  
P. Harvey G. &  
Elizabeth Virginia Bogle  
Oc. Farmer  

Edna Nye Tickle  
A. 21 S. Bland  
P. Dan'l Lineberry &  
Mary Melissa Bogle  
M. J. H. Hoge  

Date: 4-17-1890  
Jno. Wesley Neel  
A. 21 S. Bland  
P. Peter P. & Lauelett  

Oc. Farmer  

Jennie M. Neel  
A. 21 S. Tazewell  
P. Cynthia  
(now Daugherty)  
M. E. Studebaker  

Date: 4-19-1890  
Walter Bowles  
A. 21 S. Wythe  
P. Elizabeth  
(now Richardson)  
Oc. Farmer  

Mahulda A. Muncy  
A. 21 S. Bland  
P. Wm H. & Hellen  

M.  

Date: 4-25-1890  
Lewis Neel Wiley  
A. 44 W. Tazewell  
P. John & Elanor  
Oc. Farmer  

Sallie Myers  
A. 24 S. Bland  
P. John  
M. Peter R. Suiter  

Date: 5-1-1890  
Rob't Lee Meredith  
A. 27 S. Carroll  
P. Anderson & Mary  
Oc. Miner  

Minnie Belle Lampert  
A. 19 S. Bland  
P. Geo W. & Sallie A.  
M. F. F. Repass

Date: 5-6-1890
Jno Winton Stafford    Flora Lelia Wohlford
A. 28 S. Bland    A. 21 S. Bland
P. Ballard P. & Mary    P. Gordon & Matilda
Jane Henderson    Ann Byrnes
Oc. Carpenter    M. J. T. Taylor

Date: 5-6-1890
Jezreel Robinette Mustard Ina Cosby Wohlford
A. 24 S. Bland    A. 20 S. Bland
P. James Harvey &    P. Gordon & Matilda
Marshall Marcie Robinett Ann Byrnes
Oc. Farmer    M. J. T. Taylor

Date: 5-7-1890
Giles Menelius  Johnson  Lucinda Jane Mustard
A. 29 S. Giles    A. 26 S. Bland
P. Jno L. & Jane Stafford  P. Jas. Harvey & Marcia Robinett
Oc. Farmer    M. J. T. Taylor

Begin Page 30 of Original Book
Date: 5-14-1890
John Wm Carver    Lucy May  Clark
A. 25 S. Bland    A. 16 S. Bland
P. Dan'l T. & Martha C.  P. Rufus W. & Nancy L
Oc. Farmer    M. John A. Smith

Date: 5-26-1890
Wm. A. Hager    Sarah A. Gleason
A. 34 S. Bland    A. 16 S. Giles
P. Jacob J. & Margaret    P. Patrick & Margaret E.
Oc. Farmer    M. Peter R. Suiter

Date: 5-29-1890]
W. Stuart Foglesong    Mary Elizabeth Kimberling
A. 22 S. Bland    A. 27 S. Bland
P. Henry  S. & Mary Ann  P. Henry & Barbara
Oc. Farmer    M. J. Mahood

Date: 6-8-1890
Jefferson Fletcher Suiter  Eunice S. Groseclose
A. 21 S. Bland    A. 22 S. Bland
P. Sally Jane & Geo W.    P. John & Emaline
Oc. Farmer    M. James Mahoney

Date: 6-11-1890
Ballard P. French    Ollie Sarver
A. 20 S. Bland    A. 17 S. Craig
P. Rufus A. & Fannie    P. John & Joanna
Oc. Farmer    M. R. M. Ashworth

Date: 6-11-1890
Benjamin F. Starling    Sarah Stowers
A. 20 S. Bland    A. 22 S. Bland
P. John & Sarah    P. Geo W. & Polly
Oc Farmer    M. Peter R. Suiter

Date: 6:15-1890
James Montreal Sheppard  Nannie Jane Neel
A. 39 W. Bland    A. 39 W. Bland
P. E. A. & Rhoda    P. Jas. W. & Hester A. Harmon
Oc. Farmer    M. J. M. Romans

Date: 6-24-1890
Wm Harrison Worth    Cynthia Mary Grayson
A. 29 S. Pittsylvania    A. 24 S. Bland
P. Wm. H. & Susan J.    P. Andrew J. & Rosalie V.
Oc. Lawyer    M. C. W. Kelley

Date: 7-28-1890
Chas. Henry Kegley    Norah B. Hanshew
A. 22 S. Smyth    A. 18 S. Bland
P. Thos J. & Mary J.    P.S. S. & Morenses V.
Oc. Farmer    M. F. F. Repass

Date: 7-30-1890
Wade Caldwell    Mary H. Hager
A. 25 S. Montgomery    A. 19 S. Bland
P. James & Eunicey    P. J. R. & Mary C.
Oc. Farmer    M. R. M. Ashworth

Date: 7-31-1890
Andrew Jackson Bolden  Malissa Catherine Louisa Suiter
A. 36 W. Patrick    A. 28 S. Bland
P. Andrew W. & Lucinda P. Peter R. & Margaret R.
Oc. Mechanic-Gunsmith  M. Peter R. Suiter

Date: 8-23-1890
Chas Fitzroyal Snead    Eliza Jane  Bird
A. 46 W. Chesterfield    A. 54 W. Montgomery
P. Jno H. & Sallie    P.
Oc. Carpenter    M. C. W. Kelley

Date: 8-24-1890
Jno Wesley Dunagan    Hattie G. Price
A. 30 S. Bland    A. 21 S. Bland
P. Rural & Mary    P. I. K. & Ellen
Oc. Farmer    M. J. M. Romans

Date: 9-7-1890
Henry P.Lampert | Sarah Adeline Lampert
A. 21 S. Bland | A. 19 S. Bland
P. Polly A. Lampert | P. Hiram & Letitia
Oc. Farmer | M. A. Bittie? Groseclose

Date: 9-14-1890
Chas. Augustus Umbarger | Mary Jane Pattison
A.25 S. Bland | A. 35 S. Bland
P. Thos P. & Elizabeth A. | P. Wm. & Elizabeth
Oc. Farmer | M. James Mahood

Date: 9-16-1890
Jno Trigg Halsey | Sarah Elizabeth Lambert
A. 44 W. Wythe | A. 33 W. Mercer, WV
P. Jno T. & | P. Allen P. &
Sarah Elizabeth | Francis L.Meadows
Oc. Farmer | M. A. Q. Harman

Date: 9-17-1890
Jno H. Lambert | Fanny Belle French
A. 20 S. Ohio | A. 14 S. Bland
P. Ed. S. & Mary | P. Rufus A. & F. J.

Oc. Farmer | M. R. M. Ashworth

Date: 9-18-1890
Dunn Bogle Newberry | Arbanna Hancock
A. 48 S. Bland | A. 22 S. Bland
P. A. T. & Elizabeth | P. P. T. & Therasa Wyrick
Oc. Farmer | M. G. W. Penley

Date: 9-24-1890
C. W. Dunn | Bettie Lee Williams
A. 33 S. Bland | A. 23 S. Pittsylvania
P. Joseph & Sarah | P. Rob't W. & Elizabeth P.
Oc. Merchant | M. Jno E. Naff

Date: 9-24-1890
Wayman Harman | Luemma Josephine
Thompson | Blankenship
A. 39 S. Bland | A. 23 S. Bland
P. Jas & Abagail | P. Perry & Ardelia
Oc. Farmer | M. W. R. Miller

Date: 9-25-1890
Geo Washington | Adeline Conner
Blankenship |
A. 25 S. Bland | A. 23 S. Bland
P. Washington & Julia | P. Nancy Conner
Oc. Farmer | P. Jno P. Roach

Date: 10-8-1890
Rob't. Wilson Buchanan | Lula M. Thorn
A. 28 S. Smyth | A. 21 S. Bland
P. Thompson & Lucy | P. Gordon C. & Agnes
Oc. Farmer | M. Jno P. Roach

Date: 10-19-1890
Chas Watson Roland | Druzilla M. Stowers
A. 19 S. Bland | A. 30 S. Bland
P. F. M. & Maryland Louisa | P. Sims S. & Jane
Oc. Farmer | M. Peter R. Suiter

Date: 11-20-1890
Walter Buford Janney | Sarah J. Brown
A. 21 S. Floyd | A. 24 S. Tazewell
P. Moses & Ruth | P. James B. & Susan
Oc. Farmer | M. J. M. Romans

Date: 11-20-1890
Albert Wisdom Purkey | Eliza Margaret Burress
A. 21 S. Bland | A. 15 S. Bland
P. Wm & Suda | P. Thos J. & Mary Ann
Oc. Farmer | M. J. A. H. Shuler

Date: 11-23-1890
Jas Bradley Brown | Sidney Munsey
A. 67 W. Surrey, NC | A. 67 W. Surrey, NC
P. Jno E. & Mary | P. Sam'l & Mary Wall
Oc. Farmer | M. Geo W. Penley

Date: 11-25-1890
Jas Washington Harman | Norah Patton
A. 60 W. Bland | A. 22 S. Bland
P. Elias & Mary | P. Rob't & Mary
Oc. Physician | M. Geo W. Penley

Date: 11-26-1890
Franklin Edward Crigger | Margaret Rebecca Siria
A. 23 S. Tazewell | A. 20 S. Tazewell
P. Jno & Julia | P. Fontain & Margaret
Oc. Carpenter | M. James Mahood

Date: 11-28-1890
Jno Edward Atwell | Laura Jane Baumgardner
A. 21 S. Tazewell | A. 21 S. Bland
P. C. D. & M. V. | P. M. L. & M. E.
Oc. Farmer | M. F. F. Repass

Date: 12-4-1890
Chas Lawrence Leslie          Virginia Frances Burton
A. 25 D. Wythe                A. 22 S. Bland
P. J. W. & M. A.              P. J. T. & M. E.
Oc. Farmer                    M. Peter R. Suiter

Date: 12-25-1890
Jas W. Baker                  Nellie Belle Kidd
A. 22 S. Ash, NC              A. 22 S. Bland
P. Levi & Louisa              P. Chapman & Jemima

Oc. Farmer                    M. John A. Smith

Date: 12-25-1890
Arthur Gordon(B)              Elizabeth Harman(B)
A. 25 S. Wythe                A. 19 S. Mercer, WV
P. Mack & Ellen               P. Rob't & Matilda
Oc. Farmer                    M. J. A. H. Shular

Date: 1-1-1891
Wm. Payton Porter             Sarah Frances Pattison
A. 43 W. Wythe                A. 19 S. Bland
P. Dan'l & Polly              P. Virginia Pattison
Oc. Brickmason                M. J. A. H. Shular

Date: 1-7-1891
Silvester Staugen Hoback  Americus Fannie Raines
A. 23 S. Wythe                A. 25 S. Bland
P. John & Matilda             P. Sam'l & Louisa
Oc. Farmer                    M. J. M. Romans

Date: 1-28-1891
Geo Robinett Brown            Mary S. McGinnis
A. 21 S. Bland                A. 19 S. Bland
P. B. P. & Lucinda            P. Jno W. & Elizabeth
Oc. Farmer                    M. C.W. Kelley

Date: 2-5-1891
Isaac Franklin Dehart         Cynthia M. Stafford
A. 37 W. Bland                A. 25 S. Bland
P. Isaac & N. Mary L.         P. Wm. & Mahulda
Oc. Farmer                    M. W. R. Miller

Date: 3-8-1891
Raymond Clinton Repass  Juliett Elizabeth Kitts
A. 30 S. Bland                A. 19 S. Bland
P. Elias &                    P. Sam'l L. & August A.M.
Adaline C. Groseclose
Oc. Farmer                    M. F. F. Repass

Date: 12-25-1890
Wm. Austin Sarver             Viola Catherine Taylor
A. 21 S. Pulaski              A. 16 S. Mason, WV
P. Wm. & Virginia             P. C. B. & Victoria
Oc. Farmer                    M. T. R. Morris

Date: 12-25-1890
Harvey Boston Shufflebarger  Margaret Luemma Thompson
A. 26 S. Bland                A. 20 S. Bland
P. Newton S. &                P. David Flemming &
Ann Wygal                     Catherine Young Munsey
Oc. Farmer                    M. John A. Smith

Begin Page 31 of Original Book
Date: 1-1-1891
Edward Bishop                 Virginia Woodyard
A. 23 S. Montgomery           A. 18 S. Giles
P. Asa & Martha               P. John & R. V.
Oc. Farmer                    M. T. R. Morris

Date: 1-15-1891
Miller H. McNeil              Louisa Ellen Smith
A. 27 S. Bland                A. 21 S. Bland
P. Wm. & Lucinda              P. Obediah & Dicy S.
Oc. Farmer                    M. Jno P. Roach

Date: 1-22-1891
James Emory Ratliff           Maggie Isabelle. Painter
A. 39 D. Bland                A. 39 S. Wythe
P. Wayman & Polly             P. Jas. C. & Eliza
Oc. Carpenter                 M. J. A. H. Shular

Date: 1-29-1891
Chas Wm. Hanshew              Lettie Maud Umbarger
A. 20 S. Bland                A. 18 S. Bland
P. Dan'l & Polly              P. Thos. P. & Elizabeth
Oc. Farmer                    M. F. F. Repass

Date: 2-19-1891
Wm. Thos. Nunn           Sarah Elizabeth Louella Miller
A. 23 S. Bland                A. 16 S. Bland
P. B. L. & Emma               P. J. W. & Rhoda
Oc. Farmer                    M. Will Rice Miller

Date: 3-17-1891
Enoch Dunagan                 Ella Mary Fanning
A. 25 S. Surrey, NC           A. 18 S. Bland
P.Lewis & Nancy               P. W. W. & Cynthia
Oc. Farmer                    M. A. A. Ashworth

66

Date: 4-22-1891
Rob't Vernon Wohlford    Snowie Va. Melvin
A. 21 S. Bland           A. 19 S. Bland
P. George & Jane         P. E. M. & Mintie

Oc. Farmer               M. J. T. Taylor

Date: 5-3-1891
Fayette Monroe Repass    Laura Elizabeth Catherine Buck
A. 35 S. Bland           A. 25 S. Bland
P. John & Minerva        P. Felix & Margaret
Oc. Farmer               M. D. Billie⁹ Groseclose

Date: 6-3-1891
Wm. Harvey Nisewander    Flora Agnes Dehart
A. 23 S. Bland           A. 18 S. Bland
P. Harvey & Susan        P. Franklin & Semphonia
Oc. Laborer              M. J. T. Taylor

Date: 6-4-1891
Henry Peck Devor         Delva Relier Kidd
A. 26 S. Bland           A. 18 S. Bland
P. Henryy & Louisa       P. H. C. & Jemima
Oc. Farmer               M. Jno A. Smith

Date: 6-11-1891
George Thos. Bird        Cora Louisa Burton
A. 25 S. Bland           A. 19 S. Bland
P. Benj. Valentine &     P. Chas Russell &
Catherine Cole Saunders  Virginia Caroline Kitts
Oc. Farmer               M. A. A. Ashworth

Date: 7-2-1891
Jos Graham Bogle         Nannie Brown Umbarger
A. 21 S. Bland           A. 17 S. Bland
P. Lorenza Dow &         P. T. P. & Elizabeth
Charlotte Waddle
Oc. Farmer               M. James Mahoney

Date: 8-20-1891
Hiram Kelley Lambert     Nancy Belle Hager
A. 18 S. Gallie, OH      A. 21 S. Bland
P. E. S. & Mary          P. J. J. & Margaret J.
Oc. Farmer               M. A. A. Ashworth

Date: 9-9-1891
Lee Kyle Morehead        Emmarilla Catherine Miller
A. 23 S. Bland           A. 18 S. Bland
P. Dan'l F. & Isabelle   P. Abraham Woodson
Elizabeth Saunders       & Ailsey Munsey
Oc. Farmer               M. J. M. Romans

Date: 4-29-1891
Rob't Gray Mustard       Eva Annette Moore
A. 24 S. Bland           A. 19 S. Bland
P. Wm. S.&               P. Luther H. & Laura
Paulina Tynes
Oc. Farmer               M. J. M. Romans

Date: 5-3-1891
Henry Edward Peery       Jennie Groseclose
A. 23 S. Bland           A. 22 S. Bland
P. Jesse & Angeline      P. Wm. H. & Mary
Oc. Merchant             M. D. Billie? Groseclose

Date: 6-4-1891
Jas. Neel Finley         Eugenia M. Price
A. 26 S. Bland           A. 20 S. Bland
P. Jackson W. & Nannie   P. Isahah K. & Elvira
Oc. Laborer              M. W. R. Miller

Date: 6-10-1891
Buford H. Woody(B)       Mary Harman(B)
A. 35 W. Pulaski         A. 22 S. Bland
P.Uncle Ben & Aunt Tish  P. Jane Harman
Oc. Laborer              M. W. R. Miller

Date: 6-15-1891
George Alex. Kidd        Elizabeth Evaline Kidd
A. 49 W. Montgomery      A. 32 D. Bland
P. Elisha & Margaret     P. Jas M. & Margaret A.

Oc. Farmer               M. Jno A. Smith

Date: 8-5-1891
Geo Henry Harman         Callie V. Groseclose
A. 21 S. Smyth           A. 17 S. Bland
P. Hezekiah & Serrena    P. Jonas H. & Mary M

Oc. Farmer               M. James Mahoney

Date: 9-5-1891
Jas. Raulston Bogle      Mary Jane Pruett
A. 30 S. Bland           A. 26 S. Bland
P. Jas. B. & Susan Raulston  P. Jas M. & Elizabeth A.
Oc. Merchant             M. Geo W. Penley

Date: 9-12-1891
Rob't J. Terry           Nickie Belle Neel
A. 29 S. Bland           A. 17 S. Bland
P. Wm. & Peggy           P. Wm. C. & Rhoda J.

Oc. Farmer               M. Peter R. Suiter

67

Date: 9-13-1891
David French                   Willie M. French
A. 19 S. Bland                 A.   S. Giles
P.J. G. & Polly                P. A. J. & Juda
Oc. Farmer                     M. T. R. Morris

Date: 10-7-1891
Barnitz Lemuel Tickle          Rosa Mariam Kitts
A. 22 S. Bland                 A. 18 S. Bland
P. Hezekiah C. &               P. Wm. Ray &
Caroline Matilda Farmer        Nannie Edith Burton
Oc. Farmer                     M. John H. Hoge

Date: 10-17-1891
Chas. A. Bailey                Cora Della Ashworth
A. 18 S. Mercer, WV            A. 18 S. Bland
P. A. J. & Hanna L.            P. R. M. & Sarah E.
Oc. Engineer                   M. G. W. Houchins

Date: 10-21-1891
Randolph McGinnis              Elizabeth F. Ingram
Davis
A. 26 S. Bland                 A. 26 S. Bland
P. Hiram G. & Cosby J.         P. Wm. & Prudence
Oc. Farmer                     M. G.W.K. Green

Date: 10-29-1891
Chas Williams  Davis           Louisa Va. Davis
A. 25 S. Bland                 A. 21 S. Bland
P.S. C. & Eliza                P. Henry & Margaret
Oc. Farmer                     M. C. L. Stradley

Date: 11-10-1891
Wm. Davis Eagle                Nannie Jane  Chandler
A. 23 S. Bland                 A. 15 S. Bland
P. S. M. & Martha              P. Pears & Sallie Ann
Oc. Carpenter                  M. J. A. H. Shular

Date: 11-12-1891
Jno Wm. Burton                 Madella Jane Repass
A. 22 S. Bland                 A. 21 S. Bland
P. Penleton & Jane             P. F. F. & Malinda

Oc. Farmer                     M. J. A. H. Shular

Date: 11-26-1891
Wm. R. Wheeler                 Mary Emaline French
A. 21 S. Bland                 A. 19 S. Bland
P. Rob't N. & Nannie           P. G. P. & Sarah
Oc. Farmer                     M. Chas. C. Pulliam

Date: 10-1-1891
Jas. Franklin Thompson         Ibbie Frances Hounshell
A. 22 S. Bland                 A. 21 S. Bland
P. J. Winton & Margaret        P. Henry & Martha Jane
Oc. Farmer                     M. H. G. Davis

Date: 10-15-1891
Samuel Snow Corder             Mary Lucy Hudgins
A.29 W. Bland                  A. 21 S. Montgomery
P. Benjamin& Julia             P. Jno A. & Victoria A.

Oc. Engineer                   M. T. R. Morris

Date: 10-20-1891
Reece Samuel Gillespie         Nancy Adeline Tibbs
A. 22 S. Tazewell              A. 22 S. Bland
P. John Nelson  & Kate         P. Henry & Sophia
Oc. Farmer                     M. H. G. Davis

Date: 10-21-1891
Jas. Walker  Brookman          Lillie Viola Thompson

A. 29 S. Alleganey             A. 19 S. Bland
P. Walker & Annie              P.  A. N. & Harriet
Oc. Engineer                   M.  J. A. H. Shular

Date: 11-4-1891
Edward Lee Nisewander          Betty Hughes
A. 27 S. Bland                 A. 22 S. Bland
P. Alex & Mary                 P. Crockett
Oc. Carpenter                  M.  J. T. Taylor

Date: 11-12-1891
Ballard Woodson Miller         Roxie Belle Pruitt
A. 22 S. Bland                 A. 19 S. Bland
P. Abraham W & Alsie           P.  J. M. & Elizabeth
Oc. Farmer                     M.  Geo W. Penley

Begin Page 32 of Original Book
Date 11-18-1891
Wm. Isaac Umbarger             Sarah Margaret Bruce
A. 25 S. Wythe                 A. 24 S. Bland
P. Rufus & Eliza               P. J. Henderson &
                               Margaret
Oc. Farmer                     M. J. A. H. Shular

Date: 12-3-1891
Amos Holland                   Lucy Maria James
A. 20 S. Franklin              A. 21 S. Bland
P. John & Rutha                P. Anderson & Maria
Oc. Farmer                     M. W. R. Miller

Date: 12-3-1891
Chas. Wesley Snodgrass  Laura Alice Pruett
A. 22 S. Mercer WV      A. 16 S. Bland
P. Jno. C. & Araminta   P. Henry P. & Mary E.
Oc. Farmer              M. P. R. Suiter

Date: 1-24-1892
Wm. Garrett Elliott     Rosa Jane Cassell
A. 35 S. Smyth          A. 19 S. Bland
P. Wm. A. & Martha      P. Jas F. & Christina
Oc. Mill Wright         M. J. W. Strickler

Date: 2-4-1892
Lafayette Fry           Mary J. Davis
A. 29 S. Wythe          A. 28 S. Bland
P. Abram & Judith       P. Hiram G. and Cosby Jane
Oc. Farmer              M. G.W.K. Green

Date: 3-2-1892
Jas Milton French       Cora French
A. 24 S. Bland          A. 17 S. Bland
P.Preston               P. Rufus A. & Frankie Jane

Oc. Farmer              P. R. M. Ashworth

Date: 3-10-1892
Jno. Allen Compton      M. Josie Thorn
A. 39 W. Bland          A. 37 S. Bland
P. Wm. W. & Nancy C.    P. Gordon C. & Agnus

Oc. Farmer              M. J.A. H. Shular

Date: 3-10-1892
Wiley Jackson Compton   Mary Lee Hoge
A. 28 S. Bland          A. 22 S. Wise
P. Wm W. & Nancy C.     P. Dan'l Stafford & Eliz. Jane
Oc. Farmer              M. J. H. Hoge

Date: 3-22-1892
Sam'l Sidney Kidd       Cynthia L. Wynn
A. 21 S. Burks Garden   A. 16 S. Bland
P. A. R. & Charlotte    P. A. W. & A. E.
Oc. Farmer              M. Jno A. Smith

Date: 4-21-1892
Andrew Albert           Elender Elizabeth Harman
Kimberling
A. 29 S. Bland          A. 21 S. McDowell, WV
P. Franklin & Rebecca J. P. Dan'l C. & Barbara J.
Oc. Farmer              M. James Mahoney

Date: 12-3-181
John Barns Gregory      Lula Caroline Stowers
A. 23 S. Bland          A. 21 S. Bland
P. R. S. & Julia        P. Isaac F. & Virginia
Oc. Farmer              M. G. W.K. Green

Date: 2-1-1892
Taylor Gordon           Julia Harman (B)
A. 18 S. Bland          A. 17 S. Bland
P. Mack & Ellen         P. Rob't W. & Matilda
Oc. Farmer              M. Geo W. Penley

Date: 2-23-1892
Wm Andrew Woodyard      Julia Ann Dunagan
A. 40 W. Giles          A. 32 W. Giles
P. Ephriam & Charity    P. Addison & Elizabeth
Oc. Farmer              M. J. T. Taylor

Date: 3-9-1892
Newton Anderson Bruce   Bertha Maud Thompson
A. 30 W. Wise           A. 18 S. Bland
P. J. Henderson &       P. H. N. & Harriett
Margaret Anderson Hoge
Oc. Farmer              M. J.A.H. Shular

Date: 3-10-1892
Ballard Preston Stafford Elizabeth Shannon Thorn
A. 56 W. Bland          A. 32 S. Bland
P. Ralph &              P. Gordon C. &. Agnus
Mary Margaret Orr
Oc. Farmer              M. J.A.H. Shular

Date: 3-17-1892
Wm Riley Kitts          Nannie Belle Thompson
A. 21 S. Bland          A. 20 S. Bland
P. Joseph & Emma        P. Wayman & Mary
Oc. Farmer              M. J. A. H. Shular

Date: 4-14-1892
John Christopher Rhudy  Rebecca Jane Wilson
A. 31 S. Burks Garden   A. 26 S. McDowell, WV
P. Jacob & Catherine    P. Jno L. & Elizabeth
Oc. Farmer              M. J. W. Strickler

Date: 5-12-1892*
Jas. Harvey Patton      Darthula Brookman

A. 25 S. Bland          A. 21 S. Bland
P. Rob't & Mary         P. James & Harriet
Oc. Farmer              M. J.T. Taylor

Date: 5-22-1892?
James Milton Pruett, Jr.  Cora Inez Helvey
A. 21 S. Giles          A. 19 S. Bland
P. Jas. M. & Araminta   P. Jno. C. &
Elizabeth Fanning       Lee Lizzie Elizabeth Bruce
Oc. Farmer              M. W. R. Miller

Date: 5-22-1892
Ballard Graham Kitts    Ollie Norabelle Harman
A. 33 W. Bland          A. 20 S. Bland
P. Jas Washington       P. Jno Wesley & Martha
& Mary Prunty           Jane Burton
Oc. Farmer              M. J. H. Hoge

Date: 5-24-1892
J. W. Sarver            Genevie Clark
A. 23 S. Craig          A. 17 S. Bland
P. John Clark & Joanna  P. Richard & Susan

Oc. Farmer              M. R.M. Ashworth

Date: 6-1-1892
John Harvey Miller      Minnie Wright
A. 22 S. Bland          A. 22 S. Bland
P. Lorenzo John &       P. David Oliver
Martha L.               & Martha J.
Oc. Farmer              M. W. R. Miller

Date: 6-1-1892
Walter Green Detimore   Martha Jane Harman
A. 30 D. Monroe, WV     A. 30 W. Bland
P. Jacob A. &           P. Sara Rhineheart
Martha Jane
Oc. Farmer              M. Armestead A. Ashworth

Date: 6-1-1892
John Christian Detimore  Nannie Eliz. Carr
A. 22 S. Knawah, WV      A. 27 S. Bland
P. Jacob A. & Martha Jane  P. Jno. Wesley & Sarah
                         Elizabeth Moore
Oc. Blacksmith           M. A. A. Ashworth

Date: 6-8-1892
Geo. Stuart Conner      Matilda Jane Mustard
A. 33 S. Bland          A. 32 S. Bland
P. Nancy Conner         P. Harvey & Mariah
Oc. Farmer              M. J. T. Taylor

Date: 6-16-1892
Tobias Dan'l Parcell    Minnie Belle Davis
A. 23 S. Franklin       A. 16 S. Bland
P. John & Mary          P. Henry & Margaret
Oc. Laborer             M. J. M. Ashworth

Date: 6-22-1892
Wm Carnhan Hedrick      Lora Organ Bird
A. 31 W. Tazewell       A. 25 S. Bland
P. Wm & Zilla           P. Wm & Eliza
Oc. Editor & Printer    M. A. A. Ashworth

Date: 7-27-1892
Creed Fulton Fannon     Sarah Minerva Thompson
A. 34 S. Bland          A. 23 S. Tazewell
P. Acles & Sarah        P. James
Oc. Hotel Keeper        M. A. A. Ashworth

Date: 8-2-1892
Bristow Adams (B)       Edmonia Tines (B)
A. 26 S. Prince Edward  A. 19 S. Bland
P. Bristow & Jane       P. A. J. & Julia
Oc. Switchman, RR       M. J. H. Gardner

Date: 8-3-1892
Murdock Street Bridges  Georgia Ina Henderson
A. 38 W. NC             A. 24 S. Bland
P. Stephen A. & Kara    P. Elias & Rhoda
Oc. Farmer              M. J W. Repass

Date: 8-9-1892
Willis Grant Lindamood  Martha Bostonia Kitts
A. 21 S. Bland          A. 20 S. Bland
P. Jno. A. & Martha Jane  P. Newt. Montgomery &
                        Ellen Brown Baumgardner
Oc. Farmer              M. H. G. Davis

Date: 8-24-1892
Wm. Saunders Terry      Eugenia Thomas King
A. 27 W. Smyth          A. 18 S. Bland
P. Wm. & Eliza          P. Wm. T. & Nancy L.
Oc. Miner               M. C. L. Stradley

Date: 8-30-1892
Hiram Whalen            Elizabeth Powers
A. 54 S. Pulaski        A. 38 S. Bland
P. Paulina Whalen       P. John & Julia Ann
Oc. Farmer              M. Jno P. Roach

Date: 9-8-1892
Kemper Graham Munsey    Mintie Maria Lampert
A. 19 S. Bland          A. 18 S. Bland
P. Wm H. & Helen        P. Henry T. & Mary E.
Oc. Farmer              M. F. F. Repass

Date: 9-8-1892
Elbert Floyd Blessing / Locky Belle Groseclose
A. 21 S. Wythe / A. 22 S. Bland
P. Jno A. & Eliza J. / P. John & Emaline
Oc. Brickmason / M. James Mahoney

Date: 8-13-1892
Estell French / Genoa Isabelle Lambert
A. 21 S. Giles / A. 19 S. Bland
P. Isaac & Rebecca / P. A. A. & Mary Ekiz.
Oc. Farmer / M. R. M. Ashworth

Date: 10-12-1892
Sam'l Geo. Damerl (B) / Mary Agnus Hobbs (B)
A. 54 W. Floyd KY / A. 21 S. Bland
P. Dave & Cloe Ann / P. Thos & Lettie
Oc. Farmer / M. W. R. Miller

Date: 8-26-1892
Jno Jasper Bland / Ella Catherine Tickle
A. 41 W. Giles / A. 21 S. Bland
P. Isaac & Sarah / P. Peter C. & Mary
Ann Hearn / Ann Journell
Oc. Farmer & Miller / M. Jas A. Smith

Date: 11-2-1892
Chas. Watson Nunn / Margaret Ellen Lawrence
A. 21 S. Bland / A. 17 S. Montgomery
P. B. L. & Martha E. L. / P. Wm. & Catherine
Oc. Farmer / M. W. R. Miller

Date: 11-9-1892
Wm. Bascomb Keeling / Roanna Bee Linkcus
A. 19 S. Bland / A. 17 S. Mercer, WV
P. A. J. & F. H. / P. J. G. & Mary Ann
Oc. Farmer / M. R. M. Ashworth

Date: 11-17-1892
Joseph Patton Munsey / Emily Florence Kitts
A. 21 S. Bland / A. 21 S. Bland
P. Jas. Harvey / P. Andrew Jas.
& Margaret L. Hutsell / & Nancy Bower Bogle
Oc. Farmer / M. J. A. H. Shular

Date: 12-13-1892
Wiley Havens / Victoria Agnus Pawley
A. 23 S. Bland / A. 18 S. Bland
P. Jane Havens / P. Isaac P. & Rebecca
Oc. Farmer / M. J. A. H. Shular

Date: 9-8-1892
Elbert Martin Catron / Mollie Elizabeth Burket
A. 26 S. Smyth / A. 16 S. Smyth
P. Joseph & Sarah / P. Wm. H. & N. C.
Oc. Farmer / M. F. F. Repass

Begin Page 33 of Original Book
Date: 10-12-1892
Clark Waggoner Neel / Ella Linnetta Walker
A. 24 S. Tazewell / A. 17 S. Bland
P. R. R. & Mary E. / P. Thos F. & Julia A.
Oc. Farmer / M. D.A. Leffel

Date: 10-26-1892
Jas. Wesley Fortner / Laura Catherine Wilson
A. 21 S. Wythe / A. 21 S. Bland
P. John & Nancy / P. Joseph & Darthula
Oc. Farmer / M. F. F. Repass

Date: 8-27-1892
Jas Edward Keith / Lillie V. Bogle
A. 27 S. Adams, Pen / A. 23 W. Bland
P. Jacob & Caroline / P. Braxton H. &
Adaline Suiter Penley
Oc.Plasterer / M. G. W.K. Green

Date: 11-8-1892
Timothy Mitchell French / Eliza Jane Clark
A. 20 S. Bland / A. 17 S. Bland
P. Wm P. & Elizabeth / P. Richard M.
Oc. Farmer / M. R. M. Ashworth

Date: 11-16-1892
Benj. Frank. Carnihan Wilson / Ellen Rose Stowers
A. 31 S. Wythe / A. 31 S. Bland
P. Thos O. & Missouri J. / P. Wm & Christina
Oc. Farmer / M. Jas Mahoney

Date: 11-24-1892
Jas Matthew Fanning / Nannie Jane Mustard
A. 57 S. Giles / A. 22 S. Bland
P.Jos & Jane / P. Wm P. & Louisa
Bogle / Robinett
Oc. Farmer / M. J. A. H. Shular

Date: 12-21-1892
Wm. Clark Barny / Roxie Imogene Thompson
A. 31 S. Washington / A. 22 S. Bland
P. Hugh & Sarah Ann / P. A. N. & Harriet
Oc. Dentist / M. D. Emory Hawk

Date: 12-25-1892
Wm. Washing. Ramsey    Ida Viola Wright
A. 20 S. Bland         A. 16 S. Bland
P. Wm H. & Polly A.    P. D.W.M. & Ann

Oc. Farmer             M. J. T. Taylor

Date: 12-22-1892?
Jas Andrew Burton      Cora Ethel Corder
A. 24 S. Bland         A. 17 S. Bland
P. Jas. Thos. &.       P. Jas. Larkin & M. Josa
Mary E. Munsey
Oc.                    M. Geo W. Penley

Date: 1-25-1893
Stephen Dick. Humphries   Cora May Tickle
A. 22 S. Carroll       A. 16 Bland
P. Geo P & Mary F.     P. Gordon H. & Christina G.
Oc. Farmer             M. J. A. H. Shular

Date: 2-6-1893
Harvey Hoge Wolf       Minnie Stowers
A. 22 S. Giles         A. 21 S. Bland
P. George & Eliza      P. George & Polley
Oc. Farmer             M. Peter R. Suiter

Date: 2-22-1893
Chas Brown Suiter      Annie Frances Akers
A. 21 S. Bland         A. 24 S. Pulaski
P. Wm & Sarah          P. Dandridge & Parthena
Oc. Plumber            M. P. R. Suiter

Date: 3-1-1893
Wm Robinett Pendleton  Nancy Powers
A. 28 S. Bland         A. 25 S. Bland
P. James & Adelia      P. Hickman & Jane
Oc. Farmer             M. J.T. Taylor

Date: 3-23-1893
Augustus Wolf          Minnie C. Robinett
A. 22 S. Giles         A. 19 S. Bland
P. George & Eliza      P. M. D. & Sarah
Oc. Farmer             M. P. R. Suiter

Date: 4-2-1893
Andrew Jackson         Minnie Belle Harman
Foglesong
A. 25 S. Bland         A. 23 S. Bland
P. Elias & Sophia      P. P. W. & A. V.
Oc. Farmer             M. G.W.K. Green

Date: 12-27-1892
Thomas Jackson Muncy   Fannie Belle Banks
A. 27 S. Bland         A. 24 S. Tazewell
P. Andrew Jackson &    P. C. C. & A. E.?
Sarah J.Peery
Oc. Lawyer             M. J. A. H. Shular

Date: 1-4-1893
Chester Snow Crawford  Nannie May Harman
A. 32 . Bland          A. 28 S. Bland
P. Wm & Catherine      P. J. W.

Oc. Carpenter          M. John P. Roach

Date: 2-5-1893
Wm. Albert Wesley White   Daisy Mabel Wynn
A. 22 S. Surry, NC     A. 14 S. Bland
P. D. G. White         P. Joseph & Kate
Oc. Farmer             M. John A. Smith

Date: 2-22-1893
Monroe Kirby           Geneva Alice Stowers
A. 37 S. Bland         A. 28 S. Bland
P. Stephen & Margaret Ann   P. Wm & Ellen
Oc. Farmer             M. J. A. H. Shular

Date: 2-22-1893
Isaac Luther Bailey    Nora Zella Akers
A. 22 S. Mercer, WV    A. 19 S. Pulaski
P. Ballard P. & Sarah E.   P. Dandridge & Parthena
Oc. Farmer             M. P. R. Suiter

Date: 3-8-1893
Sam'l David Carver     Martha Jane Tabor
A. 21 S. Tazewell      A. 15 S. Bland
P. Dan'l T. & Martha   P. James & Louvena V.
Oc. Farmer             M. Peter R. Suiter

Date: 3-25-1893
Chas. Lawrence Leslie  Martha Dora I. Burton
A. 27 W. Wythe         A. 22 S. Bland
P. J. W. & M. A.       P. Jas T. & Mary Elizabeth
Oc. Farmer             M. J. A. H. Shular

Date: 4-23-1893
Richard Green          Elizabeth Damerl (B)
Ramsey (B)
A. 25 W. Bland         A. 20 S. Bland
P. Richard & Matilda   P. Sam'l & Delila
Oc. Farmer             M. W. R. Miller

72

Date: 4-23-1893
Amos Page (B)              Rebecca Josephine Hobbs (B)
A. 27 S. Pulaski           A. 15 S. Bland
P. Jacob & Eliza           P. Thomas & Lettie
Oc. Public Works           M. J. T. Taylor

Date: 4-26-1893
Rees Thompson Finley       Louisa Barnett
A. 35 W. Tazewell          A. 39 S. Tazewell
P. Thos & Martha           P. Arch & Julia Ann
Oc. Farmer                 M. James Mahoney

Date: 5-18-1893
David Spencer Ritter       Sarah Elizabeth Halsey
A. 50 W. Pulaski           A. 35 W. Mercer, WV
P. George & Margaret       P. Allen & Fannie Meadows
Oc. Farmer                 M. C. W. Kelley

Date: 6-22-1893
James Estell Neel          Girldine A. Tade
A. 26 S. Bland             A. 18 S. Montgomery
P. H. P. & Lydia           P. Jos S. & Martha
Oc. Carpenter              M. P. R. Suiter

Begin Page 34 of Original Book
Date: 7-13-1893
Comie Davis                Nannie Ellen Carr
A. 21 S. Bland             A. 17 S. Bland
P. Henry & Margaret        P. John J. & Elizabeth
Oc. Farmer                 M. Jas M. Ashworth

Date: 7-27-1893
Wm Henry Wheeler           Emma Susan Richardson
A. 18 S. Giles             A. 15 S. Giles
P. C. F. & Sarah C.        P. A. R. & S. V.
Oc. Farmer                 M. P. R. Suiter

Date: 8-16-1893
Henry Preston              Catherine Jane Willis
A. 21 S. Guilford, NC      A. 20 S. Giles
P. Jonathan & Betsy Jane   P. Sam'l L. & Louemma C.
Oc. Farmer                 M. R. M. Ashworth

Date: 9-6-1893
James Henry Mc Coy         Lola Edith Repass
A. 32 S. Montgomery        A. 23 S. Bland
P. Jas Newton &            P. John & Minerva
Margaret Ellen
Oc. Carpenter              M. G. A. Maiden

Date: 4-26-1893
Thos. Lockhert             Belle Gregory Shufflebarger
A. 20 S. Bland             A. 21 S. Bland
P. Newton & Ann            P. T. E. & Martha
Oc. Farmer                 P. W. I.. Fogleman

Date: 4-27-1893
Dr. Emory Willis Peery     Ina Angeline Groseclose
A. 26 S. Tazewell          A. 21 S. Bland
P. Thos & Sarah            P. H. C. & L. V.
Oc. Physician              M. John C. Repass

Date: 6-1-1893
Cephas Lawrence            Alice B. Henniger
A. 24 D. Montgomery        A. 17 S. Smyth
P. George & Ellen          P. Alex & Manda
Oc. Farmer                 M. John A. Smith

Date: 7-6-1893
Sam'l Gleaves Shrader      Bettie Henderson
A. 28 D. Grayson           A. 32 S. Bland
P. Joseph & Sarah          P. Elias & Rhoda
Oc. Farmer                 M. G. W. K. Green

Date: 7-17-1893
Harvey Crawford            Sally Eddie Josephine Wiley
A. 35 W. Mercer, WV        A. 26 W. Bland
P.                         P. John & Sophia
Oc. Laborer                M. F. F. Repass

Date: 8-10-1893
John Stephen Hunt          Emma Lampert
A. 26 S. Tazewell          A. 18 S. Bland
P. Geo W. & Sallie B.      P. Wm. H. & Mary E.
Oc. Farmer                 M. R. M. Ashworth

Date: 8-31-1893
James R. Weatherly         Mandana Hager
A. 20 S. Washington        A. 21 S. Bland
P. Jos W. & Susan T.       P. Jacob J. & Margaret J.
Oc. Farmer                 M. R. M. Ashworth

Date: 9-28-1893
Joseph Longstreet Bogle    Roxie Annie Pauley
A. 29 S. Bland             A. 20 S. Bland
P. John & Julia A.         P. Addison B. & Minnie

Oc. Farmer                 M. J. A. H. Shular

Date: 10-5-1893
Paris Geo. Lampert    Louemma Jane. Cox
A. 27 D. Bland    A. 17 S. Bland
P. Elizabeth Lampert    P. A. M. & Catherine
Oc. Farmer    M. J. Mahood

Date: 10-5-1893
Simon Kenton Groseclose    Sarah Josephine Muncy
A. 27 S. Bland    A. 31 S. Bland
P. Wm. H. & Mary Jane    P. Andrew J. & Sarah Jane
Oc. Farmer    M. J. B. Greever

Date: 10-15-1893
James Madison    Amanda Mc Farland
Stowers, Jr.
A. 53 W. Bland    A. 31 S. Bland
P. Hickman & Sarah    P. Rause. & Jane
Oc. Farmer    M. J. Mahood

Date: 10-19-1893
Jas. William Lampert    Thirsay Jane Lindamood
A. 24 S. Bland    A. 19? S. Bland
P. W. W. & Rhoda E.    P. John H. & Jane
Oc. Farmer    M. J. Mahood

Date: 10-22-1893
John Allen Ashford    Lula Belle Peak
A. 25 S. Pulaski    A. 19 S. Wythe
P. John & Elizabeth    P. Leander & Nancy Matilda
Oc. Farmer    M. J. Mahood

Date: 10-28-1893
Bruce Carrington Banks    Annie Evlyn Green
28 S. Craig    A. 25 S. Bland
P. Clement C. & Annie E.    P. Robt' C. & Addie V.
Oc. Merchant    M. Geo. Wash. Penley

Date: 11-1-1893
Wm. Howe Hoge    Louvicie Jerusha Mustard
A. 40 W. Pulaski    A. 24 S. Bland
P. Wm. E. & Jane    P. James Harvey &
   Marshall Marcie Robinett
Oc. Farmer    M. J. H. Hoge

Date: 11-10-1893
George Lockhert Smith    Belle B. Woodyard
A. 21 S. Bland    A. 18 S. Bland
P. John A. & Julia A.    P. John & R. V.

Oc. Farmer    M. Peter R. Suiter

Date: 11-22-1893
Sam'l Levi Cassell    Edna Dove Davis
A. 26 S. Wythe    A. 20 S. Bland
P. John & Elizabeth    P. Sam'l C. & Eliza Agnus
Oc. Farmer    M. M. C. Graham

Date: 11-29-1893
Chas. Abram Crabtree    Susan Alverta Foglesong
A. 27 S. Bland    A. 21 S. Bland
P. Rees & Polley    P. Henry & Mary Ann
Oc. Farmer    M. J. Mahood

Date: 12-20-1893
Robt. Lee Andrews    Laura Ellen Wheeler
A. 21 S. Mercer, WV    A. 17 S. Giles
P. A. J. & Nancy Ann    P. C. F. & Sarah C.
Oc. Farmer    M. R. M. Ashworth

Date: 12-24-1893
Allen Jefferson Neel    Nancy Elizabeth Tibbs
A. 20 S. Bland    A. 21 S. Bland
P. Alex & Mary Magdalena    P. Peter & Ann
Oc. Farmer    M. F. F. Repass

Date: 12-26-1893
Albert Franklin Updyke    Bertha Seigler Mustard
A. 21 S. Bland    A. 20 S. Bland
P. Albert Gallitan    P. John Jasper
& Mary Agnes Smith    &Francis Stuart
Oc. Farmer    M. J. T. Taylor

Date: 1-23-1894*
Andrew Shields (B)    Ollie Davidson (B)
A. 22 S. Bland    A. 22 S. Bland
P. Richard & Lucy    P. Hugh & Alsie

Oc. Farmer    M. R. M. Ashworth

Date: 1-17-1894
Wm Henry Hounshell    Ida L. Kitts
A. 27 S. Bland    A. 20 S. Bland
P. Henry L. & Martha J.    P. Austin & Eve
Oc. Farmer    M. H. G. Davis

Date: 1-17-1894
Nicholas Barnett Farmer(B)    Mary Eugene Bowls (B)
A. 22 S. Wythe    A. 20 S. Wythe
P. Stephen M. & Fanny R.    P. Bettie Richardson
Oc. Farmer    M. G.W.K. Green

Date: 1-17-1894
Thos Jackson Vaughn   Eliza Burton
A. 33  D. Wythe       A. 40 S. Pulaski
P. William & Elizabeth   P. James & Jane
Oc. Farmer           M. A. A. Ashworth

Date: 1-21-1894
Lee Monroe  Cox      Susan M. Groseclose
A. 21 S. Bland       A. 21 S. Bland
P. George & Martha   P. Jacob & Nancy
Oc. Farmer           M. F. F. Repass

Date: 2-8-1894
Albert Crockett Stowers   Martha Rebecca Lampert
A. 18 S. Bland       A. 22 S. Bland
P.James & Polly      P. James A. & Nancy
Oc. Farmer           M. F. F. Repass

Date: 2-12-1894
Wm. Hedrick Hushour   Marcia Ann Hancock
A. 23 S. Grayson     A. 16 S. Bland
P. Peter & Malinda   P. Geo W. & Sarah J.
Oc. Mechanical Engineer M. J. A. H. Shular

Date: 2-14-1894
Daniel Adam. Crow    Mary C. Foglesong
A. 39 W. Bland       A. 30 W. Bland
P. John & Catharine  P. Peter & Jemima
Oc. Farmer           M. H. G. Davis

Date: 3-7-1894
Chas Rufus Helvey    Annie Laura  Stowers
A. 24 S. Bland       A. 19 S. Bland
P. Wm B. & Elizabeth J.   P. Grayson W. & Lucinda
Oc. Farmer           M. R. M. Ashworth

Date: 3-15-1894
Allen Taylor Neece   Mollie Gray Repass
A. 22 S. Bland       A. 22 S. Bland
P. James & Sarah     P. Russell & Jane
Oc. Farmer           M. G.W. K. Green

Date: 3-29-1894
Luther Henry Lawrence   Martha Matilda  Robinett
A. 23 S. Floyd       A. 25 S. Bland
P. George  & Ellen   P. Patton C. & Malissa J.
Oc. Farmer           M. Peter R. Suiter

Date: 1-18-1894
Jezereel Taylor Waddle   Laura Belle Kitts
A. 40 S. Wythe       A. 20 S. Bland
P. Joseph & Rhoda    P. Harold Mathews & Causby
Oc. Farmer           M. J. Mahood

Date: 1-31-1894
John Preston Stowers   Nancy Jane Robinett
A. 27 S. Bland       A. 26 S. Bland
P. Geo. W. & Mary A.   P. Jefferson & Rebecca
Oc. Farmer           M. G.W.K. Green

Date: 2-9-1894
Asa Gray Lambert     Lucinda Elizabeth  Hager
A. 24 S. Bland       A. 17 S. Bland
P. Edward & Mary A.   P. Jacob J. & Margaret J.
Oc. Miner            M. R. M. Ashworth

Date: 2-14-1894
Jerome Blair Kitts   Lucy Ella Humphreys
A. 22 S. Bland       A. 16 S. Carroll
P. Ganam & Abagail   P. Geo & Mary F.
Oc. Farmer           M. G.W.K. Green

Date: 3-4-1894
Joshua Green French   Hallie Brown Burton
A. 25 S. Giles       A. 19 S. Bland
P. A. J. & Juda      P. Travis  & Mary H.
Oc. Farmer           M. R. M. Ashworth

Date: 3-14-1894
John Washington Kidd   Lizzie Stowers
A. 30 S. Bland       A. 26 S. Bland
P. James M. & Margaret   P. Wm. & Ellen
Oc. Farmer           M.  G.W.K. Green

Begin page 35 of Original Book
Date: 3-19-1895
James A. Andrews     Margaret V. Willis
A. 27 S. Bland       A. 21 S. Giles
P. Jackson & Nancy   P. S. L. & Louemma C.
Oc. Farmer           M.  No Return

Date: 4-4-1894
Ruell McGuire Dunagan   Eucina Florence Wyrick
A. 64 W. Surry, NC   A. 16 S. Bland
P. Cidda Dunnagan    P. R. B. & L. V.
Oc. Farmer           M.  Geo W. Penley

Date: 4-8-1894
Marion Lafayette Hornbarger / Fannie E. Tabor
A. 22 S. Bland / A. 28 S. Bland
P. Wm. P. & Mary C. / P. James & Christina

Oc. Farmer / M. W. I. Fogleman

Date: 4-12-1894
Jas. Henry Hancock / Margaret Luemma Tickle
A. 23 S. Bland / A. 18 S. Bland
P. Geo W. & Julia / P. Jackson Nye & Mary Ann Waggoner
Oc. Farmer / M. J. A. H. Shular

Date: 4-16-1894
Franklin P. Kidd / Matilda J. Kidd
A. 21 S. Raleigh, WV / A. 23 S. Bland
P. Geo. & Elizabeth / P. Jas M. & Margaret
Oc. Farmer / M. G.W.K. Green

Date: 4-18-1894
Ben. H. King / Dora Starling
A. 23 S. Tazewell / A. 21 S. Bland
P. Rebecca / P. Geo. W. & Rebecca J
Oc. Farmer / M. W. I. Fogleman

Date: 4-19-1894
Sam'l Jos. Patterson / Margaret Jane Tibbs
A. 20 S. Bland / A. 16 S. Bland
P. Elizbeth Cameron / P. Peter & S. A.
Oc. Farmer / M. F. F.Repass

Date: 4-20-1894
Wm.Garland Harman / Nancy E. Lillie Wyrick
A. 39 W. Bland / A. 20 S. Bland
P. Addison & Elizabeth / P. Alenanine & Tolitha M.
Oc. Carpenter / M. John P. Roach

Date: 4-25-1894
Wm. Wallace McNeil / Emma Wingfield Moore
A. 23 S. Giles / A. 24 S. Giles
P. D. O. & Sarah E. / P. W. W. & Louisa
Oc. Merchant / M. J. T. Taylor

Date: 4-30-1894
Stephen Akers / Annie Sturdivant
A. 22 S. Wythe / A. 18 S. Wilkes, NC
P. Calvin & Jane Moore / P. R. C. & Julia
Oc. Farmer / M. J. Mahood

Date: 5-17-1894
Jno Harvey Blankenship / Mary Hamilton
A. 28 S. Mercer, WV / A. 20 S. Bland
P. Daniel & Mary Eliz. / P. Thos & Elizabeth
Oc. Farmer / M. Geo W. Penley

Date: 5-24-1894
Thos. Wesley Rose / Mary Va. Kitts
A. 17 S. Ind / A. 24 S. Bland
P. French & Mattie / P. Newton M. & Ellen B.
Oc. Farmer / M. A. G. Davis

Date: 5-29-1894
Addison Winton Kidd / Laura Jane Munsey
A. 58 W. Bland / A. 28 S. Bland
P. George & Evaline / P. William & Clara
Oc. Farmer / M. J. A. H. Shular

Date: 5-30-1894
Sam'l Pierson Pruett / Minta Alice Linkous
A. 23 S. Bland / A. 16 S. Bland
P. Isaac & Lucinda / P. J. G. & Mary M.
Oc. Farmer / M. J. M. Ashworth

Date: 5-30-1894
Charles Lewis Jones / Maud Painter
A. 20 S. Smyth / A. 18 S. Bland
P. Wm L. & Melda Jane / P. Geo. D. & Bettie
Oc. Farmer / M. J. A. H. Shular

Date: 6-5-1894
James Augustus Huddle / Lola Monteg Kitts
A. 42 W. Wythe / A. 21 S. Bland
P. David & Mary / P. Sam'l L. & Augusta M.
Oc. Farmer / M. F. F. Repass

Date: 6-13-1894
James Harvey Andrews / Angline Suiter
A. 27 S. Bland / A. 26 S. Bland
P. Jackson & Nancy / P. William & Sarah
Oc. Farmer / M. Peter R. Suiter

Date: 6-27-1894
Obediah Sexton / Josa Carr
A. 22 S. Bland / A. 20 S. Bland
P. French & Susan / P. Margaret Carr
Oc. Farmer / M. W. R. Miller

Date: 7-5-1894
Geo. Washington Cox     Missouri T. Tibbs
A. 23 S. Bland     A. 18 S. Bland
P. A. M. & Catherine     P. Peter & Ann
Oc. Farmer     M. F. F. Repass

Date 7-25-1894
Wm. Hicks Nisewander     Cly'de C. Havens
A. 23 S. Bland     A. 17 S. Bland
P. Alex & Mary A.     P. Alex & Elizabeth
Oc. Farmer     M. W. R. Miller

Date: 8-29-1894
Wythe Grayson Waddle     Bettie Stowers
A. 46 S. Bland     A. 24 S. Bland
P. Jas F. & Nancy     P. Peter R. & Arminta
Oc. Farmer     M. W. I. Fogleman

Date: 9-1-1894
John Harvey Millirons     Sumilda Etta Shrader
A. 27 S. Giles     A. 21 S. Bland
P. Jno J. & Barbara A.     P. Jas M. & Emma C.

Oc. Farmer     M. T. C. Pulliam

Date: 9-5-1894
Wm. David Kimberling     Blanche Maud Barnett
A. 29 S. Bland     A. 18 S. Bland
P. Stephen & Eliza     P. Lou Barnett
Oc. Farmer     M. H. G. Davis

Date: 9-12-1894
Rob't Lee Hall     Daisy Myrtle Bennett
A. 21 S. Bland     A. 14 S. Bland
P. Sam'l H & Mary Susan     P. Mary B. Bennett
Oc. Carpenter     M. J. A. H. Shular

Date: 9-20-1894
Ennis Carson Wyrick     Carrie Rider
A. 23 S. Patterson, WV     A. 19 S. Bland
P. S. G. H. & Victoria     P. Geo F. & Julia
Oc. Farmer     M. J. T. Taylor

Date: 10-10-1894
John J. Kimberlin     Jennie Belle Foglesong
A. 39 S. Bland     A. 23 S. Bland
P. Henry & Barbara     P. Henry S. & Mollie

Oc. Farmer     M. J. Mahood

Date: 7-14-1894**
Shep. Havens     Lizzie Mustard
A. 21 S. Bland     A. 19 S. Bland
P. Elizabeth Havens     P. Minerva Mustard
Oc. Farmer     M. No Return

Date: 8-9-1894
Dan'l Green Crouch     Louise Delila Barnett
A. 33 W. Mercer, WV     A. 25 S. Tazewell
P.     P. John & Louisa
Oc. Farmer     M. Peter R. Suiter

Date: 8-28-1894
Rufus Lee Millirons     Annie Kate King
A. 19 S. Pulaski     A. 21 S. Bland
P. William & Julia     P. Wm. T. & Nancy
Oc. Teacher     M. J. B. Greever

Date: 9-5-1894
John David French     Elizabeth Ann Morehead
A. 35 S. Bland     A. 24 S. Bland
P. Giles P. & Sarah     P. Dan'l F. &
    Isabelle Elizabeth H.Saunders
Oc. Farmer     M. W. R. Miller

Date: 9-5-1894
John Alfred Fox     Martha Jane Rhinehart
A. 27 S. Bland     A. 19 S. Bland
P. Mathias A. & Ann C.     P. Eliza Rhinehart
Oc. Farmer     M. W. I. Fogleman

Date: 9-13-1894
Jas. J. Kegley     Ibbie Eunice Hanshew
A. 23 S. Smyth     A. 17 S. Bland
P. T. J. & M. J.     P. Sam'l S. & Markum V.
Oc. Farmer     M. F. F. Repass

Date: 9-26-1894
John Stuart Crow     Eva Nickatie Baugh
A. 18 S. Bland     A. 21 S. Tazewell
P. Jonas M. & Christina     P. D. M. & Nickatie J. C.
Oc. Farmer     M. H. G. Davis

Date: 10-24-1894
Wm. Alex. Suiter     Lulu B. Bishop
A. 25 S. Bland     A. 20 S. Montgomery
P. Peter R. &     P. Jacob C. & Elizabeth
Margaret Rebecca
Oc. Farmer     M. Peter R. Suiter

Date: 11-1-1894
Frank Preston Crigger    Alice Lindamood
A. 46 W. Smyth           A. 33 W. Bland
P. Reuben & Mary         P. Ganam & Abigail Kitts
Oc. Farmer               M. J. Mahood

Date: 11-20-1894
Wm. Alex Hamilton        Josie A. Tickle
A. 24 S. Bland           A. 22 S. Bland
P. Elizabeth Hamilton    P. Peter C. & Mary Ann Journell
Oc. Farmer               M. H. C. Clemons

Date: 11-28-1894
Jas. Pearson Crutchfield Kate Barnett
A. 38 W. Smyth           A. 24 S. Tazewell
P. Wm & Elizabeth        P. Arch & Jemima
Oc. Farmer               M. H. G. Davis

Date: 12-19-1894
Gordon Lewis Meador      Mary Ann Kidd
A. 23 S. Summers, WV     A. 19 S. Bland
P. Silvester & Mary J.   P. Wm. S. & Elvira
Oc. Farmer               M. P. R. Suiter

Date: 12-27-1894
Chas Brady Wolf          Cora Eddie Nunn
A. 22 S. Giles           A. 16 S. Bland
P. Geo. & Eliza          P. W. G. & Lizzie
Oc. Farmer               M. P. R. Suiter

Date: 12-27-1894
Jos Marion Baumgardner   Margaret Eliz. Atwell
A. 21 S. Bland           A. 23 S. Tazewell
P. Martin L. & Mary E.   P. Putnam D. &Victoria
Oc. Farmer               M. F. F. Repass

Date: 1-17-1895
Jacob B.rown Moore       Frances Bird
A. 39 W. Bland           A. 38 S. Bland
P. Richard & Elizabeth   P. John R. & Susan
Oc. Farmer               M. R. L. Newberry

Date: 1-30-1985
James Edward Woodyard    Melissa Rosalie Smith
A. 22 S. Giles           A. 27 S. Bland
P. John & Rebecca        P. J. A. & Julia A.
Oc. Farmer               M. P. R. Suiter

Date: 11-1-1894
Terry Franklin Devor     Sallie Belle Stowers
A. 27 S. Bland           A. 17 S. Bland
P. John & Sarah E.       P. Isaac F. & Virginia
Oc. Farmer               M. Jno A. Smith

Date 11-21-1894
Henry  S. Lefler         Dora A. Akers
A. 21 S. Wythe           A. 19 S. Bland
P. Jos H. & Frances A.   P. Moses & Sallie
Oc. Farmer               M. W. C. Crockett

Begin Page 36 of Original Book
Date: 11-29-1894
China Winton Lampert     Cannie Cemettis Muncy
A. 21 S. Bland           A. 24 S. Bland
P. Geo W. & Sarah A.     P. Wm. H. & Hellen
Oc. Farmer               M. H. C. Clemmens

Date: 12-22-1894
Benj. Clark Osborne      Poca Florence  Stafford
A. 31 S. Washington      A. 22 S. Bland
P. Rob't & Elizabeth     P. Jas M. & Vica Melvin
Oc. Farmer               M. P. R.Suiter

Date: 12-27–1894
Bossie Fitzroyal Snead   Rosa L. Andrews
A. 21 S. Bland           A. 18 S. Grayson
P. Chas F. & Catherine   P. W. R. & S. A.
Oc. Carpenter            M. H. C. Clemmens

Date: 1-3-1895
Jos.  Marion Starling    Alice F. Sarver
A. 24 S. Bland           A. 20 S. Craig
P. John & Sallie         P. John & Joanna
Oc. Farmer               M. P. R. Suiter

Date 1-24-1895
Chas. Milton Robinett    Mollie Belle Stowers
A. 22 S. Bland           A. 23 S. Bland
P. M. D. & Sarah L.      A. Grayson & Lucinda
Oc. Farmer               M. P. R. Suiter

Date: 2-6-1895
Chas L. Jarrell          Mary Va. Davis
A. 21 S. Mercer, WV      A. 20 S. Bland
P. Washington & J. B.    P. E. A. & Z.A.
Oc. Farmer               M. J. M. Ashworth

Date: 2-20-1895
Franklin Seldon Stowers  Fannie Belle Wilson
A. 25 S. Bland          A. 24 S. Bland
P. Wm. & Ellen          P. Thos O. & M. J.
Oc. Farmer              M. C. L. Stradley

Date: 3-21-1895
Chas Edward Hancock     Mary Etta Humphreys
A. 24 S. Bland          A. 20 S. Parson, NC
P. Pleasant & Thriza V. P. Geo. & Mary F.
Oc. Farmer              M. H. C. Clemmens

Date: 4-1-1895
James Marion Crow       Letitia E. Syra
A. 46 W. Wythe          A. 23 S. Washington
P. John & Catherine     P. Fountain & Margaret
Oc. Farmer              M. H. G. Davis

Date: 4-14-1895
George Leffler          Victoria Willis
A. 22 S. Giles          A. 22 S. Giles
P. James & Elizabeth    P. Samuel & Louemma
Oc. Running a Saw Mill  M. P. R. Suiter

Date: 4-30-1895
Harvey T. Hamblin       Viola Alice Price
A. 28 S. Giles          A. 19 S. Bland
P. David Y. & Nancy J.  P. Isaiah K. & Elvira J.
Oc. Farmer              M. W. R. Miller

Date: 5-1-1895
Sam'l Blair Robinett    Nellie Gray Carr
A. 24 S. Bland          A. 17 S. Bland
P. Jas. S. & Ella R.    P. John E. & Mattie
Oc. Farmer              M. Geo W. Penley

Date: 6-3-1895
Albert Patton Lee Wilson Rachel Grace Tilson
A. 26 S. Bland          A. 24 S. Bland
P. Jas M. C.& Amanda J. P. H. H. & M. J.

Oc. Farmer              M. J. Mahood

Date 6-5-1895
Wm Allen Taylor Newberry Ida Kate Kegley
A. 27 S. Bland          A. 19 S. Bland
P. Harman & Mary        P. Jas. Gordon &
Ann McDonald            Fannie Bird
Oc. Farmer              M. H. C. Clemmons

Date: 6-6-1895
Wm. Edward Pattison     Alice Hamilton
A. 32 W. Bland          A. 26 S. Bland
P. Newton & Gennie      P. Thomas & Elizabeth

Oc. Farmer              M. G. W. Penley

Date: 6-12-1895
Jesse Archiebald Munsey Josie Ellen Green
A. 26 S. Bland          A. 24 S. Bland
P. A. J. & Sarah J.     P. Rob't Crutchfield &
                        Addie V. Magruder
Oc. Farmer              M. H. C. Clemmons

Date: 6-26-1895
Geo Sam'l Augustus      Ada Chewning
Hamilton
A. 21 S. Bland          A. 21 S. Giles
P. Elizabeth Hamilton   P. Lafayette & Melissa
Oc. Farmer              M. A. A. Ashworth

Date: 6-27-1895
Chas Henry Mustard      Mary Ewald
A. 25 S. Bland          A. 20 S. Bland
P. Wesley Newton &      P. Gregory A.& Theressa A.
Elizabeth Caroline Newberry
Oc. Merchant            M. H. C. Clemens

Date: 7-7-1895
Joseph Edward Warner    Nannie Taylor
A. 24 S. Bland          A. 18 S. Bland
P. David Calhoun &      P. Green &
Margaret Mahulda Jones  Stacey "Lucy" Rider
Oc. Farmer              M. Robt L. Newberry

Date: 8-1-1895
James Milton French     Jannie Louisa Robinson
A. 22 S. Bland          A. 23 S. Mercer, WV
P. Rufus A. &           P. Henry & Emma
Frankie J.
Oc. Farmer              M. J. M. Ashworth

Date: 8-21-1895
William Crockett Kitts  Lena Abagail Repass
A. 23 S. Bland          A. 15 S. Bland
P. And. Jack. & Hester T. P. Russell & Martha J.
Oc. Farmer              M. H. C. Clemens

Date: 8-27-1895
Whitley A. Madison Wolf Margaret Texas Fox
A. 21 S. Giles          A. 23 S. Bland
P. Geo. A. & Eliza Jane P. M. A. & Ann C.
Oc. Farmer              M. W. I. Fogleman

Date: 8-28-1895
Frank Gordon Tabor | Hester Alveda Rosella Wolf
A. 20 S. Mercer, WV | A. 20 S. Bland
P. James & L. V. | P.Geo A. & Eliza Jane
Oc. Farmer | M. W. I. Fogleman

Date: 8-30-1895*
John Henry Dunford | Jennie Melvin
A. 43 W. Giles | A. 21 S. Mercer, WV
P. Albert & Eliza | P. Mariah Melvin
Oc. Farmer | M. J. T.Taylor

Date: 9-4-1895
Wm. Paris Umbarger | Crate Penley
A. 24 S. Smyth | A. 22 S. Bland
P. Alex & Susan | P. Geo Wash. & Adeline Suiter
Oc. Farmer | M. H. C. Clemens

Date: 9-18-1895
George A. Baugh | Leila E. Harman
A. 25 S. Bland | A. 18 S. Bland
P. Thomas & Susan | P. Wm. Neal & Orlena
 | Shockley Farmer
Oc. Farmer | M. Robert S. Sheffey

Date: 10-9-1895
Chas McDonald Bane | Mary Eliza Chumbley
A. 23 S. Giles | A. 20 S. Pulaski
P. Rob't H. & Fannie | P. Shepard C. & Lucy Hoge
McDonald
Oc. Farmer | M. Geo. H. Gilmer

Begin page 37 of Original Book
Date: 10-20-1985
Emory Jackson (B) | Belle Samson (B)
A. 21 S. Bland | A.   S. Wythe
P. Winston & Lettie | P. Babe Surratt & ?? Saunders
Oc. Farmer | M. Geo W. Penley

Date: 12-12-1895
Thompson Crockett | Emmer Penley
Havens
A. 35 S. Bland | A. 25 S. Bland
P. John & Joanna A. | P. Braxton H. & Adaline Suiter
Oc. Farmer | M. J. F. Matheson

Date: 12-18-1895
Rob't Ward Lawrence | Mary Elizabeth Miller
A. 20 S. Montgomery | A. 17 S. Bland
P. Wm. A. & Catherine | P. Wm. R. & Emma  J.
Oc. Farmer | M. D. H. Carr

Date: 9-1-1895
Emmet Sidney Gross | Rhoda Virginia Hicks
A. 22 S. Bland | A. 23 S. Lee
P. Harvey & Mary | P. Russell S. & Matilda
Oc. Farmer | M. W. I. Fogleman

Date: 9-4-1895
Addison Harman | Rose Havens
A. 24 S. Bland | A. 21 S. Bland
P. Addison & Elizabeth | P. Alex & Elizabeth
Oc. Farmer | M. W. R. Miller

Date: 9-12-1895
Rob't Ray Burress | Margaret Christina Tabor
A. 35 W. Bland | A. 18 S. Mercer, WV
P. Rayburn & Rosanna | P. James & L. V.
Oc. Farmer | M. John A. Smith

Date: 10-2-1895
Jackson S. Bird | Araminta A. Lawrence
A. 28 S. Bland | A. 23 S. Montgomery
P. Stephen W. & Melissa A. | P. George & Martha

Oc. Farmer | M. W. T. Fogleman

Date: 10-14-1895
Millard Lee French | Allie B. Robinett
A. 24 S. Bland | A. 22 S. Bland
P. W. P. & Elizabeth | P. Daniel & Ellen
Oc. Farmer | M. J. M. Ashworth

Date: 11-17-1895
James Franklin Wynn | Rosie Etta Kidd
A. 22 S. Bland | A. 18 S. Bland
P. Joseph & M. C. | P. J. M. & M. A.
Oc. Farmer | M. John A. Smith

Date: 12-16-1895
William Thos. Davis | Minnie Caldoniia Collins

A. 23 S. Bland | A. 19 S. Bland
P. Sam'l & Minerva | P. James & Lizzie
Oc. Farmer | M. A. A. Ashworth

Date: 12-19-1895
John Nelson Thompson | Mattie Neel
A. 34 S. Wythe | A. 19 S. Bland
P. David & Nancy | P. A. J. & Jane
Oc. Farmer | M. P. R. Suiter

80

Date: 12-25-1895
Isaac Wesley Kidd    Nannie Belle Thompson
A. 30 W. Bland       A. 27 W. Tazewell
P. Henry C. & Jemima P. Andrew W. & Abagail
Oc. Farmer           M. John A. Smith

Date: 12-26-1895
Pearis Beverly       Belle James (B)
Charlton (B)
A. 20 S. Mercer, WV  A. 21 S. Bland
P. Noah & Sarah A.   P. Harvey & Hannah
Oc. Farmer           M. D. H. Carr

Date: 1-2-1896
Jas. Henderson Burton Daisy Mitchell
A. 25 S. Bland       A. 19 S. Bland
P. Pendleton & Eliz. J. P. Timothy E. & Ardelia
Oc. Farmer           M. J. T. Taylor

Date: 2-12-1896
Geo. Wm. Burton      Elizabeth C. Hancock
A. 20 S. Bland       A. 30 S. Bland
P. Jas T. & Mary E.  P. Mary Jane Hancock
Oc. Farmer           M. D. H. Carr

Date: 2-26-1896
Rob't C. Kidd        Bettie J. Starling
A. 24 S. Bland       A. 17 S. Bland
P. Wm C. & Allie     P. G. W. & Rebecca J.
Oc. Farmer           M. P. R. Suiter

Date: 4-1-1896
Jas. Wm. Walters     Sallie Belle Robinett
A. 22 S. Bland       A. 20 S. Bland
P. Russell & Nancy   P. M. D. & Sarah L.
Oc. Farmer           M. P. R. Suiter

Date: 4-23-1896
Jas. Wm. Looney      Sallie O. Warner
A. 21 S. Giles       A. 20 S. Bland
P. Henry & Emily J.  P. D. C. & Margaret
Oc. Farmer           M. D. H. Carr

Date: 6-17-1896
Walter Lee Umbarger  Emma Eunice Newberry
A. 29 S. Giles       A. 29 S. Bland
P. E. T. & L. A.     P. Henley Chapman &
                     Mollie E. Steel
Oc. Teacher          M. D. H. Carr

Date: 12-25-1895**
Earsten Sheppard Havens Lizzie Mustard
A. 22 S. Bland       A. 20 S. Bland
P. Lizzie Havens     P. Minerva Mustard
Oc. Farmer           M. Robert L. Newberry

Date: 1-1-1896
Wm. Edley Umbarger   Lillie Pauline Wilson

A. 23 S. Wythe       A. 24 S. Bland
P. Wm. Edley & Martha E. P. Thos O. & Missouri J.
Oc. Farmer           M. C. L. Stradley

Date: 1-8-1896
Hoge Tyler Nisewander India Sublett
A. 22 S. Bland       A. 16 S. Bland
P. Alex & Mary       P. Delia Pendleton
Oc. Miner            M. W. R. Miller

Date 2-20-1896
Thos M. Tibbs        Eviline Noonkester
A. 25 S. Bland       A. 20 S. Carroll
P. Peter & Ann       P. Michael & Nancy
Oc. Farmer           M. F. F. Repass

Date: 3-19-1896
Wm. Andrew Day       Robertie May French
A. 22 S. Giles       A. 20 S. Bland
P. Lewis M. & Barbara P. Giles P. & Sarah
Oc. Farmer           M. W. R. Miller

Date: 4-9-1896
Chas H. Lindamood    Lillie Texas Perkey
A. 29 S. Bland       A. 20 S. Bland
P. John H. & Martha Jane P. Wm. A. & Sophia M.
Oc. Farmer           M. H. G. Davis

Date: 5-3-1896
A. D. Simpson        Carrie E. Riggsby
A. 22 S. Tazewell    A. 22 S. Smyth
P. Hack & Jane       P. W. M. & Mary
Oc. Farmer           M. C. Mitchell

Date 7-3-1896
John H. Mullins      Sarah A. Whitt
A. 23 S. TN          A. 22 S. Tazewell
P.                   P. John & Mahala J.

Oc. Farmer           M. Not Returned

Date: 7-15-1896
Wm. Miller Patton       Poca Dallas Pauley
A. 19 S. Bland          A. 17 S. Bland
P. Rob't & Mary         P. I. P. & R. B.
Oc. Farmer              M.  Geo W. Penley

Date: 8-2-1896
John H. Atwell          Carrie E. D. Umbarger
A. 19 S. Smyth          A. 18 S. Bland
P. James E. & Eliza     P. Thos. P. & Elizabeth
Oc. Farmer              M. F. F. Repass

Date: 9-14-1896
Sand. F. Tibbs          Odessa I. Repass
A. 20 S. Bland          A. 20 S. Bland
P. Henry T. & Sophia    P. Elias & Adaline E.
Oc. Farmer              M. F. F. Repass

Date: 10-7-1896
James H. Bogle          Della C. Bailey
A. 28 S. Bland          A. 17 S. Bland
P. Jno & Julia A. Bralley P. James M. & Julia H.
Oc. Physician           M. J. M. Ashworth

Date: 10-15-1896
James F. Cassell        Mary E. Spangler
A. 47 W.  Smyth         A. 24 S. Minnasota
P. John M. & Frances    P. And. J. & Angeline
Oc. Farmer              M. J. F. Matheson

Date: 11-1-1896
Geo. Stuart Atwell      Essie A. Tibbs
A. 21 S. Tazewell       A. 22 S. Bland
P. Putnam D. & M. V.    P. Jas. A. & Mary
Oc. Farmer              M. H. G. Davis

Date: 11-18-1896
Sam'l C. Warner         Blanche D. Repass
A. 26 S. Bland          A. 29 S. Bland
P.D.C. & Mahulda        P. John & Minerva
Oc. Physician           M.  J. F. Matheson

Date: 12-2-1896
Wm. T. Pruett           Osternine Neel
A. 38 W. Bland          A. 23 S. Bland
P. Henry & Martha       P. Jackson & Jane
Oc. Farmer              M. P. R. Suiter

Date: 7-30-1896
Isaac Ed. French        Cora A. Chapman
A. 22 S. Bland          A. 16 S. Bland
P. Giles P. & Sarah     P. Jas. Wm. & Mary O.
Oc. Farmer              M. S. V. Morris

Date: 8-16-1896
James Emmett Cox        Eliza K. Waddle
A. 22 S. Bland          A. 21 S. Bland
P. A. M. & Catherine    P. Paris & Mary M.
Oc. Farmer              M. J. Mahood

Date: 9-20-1896
Harman Ingram           Sallie K. Davis
A. 30 S. Bland          A. 22 S. Bland
P. Wm. & Pruny          P. Hiram G. & Cosby Jane
Oc. Farmer              M. J. Mahood

Date: 10-7-1896
Wm. H. Spiller (B)      Mora M. Harman (B)
A. 19 S. Bland          A. 18 S. Mercer, WV
P. Pauline H. Hatch     P. Matilda Harman
Oc. Brakeman            M. D. H. Carr

Date: 10-22-1896
Miller Hoge Thompson    Mollie Kate Ashworth
A. 23 S. Bland          A. 26 S. Bland
P. Josh. B. & Margaret  P. Wm. B. & Martha
Oc. Carpenter           M. A. A. Ashworth

Date: 11-12-1896
Jacob S. Dillman        Pinkie E. Lampert
A. 21 S. Bland          A. 20 S. Bland
P. Geo. W. & Lucinda    P. R. Floyd & Marcia
Oc. Farmer              M. H. G. Davis

Date: 12-2-1896
Geo W. Jones            Mary E. Goff
A. 25 S. Bland          A. 20 S. Bland
P. Ellen Jones          P. Chas.
Oc. Farmer              M.  D. H. Carr

Begin Page 38 of Original Book
Date: 12-16-1896
Leonard Waddle          Lou/Lon. Kitts
A. 33 S. Bland          A. 31 S. Bland
P. Michael & Margaret   P. Ganam & Abigail
Oc. Teacher             M.  J. F. Matheson

Date: 12-16-1896  
Jas. H. Lampert  
A. 23 S. Blalnd  
P. Jas A. & Nancy  
Oc. Farmer  

Ossie Tibbs  
A. 18 S. Bland  
P. Jas. A. & Mary  
M. H. G. Davis  

Date: 12-30-1896  
John H. Nunn  
A. 19 S. Bland  
P. B. L. & Martha E.  
Oc. Farmer  

Louemma E. Miller  
A. 16 S. Bland  
P. C. W. & Lou.  
M. W. R. Miller  

Date: 12-30-1896  
Rob't L. Sparks  
A. 24 S. Tazewell  
P. Hugh & Nancy  
Oc. Farmer  

Laura L. Robertson  
A. 27 S. Montgomery  
P. Harvey & Emmiemiah?  
M. J. M. Ashworth  

Date: 12-31-1896  
Jas. Arthur Reedy  
A. 23 S. Grayson  
P. J. M. & R. J.  
Oc. Mail Carrier  

Susan Forkner  
A. 23 S. Bland  
P. John  
M. J. F. Matheson  

Date: 12-31-1896  
Wm. Trigg Farmer  
A. 20 S. Wythe  
P. S. M. & Fannie  
Oc. Farmer  

Maggie E. Saddler  
A. 20 S. Bland  
P. Geo. S. & Belle  
M. J. F. Matheson  

Date: 1-6-1897  
Wm. S. Lampert  
A. 21 S. Bland  
P. James A. & Nancy  
Oc. Farmer  

Daisy L. Lindsey  
A. 19 S. Wilson, TN  
P. George & Amita  
M. C. L. Stradley  

Date: 1-10-1897  
Jocob Groseclose  
A. 61 W. Bland  
P. Jacob & Susan  
Oc. Farmer  

Elizabeth Groseclose  
A. 65 W. Bland  
P. Jno & Mary Crabtree  
M. C. W. Cassell  

Date: 1-20-1897  
Crockett A. Wilson  
A.    S. Bland  
P. Joseph & Darthulia  
Oc. Farmer  

Texie Wright  
A.    S. Bland  
P. Dan'l O. & M. J.  
M. License not returned  

Date: 1-21-1897  
Ballard Preston Stowers  
A. 29 S. Bland  
P. Peter R. & Araminta  
Oc. Farmer  

Missouri Caldwell  
A. 27 S. Bland  
P. Noah & Sarah  
M. Samuel S. Weatherly  

Date: 3-9-1897  
J. Wih? Witten  
A. 24 S. Tazewell  
P. A.S. & Lucinda  
Oc. Farmer  

Mimmi Wilson  
A. 22 S. Bland  
P. Thos O. & Missouri E.  
M. C. L. Stradley  

Date: 3-11-1897  
Geo S. Bishop  
A. 20 S. Floyd  
P. Jacob & Elizabeth  
Oc. Farmer  

Sallie M. Davis  
A. 18 S. Bland  
P. Ed'wd A. & Zarilda  
M. Samuel S. Weatherly  

Date: 3-13-1897  
Wm. B. Edwards (B)  
A. 33 W. Franklin  
P. Carter & Grace  
Oc. Teacher  

Nannie L. Gordon (B)  
A. 20 S. Bland  
P. Mack & Ellen  
M. J. F. Matheson  

Date: 3-30-1897  
Joseph Foglesong  
A. 61 W. Wythe  
P. Simon & Christina  
Oc. Farmer  

Bittie Groseclose  
A. 50 S. Wythe  
P. Absalom & Sarah  
M. C. W. Cassell  

Date: 4-7-1897  
Braxton H. Penley  
A. 67 W. Buncumbe, NC  
P. Wm. S. & Margaret  
Oc. Farmer  

Addie E. Fannon  
A. 51 S. Bland  
P. Acles & Sarah  
M. G. W. Penley  

Date: 4-10-1897  
Wiley Winton Bruce  
A. 28 S. Bland  
P. James H. & M. M.  
Oc. Farmer  

Dora E. Umbarger  
A. 21 S. Bland  
P. John F. & Rachel  
M. H. G. Davis  

Date: 4-17-1897  
Jacob I. Lampert  
A. 22 S. Bland  
P. Geo W. & Lucinda  
Oc. Farmer  

Bertha D. Dillman  
A. 16 S. Tazewell  
P. Wm. W. & Rhoda  
M. H. G. Davis

Date: 4-29-1897
Robert Lee King
A. 25 S. Pulaski
P. Johnston & Lucinda
Oc. Farmer

Hallie N. Rider
A. 21 S. Bland
P. Thos A. & Jennie A.
M. J. P. Roach

Date: 5-2-1897
Geo E. Burgher
A. 28 S. Tazewell
P. James & Susan
Oc. Farmer

Verni C. Tibbs
A. 22 S. Smyth
P. Peter & Ann
M. F. F. Repass

Date: 5-3-1897
John W. Hilton
A. 24 S. TN
P. James & Mahala
Oc. Farmer

Martha Prince
A. 27 S. WV
P. Floyd S. & Margaret
M. J. M. Ashworth

Date: 6-15-1897
Geo W. Rogers
A. 24 S. Scott
P. Jame J. & Catherine
Oc. Farmer

Hattie H. Tilson
A. 21 S. Bland
P. Harvey H. & Mary Jane
M. C. W. Cassell

Date: 7-15-1897
Sandy P. White
A. 23 S. NC
P. Thomas & Dicey
Oc. Farmer

Lillie A. Lawrence
A. 17 S. Floyd
P. Geo W. & Ellen
M. Samuel S. Weatherly

Date: 8-25-1897
Stuart Frazier Stowers
A. 24 S. Bland
P. Isaac F. & Virginia
Oc. Farmer

Julia N. Bailey
A. 17 S. Bland
P. Dan'l M. & Bettie
M. Samuel S.Weatherly

Date: 8-31-1897
Robert Cruff
A. 21 S. Montgomery
P. Henry D. & Lucinda
Oc. Farmer

V. N. Hamblin
A. 16 S. Bland
P. Wm & Ollie
M. J. H. Jones

Date: 9-12-1897
Wm. G. Neece
A. 27 W. Wythe
P. Wayman L. & Eliza
Oc. Farmer

Roxie M. Umbarger
A. 19 S. Bland
P. Henry & Mary J.
M. J. Mahood

Date: 9-26-1897
Wiley Winton Smith
A. 23 S. Smyth
P. T. J. & M. J.
Oc. Farmer

Rosa A. Cumiford
A. 23 S. Bland
P. Margaret
M. Samuel S. Weatherly

Date: 9-26-1897
Dexter S. Groseclose
A. 28 S. Bland
P. Henry & Mary
Oc. Farmer

Victoria Wilson
A. 26 S. Bland
P. John L. & Elizabeth
M. H. G. Davis

Date: 10-3-1897
Daniel Levi Harman
A. A. 24 S. Bland
P. Addison F. &
Sarah Elizabeth Ellis
Oc. Miner

Cynthia Va. Fanning
A. 22 S. Bland
P. Wm. & Cynthia

M. A. A. Ashworth

Date: 10-4-1897
Edward Wilson
A. 17 S. Bland
P. Samuel & Rebecca

Oc. Farmer

Hallie Fletcher
A. 17 S. Bland
P. John F. & Mary E.

M. W. R. Miller

Date: 10-6-1897
Rob't Ezra Munsey
A. 23 S. Bland
P. Jas Harvey &
Margaret L Hutsell
Oc. Farmer

Agnes Gertrude Updyke
A. 26 S. Bland
P. Albert Galatin&
Mary Agnes Smith
M. D. H. Carr

Date: 10-23-1897
Henry Thomas Wall
A. 24 D. Surry, NC
P.Henry J. & Lucinda

Oc. Farmer

Celia Sutphin
A. 22 S. Carroll
P. L. L. & E. S.

M. D. H. Carr

Date: 10-23-1897
Thos. M. Hall
A. 44 W. Giles
P. Wm. R. & Charlotte
Oc. Farmer

Martha Peak
A. 16 S. Bland
P. Leander & Nancy M.
M. J. Mahood

Date: 11-7-197
Joseph Reed
A. 68 W. Stokes, NC
P. Josiah & Mary
Oc. Carpenter

Ellen Gordon
A. 39 W. Bland
P. John & Julia Powers
M. J. T. Taylor

Date: 11-10-1897
Green Ramsey (B)     Hulda Jackson (B)
A. 29 S. Franklin     A. 34 W. Tazewell
P. Richard& Matilda     P. Buck & Kizzie Charlton

Oc. Farmer     M. C. W. Cassell

Date: 12-8-1897
Elliott O. Bernard     Emma N. McNeil
A. 25 S. Pulaski     A. 23 S. Bland
P. Sam'l H. & Eliz. P.     P. Dan'l O. & Sarah E.

Oc. Farmer     M. J. T. Taylor

Begin Page 39 of Original Book
Date: 12-24-1897
James N. Patterson (B)     Alice Ferguson (B)
A. 28 S. Mercer, WV     A. 18 S. Franklin
P. Ballard & Roxie     P. M. H. & M. F.
Oc. Rail Roading     M. F. Meadows

Date: 12-25-1897
Joseph C. Painter     Irene M. Chandler
A. 27 S. Bland     A. 15 S. Bland
P. Maggie Painter     P. P. H. & Sally Ann
Oc. Farmer     M. D. H. Carr

Date: 1-6-1898
John Joseph Igo     Nancy J. Wilburn
A. 32 W. Tazewell     A. 33 S. Tazewell
P. Dennis & Elizabeth     P. John J. & Sarah J.
Oc. Farmer     M. C. E. Painter

Date: 2-15-1898
Jas. Peter Kellinger     Lena May Kelley
A. 24 S. Smyth     A. 20 S. Smyth
P. G. D. H. & Margaret A.P. Jno P. & Mary
Oc. Salesman     M. J. J. Sherer

Date: 4-13-1898
Geo Milton Chandler     Vessa Virginia Hall
A. 18 S. Bland     A. 16 S. Bland
P. P. H. & Sally A.     A. S. H. & Mary S.
Oc. Farmer     M. C. W. Cassell

Date: 4-19-1898
Chas Miller Jones     Rosa Ellen Totten
A. 30 S. Wise     A. 20 S. Tazewell
P. Wm. & Mary E.     P. Jno J. & Elizabeth

Oc. Farmer     M. D. M. Shupe

Date: 11-28-1897
Geo W. Roberts     Nannie E. Carr
A. 37 S. Bland     A. 32 D. Bland
P. Wm. & Elizabeth     P. Jno Wesley Harman
    & Sarah Virginia Moore
Oc. Farmer     M. J. F. Matheson

Date: 12-22-1897
Miller W. Kitts     Emma J. Burton
A. 31 W. Bland     A. 20 S. Bland
P. Jacob F.& Luthera     P. Jas Thos. & Mary Eliz.
Bruce     Munsey
Oc. Farmer     M. D. H. Carr

Date: 12-25-1897
John W. E. Pauley     Polly Ann Waddle
A. 28 D. Bland     A. 29 S. Bland
P. I. P. & Rebecca     P. Randolph & M. J.
Oc. Farmer     M. D. H. Carr

Date: 12-29-1897
Thos W. Newberry     Minta C. Kegley
A. 27 S. Bland     A. 23 S. Bland
P. Henry & Lizzie     P. Jas Gordon & Fannie
Oc. Farmer     M. D. H. Carr

1-27-1898
Harman Ramsey     Almedia Lawrence
A. 21 S. Bland     A. 17 S. Montgomery
P. Chas. & Willie     P. Wm. & Catherine
Oc. Farmer     M. William R. Miller

Date: 2-24-1898
Jas. Welsey Willis     Marie Henderson Tabor
A. 32 W. Giles     A. 17 S. Bland
P. Wm V. & Margeret     P. James & Virginia
Oc. Farmer     M. John A. Smith

Date: 4-21-1898
Roach Pauley     Mollie Melissa Lampert
A. 27 S. Bland     A. 19 S. Bland
P. T. G. & Telia A.     P. Jane Lampert
Oc. Farmer     M. J. F. Jones

Date: 4-20-1898
Wythe Newberry Brown     Mary Edith Newberry
A. 27 S. Bland     A. 25 S. Bland
P. Ballard Preston &     P. Henley Chapman &
Lucinda Robinett     Mollie E. Steel
Oc. Farmer     M. George W. Penley

Date: 4-21-1898
Wm. Witten Carver     Annie Wynn
A. 46 D. Bland     A. 26 S. Bland
P. Rob't & Katie     P. Jas & Catherine
Oc. Farmer     M. C. E. Painter

Date: 4-28-1898
Thos Robinson (B)     Laura Showalter (B)
A. 21 S. Giles     A. 20 S. Pulaski
P. John & Charlotte     P. Wm. & Marg.
Oc. Rail Roading     M. W. H. Perkins

Date: 5-25-1898
John M. Conley     Irene E. Mitchell
A. 27 S. Giles     A. 26 S. Floyd
P. Jno W. & Jane M.     P. T. E. & Ardelia
Oc. Lumberman     M. J. T. Taylor

Date: 6-8-1898
Emory Huddle Waddle     Mable Kitts
A. 28 S. Bland     A. 24 S. Bland
P. Ran. Waddle &     P. Andrew Jackson &
Mar. J. Musser     Hester Ann Tickle
Oc. Farmer     M. C. W. Cassell

Date: 8-29-1898
Charles Clinton Davis     Willie Floyd Davis
A. 23 S. Bland     A. 20 S. Bland
P. Henry & Margaret     P. Jno T. & Mary
Oc. Sawyer     M. J. F. Jones

Date 6-30-1898
Meek Bogle Tickle     Ella Palmyra Harman
A. 27 S. Bland     A. 24 S. Bland
P. Dan'l LLineberry &     P. John Wesley &
Mary Melissa Bogle     Martha Jane Burton
Oc. Farmer     M. D. H. Carr

Date: 8-17-1898
Jno Jacob Burton     Margaret Salomia Hill
A. 26 D. Bland     A. 18 S. Bland
P. Jas T. & Mary E.     P. Maxwell & Nannie E.
Oc. Farmer     M. J. F. Jones

Date: 8-29-1898
Lewis Mason Day     Allie Hancock
A. 52 W. Tazewell     A. 25 S. Bland
P. Wm. & Rachel     P. Pleas. & Virginia
Oc. Merchant     M. John P. Roach

Date: 4-27-1898
Wm Henry Edmonds     Katie Belle Kidd
A. 26 S. Raliegh, WV     A. 18 S. Bland
P. Joel & Mary F.     P. J. M. & M. A.
Oc. Farmer     M. John A. Smith

Date: 5-4-1898
Henderson Monroe Kidd     Nannie M. Leedy
A. 30 S. Bland     A. 22 S. Bland
P. E. S. & Clara     A. Eli & Mary E.
Oc. Farmer     M. John A. Smith

Date 5-31-1898
Rufus Edgar Levitt     Sarah A. Gregory
A. 29 S. Bland     A. 29 W. Tazewell
P. Geo & Sarah J.     P. G. C. & Jane Fox
Oc. Farmer     M. John A. Smith

Date: 6-22-1898
Chas Jackson Miller Starks     Frances Mariah Hicks
A. 28 S. Bland     A. 18 S. Bland
P. J. M. & Emaline     P. J. W. & Mary

Oc. Farmer     M. D. A. Leffel

Date: 8-29-1898
Rush Dillow     Nannie Gray Pauley
A. 21 S. Bland     A. 23 S. Bland
P. Allen & Frances     P. Thos & Ann
Oc. Farmer     M. D. H. Carr

Date: 8-3-1898
Wm. Lafayette Shrader     Annie Stowers
A. 20 S. Bland     A. 23 S. Bland
P. I. N & Alpha     P. G. W. & Polly

Oc. Farmer     M. John A. Smith

Date: 8-25-1898
Elbert Taylor King     Mary E. Starling
A. 22 S. Floyd     A. 25 S. Bland
P. Jacob & Rebecca C.     P. John & Sarah
Oc. Farmer     M. C. E. Painter

Date: 8-30-1898
Emmett Brown Gilliam     Virginia Belle Walker
A. 25 S. Patrick     A. 23 S. Raliegh, WV
P. Jno W. & Mary A.     P. Wm. A. & Sarah E.
Oc. Miller     M. C. W. Cassell

Date: 9-22-1898
Jas. Wm. Kidd — Bertie Lee Hall
A. 19 S. Pulaski — A. 18 S. Tazewell
P. Jas. H. & Nancy — P. Thos M. & Jennie
Oc. Farmer — M. E. L. Addington

Date: 10-12-1898
Jno. Wm. Hoge Bird — Fannie Cora Coburn
A. 20 S. Bland — A. 24 S. Bland
P. Jas H. & M. J. — P. T. G. & C. N.
Oc. Farmer — M. J. M. Ashworth

Date: 11-9-1898
Dan. Baldwin Thompson — Julia Burrass
A. 43 W. Wythe — A. 40 W. Bland
P. Jezrell & Allie — P. Chapman Kidd

Oc. Lumberman — M. John A. Smith

Date: 11-17-1898
John Tynes (B) — Bertie Gray (B)
A. 24 S. Bland — A. 21 S. Franklin
P. Jack & Julia — P. Henry & Octavia
Oc. Farmer — M. George Lee

Date. 11-30-1898
Andrew Napoleon Bogle — Louvenia Pruett
A. 42 S. TN — A. 16 S. Bland
P. Jas Buchanan & — P. Jas Milton &
Elizabeth Jane Munsey — Elizbeth A. Fanning
Oc. Farmer — M. W. C. Crockett

Date: 12-28-1898
Andrew Jackson Hayton — Mary Dell Kitts
A. 30 S. Smyth — A. 23 S. Bland
P. Peter — P. Samuel L. & Augusta M.
Oc. Mechanic — M. E. L. Addington

Date: 1-11-1899
William S. Stowers — Roxie L. J. Kitts
A. 20 S. Bland — A. 17 S. Bland
P. E. G. & Mary E. — P. Arthur Maden & Earsley J.
Oc. Farmer — M. Jas. Mahood

Date: 2-18-1899
Wm. L. Waddle — Mary L. Hall
A. 24 S. Smyth — A. 24 S. Tazewell
P. Paris & Mary F. — P. Thos. M. & Mary M.
Oc. Farmer — M. E. L. Addington

Date: 10-6-1898
Elbert Elverson Noonkester — Elizabeth Belle Tibbs
A. 20 S. Carroll — A. 20 S. Bland
P. Michael & Nancy A. — P. H. T. & Sophia
Oc. Farmer — M. F. F. Repass

Date: 10-20-1898
Rob't Jackson Brookman — Emma Jane Patton
A. 25 S. Pulaski — A. 24 S. Bland
P. James & Harriett — P. Rob't & Mary
Oc. Farmer — M. John P. Roach

Date: 11-9-1898
Melicue Samuel Irvin Townley — Rebecca Alice Duncan
A. 24 S. Amherst — A. 17 S. Floyd
P. Jno. Wm. Summerfield — P. Ananias & Adaline?
Mary Katherine Harman — Evaline Wood
Oc. Farmer — M. George W. Penley

Date: 11-26-1898
Walter Watson Painter — Emma Louella Pardue
A. 26 S. Bland — A. 26 S. Wilkes, NC
P. Maggie Ratliff — P. J. W. & Fannie
Oc. Farmer — M. W. C. Crockett

Begin Page 40 of Original Book
Date: 12-21-1898
Geo. Estell Stafford — Beulah Ada Bernard
A. 26 S. Bland — A. 22 S. Bland
P. Ballard P. & — P. Sam'l H. & Elizabeth
Mary E. J. — Pelter
Oc. Carpenter — M. J. T. Taylor

Date: 1-1-1899
Clyde Dunnagan — Martha J. Delimore
A. 22 S. Bland — A. 36 D. Bland
P. Wm. & Mary — P. ??? Rhinehart
Oc. Farmer — M. Geo W. Penley

Date: 1-18-1899
Cyrus M. Meadows — Osa E. Gibson
A. 20 S. Giles — A. 21 S. Bland
P. Mildred Meadows — P. E. B. & A. Bettie
Oc. Farmer — M. C. E. Painter

Date: 2-22-1899
Eugene B. Edmondson — Birdie M. Robinett
A. 25 S. Memphis, TN — A. 24 S. Bland
P. Henry & Sophia — P. Jas. S. & Ella
Oc. Farmer — M. G. W. Penley

Date: 3-9-1899
Robt. J. Pugh  Rachel A. Farmer
A. 44 W. Giles  A. 24 S. Bland
P. Geo W. & Elizabeth P. S. M. & Fannie

Oc. Carpenter  M. W. C. Crockett

Date: 3-15-1899
L. M. Thomas  Leona Tracy
A. 23 S. Mercer, WV A. 19 S. Giles
P. Green & Annie  P. G. P. Tracy
Oc. Farmer  M. W. C. Crockett

Date: 4-12-1899
Hugh P. Bolling  Surrilda V. Stowers
A. 28 S. Tazewell  A. 26 S. Bland
P. Andrew & Barbara P. Geo W. & Sarah J.
Oc. Farmer  M. John A. Smith

Date: 4-26-1899
Daniel S. Wolf  Ada Kidd
A. 22 S. Bland  A. 24 S. Bland
P. Geo & Eliza  P. G. W. & M. C.
Oc. Farmer  M. John A. Smith

Date: 5-20-1899
James H. Wilson, Jr. M. Ada Va. Stowers
A. 23 S. Mercer, WV A. 24 S. Bland
P. Jas. H. & Marinda P. I. F. & Virginia
Oc. Farmer  M. C. E. Painter

Date: 5-30-1899
John R. Hutchins Rebecca E. Keeling
A. 24 S. Bland  A. 24 S. Bland
P. Wm. & Lou.  P. A. J. & Fannie
Oc. Farmer  M. W. R. Miller

Date: 6-14-1899
Thos Hoge McNiel Victoria M. Wholford
A. we S. Bland  A. 22 S. Bland
P. D. O. & Sarah E. P. Gordon &
    Matilda Ann Byrnes
Oc. Merchant  M. J. T. Taylor

Date: 6-29-1899
Harvey W. Richardson Victoria V. Robertson
A. 23 S. Giles  A. 20 S. Giles
P. A. R. & S. V.  P. Geo W. & Susan E.
Oc. Farmer  M. C. E. Painter

Date: 3-15-1899
Smith N. Penley  Eva H. Robinett
A. 29 S. Asheville, NC A. 25 S. Bland
P. Geo Wash. &  P. Jas & Ella
Adaline Robinett
Oc. Farmer  M. G. W. Penley

Date: 4-5-1899
William Preston (B) Mora Spiller (B)
A. 23 S. Bland  A. 21 W. Mercer, WV
P. Boda & Nancy  P. Matilda Harman
Oc. Laborer  M. W. C. Crockett

Date: 4-19-1899
Wm. A. Gray (B)  Amanda Shields (B)
A. 29 W. Franklin  A. 21 S. Bland
P. Henry & Octavia P. Richard & Lucy
Oc. Farmer  M. J. M. Ashworth

Date: 5-10-1899
John M. Wynn  Gracie Burton
A. 31 S. Bland  A. 25 S. Bland
P. Wm. & Millie  P. J. T. & Mary E.
Oc. Furnace-man. M. George W. Penley

Date: 5-24-1899
John H. Blessing  Stella M. Kidd
A. 22 S. Wythe  A. 17 S. Bland
P. J. W. & Elizabeth P. A. T. & Roda J.
Oc. Farmer  M. John A. Smith

Date: 6-1-1899
Chas R. Grayson  Lucy Ewald
A. 23 S. Bland  A. 20 S. Wythe
P. A. J. & Rosa V.  P. G. A. & Theressa
Oc. Farmer  M. W. C. Crockett

Date: 6-28-1899
Julius W. Kidd  Susan J. Kidd
A. 25 S. Bland  A. 18 S. Bland
P. A. I. Rhoda J.  P. S. H. & L. A.

Oc. Farmer  M. John A. Smith

Date: 6-29-1899
Jos T. Richardson Cordelia Willis
A. 19 S. Giles  A. 22 S. Giles
P. A. R. & S. V.  P. S. L. & Emma
Oc. Farmer  M. C. E. Painter

Date: 7-12-1899
Chas. W. Fletcher        Aldora C. Austin
A. 21 S. Bland           A. 24 S. Floyd
P. Jno F. & Mary E.      P. W. G. & Elizabeth

Oc. Farmer               M. W. C. Crockett

Date: 7-23-1899
Ulysses Grant Tickle     Lottie Va. Tickle
A. 26 S. Bland           A. 25 S. Bland
P. Jackson Nye &         P. Dan'l Lineberry
Mary Ann Waggoner        Mary Melissa "Polly" Bogle
Oc. Farmer               M. W. C. Crockett

Date: 8-2-1899
Geo. H. Stowers          Julia A. Pruett
A. 20 S. Bland           A. 20 S. Bland
P. Jos H. & Ellen        P. Harvey & Nancy J.
Oc. Farmer               M. W. K. Neel

Date: 8-10-1899
Benj. S. Corder          Frances B. Davis
A. 22 S. Bland           A. 19 S. Bland
P. Jas & Josephine       P. J. W. & Nancy J.
Oc. Farmer               M. John P. Roach

Date: 8-16-1899
Walter N. Vermillion     Nellie Burton
A. 30 S. Washington      A. 18 S. Bland
P. J. W. & L. H.         P. Travis & Mary H.
Oc. Stonecutter          M. C. E. Painter

Date: 10-12-1899
Sam'l L. Willis          Ruthy Martin
A. 50 W. Giles           A. 41 S. Franklin
P. Wm. H. & Margaret     P. Hez. & Sarah
Oc. Farmer               M. J. M. Ashworth

Date: 10-18-1899
William J. Dunn          Ettia M. Hornbarger
A. 24 S. Bland           A. 20 S. Bland
P. W. G. & S. J.         P. W. P. & Mary
Oc. Farmer               M. John A. Smith

Date: 11-1-1899
Ed. S. Stowers           Maggie M. Hall
A. 23 S. Bland           A. 16 S. Bland
P. E. G. & Mary          P. Wm. & Sarah

Oc. Farmer               M. James Mahood

Date: 7-18-1899
Wm. Gordon Wright        Macy M. Spangler
A. 23 S. Bland           A. 18 S. Bland
P. David Oliver &        P. W. J. & Darthulia
Martha Jane Morehead
Oc. Farmer               M. J. Mahood

Date: 8-2-1899
George Lee               Mollie J. Bean
A. 21 S. Smyth           A. 23 S. Bland
P. Rob't & Mary          P. J. S. C. & Margaret M.

Oc. Farmer               M. F. F. Repass

Date: 8-9-1899
Harley H. Kidd           Ollie Yost
A. 20 S. Bland           A. 19 S. Tazewell
P. A. R. & Lettie        P. D. P. & Mary K.
Oc. Farmer               M. John A. Smith

Date: 8-15-1899
Wm. R. H. Munsey         Nora M. Harman
A. 26 S. Bland           A. 17 S. Tazewell
P. Davis H. & Julia      P. Blain & Virginia
Oc. Farmer               M. G. W. Penley

Date: 8-30-1899
John R. Wilson           Rosa Wilson
A. 21 S. Bland           A. 24 S. Bland
P. Elias & Polly         P. Jno L. & Elizabeth
Oc. Farmer               M. E. L. Addington

Date: 12-17-1899
Chas. L. Jones           Nannie L. Cassell
A. 30 S. Wythe           A. 24 S. Bland
P. D. C. & F. E.         P. Jas F. & Christina
Oc. Salesman             M. C. Willis Cassell

Begin Page 41 of Original Book
Date: 10-25-1899
Geo. L. Robinett         Minnie B. Foglesong
A. 22 S. Bland           A. 27 W. Bland
P. Jas S. & Ella         P. P. W. & Louisa Harman
Oc. Farmer               M. Geo. W. Penley

Date: 11-29-1899
Esca Mitchell            Minnie F. Miller
A. 22 S. Bland           A. 19 S. Bland
P. Timothy Elijah &      P. J. W. & Rhoda
Ardelia Jane Wohlford
Oc. Farmer               M. J. T. Taylor

Date: 12-6-1899
James J. Umbarger          Laura McFarland
A. 40 W. Bland            A. 24 S. Bland
P. Wm. & Christina        P. L. D. & Jane
Oc. Farmer               M. F. F. Repass

Date: 12-20-1899
Geo Chas. Fanning         Lelia Grace Mustard
A. 20 S. Bland           A. 22 S. Bland
P. George W. &           P. John Jasper &
Matilda H. Davidson       Frances Stuart
Oc. Farmer               M. J. T. Taylor

Date: 12-25-1899
Jas H. Spangler          Bertha M. Ramsey
A. 23 S. Bland           A. 16 S. Bland
P. W. J. & Darthulia      P. Wm. H. & Polly
Oc. Farmer               M. W. R. Miller

Date: 12-28-1899
Giles R. Fanning          Annie L. Harless
A. 20 S. Bland           A. 23 S. Giles
P. W. W. & Cynthia        P. W. T. & Minerva
Oc. Farmer               M. A. A. Ashworth

Date: 1-17-1900
Henry P. Stowers          Annie T. Robinett
A. 21 S. Bland           A. 21 S. Bland
P. Elbert & Ludemia       P. F. M. & Larilette
Oc. Farmer               M. Jas. Mahood

Date: 2-18-1900
John H. Crabtree          Mary V. Groseclose
A. 34 W. Tazewell        A. 27 S. Bland
P. W. J. & Nancy         P. Henry & Mary L.

Oc. Lumberman            M. Sam'l S. Weatherly

Date: 3-14-1900
Wm. W. Goad              Gertrude Harman
A. 20 S. Carroll         A. 18 S. Bland
P. Andrew J.             P. R. J. & Zildy
Oc. Farmer               M. W. C. Crockett

Date: 5-6-1900
Chas L. Kinder           Julia F. Atwell
A. 21 S. Bland           A. 17 S. Smyth
P. J. M. & Sophia        P. Jas. E. & Eliza
Oc. Farmer               M. R. R. Sowers

Date: 12-6-1899
Tildon G. Catron          Helena E. Groseclose
A. 23 S. Smyth           A. 20 S. Bland
P. Jacob & Mary          P. J. H. & M. M.
Oc. Farmer               M. S. S. Weatherly

Date: 12-21-1899
Thos Grayson Dillow       Margaret Luema Hancock
A. 21 S. Bland           A. 22 D. Bland
P. Wm. Addison &         P. Jackson Nye Tickle &
Elizabeth Waddle         Mary Ann Waggoner
Oc. Farmer               M. A. A. Ashworth

Date: 12-29-1899
Wm. G. Ferrell           Maggie J. Callahan
A. 29 S. Pulaski         A. 25 S. Bland
P. W. B.P. & Rebecca      P. I. T. & Mary V.
Oc. Clerk in store       M. S. S. Weatherly

Date: 1-10-1900
Bane Neece               Laura A. Kitts
A. 23 S. Bland           A. 20 D. Bland
P. Jas M. & Sarah     P. Russell & Martha J. Repass
Oc. Farmer               M. W. C. Crockett

Date: 2-15-1900
H. B. Nunn               Matilda Smith
A. 24 S. Bland           A. 20 S. Wythe
P. B. L. & Martha L.      P. B. M. Smith
Oc. Farmer               M. W. C. Crockett

Date: 3-8-1900
Henry A. W. Arrington     Alva May Thomas
A. 40 W. Franklin        A. 18 S. Bland
P. Chas & Sarah          P. Rob't G. &
                         Susan Va. Woodyard
Oc. Farmer               M. J. T. Taylor

Date: 4-25-1900
Dexter S. Waddle          Margaret E. Fortner
A. 21 S. Bland           A. 17 S. Bland
P. Harvey I. & Rhoda      P. Sam. T. & Mary L.
Oc. Farmer               M. W. C. Crockett

Date: 5-9-1900
John Mason Bennett        Mary Florence Bogle
A. 25 S. Bland           A. 20 S. Bland
P. W. A. & Bettie        P. R. D. & Annie B.
Oc. Farmer               M. R. R. Sowers

Date: 5-13-1900
Thos J. Chandler    Stella M. Mitchell
A. 21 S. Bland    A. 18 S. Bland
P. Jno W. & R. C.    P. Jerome Mitchell & Octavia Smith
Oc. Farmer    M. J. M. Maiden

Date: 5-20-1900
Jas Henry Hancock    Callie Brown
A. 28 D. Bland    A. 31 W. Bland
P. Geo W. & Julia A.    P. Henry & Elizabeth Newberry
Oc. Farmer    M. A. A. Ashworth

Date: 5-30-1900
Geo W. Love    Sallie A. Walker
A. 23 S. Mercer, WV    A. 24 S. Bland
P. Jas. & Frances    P. Chs. E. & Louisa M.
Oc. Bookkeeper    M. D. A. Daugherty

Date: 6-6-1900
James R. Sea (B)    Susan J. Charlton (B)
A. 50 W. Pulaski    A. 24 S. Mercer, WV
P. Jacob & Cornelia    P. Noah & Sarah
Oc. Farmer    M. Rev. R. W. Hills

Date: 7-18-1900
Andrew A. Overbey    Ada G. Foglesong
A. 27 S. Smyth    A. 17 S. Bland
P. Jno. H. & Emaline    P. H. S. & Mollie A.
Oc. Carpenter    M. R. R. Sowers

Date: 8-9-1900
Edward L. Noonkester    Lucretia Atwell
A. 23 S. Carroll    A. 17 S. Bland
P. Michael & Nancy    P. P.? D. & Mahala V

Oc. Farmer    M. James Mahood

Date: 8-23-1900
Stuart L. Tickle    Ida Jane Burton
A. 21 S. Bland    A. 18 S. Bland
P. Gordon H. & Ellen    P. Giles Henderson &
Dillman    Callie Dixie Kitts
Oc. Farmer    M. W. C. Crockett

Date: 9-2-1900
J. W. Brown    Lucy Annie Lintiman
A. 68 W. Cumberland    A. 46 W. Craig
P. Rob't & Sarah    P. Wm. M. & Lucy Ann Bishop

Oc. Farmer    M. W. K. Neal

Date: 5-16-1900
Dan'l W. Shrader    Alice C. Walker
A. 25 S. Bland    A. 19 S. Mercer, WV
P. T. N. & Alpha    P. Conrad & Emma
Oc. Farmer    M. John A. Smith

Date: 5-19-1900
Hickman Spiller (B)    Callie Davidson (B)
A. 44 S. Wythe    A. 23 D. Mercer, WV
P. Hick. & Esther    P. Hills Jones
Oc. Farmer    M. W. C. Crockett

Date: 6-7-1900
I. M. Hager    Cora Burton
A. 24 S. Bland    A. 16 S. Giles
P. J. J. & Margaret    P. Jno F. & Dicy
Oc. Farmer    M. John A. Smith

Date: 7-4-1900
Lewis G. Shrader    Lola B. Stowers
A. 21 S. Bland    A. 18 S. Bland
P. Jos M. & Emily    P. Geo W. & Mary
Oc. Farmer    M. John A. Smith

Date: 7-24-1900
A. Mathias F. Neal    Naomi Kirby
A. 45 W. Tazewell    A. 31 S. Montgomery
P. Elgin & Annie    P. Jas & Mary
Oc. Carpenter    M. J. M. Maiden

Date: 9-22-1900
Walter Lee Kitts    Sultana R. Muncy
A. 31 S. Bland    A. 25 S. Bland
P. Hyman Matthew &    P. Wm. H. & Helen V.
Crosby D. Kitts
Oc. Farmer    M. R. R. Sowers

Date: 8-23-1900
Chas. J. Ramsey    Ida M. Spangler
A. 25 S. Bland    A. 21 S. Bland
P. Wm. H. & Polly A.    P. Wm. J. & Darthulia

Oc. Farmer    M. J. T. Taylor

Date: 9-20-1900
Sam'l Clay Bogle    Malinda M. Cameron
A. 28 S. Bland    A. 18 S. Bland
P. Freeling Clay &    P. J. W. & E. C.
Martha Jane Bogle
Oc. Farmer    M. John A. Smith

Date: 9-30-1900
John Fortner                    Jane Pauley
A. 65 W. NC                     A. 35 S. Bland
P. Hugh & Rachel                P. Thos G. & Martelia
                                Ann <u>Kitts</u>
Oc. Farmer                      M. K. H. Hackler

Date: 10-3-1900
Miller F. Day                   Lou Pearl Wyrick
A. 19 S. Giles                  A. 18 S. Bland
P. L. M. & Barbara              P. Ralph S. & Anabelle
                                Hancock
Oc. Farmer                      M. W. C. Crockett

Date: 10-5-1900
Chas. W. Warner                 Abigail J. Munsey
A. 24 S. Bland                  A. 18 S. Giles
P. D. C. & Hulda                P. Wm. & Matilda E.
Oc. Farmer                      M. W. C. Crockett

Date: 10-16-1900
C. A. Hagan                     Nellie Thompson
A. 30 S. Floyd                  A. 21 S. Bland
P. Abram & Sallie               P. A. N. & J. Harriet
Oc. Saddler                     M. W. C. Crockett

Date: 10-17-1900
Earsten Sheppard Havens Lillie Woods
A. 26 W. Bland                  A. 19 S. Patrick
P. Elizabeth                    P. Winfield & Lydia
Oc. Farmer                      M. J. T. Taylor

Date: 10-25-1900
Clarence W. Lampert             Lucretia Lampert
A. 19 S. Bland                  A. 17 S. Bland
P. Jas. A. & Clementine         P. W. W. & Rhoda
Oc. Farmer                      M. W. C. Crockett

Date: 11-6-1900
Wesley Morrell                  Mamie Hart
A. 23 S. McDonough, Ill         A. 19 S. Bland
P. Basil & Mattie               P. W. R. & M. V.
Oc. Farmer                      M. W. C. Crockett

Date: 11-21-1900
Clovis B. Wilson                Lousia C. Pruett
A. 22 S. Bland                  A. 16 S. Bland
P. C. H. & Eliza E.             P. J. M. & Elizabeth
Oc. Farmer                      M. T. C. Pulliam

Date: 11-28-1900
Sylvester V. Willis             Victoria Linkous
A. 33 W. Giles                  A. 23 S. Bland
P.                              P. Jno & Isabelle
Oc. Carpenter                   M. W. K. Neel

Date: 12-12-1900
John H. Nunn                    Carrie E. Lambert
A. 22 S. Bland                  A. 19 S. Bland
P. B. L. & Martha L.            P. S. K. & Virginia A.
Oc. Farmer                      M. W. R. Miller

Date: 12-6-1900
Jas H. Clemons                  Emma J. Pugh
A. 19 S. Wythe                  A. 19 S. Bland
P. Chas. & Susan C.             P. R. J. & Sarah J.
Oc. Farmer                      M. J. T. Taylor

Date: 12-10-1900
Hugh M. Fugate                  Ibbie L. T. Repass
A. 24 S. Scott                  A. 26 S. Bland
P. Harvey & Elizabeth           P. F. F. & Malinda
Oc. Farmer                      M. E. L. Addington

Date: 12-25-1900
Isiah W. Wright                 Anna B. Harman
A. 20 S. Bland                  A. 16 S. Bland
P. D. M. & Sarah A.             P. W. N. & Orlenia

Oc. Farmer                      M. W. C. Crockett

Date: 12-25-1900
John M. Scott                   Cynthia Mary Bogle
A. 25 S. Bland                  A. 22 S. Bland
P. E. M. & Mary A.              P. Lorenza Dow &
                                Charlotte <u>Waddle</u>
Oc. Farmer                      M. R. R. Sowers

Date: 12-26-1900
Calvin J. Whisman               Amanda J. Kitts
A. 24 W. Smyth                  A. 22 S. Bland
P. Wiley H. & C. C.             P. Hyman M. & Crosby

Oc. Farmer                      M. Rob't B. Hudson

Date: 12-26-1900
Robt. H. Kitts                  Bertha J. Davis
A. 26 S. Bland                  A. 20 S. Bland
P. Jacob F. & Cynthia J.        P. Henry & Margaret
<u>Wyrick</u>
Oc. Farmer                      M. W. H. Day

Date: 12-27-1900
Hiram G. Fox                  Nannie C. Crabtree
A. 50 W. Smyth                A.   S. Wythe
P. Jno. & Margaret            P.
Oc. Farmer                    M. J. T. Huddle

Date: 1-9-1901
John Henry Crabtree           Sarah N. E. Shannon
A. 20 S. Tazewell             A. 20 S. Tazewell
P. G. W. & Susan              P. Wiley & Sallie J.

Oc. Farmer                    M. W. K. Neel

Date: 1-31-1901
John Henry Epperson           Ida Josephine Corder
A. 29 S. Bland                A. 18 S. Bland
P. Ed. & Drucilla             P. Jas Larkin & Minerva J.
Oc.Farmer                     M. W. C. Crockett

Date: 2-13-1901
Oscar Brown Kelley            Nancy Eller Fortner
A. 21 S. Bland                A. 16 S. Bland
P. M. J. & Mollie             P. S. T. & Mary E.
Oc. Farmer                    M. W. C. Crockett

Date: 2-24-1901
John W. Woods                 Hattie Havens
A. 22 S. Patrick              A. 15 S. Bland
P. Winfield & Mary            P. Elizabeth
Oc. Farmer                    M. J. T. Taylor

Date: 3-7-1901
Lafayette Grayson             Irene Williams
A. 40 W. Bland                A. 22 S. Henry
P. A. J. & Rosalie            P. Wm. M. & Mollie H.
Oc. Farmer                    M. W. C. Crockett

Date: 4-1-1901
James Jackson Brown           Lanna Catherine Bane
A. 34 W. Bland                A. 30 W. Bland
P. America                    P. Jas & Darthulia Wilson
Oc. Farmer                    M. R. R. Sowers

Date: 4-9-1901
Wm. Henry Walker              Lelia S. Walker
A. 21 S. Tazewell            A. 20 S. Bland
P. Wm. P. & Margaret A. P. C. E. & Mary S.
Oc. Saw Milling               M. T. E. Weaver

Date: 1-2-1901
John Wm. Bruce                Hattie Ellen Leedy
A. 21 S. Bland                A. 18 S. Bland
P. J. H. D. & Mary J.         P. Eli & Mary E.
Oc. Farmer                    M. John A. Smith

Date: 1-24-1901
Sam'l Dunn Mustard            Mary Blanche Fry
A. 22 S. Bland                A. 20 S. Bland
P. Wm. Sam'l &                P. Stephen V. & Elizabeth
Hester Adaline Newberry
Oc. Farmer                    M. W. C. Crockett

Date: 2-13-1901
Rush Floyd Robinett           Fannie D. Stowers
A. 23 S. Bland                A. 24 S. Bland
P. M. J. & Rebecca J.         P. Geo W.ash. & Sarah
Oc. Farmer                    M. John A. Smith

Date: 2-13-1901
Jos  Sharitz Umbarger         Ellen Ora Brown Epperson
A. 49 W. Wythe                A. 35 S. Bland
P. Joel & Rhosia              P. Ed. & Drucilla
Oc. Farmer                    M. W. C. Crockett

Date: 3-3-1901
Isaac Frank Dehart            Kizzie Ward Strock
A. 23 S. Bland                A. 24 S. Bland
P. Bolivar & Mary             P. Jno F. & Julia Price
Oc. Farmer                    M. W. C. Crockett

Date: 3-20-1901
Charles Norman Kirby          Lou E. Farley
A. 30 S. Bland                A. 26 S. Wythe
P. Jno W. & Cynthia           P. F. H. & Nancy M.
Oc. Farmer                    M. R. R. Sowers

Date: 4-1-1901
John Mitchell Ramsey          Emma Georgettie Spangler
A. 19 S. Bland                A. 25 S. Bland
P. W. H. & Polly A.           P. Jas & Darthulia
Oc. Farmer                    M. R. R. Sowers

Date: 4-10-1901
Arnold Patton                 Ida M. Austin
A. 22 S. Bland                A. 21 S. Floyd
P. Belle Patton               P. Wm. G. & Elizabeth
Oc. Farmer                    M.   John P. Roach

Date: 4-10-1901
Robt Lineberry Tickle      Lillie Belle Harman
A. 24 S. Bland             A. 22 S. Bland
P. Dan'l Lineberry &       P. Orsova Cecil &
Mary Melissa Bogle         Mary Ann Robinson
Oc. Farmer                 M. W. C. Crockett

Date: 1-9-1901**
Estel P. Lambert           Callie A. French
A. 23 S. Bland             A. 20 S. Bland
P. A. A. & Elizabeth       P. Giles P. & Sarah
Oc. Farmer                 M. T. E. Weaver

Date: 6-19-1901
John Wm. Thompson          Rosa Belle Foglesong
A. 28 S. Bland             A. 24 S. Bland
P. David Flemming &        P. Christopher &
Catherine Young Munsey     Mollie A. Herron
Oc. Farmer                 M. S. S. Weatherly

Date: 7-21-1901
Wm. J. Evick               Maggie Mary Gibson
A. 27 S. Coreda, WV        A. 20 S. Bland
P. W. C. & Addie           P. J. V. & C. V.
Oc. Painter                M. John A. Smith

Date: 8-21-1901
Edward Woodson Shrader     Ada E. Stowers
A. 29 S. Bland             A. 25 S. Bland
P. J. M. & Emily           P. Geo W. & Polly
Oc. Farmer                 M. T. E. Weaver

Date: 9-1-1901
Geo Grayson Wilkinson      Daisy Louisa Fanning
A. 22 S. Carroll           A. 22 S. Bland
P. Rush F. & Nancy J.      P. Wm. W. & Martelia M.
Oc. Farmer                 M. J. T. Taylor

Date: 9-25-1901
Steward Otto Caldwell      Pearlie Grace Sarver
A. 27 S. Mercer, WV        A. 18 S. Bland
P. N. N. & Sarah           P. C. M. & Martha A.
Oc. Farmer                 M. T. E. Weaver

Date: 10-9-1901
Lester Norman Chandler     Nina Jane Wright
A. 21 S. Bland             A. 17 S. Bland
P. Jno W. & Rona C.        P. Doc Wm. McComas
                           & Sarah A. Bruce
Oc. Farmer                 M. Samuel V. Morris

Date: 4-14-1901
Edward Ritter              Alice G. Davis
A. 19 S. Pulaski           A. 19 S. Bland
P. D. S. & Hattie L.       P. Henry & Margaret

Oc. Lumberman              M. W. H. Troy?

Date: 6-13-1901
Moton Minnis               Alice James
A. 25 S. Bland             A. 25 S. Bland
P. Jas. & Sallie           P. Harry & Hannah
Oc. Farmer                 M. W. C. Crockett

Date: 7-10-1901
Emory Jackson (B)          Julia Ann Green (B)
A. 27 D. Bland             A. 20 S. Bland
P. Wint. & Lettie          P. Calib & Vina

Oc. Farmer                 M. W. C. Crockett

Begin Page 43 of Original Book
Date: 8-11-1901
Walter Brown Blankenship   Jennie Belle Robinett
A. 24 S. Bland             A. 17 S. Bland
P. Wash. & Julia           P. Chas & Nickatie
Oc. Farmer                 M. S. V. Morris

Date: 8-29-1901
Walter Simon Foglesong     Virginia Victoria Groseclose
A. 26 S. Bland             A. 24 S. Bland
P. Henry S. & Mollie A.    P. H. C. & L. V.
Oc. Farmer                 M. Rob B. Hudson

Date: 9-19-1901
Jas Blanton Kirby          Hattie Collins
A. 21 S. Bland             A. 19 S. Bland
P. Jno W. & Cynthia E.     P. Sam'l & Margaret
Oc. Farmer                 M. G. A. Connor

Date: 9-25-1901
Hiram Addison Hetherington Sallie Gertrude Bird
A. 26 S. Giles             A. 21 S. Bland
P. G. S. & Mary E.         P. J. H. & M. J.
Oc. Farmer                 M. W. C. Crockett

Date: 10-30-1901
Elbert Marvin Munsey       Lola Kate Foglesong
A. 23 S. Bland             A. 23 S. Bland
P. Jas. Harvey &           P. Christopher &
Margaret L. Hutsell        Mollie A. Herron
Oc. Farmer                 M. S. S. Weatherly

Date: 11-10-1901
Sam'l. V. Ingram          Ettie Waddle
A. 35 S. Bland            A. 27 S. Bland
P. Wm. & Prudy            P. Harvey I & Rhoda B.

Oc. Farmer                M. R. R. Sowers

Date: 11-24-1901
John Henry Keen (B)       Lettie Johnson (B)
A. 59 D. Rockingham,NC    A. 32 S. Bland
P. Simpson Brown &        P. Bud.? & Harriet
Zilpha Keen
Oc. Farmer                M. A. A. Ashworth

Date: 11-28-1901
William Henry Campbell    Mary Adaline Lambert
A. 45 S. Albany, NY       A. 20 S. Bland
P. Wm. Henry & Maud       P. Jas L. & Angline
Oc. Painter               M. R. R. Sowers

Date: 12-4-1901
Leander Dolphni Wyrick    Ida May Hancock
A. 21 S. Mercer, WV       A. 17 S. Bland
P. Sanders & Nancy        P. Wm. Leroy & Mary C.
Oc. Farmer                M. Jacob Smith

Date: 12-19-1901
Wm. Nelson Stinson        Ann Ola Tuggle
A. 26 S. Bland            A. 20 S. Bland
P. S. E. & Mary E.        P. J. M. & Matilda

Oc. Farmer                M. J. F. Hash

Date: 12-19-1901
Otto Verona Harman        Katherine Eve Bogle
A. 25 S. Bland            A. 28 S. Bland
P. Orsova Cecil           P. Lorenza Dow
& Mary Ann Robinson       & Charlotte Waddle
Oc. Farmer                M. F. F. Repass

Date: 12-24-1901
James Henry Harrison Wolf Annie Atwell
A. 24 S. Smyth            A. 22 S. Tazewell
P. G.W.S. & Sarah C.      P. P. D. & M. V.
Oc. Farmer                M. W. H. Troy

Date: 12-25-1901
Thos A. G. Akers          Callie Maiden Hanshew
A. 20 S. Smyth            A. 20 S. Bland
P. Jno L. & Mary A. R.    P. Sam'l S. & M. V.
Oc. Farmer                M. Rob. B. Hudson

Date: 12-25-1901
Edward Holly Waddle       Grace Adaline Steel
A. 27 S. Bland            A. 24 S. Bland
P. Wm. G. & Mary C.       P. H. W. & Josephine
Oc. Farmer                M. W. C. Crockett

Date: 12-25-1901
Geo. Wash. Woodyard       Lula May Linkous
A. 21 S. Bland            A. 19 S. Bland
P. Jno & Rebecca          P. Isabella Linkous
Oc. Farmer                M. J. F. Hash

Date: 12-25-1901
Wiley Abner Chewning      Florence Hamilton
A. 20 S. Giles            A. 18 S. Bland
P. LaF. & M. J.           P. Elizabeth Hamilton
Oc. Farmer                M. A. A. Ashworth

Date: 12-26-1901
Wm. Wade Neece            Edith Blanche Houndshell
A. 28 S. Bland            A. 21 S. Bland
P. Jas M. & Sarah         P. Jos & Margaret A.
Oc. Farmer                M. W. C. Crockett

Begin Page 44 of Original Book
Date: 1-5-1902
Thomas Black (B)          Julia Showalter(B)
A. 19 S. Pulaski          A. 22 S. Pulaski
P. Jno & Kitty            P. Thos & Mary

Oc. Railroading           M. Rev. R.W. Hill

Date: 12-31-1901
Thos Thurman Harman       Lucy Louvicia Mustard
A. 21 S. Bland            A. 18 S. Bland
P. Paris & Martha         P. Joshua Nye & Mary Jones
(Now Dunagan)
Oc. Farmer                M. W. C. Crockett

Date: 1-7-1902
David Avne Ritter         Della Roxey Hamblin
A. 26 S. Pulaski          A. 21 S. Bland
P. D. S. & Hattie         P. Jno S. & Sarah
Oc. Farmer                M. T. S. Johnson

Date: 1-8-1902
Wiley Hobbs (B)           Minnie Edwards (B)
A. 26 S. Bland            A. 23 W. Bland
P. Thos. & Lydia          P. Mack & Ellen Gordon
Oc. Farmer                M. W. C. Crockett

Date: 1-23-1902  
Sam'l Madison Corder    Effie Pearl Hancock  
A. 21 S. Bland               A. 23 S. Bland  
P. Jas. L. & Minerva J.    P. M. L. & M. V.  
Oc. Farmer                M. W. C. Crockett  

Date: 1-29-1902  
Morris Dupree Repass    Gray Virginia Umbarger  
A. 23 S. Bland               A. 17 S. Bland  
P. Fredric F. & Malinda C. P. T. P. & Eliz. A.  
Oc. Farmer                M. W. H. Troy  

Date: 2-12-1902  
Jno David Fortner    Ida Dillman  
A. 21 S. Bland               A. 16 S. Bland  
P. Sam'l T. & Mary E.    P. Geo. & Lucinda  

Oc. Farmer                M. W. C. Crockett  

Date: 2-26-1902  
Milton Wade Farmer    Martha Lou Starling  
A. 23 S. Bland               A. 20 S. Bland  
P. Stephen M. & Fannie R. P. G. W. & Rebecca  
Oc. Farmer                M. John A. Smith  

Date: 3-5-1902  
Kelly Lee Pruett    Agnes Virginia S.Wolf  
A. 20 S. Bland               A. 21 S. Bland  
P. Nancy Jane Pruett    P. Geo & L. J.  
Oc. Farmer                M. J. T. Hash  

Date: 3-12-1902  
Andrew Jackson Robinett Lillie Linkous  
A. 30 S. Bland               A. 16 S. Bland  
P. Prudence Robinett    P. W. J. & Hester  

Oc. Farmer                M. John A. Smith  

Date: 4-30-1902   (Giles)  
John Calvin Melvin    Julia Louellen Mustard  
A. 35 S. Bland               A. 26 S. Bland  
P. Stanford & Mary    P. Harvey &  
Patterson                Marshall Marcia Robinett  
Oc. Farmer                M. W. C. Crockett  

Date: 5-28-1902  
Wm. Thomas Pruett    Sallie Margaret Stowers  
A. 43 W. Bland               A. 38 D. Bland  
P. Henry & Martha    P. Russell & Nancy Walters  
Oc. Farmer                M. J. F. Hash  

Date: 1-29-1902  
John Davis    Kate Chandler  
A. 22 S. Bland               A. 18 S. Bland  
P. J. D. & Margaret    P. J. W. & R. C.  
Oc. Farmer                M. W. C. Crockett  

Date: 2-2-1902  
Frank Haymaker French    Elcy Vicoria Muncy  
A. 17 S. Giles               A. 20 S. Bland  
P. Issac & Rebecca    P. Wm. & Matilda E.  
Oc. Farmer                M. W. R. Miller  

Date: 2-12-1902  
John Marshall Morehead Edna Kate Helvey  
A. 39 W. Bland               A. 27 S. Bland  
P. Dan'l Franklin    P. Wm B. &  
& Isabell Eliz.Saunders    Elizabeth Wheeler  
Oc. Farmer                M. F. F. Repass  

Date: 2-26-1902  
Lewis Stephens (B)    Cora B. Charlton (B)  
A. 26 S. Franklin              A. 21 S. Mercer, WV  
P. Jno & Sarah    P. Jas & Sarah  
Oc. Farmer                M. Cert. not signed;  
                      name of Rev. R. W. Hill in body of cert.  

Date: 3-12-1902  
Stephen Whitly Fox    Bertha Hester Kidd  
A. 27 S. Bland               A. 17 S. Bland  
P. M. A. & N. C.    P. A. R. & Charlotte  
Oc. Farmer                M. John A. Smith  

Date: 4-3-1902  
Walter Harvey Neel    Ninevah "Ninnie"Jane Bogle  
A. 24 S. Bland               A. 25 S. Bland  
P. Alex & Mollie    P. Freeling Clay Bogle  
                      & Martha J. Bogle  
Oc. Farmer                M. John A. Smith  

Date: 5-20-1902  
Ballard Preston McFarland    Blanche Dakota Warner  
A. 47 W. Bland               A. 36 W. Bland  
P. L. D. & Jane    P. Jno & Minerva Repass  

Oc. Farmer                M. R. R. Sowers in Giles  

Date: 5-27-1902  
Anaziah Henderson Blankenship Stella Myrtle Dillow  
A. 21 S. Mercer, WV         A. 19 S. Bland  
P. E. H. & Eliz.    P. Wm. K. & Eliz. M.  
Oc. Miner                M. W. C. Crockett

Date: 6-25-1902
Estel Dunn Mustard          Florence Estella Groseclose
A. 30 S. Bland              A. 24 S. Bland
P. Wiley Newton &           P. A. D. & Parthia A.
Eliz. Caroline Newberry
Oc. Farmer                  M. Robt. B. Hudson

Date: 6-26-1902
Geo Frank Stowers           Naomi Carver
A. 25 S. Bland              A. 23 S. Bland
P. Geo. W. & Mary A.        P. W. W. & Amanda
Oc. Farmer                  M. J. T. Hash

Date: 8-20-1902
Ira Howard Gilliam          Margaret Mary Ann Suiter
A. 24 S. Pulaski            A. 22 S. Bland
P. J. E. & Mandy?           P. P. R. & Margaret
Oc. Saw Milling             M. J. F. Hash

Date: 9-3-1902
Arless Wash. Stowers        Nannie Chole Kirby
A. 20 S. Bland              A. 20 S. Bland
P. Jno C. & Jane            P. Jno W. & Cynthia
Oc. Farmer                  M. W. C. Crockett

Date: 9-7-1902
Lorenzo D. McFarland, Jr. Jessie Bales
A. 25 S. Tazewell           A. 13 S. Tazewell
P. L. Dow & Jane            P. S. S. & B. A.
Oc. Farmer                  M. F. F. Repass

Date: 9-16-1902
Chas W. Tabor               Ida V. Blankenship
A. 24 S. Tazewell           A. 19 S. Bland
P. Wm. J. & Eliz.           P. Wm. E. & Rhoda A.
Oc. Farmer                  M. J. F. Hash

Date: 9-18-1902
Ellison C.Polk              Willie A. Graves
A. 32 W. Hampton, SC        A.31 S. Bland
P. J. L. & E. A.            P. B. D. & Nancy
Oc. Paymaster on R. R.      M. W. C. Crockett

Date: 9-27-1902
Rob't. Madison Cox          Eliza Gracie Cox
A. 25 S. Lee                A. 18 S. Bland
P. A. M. & Catherine        P. Geo. C. & Martha
Oc. Farmer                  M. F. F. Repass

Date: 6-25-1902
Jno Wm. Hoge Bird           Lizzie Irvin
A. 24 W. Bland              A. 27 D. Giles
P. J. H. & M. J.            P. P. & Malinda Anderson
Oc. Farmer                  M. J. F. Hash

Date: 7-10-1902
Jno Ira Hall                Mintie Kitts
A. 21 S. Bland              A. 22 S. Bland
P. Lewis B. & Emily         P. Geo. W. & Martha
Oc. Farmer                  M. R. R. Sowers

Date: 8-21-1902
Sam'l F. Neel               Lelia M. Greever
A. 22 S. Tazewell           A. 22 S. Tazewell
P. Jno. A. & Elizabeth      P. Jno H. & Lettie
Oc. Farmer                  M. D. S. Fox

Date: 9-4-1902
Ephiram Ray Kidd            Julia Crockett Smith
A. 28 S. Bland              A. 21 S. Bland
P. A. T. & R. J.            P. Jno A. & Julia A.
Oc. Farmer                  M. J. F. Hash

Date: 9-12-1902
Sam'l Booten Warden         Myrtle Mary Britts
A. 26 S. Pulaski            A. 21 S. Bland
P. Stuart & Josie           P. Clifton & Mary
Oc. Miner                   M. W. C. Crockett

Date: 9-17-1902
Jas. Walker Lampert         Emma Jane Hall
A. 25 S. Bland              A. 17 S. Tazewell
P. Henry T. & Mary E.       P. Thos M. & Harriet C.
Oc. Farmer                  M. F. F. Repass

Date: 9-24-1902
Benjamin Terry              Laura May Hancock
A. 28 S. Smythe             A. 15 S. Bland
P. Wm. & Eliza              P. M. W. & Mahala
Oc. Farmer                  M. Jacob Smith

Date: 10-2-1902
Chas Mathias Hounshell Lillie May Peak
A. 25 S. Bland              A. 17 S. Bland
P. Henry B. & Martha J.     P. Anderson & Sophia
Oc. Farmer                  M. W. C. Crockett

Date: 10-9-1902
Andrew Bane Woolwine   Mannie E. Groseclose
A. 28 S. Giles          A. 21 S. Bland
P. C. C. & Josephine    P. H. C. & L. V.
Oc. Physician           M. Rob. B. Hudson?

Date: 10-26-1902
Wm. Peyton Mathews      Ida May French
A. 27 S. Carroll        A. 22 S. Bland
P. A. W. & C. V.        P. Jno D. & Willie A.
Oc. Artist              M. Samuel V. Morris

Date: 11-24-1902
Jno Henry Mullins       Mary Peak
A. 28 S. Hawkins, TN    A. 20 S. Bland
P. Mark & Rachel        P. Leander & Mary
Oc. Farmer              M. J. H. Wyse?

Date: 11-27-1902
Geo D. Howard           Nannie A. Hoilman
A. 53 S. New Haven, CT  A. 39 S. Bland
P. Jas & Lucy           P. Jno H. & Jane
Oc. Polisher            M. J. T. Taylor

Date: 12-21-1902
Simon Peter Atwell      Margaret Russell Bogle
A. 21 S. Tazewell       A. 21 S. Bland
P. P. D. & M. V.        P. L. D. & Charlotte
Oc. Farmer              M. F. F. Repass

Date: 12-24-1902
Lorenzo Jno Wilkinson   Debirtia Hancock
A. 40 W. Bland          A. 25 S. Bland
P. Thos. & Malinda      P. Pleas. & Thirza
Oc. Farmer              M. C. L. Stradley

Date: 12-25-1902
Kennon Newman           Lettie Hanshew
A. 21 S. Wythe          A. 15 S. Bland
P. Jno & Eliza          P. Jno T. & M. L.
Oc. Sawmilling          M. W. H. Troy

Begin Page 46 of Original Book
Date: 1-1-1903
Jno. W. Burton          Belle R. Lambert
A. 26 S. Linclon, WV    A. 16 S. Bland
P. H. B. & M. C.        P. S. K. & Virginia A.
Oc. Farmer              M. J. F. Hash

Date: 10-15-1902
Hugh Pruett             Pearlie Roasette Nunn
A. 23 S. Bland          A. 19 S. Bland
P. J. M. & Eliz.        P. B. L. & M. E.
Oc. Farmer              M. J. T. Taylor

Date: 11-15-1902
Jas Lemuel Akers        Maggie Willis
A. 39 W. Giles          A. 21 S. Giles
P. Dandride & Parthena  P. W. A. & Rebecca
Oc. Farmer              M. Jones F. Hash

Begin Page 45 of Original Book
Date: 11-27-1902
Chas Kenndy Bruce             Susan Ettie Foglesong
A. 35 S. Bland                A. 27 S. Bland
P. Jehiel M. & Margaret J.    P. Christopher & Mary E.
Oc. Farmer                    M. R. R. Sowers

Date: 12-18-1902
Jno David Umbarger      Minnie Ettie Foglesong
A. 28 S. Bland          A. 28 S. Bland
P. Wm. & Christina      P. Henry H. & M. N.
Oc. Carpenter           M. R. R. Sowers

Date: 12-24-1902
Jno David DeHart        Lillie Grace Wright
A. 27 S. Pulaski        A. 24 S. Bland
P. Jas B. & Mary C.     P. Chas M. & Cecelia S.
Oc. Farmer              M. C. L. Stradley

Date: 12-24-1902
Estell Hoge Millirons   Ellen Augusta Akers
A. 21 S. Pulaski        A. 23 S. Bland
P. Wm. & Julia          P. Moses & Sallie P.
Oc. Farmer              M. J. V. Hall

Date: 12-24-1902
Thos Rufus Kelley            Maud Petree Bruce
A. 38 S. Giles               A. 21 S. Bland
P. M. W. & Frances M.        P. J. W. & Elizabeth
Oc. Commercial Travler       M. Eugene Blake

Date: 1-1-1903
Millard Baskerville Nunn  Fanny Mae Lambert
A. 22 S. Bland            A. 18 S. Bland
P. B. L. & M. E.          P. S. K. & Virginia A.
Oc. Farmer                M. J. F. Hash

Date: 12-31-1902 James Goins A.18 S. Bland P. Nat. & Biddy. V. Married (Left out)**
Lillie Belle Kelly A. 15 S. Bland P. J. D. & Rebecca Oc. Farmer M. J. E. Bruce

Date: 1-1-1903
Luther B. Scott                 Bertha E. Foglesong
A. 24 S. Bland                  A. 19 S. Bland
P. E. M. & Mary                 P. Christopher & Mary E.
Oc. Farmer                      M. W. H. Troy

Date: 1-18-1903
Wesley W. Lampert               Laura J. Hounshell
A. 55 S. Bland                  A. 41 S. Bland
P. Jas & Mandana                P. H. B. & Martha
Oc. Farmer                      M. G. A. Connor

Date: 2-25-1903
Clarence Dailey Hubble          Martha J. Farley
A. 22 S. Tazewell               A. 21 S. Tazewell
P. J. M. C. &                   P. R. T. & Margaret
Amanda E. V.
Oc. Farmer                      M. W. H. Troy

Date: 3-26-1903
Geo Lockard Smith               Susan Willis
A. 30 W. Bland                  A. 19 S. Bland
P. John & Julia                 P. Alex & Rebecca
Oc. Farmer                      M. J. F. Hash

Date: 4-1-1903
Wm. Henry Bean                  Mary Va. Kimberling
A. 27 S. Bland                  A. 35 S. Bland
P. J. S. C. & Margaret          P. Stephen & Eliza
Oc. Farmer                      M. F. F. Repass

Date: 4-19-1903
Harman Dillman                  Teddy Gertrude Waddle
A. 25 S. Bland                  A. 21 S. Bland
P. Geo. W. & Lucinda J.         P. Wm. G. & Mary
Oc. Farmer                      M. James Mahood

Date: 5-13-1903
Chas. Watson Compton            Lula B. Kegley
A. 25 S. Bland                  A. 21 S. Bland
P. F. M. & Rhoda                P. J. G. & E. Fannie
Oc. Farmer                      M. C. L. Stradley

Date: 5-20-1903
Noah Dow Dillow                 Mary S. Burton
A. 21 S. Bland                  A. 18 S. Bland
P. Emily Dillow                 P. Giles Henderson
                                Callie Dixie Kitts
Oc. Farmer                      M. J. E. Bruce

Date: 1-2-1903
Chas. Newton Hall               Mary Bell Bennett
A. 23 S. Bland                  A. 36 S. Bland
P. Sam'l H. & Mary S.           P. Jno A. & Jane
Oc. Laborer                     M. C. L. Stradley

Date 2-22-1903
Geo. Marvin Cox                 Nannie Texas Brown
A. 22 S. Bland                  A. 18 S. Bland
P. Geo C. & Martha              P. Elijah & M. B.
Oc. Farmer                      M. John A. Smith

Date 3-19-1903
Chas. Rob't Blankenship         Zona Fanning
A. 24 S. Bland                  A. 19 S. Bland
P. Wash. & Julia                P. W. W. & M. M.
Oc. Farmer                      M. J. F. Hash

Date: 3-29-1903
Roach Shields (B)               Fannie Ferguson (B)
A. 21 S. Bland                  A. 21 S. Bland
P. Dick & Lucy                  P. M c & Mary
Oc. Farmer                      M. F. D. Johnson

Date: 4-12-1903
McDowell Clingenpeel            Jennie Prudence Graves
A. 33 S. Floyd                  A. 29 S. Bland
P. Marion & Josephine M.        P. B. D. & Nancy
Oc. Teacher                     M. C. L. Stradley

Date: 5-6-1903
Wm. Reason Oxley                Evelyn Bird Thompson
A. 26 S. Mercer, WV             A. 20 S. Bland
P. Benj. H. & Nancy M.          P. A. N. & J. Harriet
Oc. Farmer                      M. J. E. Bruce

Date: 5-21-1903
E. S. Hancock                   Emily L. Corder
A. 23 S. Bland                  A. 18 S. Bland
P. Geo W. & Sarah               P. Jas. Larkin & Minerva
Oc. Farmer                      M. J. V. Hall

Date: 5-31-1903
Wm Fanning                      Naomi Ellen Stowers
A. 21 S. Bland                  A. 21 S. Bland
P. Geo & Isabella               P. W. G. & Lucinda E.
Oc. Farmer                      M. Samuel V. Morris

Date: 6-10-1903
John Whitman Smith     Mary India Dunn
A. 35 W. Wythe         A. 20 S. Bland
P. Obdiah & Dicie S.   P. Wm. G. & Jane
Oc. Farmer             M. J. E. Bruce

Date: 6-24-1903
Wm. Andrew Davis       Laura Alice Riggsby
A. 29 S. Tazewell      A. 28 S. Bland
P. R. G. & Mary E.     P. W. M. & Mary M.
Oc. Farmer             M. W. G. Troy

Date: 7-19-1903
Jno C. Carpenter       Emma J. Davis
A. 50 S. North Hampton A. 23 S. Bland
P. J. C. & Eliza       P. E. A. & Zarilda

Oc. Farmer             M. J. F. Hash

Date: 7-31-1903
Rob't. Underwood       Maud Gibson
A. 24 S. Franklin      A. 21 S. Bland
P.                     P. J. V. Gibson
Oc. Lawyer             M. J. F. Hash

Date: 8-20-1903
Wm. Henderson Thomas   Birdie Mae Kitts
A. 24 S. Bland         A. 20 S. Bland
P. C. C. & Nannie      P. Breckenridge Harvey &
                       Emma Caroline Bowles
Oc. Farmer             M. A. A. Ashworth

Date: 9-16-1903
L. P. Wohlford         Cannie Sheppard
A. 30 S. Bland         A. 21 S. Bland
P. G. W. & Jane?       P. H.E. & Bessie
Oc. Miller             M. J. T. Taylor

Date: 9-30-1903
Wilburn T. Stitt       Clara E. Walker
A. 23 S. Tazewell      A. 18 S. Bland
P. J. C. & Mary A.     P. Chas. E. & L. M.
Oc. Sawyer             M. W. B. Belcher

Date: 10-6-1903
Lewis A. Thomas        Dora Pruett
A. 24 S. Mercer, WV    A. 19 S. Bland
P. Wayman & Sarah      P. Jno & Sarah
Oc. Farmer             M. John A. Smith

Date: 6-16-1903
C. Nicklas Kimbleton   Naomi Harman
A. 27 S. Pulaski       A. 18 S. Bland
P. Chas. Thos. & Charity  P. Paris & Martha J.
Oc. Rail Roading       M. Geo W. Penley

Date: 7-1-1903
Will Lawrence          Julia Starling
A. 20 S. Bland         A. 19 S. Balnd
P. Wm. & Catherine     P. Jno Sarah
Oc. Farmer             M. John A. Smith

Date: 7-19-1903
Jas. Walter Fanning    Insie Ethel "Dink" Harman
A. 33 S. Bland         A. 27 S. Bland
P. Wm. & Cynthia       P. Jno Wesley
                       & Martha Jane Burton
Oc. Farmer             M. A. A. Ashworth

Date: 8-5-1903
T. L. Shrader          Susie A. Thompson
A. 21 S. Bland         A. 20 S. Bland
P. S. G. & Kate        P. M. A. & M. J.
Oc. Farmer             M. J. F. Hash

Date: 9-16-1903
John Thurman Willis    Hattie Martin
A. 20 S. Giles         A. 15 S. Bland
P. Samuel & Louemma    P. Ruthy Martin

Oc. Farmer             M. W. B. Belcher

Date: 9-19-1903
John H. Gordon (B)     Hattie Johnson (B)
A. 22 S. Bland         A. 14 S. Bland
P. Mc & Ellen          P. Lettie & Buf.
Oc. Farmer             M. Chas E.. Anderson

Date: 9-30-1903
David Tolbert          Nancy Ellen Nunn
A. 20 S. Bland         A. 16 S. Mercer, WV?
P. J B. & Mariah       P. Guss & Lizzie
Oc. Farmer             M. W. B. Belcher

Date: 10-14-1903
John C. French         Dolly McNeil
A. 39 S. Mercer, WV    A. 24 S. Bland
P. G. C. & Mary A.     P. Jacob McNeil
Oc. Lumberman          M. Robt. B. Hudson

Date: 10-25-1903
Wm. Marion Hurt          Dessie N. Duncan
A. 24 S. Tazzewell       A. 22 S. Craig
P. G. W. & Sallie        P. Silas N. & Sallie
Oc. Machinist            M.  John A. Smith

Date: 11-25-1903
Chas Hayton              Lena R. Umbarger
A. 27 S. Smyth           A. 19 S. Bland
P.  Peter                P. R. M. & E. J.
Oc. Carpenter            M. A. H. Gentry

Date: 11-29-1903
Dan'l M. Lambert         Mary Shrader
A. 21 S. Bland           A. 24 S. Bland
P. A. A. & Eliz.         P. I. N. & Alpha

Oc. Farmer               M. G. A. Corner

Begin Page 47 of Original Book
Date: 12-16-1903
Robt. B. Hager           Nancy Eliz. Woodyard
A. 25 S. Bland           A. 19 S. Bland
P. Wm & Martha           P. Jno & Rebecca
Oc. Farmer               M. G. A. Corner

Date: 1-1-1904
John Wm. Tibbs           Belle Lampert
A. 28 W. Smyth           A. 17 S. Bland
P. F. M. & S. J.         P. Jas. L. & Angeline
Oc. Farmer               M. F. M. Shupe

Date: 1-6-1904
Wm. J. Groseclose        Lillie M. Kinzer
A. 31 S. Bland           A. 26 S. Bland
P. J.A.T. & Eliza J.     Geo. W. & Ann E.
Oc. Farmer               M. A. H. Gentry

Date: 1-26-1904
Jas. Milton Hughes       Virginia Austin
A. 47 W. Giles           A. 27 S. Montgomery
P. Andrew & Lydia        P. Wm. G. & Elizabeth A.
Oc. Farmer               M. J. T. Taylor

Date: 3-3-1904
Dan'l Wm. Stowers        Beatrice Duncan
A. 20 S. Bland           A. 18 S. Bland
P. J. H. & Ellen         P. Silas N. & Mellissa

Oc. Farmer               M. John A. Smith

Date: 11-5-1903
Waldo Mamsdville?Dickason (B)  Lizzie Belle Tynes (B)
A. 23 S. Mercer, WV      A. 18 S. Bland
P. Jno & Ellen           P. A. J. & Emma
Oc. Farmer               M.  G. H. Pettis

Date: 11-26-1903
Jas. A. Starling         Abbie Lawrence
A. 26 S. Bland           A. 19 S. Montgomery
P. Jno & Sarah           P. W. A. & Catherine
Oc. Farmer               M. G. A. Corner

Date: 12-9-1903
Jacob D. Trent           Ora Blanche Painter
A. 21 S. Campbell        A. 21 S. B.and
P. Thos H. & C. S.       P. Geo Dabney
                         & Eliz. Nancy Tickle
Oc. Sawmilling           M. C. L. Stradley

Date: 12-23-1903
Meek Hoge Davis          Ressa Chloe Kitts
A. 25 S. Bland           A. 25 S. Bland
P. Jas W. & Mary J.      P. Jacob F. & Cythia J.
Oc. Sawmilling           M.  J. E. Bruce

Date: 1-6-1904
J. D. Goodwin            Mary Dillman
A. 20 S. Tazewell        A. 20 S. Bland
P. S. P. & Flo A.        P. A. J. & America
Oc. Sawmilling           M.  James Mahood

Date: 1-20-1904
Arlington Hicks Neel     Perdica Gray Robinett
A. 23 S. Tazewell        A. 27 S. Bland
P. M. F. & H. L.         P. F. M. & Laulett
Oc. Carpenter            M. W. K. Neel

Date: 2-15-1904
M. R. Roland             Araminta Turner
A. 57 W. Floyd           A. 57 W. Bland
P. Jas. & Frances        P. M. F. & Betsy Hill
Oc. Farmer               M. C. E. Anderson

Date: 3-9-1904
Fred Jay Penley          Gracie Ellen Newberry
A. 25 S. Bunscomb, NC    A. 15 S. Bland
P. Geo Wash. &           P. Sam'l Price &
Adaline Robinett         Malissa Rose Miller
Oc. Farmer               M. George W. Penley

Date: 3-10-1904
Frank Hubert Farmer       Rebecca Jane Starling
A. 19 S. Bland           A. 20 S. Bland
P. S. M. & Fannie R.     P. G. W. & Rebecca

Oc. Farmer               M.  G. A. Corner

Date: 4-27-1904
Henry Grayson Helvey     Martha Ann Miller
A. 21 S. Bland           A. 20 S. Bland
P. Jno Crismond &        P. Rev. Will Rice &
Elizabeth                Emma Jane Morehead
Oc. Farmer               M.  S. V. Morris

Date: 5-18-1904
Harry King               Bessie LeFew
A. 21 S. Pulaski         A. 20 S. Bland
P. Jno N. & Martha L.    P. Jas & Priscilla
Oc. Farmer               M.  J. T. Taylor

Date: 5-25-1904
Wm. Harvey Foglesong     Lena Brown Wilson
A. 24 S. Bland           A. 24 S. Bland
P. Chris. & Mollie       P. Thos. O. & Missouri
Oc. Minister             M. C. L. Stradley

Date: 6-8-1904
Chas Byrnes Wohlford     Maud Eliz. Kegley
A. 29 S. Bland           A. 24 S. Bland
P. Gordon &              P. James Gordon &
Matilda Ann Byrnes       Fannie E. Bird
Oc. Farmer               M. C. L. Stradley

Date: 6-30-1904
Wm. Henry Harrison       Mary Eliz. Burton
Munsey
A. 63 W. Bland           A. 58 W. Bland
P. Jas. & Jemima         P. Jacob & Martha Munsey
Oc. Farmer               M. C. E. Anderson

Date: 7-20-1904
Wm. Alex. Davidson       Nannie  Jane Compton
A. 28 S. Bland           A. 28 S. Bland
P. Jno. A. & Mattie J.   P. F. M. &  Rhoda
Oc. Farmer               M. J. E. Bruce

Date: 8-10-1904
Clyde A. Stinson         Quennie B. Strock
A. 20 S. Bland           A. 22 S. Bland
P. Jno & Hester          P. Jno F. & Julia Price
Oc. Farmer               M. C. L. Stradley

Date: 3-15-1904
Walter Gordon Mustard    Julia Mae Fanning
A. 30 S. Bland           A. 26 S. Bland
P. Harvey R. &           P. Geo.W. &
Mariah Wohlford          Matilda H.
Oc. Merchant             M.  J. T. Taylor

Date: 4-27-1904
Sam'l Rob't Pruett       Louisa Huffman
A. 21 S. Bland           A. 19 S. Craig
P. Wm. & Sallie          P. Jas. A. & Phebe C.

Oc. Farmer               M.  John A. Smith

Date: 5-25-1904
Beverly E. Davis         Pollie C. Wilson
A. 28 S. Bland           A. 19 S. Bland
P. Edward A. & Zarilda A. P. Barnard P. & Hester
Oc. Farmer               M. G. A. Carner

Date: 5-25-1904
Robt L. Chandler         Gussie L. Davis
A. 24 S. Bland           A. 24 S. Bland
P. Hannah Chandler       P. Jno. T. & Mary
Oc. Engineer             M. J. E. Bruce

Date: 6-26-1904
Elbert Trainer Lambert   Cora Cordelia Lambert
A. 28 A. Bland           A. 24 S. Bland
P. A. A. & Mary E.       P. W. H. & Mary E.

Oc. Farmer               M. G. A. Corner

Date: 7-17-1904
Jas W. Dillow            Ella Bruce

A. 38 S. Bland           A. 28 S. Bland
P. Sam'l & Jane          P. Newton & Lucinda
Oc. Farmer               M.  J. E. Bruce

Date: 7-21-1904
W. V. Saunders           Rillie M. French
A. 20 S. Mercer, WV      A. 17 S. Bland
P. W. B. & Manda P.      P. W. P. & Elizabeth
Oc. Farmer               M. S. V. Morris

Date: 8-20-1904
Gordon H. Peery          Lelia Lambert
A. 24 S. Tazewell        A. 22 S. Bland
P. Marion & Maggie       P. Henry W. & Martha  J.
Oc. Sawmilling           M. W. K Neel

Date: 8-21-1904
Jas. Rush Jackson            Daisy Angeline Blankenship
A. 26 S. Wythe               A. 19 S. Bland
P. Ed. & Eliza               P. Jas. P. & Jerusha
Oc. Farmer                   M. Chas E. Anderson

Date: 8-31-1904
Jas L. Miller                Mellie R. Bird
A. 20 S. Bland               A. 20 S. Bland
P. Jasper W. &               P. Austin Lecthel &
Rhoda E.                     Geneva J. Miller
Oc. Farmer                   M. J. T. Taylor

Date: 9-20-1904
Jas. Davidson Honaker        Annie Eliz. Mustard
A. 54 W. Bland               A. 38 S. Bland
P. Peter C. & Mary A.        P. Wesley Newton &
                             Eliz. Caroline Newberry
Oc. Farmer                   M. John A. Smith

Date: 9-21-1904
Andrew Jackson Stowers  Lucy A. Brown
A. 56 W. Tazewell            A. 50 W. Craig
P. Hickman & Sallie          P. Wm M. Bishop
Oc. Farmer                   M. John A. Smith

Date: 10-19-1904
Frank L. Johnson             Willie V. Pruett
A. 21 S. Giles               A. 18 S. Bland
P. Wm. Johnson               P. Jno W. & Sarah L.
Oc. Farmer                   M. John A. Smith

Begin Page 48 of Original Book
Date: 10-16-1904
Geo Wythe Waddle             Nannie Bertie Richardson
A. 37 S. Bland               A. 21 S. Bland
P. Jos & Rhoda               P. J. H. & Emma

Oc. Farmer                   M. C. E. Anderson

Date: 11-6-1904
Geo W.ash.Heath              Ella Perry
A. 24 S. Mercer, WV          A. 20 S. Tazewell
P. J. T. & Minerva           P. M. S. & Maggie
Oc. Sawmilling               M. G. A. Carner

Date: 12-1-1904
Chas. M. Robinett            Arizona Huffman
A. 34 W. Bland               A. 24 S. Craig
P. M. D. & Sarah A.          P. Jas. A. & Phebe C.
Oc. Farmer                   M. H. S. Johnston

Date: 8-25-1904
Harvey Wingo Perkins         Eva L. Clark
A. 21 S. Giles               A. 20 S. Bland
P. Jesse A. & Nancy J.       P. Jno. W. & Martha A.
Oc. Farmer                   M. S. V. Morris

Date: 9-14-1904
Gaston Bailey Stowers        Annie M. Hurt
A. 23 S. Bland               A. 22 S. Bland
P. Sims F. & Mary E.         P. Geo. W. & Sallie

Oc. Farmer                   M. G. A. Corner?

Date: 9-15-1904
Jas M. Linkous               Sallie Belle Stowers
A. 20 S. Bland               A. 20 S. Bland
P. Geo. W. & Attelia         P. Sims F. & Lizzie M.
Oc. Farmer                   M. G. A. Carner

Date: 10-5-1904
John Dunn Finley             Carrie Susan Fanning
A. 21 S. Bland               A. 23 S. Bland
P. J. W. & Nannie            P. W. W. & M. M.
Oc. Farmer                   M. J. T. Taylor

Date: 10-13-1904
Geo W. Blanchett             Dora Isabella Dillow
A. 28 S. Smyth               A. 28 S. Bland
P. Eph. & Lizzie             P. Wm. A. & Nancy E.
Oc. Laborer                  M. John A. Smith

Date: 11-3-1904
John W. Kidd                 Elizabeth May Newberry
A. 28 S. Tazewell            A. 30 S. Bland
P. R. J. & S. A.             P. Henley Chapman
                             & Mollie E. Steel
Oc. Engineer                 M. Geo W. Penley

Date: 11-24-1904
Jas Lowell Lindamood         Ollie Mahood Perkey
A. 22 S. Bland               A. 23 S. Bland
P. Jno. H. & E. C.           P. Wm. & Sophia
Oc. Farmer                   M. F. F. Repass

Date: 12-11-1904
Robt. Ephiram Lee Brick  Ida B. Robinett
A. 35 S. Bland               A. 29 S. Bland
P. Felix & Margaret A.       P. M. J. & Rebecca E.
Oc. Farmer                   M. James Mahood

Date: 12-14-1904
John H. Tibbs                     Nettie Mae Sarver
A. 22 S. Bland                    A. 23 S. Mercer, WV
P. Peter & Ann                    P. Jno & JoAnna

Oc. Farmer                        M. H. S. Johnston

Date: 12-20-1904
James Stephens                    Flora A. Flick
A. 21 S. Giles                    A. 22 S. Bland
P. Sol. B & Ibbie                 P. C. M. & Ettie
Oc. Farmer                        M. Rob. B. Hudson

Date: 12-28-1904
Edward Arthur Rose                Mary Ettie Christian
A. 22 S. McDowell, WV             A. 24 S. Bland
P. Arthur & Maggie                P. M. T. & C. C.
Oc. Car Checker                   M. W. K. Neel

Date: 1-22-1905
Wm Armistead Ashworth Julia Belle Compton
A. 27 S. Bland                    A. 20 S. Bland
P. W. B. & Martha                 P. Jno A. & Mollie B.
Oc. Farmer                        M. J. M. Ashworth

Date: 1-25-1905
Hubert Lyceugus? Suiter  Ada Lee Harman
A. 25 S. Bland                    A. 18 S. Mercer, WV
P. F. I. & Mary Grey              P. C. B. & Callie
Updyke
Oc. Farmer                        M. H. S. Johnston

Date: 2-8-1905
Wm. Robinett Penley               Rosa May Miller
A. 39 S. Bland                    A. 16 S. Bland
P. Geo W. & Adaline               P. Chas W. & Mary Lou
Oc. Farmer                        M. W. R. Miller

Date: 4-12-1905
Fitzhugh Lee Atwell               Cora Lawrence
A. 19 S. Smyth                    A. 21 S. Montgomery
P. Wm. & Belle                    P. W. A. & Catherine
Oc. Farmer                        M. H. S. Johnston

Date: 4-18-1905
J. F. Peak                        Allie Waddle
A. 26 S. Bland                    A. 26 S. Bland
P. J. A. & Sophia                 P. Chas A. & Angeline
Oc. Farmer                        M. R. B. Hudson


Date: 12-16-1904
Newton Anderson Bruce             Nannie B. Bogle
A. 43 W. Wise                     A. 42 W. Bland
P. Joshua Henderson &             P. Andrew Jas. Kitts &
Margaret Anderson Hoge            Nanie Bower Bogle
Oc. Farmer                        M. J. A. Duvall

Date: 12-24-1904
William Chandler (B)              Rossa Bullard (B)
A. 21 S. Bland                    A. 21 S. Bland
P. Hannah Chandler                P. Ransom & Cosby
Oc. Laborer                       M. C. E. Anderson

Date: 1-4-1905
Geo Milo Codding                  Nannie Moore
A. 36 W. Savoy, Mass              A. 24 S. Bland
P. Ebeneezer B. & Emily M.        P. Luther & Laura H.
Oc. Distiller of Oils             M. A. H. Gentry

Date: 1-25-1905
Henry Harman Dillow               Nannie Jane Pauley
A. 28 S. Bland                    A. 19 S. Bland
P. Wm A. & Elizabeth              P. Polly A. Pauley
Oc. Laborer                       M. J. A. Duvall

Date: 2-1-1905
Wm. Doane Green                   Mary Eliz. Bogle
A. 35 S. Bland                    A. 25 S. Bland
P. Robt. Crutchfield&             P. Nye & Cynthia Jane
Addie V. Magruder                 Harman
Oc. Farmer                        M. J.A. Duvall

Date: 3-27-1905
Jacob Humphreys                   Naomi M. McNutt
A. 62 D. Parson, NC               A. 41 W. Pulaski
P. Alex. & Lucy                   P. __ & ____ Saddler
Oc. Blacksmith                    M. Robt B. Hudson

Date: 4-12-1905
Arthur Brown Moore                Etta May Hamilton
A. 24 S. Bland                    A. 24 S. Bland
P. J. B. & Nanie                  P. Saunders & Sallie
Oc. Preacher                      M. A. H. Gentry

Date: 4-20-1905
Jas Augustus Repass               Lucinda Jane Dillman
A. 73 W. Bland                    A. 47 W. Bland
P. Stephen & Rosanna              P. ___ & ____ Hearn
Oc. Farmer                        M. F.F. Repass

Date: 4-26-1905
Sam'l Lee Repass          Ellie F. Lampert
A. 40 W. Bland            A. 23 S. Bland
P. Jas. A. & Lucinda      P. M. F. & Hester

Oc. Farmer                M. F. F. Repass

Date: 5-16-1905
Jas. Wm. Gleason          Bettie Caldwell
A. 36 S. Giles            A. 30 S. Mercer, WV
P. Patrick & Margaret E.  P. N. N. & Sarah

Oc. Farmer                M. H. S. Johnston

Date: 6-1-1905
James S. Brown            Ethel H. Miller
A. 30 S. B.and            A. 17 S. Bland
P. Ballard P. & Lucinda   P. Geo. E. & Ella H.

Oc. Railroading           M. A. H. Gentry

Date: 6-22-1905
Wadsw'th Cannon Hankla    Annie Myrtle Mahood
A. 31 S. Wythe            A. 22 S. Bland
P. Lewis P. & Ella B.     P. Jas & Amanda V.
Oc. Farmer                M. James Mahood

Date: 6-28-1905
Chas French Stowers       Emma Grace Green
A. 40 W. Bland            A. 32 S. Bland
P. Isaac F. & Virginia    P. Robt C. & Adaline
Oc. Farmer                M. J. A. Duvall

Date: 7-11-1905
Edward Jas. Pauley        Nannie Kelly
A. 22 S. Bland            A. 14 S. Carroll
P. G. P. & Sallie         P. J. D. & Rebecca
Oc. Farmer                M. C. E. Anderson

Begin Page 49 of Original Book
Date: 8-6-1905
Chas B. Pruett            Cora B. Akers
A. 23 S. Bland            A. 18 S. Bland
P.Jno W. & Sarah          P. J. L. & Nannie
Oc. Farmer                M. C. E. Anderson

Date: 8-23-1905
Oscar Peyton Copenhaver   Macae Helen Repass
A. 41 S. Smyth            A. 32 S. Bland
P. Peter & Susan C.       P. T. M. & Ibbie T.
Oc. Farmer                M. John S. Henley

Date 5-10-1905
Jas. Gordon Sifford       Vernie Snow Munsey
A. 21 S. Pulaski          A. 23 S. Bland
P. Jas. G. & Lucy K.      P. Harvey J. &
                          Catherine A. Kitts
Oc. Rural Letter Carrier  M. J. A. Duvall

Date: 5-17-1905
Otto Gordon Morehead      Ella Jackson Miller
A. 27 S. Bland            A. 20 S. Wise
P. Leanord Franklin       P. Jas. Byrnes
& Emma Louise Robinett    & Sarah Eliz. Hoge
Oc. Farmer                M. J. A. Duvall

Date: 6-14-1905
Wm. Henry Stafford        Emma Jane Wright
A. 22 S. Bland            A. 23 S. Bland
P. Ralph Montgomery &     P. Chas Monroe
Mary Eliz. Crawford       Cecilia Susan Bussey
Oc. Carpenter             M. A. H. Gentry

Date: 6-18-1905
Stephen A Smith           Hattie G. Hancock
A. 29 W. Bland            A. 16 S. Bland
P. Jno & Jane             P. Geo. W. & Eliza B.
Oc. Sawmilling            M. J. A. Duvall

Date: 7-6-1905
Thos H. Kinser            Marie Powers
A. 74 W. Montgomery       A. 58 S. Bland
P. Philip & Ann           P. Jno Powers
Oc. Farmer                M. A. H. Gentry

Date 7-19-1905
Walter Stephen Newberry   Cynthia Marcia Stuart
A. 25 S. Bland            A. 19 S. Bland
P. Henry & Laura Porter   P. Wm. B.& Sallie Mustard
Oc. Farmer                M. J. T. Taylor

Date: 8-9-1905
James Benj. Carter        Mary Alice Looney
A. 24 S. Tazewell         A. 19 S. Buchanan
P. O. B. & M. L.          P. H. J. & Frances
Oc. Farmer                M. John A. Smith

Date: 8-29-1905
J. H. Stowers             Mollie A. Huffman
A. 56 W. Bland            A. 27 S. Craig
P. Gordon & Sallie        P. Jas. A. & Pheobe
Oc. Farmer                M. H. S. Johnston

Date: 9-9-1905
Bailey Strong
A. 24 S. Monroe, WV
P. Dan'l & Mary E.
Oc. Carpenter & Painter

Nettie M. Pruett
A. 16 S. Bland
P. D. H. & Lucy J.
M. John A. Smith

Date: 9-20-1905
Wm. Saunders Beville
A. 24 S.
P. Robt N. Beville
Oc. Farmer

Price Tibbs
A. 19 S. Bland
P. Jas. & Matilda
M. F. F. Repass

Date: 9-27-1905
Floyd Gillespie Christian
A. 21 S. McDowell, WV
P. M. T. & Cosby
Oc. Railroading

Hattie Jane Carter
A. 21 S. McDowell, WV
P. M. L. & O. B.
M. L. W. Pierce

Date: 10-11-1905
Allen White
A. 24 S. Mercer, WV
P. George White
Oc. Farmer

Willie Minor? French
A. 28 W. Giles
P. A. J. & Judy
M. H. S. Johnston

Date: 10-15-1905
Luther Edmond Lampert
A. 21 S. Bland
P. Jas. A. & Clemintine
Oc. Farmer

Ina Olevi Hancock
A.    S. Bland
P. M. W. & Mahala
M. C. E. Anderson

Date: 10-20-1905
Henry Hanshew
A. 27 S. Bland
P. Sam'l & Marcum?
Oc. Farmer

Callie Hayton
A. 38 S. Smyth
P. Peter & Mary A.
M. John S. Henley

Date: 10-18-1905
Emory Hutsel Wagner
A. 23 S. Bland
P. Wm Foster &
Octavia Vivtoria Munsey
Oc. Farmer

Mollie Eliz. Morehead
A. 21 S. Bland
P. Leonard Franklin &
Emma Louise Robinett
M. A. H. Gentry

Date: 10-25-1905
Wm. N. Looney
A. 31 S. Craig
P. J. B. & Annie

Oc. Farmer

Dove Ora Wilson
A. 25 S. Bland
P. C. H. & Eliza

M. W. K. Neel

Date: 10-31-1905
John Hollins
A. 60 W. Franklin
P. Jas. & Artie
Oc. Farmer

Minta Corner
A. 30 S. Bland
P. James Corner
M. W. R. Miller

Date: 11-15-1905
Stuart Geo. Odell
A. 28 S. Mercer, WV
P. Jacob E. & Minerva
Oc. Asst. Yard Master

Ida Ann Wilson
A. 31 S. Bland
P. Thos. O. & Missouri
M. W. H. Foglesong

Date: 11-12-1905
John Hubble
A. 50 W. Smyth
P. Wm. H. & Betsey
Oc. Farmer

Minnie G. Waddle
A. 22 S. Bland
P. Paris & Mary F.
M. C. E. Anderson

Date: 11-15-1905
John R. Thompson
A. 28 S. Giles
P. I. P. & Amelia
Oc. Farmer

Lizzie Wyrick
A. 21 S. Bland
P. Ralph & L. V.
M. J. T. Taylor

Date: 11-14-1905
Chas Bishop Linkous
A. 26 S. Bland
P. Jno & Izzie

Oc. Carpenter

Lizzie Blanche Rudder
A. 27 S. Bland
P. C. M. & L.J.

M. J. A. Duvall

Date: 11-16-1905
Conley Trigg Dillow
A. 23 S. Tazewell
P. Jas. A. & Frances

Oc. Farmer

Della Eliz. Tickle
A. 21 S. Bland
P. Jack. Nye &
Mary Ann Waggoner
M. J. A. Duvall

Date: 12-6-1905
H. Kemper Rider
A. 32 S. Bland
P. Thos A. & Jennie A.
Oc. Farmer

Victoria Patton
A. 23 S. Bland
P. Robt & Mary
M. J. T. Taylor

Date: 12-7-1905
Chas. Jefferson Stitt
A. 22 S. Tazewell
P. Chas J. & Mary
Oc. Railroading

Lula Belle Atkins
A. 20 S. Mercer, WV
P. H. W. & Edna E.
M. W. K. Neel

Date: 12-24-1905
Dan'l Starling          Mary E. Hager
A. 21 S. Bland          A. 15 S. Bland
P. Jno & Sallie         P. W. A. & Sallie
Oc. Farmer              M.  Not returned withn 30 days

Date: 12-25-1905
John Rob't Wilson       Ada Agnes Dillow
A. 19 S. Tazewell       A. 21 S. Tazewell
P. J. R. & Ossie A.     P. Jas A. & Frances
Oc.Farmer               M. J. A. Duvall

Date: 12-27-1905
Jas Taylor Mitchell     Margaret Eunice Mustard
A. 25 S. Bland          A. 22 S. Bland
P. Timothy Elijah &     P. Jas. Harvey &
Ardelia Jane Wohlford   Marshall Marcia Robinett
Oc. Farmer              M. J. T. Taylor

Date: 12-27-1905
Chas R. Burton          Ressa Mary Dunagan
A. 28 S. Bland          A. 19 S. Bland
P. Pendleton & Jane     P. Wm. & Mary M.
Oc. Farmer              M. Rob. B. Hudscn

Date: 12-27-1905
Rob't Ruble             Gary Akers
A. 22 S. Tazewell       A. 17 S. Tazewell
P. Geo & Mary           P. C. K. & Elizabeth
Oc. Farmer              M. H. S. Johnston

Date: 12-27-1905
Wm. Curtis Haga         Ida Essie King
A. 23 S. Grayson        A. 24 S. Bland
P. Martin Curtis &      P. Wm. Thompson &
Sarah Jane              Nancy Louvicie
Oc. Farmer              M. J. A. Duvall

Begin Page 50 of Original Book
Date: 1-3-1906
Walter Wm. Leffel       Mary Rebecca Eliz. Hornbarger
A. 25 S. Tazewell       A. 21 S. Bland
P. Jacob P. & Frances E.  P. W. P. & Mary C.
Oc. Farmer              M. D. A. Leffel

Date: 1-21-1906
John Keen (B)           Ellen Gordon (B)
A. 59 D. Rockingham, NC  A.56 W. Wythe
P. Zilpha Keen & S. Burres  P. Hickman  Spiller
Oc. Laborer             M.  Geo W. Penley

Date: 1-24-1906
Wm. Loton Croy          Julia Lucille Stinson
A. 27 W. Giles          A. 18 S. Bland
P. David J. & Martha A.  P. John & Hester A.
Oc. Farmer              M. A. H. Gentry

Date: 1-28-1906
Levi Breckenridge Groseclose  Nannie Easter Carter
A. 32 S. Bland          A. 25 S. Tazewell
P. J. A. T. & Eliz. J.  P. W.W. & Rebecca
Oc. Farmer & Lawyer     M. John S. Henley

Date: 1-30-1906
Mc Dan'l Ferguson (B)   Cornelia E. Hogan (B)
A. 24 S. Franklin       A. 19 S. Pulaski
P. Mc. & Mary           P. H. H. & Maud
Oc. Farmer              M.  J. E. Kilgore

Date: 2-20-2906
Augustus Wade Richardson  Laura Jeanette Willis
A. 19 S. Bland          A. 19 S. Bland
P. A. R. & S. V.        P. S. L & Emma
Oc. Farmer              M. C. E. Anderson

Date: 2-24-1906
Thos W. Massie          Lillie Pruett
A. 35 W. Franklin       A. 18 S. Bland
P. Geo. & Martha        P. P. O. & Rhoda A.
Oc. Machinist           M. May not have been used?

Date: 3-1-1906
Jas. Rob't Akers        Ella Meadows
A. 21 S. Bland          A. 21 S. Bland
P. Belle Akers          P. Frank & Eliza
Oc. Farmer              M. John A. Smith

Date: 3-28-1906
Washington C. DeHart    Mary Eliz. Wiley
A. 26 S. Bland          A. 26 S. Bland
P. I. F. & Sophrina     P. E. C. & Mary M.
Oc. Farmer              M. A. H. Gentry

Date: 4-11-1906
William Gray            Emily P. King
A. 23 S. Pulsaki        A. 21 S. Bland
P. James & Ellen        P. Wm. T. & Nanzy L.
Oc. Farmer              M. J. A. Duvall

Date: 4-17-1906
Harlow Greever
Groseclose
A. 30 S. Bland
P. Geo W. & Christina
Oc. Farmer

Julia A. B. Thompson

A. 25 S. Bland
P. H. G. Thompson
M. H. S. Johnston

Date: 11-25-1906
Jas. Ward Morehead
A. 26 S. Bland
P. Leonard Franklin
& Emma Louise Robinett
Oc. Carpenter

Bessie May Helvey
A. 18 S. Bland
P. Lorenza Dow
Sarah Ann Eliz. Miller
M. A. H. Gentry

Date: 5-2-1906
David Glenn Lampert
A. 25 S. Bland
P. W. W. & S. J.

Oc. Farmer

Corsie Va. Hounshell
A. 23 S. Bland
P. Jos & Margaret

M. Rob't B. Hudson

Date: 5-23-1906
William Nye Tickle
A. 21 S. Bland
P. Jackson Nye &
Mary Ann Waggoner
Oc. Farmer

Lizzie Mabel Hancock
A. 18 S. Bland
P. Ollie Hancock

M. C. E. Anderson

Date: 6-3-1906
George Naff Hart
A. 20 S.Bland
P. Wm. R. & Marie
Oc. Farmer

Sarah Pearl Blankenship
A. 21 S. Bland
P. Berry & Addie
M. F. F. Repass

Date: 6-13-1906
Sam'l Edward Gibson
A. 23 S. Bland
P. Geo & Nancy
Oc. Farmer

Rosa Victoria Neel
A. 17 S. Bland
P.
M. H. S. Johnston

Date: 6-20-1906
Wiley Pruett
A. 20 S. Bland
P. W. T. & Nancy
Oc. Farmer

Ella Gibson
A. 20 S. Bland
P. Geo & Nancy
M. H. S. Johnston

Date: 5-9-1906
Daily Harman Nunn
A. 21 S. Bland
P. B. L. & M. E.
Oc. Farmer

Hattie J. Richardson
A. 23 S. Bland
P. C. W. & Bettie
M. George W. Penley

Date: 6-20-1906
Eugene T. King
A. 22 S. Pulaski
P. H. N. & D. E.
Oc. Laborer

Mary Veta LeFew
A. 19 S. Bland
P. J. M. & Prescilla
M. J. T. Taylor

Date: 6-20-1906
Harry W. Jones
A. 25 S. Tazewell
P. W. D. & Annie
Oc. Farmer

Mattie Kate Thompson
A. 20 S. Bland
P. Geo. W. & Martha
M. H. S. Johnston

Date: 6-24-1906
Sam'l R. Harden
A. 19 S. Bland
P. S. H. & Fannie D.

Oc. Farmer

Nora C. Edwards
A. 19 S. Bland
P. Chas.&

M. James Mahood

Date: 6-27-1906
Henry Franklin Helvey
A. 22 S. Bland
P. Jno. Kennerly &
Luvenia M. Pruett
Oc. Farmer

Woodie Belle Morehead
A. 23 S. Bland
P. Gordon Andrew &
Mary Isobell Miller
M. A. H. Gentry

Date: 6-28-1906
Geo W. Thompson
A. 20 S. Giles
P. Jas & Mary

Oc. Laborer

Orgie Pauley
A. 17 S. Bland
P. G. P. & Sallie

M. Rob't B. Hudson

Date: 7-3-1906
Joseph Dillow
A. 19 S. Bland
P. J. F. & Lonie

Oc. Laborer

Minnie Neel
A. 25 S. Bland
P. Wm. Melvin &
Barbara Jane Neel?
M. H. S. Johnston

Date: 7-26-1906
Henry Robinett
A. 22 S. Bland
P. Chas & Nickatie
Oc. Laborer

Ossa Larance
A. 17 S. Bland
P. W. A. & Cath.
M. W. B. Belcher

Date: 7-29-1906
Dan'l Starling
A. 21 S. Bland
P. Jno & Sarah
Oc. Farmer

Della Hager
A. 16 S. Bland
P. Rob't L. & Matilda
M. S. V. Morris

Date: 8-19-1906
Mazappa Cooley Tibbs — Margaret Angaline Groseclose
A. 35 W. Bland — A. 24 S. Bland
P. Jno & Christina — P. Rebecca Groseclose
Oc. Clerk in Store — M. John S. Henley

Date: 8-23-1906
A. S. Heileman — Lena Etta Kidd
A. 27 S. McDowell, WV — A. 25 S. Bland
P. Frederick & Mariah — P. G. W. & M. C.
Oc. Farmer — M. John A. Smith

Date: 8-29-1906
Wm. Pepper Kinder — Lula A. Gibson
A. 34 S. Wythe — A. 25 S. Bland
P. — P. Ed. B. & Bettie Gibson
Oc. Lumberman — M. H. J. Johnston

Date: 9-19-1906
Geo Shannon Dillow — Mellie Ludemia Dillow
A. 20 S. Bland — A. 15 S. Bland
P. Jas. A. & Frances A. — P. J. F. & A. V.
Oc. Farmer — M. J. A. Duvall

Date: 9-18-1906
Leonard D. Queen — Mary R. Fortner
A. 32 W. Braxton, WV — A. 26 S. Bland
P. Armstead & — P. Erastus M. & S. J.
Mary A. Queen
Oc. Lumberman — M. H. J. Johnston

Date: 10-4-1906
Wm. Bascomb Allen — Lillie Fay Foglesong
A. 49 W. Giles — A. 28 S. Bland
P. Wm. B. & Hannah — P. H. S. & Mollie
Oc. Farmer — M. James Mahood

Date: 10-18-1906
Henry Grayson Helvey — Naomi Steward Miller
A. 23 W. Bland — A. 16 S. Bland
P. Jno C. & Elizabeth — P. Rev. Will Rice & Emma
Bruce — Jane Morehead
Oc. Farmer — M. F. F. Repass

Date: 10-17-1906
Wylie Winton Kidd — Effie Gray Kidd
A. 37 S. Bland — A. 24 S. Bland
P. E. S. & Clara — P. J. M. & Margaret A.
Oc. Farmer — M. H. S. Johnston

Date: 10-17-1906
Jos L. Lampert — Littie Baugh
A. 26 S. Bland — A. 25 S. Tazewell
P. Henry T. & Mary — P. David M. & Nickatie L.
Oc. Farmer — M. James Mahood

Date: 10-25-1906
Wiley Addison Wolf — Rosa May Willis
A. 23 S. Bland — A. 19 S. Bland
P. Geo & Eliza — P. W. A. & Rebecca
Oc. Farmer — M. H. S. Johnston

Date: 10-23-1906
Arthur Damerel (B) — Effie Brown (B)
A. 24 S. Bland — A. 17 S. Giles
P. Sam & Eliza — P. Eva Brown
Oc. Laborer — M. J. T. Taylor

Date: 11-14-1906
Ward Sheffey Harman — Ethel Pearl Munsey
A. 22 S. Bland — A. 22 S. Bland
P. Orsova Cecil & — P. Harvey J. &
Mary Ann Robinson — Catherine A. Kitts
Oc. Farmer — M. Geo B. Draper

Date: 11-28-1906
Henry Hampton Davis — Victoria Agnes Vandegrift
A. 22 S. Bland — A. 30 W. Bland
P. Henry & Margaret — P. J. T. & Mary Davis
Oc. Farmer — M. Geo B. Draper

Date: 12-26-1906
Oliver W. Crabtree — Lula H. Davis
A. 28 S. Tazewell — A. 23 S. Bland
P. G. W. & Sue A. — P. E. A. & Zarilda
Oc. Farmer — M. W. K. Neel

Begin Page 51 of Original Book
Date: 12-28-1906
Luther Burton — Ella May French
A. 23 S. Giles — A. 16 S. Bland
P. Dock & Dicey — P. Rufus A. & Frankie J.
Oc. Farmer — M. S. V. Morris

Date: 1-5-1907
Frank Ross — Isora May Clark
A. 26 S. Italy — A. 19 S. Bland
P. — P. Jno. C. & Martha
Oc. Railroading — M. S. V. Morris

Date: 1-9-1907
Thos H. Hoilman          Nettie Harman
A. 41 S. Bland           A. 37 W. Bland
P. Jno. H. & Jane        P. Rob't & Mary Patton
Oc. Jeweler              M. J. T. Taylor

Date: 1-25-1907
Anderson Preston Fortner Ella Maria Lampert
A. 29 S. Bland           A. 25 S. Bland
P. Jno & Nancy           P. W. W. & Rhoda E.
Oc. Farmer               M. James Mahood

Date: 3-6-1907
Edmond Barbour Fry       Laura Va. Waddle
A. 23 S. Bland           A. 26 S. Bland
P. S. V. & Margaret E.   P. W. G. & Mary C.
Oc. Farmer               M. G. B. Draper

Date: 4-18-1907
James Jackson Nunn       Sallie J. Wiley
A. 27 S. Bland           A. 16 S. Bland
P. W. G. & Elizabeth     P. N. J. & Ollie C.

Oc. Farmer               M. S.W.Bourne

Date: 5-23-1907
David M. Wilson          Sallie A. Baugh
A. 39 S. Bland           A. 33 S. Tazewell
P. Thos. O. & Missouri J. P. D. M. & Nickatie
Oc. Farmer               M. L. M. Neel

Date: 6-7-1907
Isaac Wiley Dillow       Willie Gray Kitts
A. 26 S. Bland           A. 20 S. Bland
P. Sam'l & Barbara J.    P. Harvey Hiram &
                         Lucinda C. McFarland
Oc. Laborer              M. G. B. Draper

Date: 7-9-1907
Spencer Nisewander       Bertha Sublett
A. 22 S. Bland           A. 22 S. Bland
P. Henley & Rhoda        P. Jos & Minnie
Oc. Laborer              M. G. T. Jordan

Date: 7-31-1907
Jno H. Ashworth          Mabel Katherine Bruce
A. 27 S. Bland           A. 22 S. Bland
P. Wm. B. & Martha E.    P. J. W. & Lizzie
Oc. Teacher              M. W. M. Morrell

Date: 1-25-1907
Jno Lorenzo Nelson       Ada J. French
A. 24 S. Bland           A. 17 S. Bland
P. R. R. & Lizzie        P. Wm. A. & Laura
Oc. Farmer               M. W. K. Neel

Date: 2-17-1907
W. Newton Neel           Mabel Claire Bird
A. 25 S. Tazewell        A. 21 S. Bland
P. Rayburn & Mary        P. J. B. & L. V.
Oc. Sawmilling           M. S. W. Bourne

Date 3-26-1907
Arthur Gleaves Repass    Maggie M. Groseclose
A. 36 S. Bland           A. 25 S. Bland
P. I. M. & Ibbie T.      P. Jno. & Emaline
Oc. Farmer               M. L. M. Neel

Date: 4-24-1907
Jos. Hoge Hetherington   Cynthia E. Wohlford
A. 30 S. Mercer, WV      A. 24 S. Bland
P. Jos. P.  Juliet E.    P. Gordon & Matilda Ann
                         Byrnes
Oc. Lumbering            M. J. T. Taylor

Date: 5-30-1907
Thos Patton              Lucy May Hamilton
A. 19 S. Bland           A. 18 S. Bland
P. J. R. & Mary M.       P. Elizabeth Hamilton
Oc. Farmer               M. Geo B. Draper

Date: 7-3-1907
J. K. Robertson          Bessie Willis
A. 24 S. Giles           A. 21 S. Bland
P. Geo & Susan           P. Sam'l L. & Emma

Oc. Laborer              M. Geo. B. Draper

Date: 7-21-1907
Jas H. Lampert           Nannie E. Hayton
A. 35 S. Bland           A. 32 S. Bland
P. Jas. A. & Nancy       P. Thos & Ann
Oc. Farmer               M. S. M. Neel

Date: 8-7-1907
Stephen Winton Bourne    Rosa Belle Davis
A. 40 W. Grayson         A. 20 S. Bland
P. Wiley B. & Caroline   P. Edward A. & Zarilda
Oc. Minister             M. G. A. Maiden

Date: 8-14-1907
Chas W. Sluss | Annie Ella Cassell
A. 20 S. Tazewell | A. 21 S. Bland
P. Ragis Sluss | P. Jas.F. & Christina

Oc. Farmer | M. P.H.E. Derrick

Date: 9-11-1907
Chas Henry Neel | Annie Umbarger
A. 21 S. Bland | A. 20 S. Bland
P. Alex & Mary | P. Henry & Jane
Oc. Farmer | M. L. M. Neel

Date: 9-24-1907
Jno. Richard Christian | Myrtle Atkins
A. 24 S. McDowell, WV | A. 19 S. Bland
P. M. T. & Causby | P. H. W. & Edna E.

Oc. Farmer | M. H. S. Johnston

Date: 10-24-1907
Jas. Dow Wyrick | Bettie Wynn
A. 22 S. Bland | A. 30 S. Bland
P. Ralph B. & L. V. | P. Jos & Kate
Oc. Farmer | M. Returned not used

Date: 11-12-1907
Jas. T. Clark | Bertie May Burton
A.   S. Bland | A.   S. Bland
P. Richard & Susan | P. Pauline Burton
Oc. Farmer | M. S. V. Morris

Date: 11-14-1907
Jas. J. Davidson | Lena Mabel Grayson
A. 29 S. Bland | A. 23 S. Bland
P.J.no A. & Mattie J. | P. Jas F. & Lucy A.
Oc. Physician | M. Geo B. Draper

Date: 11-27-1907
Wm. Hezekiah Gollehone | Pearl McNutt
A. 28 S. Bland | A. 17 S. Balnd
P. I. T. & M. V. | P. W. T. & Nannie
Oc. Carpenter | M. L. M. Neel

Begin Page 52 of Original Book
Date: 11-28-1907
Jas Duncan Brown | Anna Myrtle Spangler
A 26 S. Tazewell | A. 23 S. Bland
P. Elijah & Malinda | P. Jas.W. & Darthulia A.
Oc. Farmer | M. James Mahood

Date: 8-28-1907
Way Penley | Agnes Wohlford
A. 31 W. Bland | A. 27 S. Bland
P. Geo Wash & | P. Gordon & Matilda
Adaline Robinett | Ann Byrnes
Oc. Farmer | M. Geo T. Jordan

Date: 9-17-1907
Jas. R. Childress | Sallie M. Owens
A. 18 S. Buchanan | A. 21 S. Buchanan
P. Jno. W. & Sarah A. | P. Floyd & Elzeny
Oc. Farmer | M. H. S. Johnston

Date: 10-23-1907
Jno Rob't Shrader | Nannie Bettie Helvey
A. 24 S. Bland | A. 18 S. Bland
P. S. G. & Katie | P. Wm. Baltzer, Jr. &
 | Elizabeth J. Wheeler
Oc. Farmer | M. S. W. Bourne

Date: 10-28-1907
Roy Eakin | Nannie Peery Christian
A. 19 S. Barbour's Creek? | A. 19 S. Tazewell
P. Jno J. & Mariah L. | P. M. T. & Causby
Oc. Railroading | M. W. K. Neel

Date: 11-12-1907
Henry King | Dora Agnes Thompson
A. 38 S. | A. 19 S. Bland
P. ___ & ___ King | P. Jas & Mary
Oc. Farmer | M. S. W. Bourne

Date: 11-21-1907
Jasper Newton Walker | Bertie Olivia Green
A. 41 S. Bland | A. 31 S. Bland
P. Thos. F. & Julia A. | P. Rob't C. & Adaline
Oc. Physician | M. Geo B. Draper

Date: 11-27-1907
Doll Ruble | Martha M. Lawrence
A. 40 W. Caball, WV | A. 36 W. Bland
P. Chas & Cynthia | P. Patton G. & Malinda Robinett
Oc. Driver? | M. S. W. Bourne?

Date: 12-2-1907
Harris Ruble | Ida May Stowers
A. 24 S. Tazewell | A. 21 S. Bland
P. Geo & Mary | P. A. C. & Amanda V.
Oc. Railroading | M. S. W. Bourne

Date: 12-4-1907
Thos Wisdon Lampert     Alice Frances Hounshell
A. 26 S. Bland          A. 21 S. Bland
P. Wesley W. & Levni J.  P. Jos & Margaret
Oc. Farmer              M. James Mahood

Date: 12-5-1907
Fred Blankenship        Ola B. Wright
A. 23 S. Bland          A. 18 S. Bland
P. Berry & Ardelia      P. M. E. & L. J.
Oc. Farmer              M. F. F. Repass

Date: 12-23-1907
James E. Ratliff        Bower Dillow
A. 53 W. Smyth          A. 60 W. Bland
P. Wayman & Polly       P. Jno & Rebecca Pauley

Oc. Carpenter           M. J. G. Reveley

Date: 12-25-1907
John Lockhart Bogle, Sr.  Nannie White Miller
A. 35 S. Bland          A. 25 S. Bland
P. John & Julia Bralley  P. Dan'l A. & Molly
                           Newberry
Oc. Farmer              M. Geo  T. Jordan

Date: 12-31-1907
David Henry Carl Pauley  Sheffey Margaret Frances Collins
A. 24 S. Bland          A. 20 S. Bland
P. Gratton Crockett &   P. Jno H. & Gilley Bradley
Mary Geneva Kitts
Oc. Farmer              M. J. E. Bruce

Date: 1-8-1908
Jas D. Helvey           Anne K. Shrader
A. 24 S. Bland          A. 23 S. Bland
P. W. B. & E. J.        P. S. G. & Kate
Oc. Farmer              M. F. F. Repass

Date: 1-15-1908
Chas. Wm. Clemons       Ella Dillow
A. 50 D. Wythe          A. 32 W. Bland
P. Ephriam & Margaret   P. W. N. & Lucinda
Oc. Laborer             M. G. B. Draper

Date: 1-17-1908
Frank Lee Dunn          Minnie Wayne McColgan
A. 24 S. Bland          A. 22 S. Bland
P. D. W. & Cynthia      A. W. F. & Mary G.
Oc. Publisher           M. G. B. Draper

Date: 2-12-1908
Hugh Flemming Miller    Margaret Jane Newberry
A. 18 S. Bland          A. 21 S. Bland
P. R. J. & Mary         P. Henry & Laura M. Porter
Oc. Farmer              M. G. B. Draper

Date: 3-2-1908
J. J. Lambert           Bettie Spangler
A. 66 W. Wythe          A. 66 W. Tazewell
P.___?___ Lambert       P. Jno. J. & Margaret Greever
Oc. Stone Mason         M. J. G. Reveley

Date: 3-25-1908
Sam'l Mullins           Mary Emma Hall
A. 21 S. Mercer, WV     A. 17 S. Bland
P. Jos & Jane           P. Sam'l H. & Mary S.
Oc. Printer             M. J. G. Reveley

Date: 3-29-1908
Hubert R. Steel         Woody Lee Farmer
A. 17 S. Bland          A. 18 S. Pulaski
P. Telia Steel          P. Jno. T. & Jennie
Oc. Farmer              M. Geo B. Draper

Date: 4-5-1908
Henley H. Harden        Mary A. Baugh
A. 29 S. Bland          A. 31 S. Tazewell
P. Sam'l H. & Frances V.  P. D. M. & Nicketie
Oc. Farmer              M. James Mahood

Date: 4-9-1908
Tobias Frank Neese      Annie McHaffee
A. 26 S. Bland          A. 27 S. Bland
P. Jas. M. & Sarah      P. Loudemia McHaffee
Oc. Farmer              M. S. V. Morris

Date: 4-12-1908
Levi W. Lambert         Linnie Jane Shrader
A. 23 S. Bland          A. 18 S. Bland
P. A. A. & Eliz.        P. S. G. & Nicketie
Oc. Farmer              M. W. A. Warner

Date: 4-16-1908
Chas S. Groseclose      Grace Williams
A. 26 S. Bland          A. 18 S. Bland
P. Jno & Emaline        P. A. J. & M. L.
Oc. Farmer              M. L. M. Neel

Date: 4-22-1908
Jno Wm. Patton      Susan Margaret Davis
A. 30 S. Bland      A. 18 S. Pulaski
P. J. R. & Mary      P. J. E. & Ollie E.
Oc. Farmer      M. J. T. Taylor

Date: 5-20-1908
Jacob Franklin Kitts      Lillie Jane Hamblin
A. 65 W. Wythe      A. 22 S. Bland
P. Andrew J. & Mary      P. W. J. & Ollie
Leedy
Oc. Farmer      M. L. M. Burris

Date: 6-2-1908
Winfield Marcellus      Lena Eliz. Crabtree
Harden
A. 25 D. Bland      A. 16 S. Bland
P. Missouri Kitts      P F. A. & S. J.
Oc. Farmer      M. L. W. Ellison

Date: 7-28-1908
Hoil Kemper Rider      Flora Belle Brown
A. 34 W. Bland      A. 20 S. Bland
P. T. A. & Jennie A.      P. J. J. & Missouri
Oc. Farmer      M. James Mahood

Date: 8-26-1908
Abraham B. Jarrett      Osciola Euclid Meadows
A. 31 S. Madison. NC      A. 30 W. Missouri
P. Jacob P. & Susana      P. E. B. & A. B. Gibson
Oc. Engineer      M. S. W. Bourne

Date: 9-8-1908
H. C. Atwell      Bessie E. Hagee
A. 20 S. Tazewell      A. 18 S. Bland
P. Willis & Belle      P. W. A. & S A.
Oc. Farmer      M. S. W. Bourne

Date: 10-4-1908
Simon Baugh      Elizabeth Turley
A. 30 S. Tazewell      A. 20 S. Tazewell
P. D. M. & Nicketie      P. Reese & Margaret U.
Oc. Farmer      M. L. M. Neel

Begin page 53 of Original book
Date: 10-29-1908
John Henry Townsand      Josie Pauley
A. 21 S. Watauga, NC      A. 20 S. Bland
P. Jno A. & Malinda      P. Creed F. & Martelia Kitts
Oc. Farmer      M. Jacob Smith

Date: 5-6-1908
Elijah Harner      Sadie A. Musser
A. 57 W. McDowell, WV      A. 34 S. Smyth
P. Adam & Elizabeth      P. G. W. & Leveni
Oc. Farmer      M. L. M. Neel

Date: 6-3-1908
Thos Millard Davis      Ada Lee Stimson
A. 23 S. Bland      A. 23 S. Bland
P. Edward A. & Zarilda      P. Sam'l L. & Mary E.
Oc. Farmer      M. S. W. Bourne

Date: 7-16-1908
Thomas Lawrence      Emma Starling
A. 18 S. Montgomery      A. 19 S. Bland
P. W. A. & Catherine      P. Jno. & Sarah
Oc. Farmer      M. S. W. Bourne

Date: 8-1-1908
Jno Calvin Ragland      Claudine Mae Pindar
A. 23 S. Petersburg      A. 21 S. New Haven, CT
P. Emmett & Rosa      P. Allen & Hattie
Oc. Theatrical Business      M. G. B. Draper

Date: 9-2-1908
Andrew Clark      Izora Stowers
A. 24 S. Bland      A. 22 S. Bland
P. Richard, Jr. & Mary J.      P. Allen & Victoria
Oc. Farmer      M. S. W. Bourne

Date: 9-13-1908
Thomas Powers      Isabelle Jones
A. 47 S. Bland      A. 38 W. Bland
P. John & Julia      P. Nancy Corner
Oc. Farmer      M. Geo T. Jordan

Date: 10-22 -1908
Wm. Henry Gibson      Mollie Ellen Richardson
A. 21 S. Bland      A. 16 S. Bland
P. Jas & Caroline V      Riley & L. V.
Oc. Farmer      M. S. W. Bourne

Date: 10-28-1908
Walter W. Cox      Mary Harner
A. 20 S. Bland      A. 20 S. McDowell, WV
P. Geo C. & Martha      P. B.W.P. & Nannie
Oc. Farmer      M. James Mahood

Date: 10-28-1908
Luther Watson Whittaker Anna E. Wright
A. 24 S. Giles
A. 22 S. Bland
P. J. W. & Jane
P. Chas. Monroe &
Cecelia Susan Bussey
Oc. Farmer
M. W. R. Miller

Date: 10-31-1908
John Alex. Newberry
Catherine Eaton
A. 21 S. Bland
A. 21 S. Giles
P. Sam'lP. & Rosa M
P. E. D. & Dora
Oc. Farmer
M. J. G. Reveley

Date: 11-12-1908
Jno Sam'l Bernard
Eulah Lee Gordon
A. 30 S. Bland
A. 20 S. Bland
P. S. H. & E. H. Pelter
P. F. M. & Ella
Oc. Farmer
M. J. T. Taylor

Date: 11-26-1908
Eli Franklin Umbarger
Minerva Katherine Walker
A. 27 S. Bland
A. 22 S. Tazewell
P. T. P. & Elizabeth A.
P. Jno S. & Nannie
Oc. Farmer
M. James Mahood

Date: 12-9-1908
Wm. Lambert
Etta May Kitts
A. 24 S. Wythe
A. 23 S. Bland
P. Mary Lambert
P. Henry Hiram & Lucinda
Lucinda McFarland
Oc. Laborer
M. James Mahood

Date: 12-23-1908
Lemuel Hezekiah Tickle Ida Louise Blankenship
A. 21 S. Bland
A. 20 S. Bland
P. Jno Nye &
P. Wm. Jack. & Lutheria
Mary Ann Waggoner
Dillow
Oc. Farmer
M. J. E. Bruce

Date: 1-26-1909
Wm. Gordon Steel
Emma Harden
A. 42 D. Bland
A. 25 S. Bland
P. Wayman & Jane
P. Sam'l H. & Francis
Oc. Farmer
M. W. D. Shupe

Date: 2-4-1909
John Thomas Baugh
Bettie Maiden Kimberlin
A. 25 S. Tazewell
A. 28 S. Bland
P. D. M. & Nicketie
P. E. H. & Louisa C.
Oc. Farmer
M. F. F. Repass

Date: 10-29-1908
John P.? Duncan
Sallie K. Herron
A. 21 S. Monroe, WV
A. 26 S. Sullivan, TN
P. Ananias & Evaline
P. Wm. & Jennie
Wood
Oc. Farmer
M. J. E. Bruce

Date: 11-4-1908
David G. Stowers
Ollie D. Clark
A. 26 S. Bland
A. 18 S. Bland
P. Allen C. & Victoria
P. R. M. & M. J.
Oc. Farmer
M. W. A. Warner

Date: 11-25-1908
Sam'l Leslie Umbarger
Vinnie Myrtle Baugh
A. 21 S. Bland
A. 18 S. Bland
P. Rufus M. & Eliza J.
P. D. M. & Nicketie
Oc. Farmer
M. James Mahood

Date: 12-2-1908
Wylie Van D. Meadows Dana C. Hambliln
A. 24 A. Bland
A. 20 S. Bland
P. J. W. & Ida
P. J. S. & Sarah C.
Oc. Farmer
M. S. M. Burris

Date: 12-23-1908
Walter Caldwell
Virgie Sarver
A. 28 S. Bland
A. 21 S. Bland
P. N. N. & Sarah A.
P. C. M. & N. J.

Oc. Farmer
M. N. B. Phillips

Begin Page 54 of Original Book
Date: 1-21-1909
Chas H. Hall
Bessie Harden
A. 19 S. Tazewell
A. 19 S. Bland
P. Thos & Jennie
P. Sam'l H. & Frances

Oc. Farmer
M. James Mahood

Date: 1-24-1909
Lafayette Grayson
Nannie Lee Bird
A. 47 W. Bland
A. 35 W. Bland
P. A. J. & R. V.
P. C. R. & Caroline Burton
Oc. Farmer
M. James Mahood

Date: 2-18-1909
Luther Bittle Spangler
Kate Ramsey
A. 22 S. Bland
A. 20 S. Bland
P. W. J. & Darthulia
P. W. H. & Polly A.
Oc. Farmer
M. N. B. Phillips

114

Date: 2-23-1909
Geo W. Starling, Jr.    Lizzie Wolf
A. 33 S. Bland    A. 24 S. Bland
P. Jno & Sarah    P. Lizzie Wolf
Oc. Farmer    M. N. B. Phillips

Date: 3-14-1909
Millard Dan'l Akers    Julia Ann Hager
A. 24 S. Bland    A. 26 S. Bland
P. J. L. & Jane    P. Wm. & Martha
Oc. Farmer    M. N. B. Phillips

Date: 3-17-1909
Edgar Terry Whittaker    Dora Frances Wright
A. 27 S. Giles    A. 22 S. Bland
P. J. W. & R. J.    P. Chas M. & Susan Bussey
Oc. Lumberman    M. Geo T. Jordan

Date: 3-18-1909
Wm. Taylor Lampert    Sallie Ellen Kirby
A. 24 S. Bland    A. 33 S. Bland
P. M. F. & Margaret    P. Jno W. & Cynthia
Oc. Farmer    M. J. G. Reyeley

Date: 4-1-1909
Ellis Arthur Lampert    Ollie Louisa Baker
A. 23 S. Bland    A. 15 S. Bland
P. Jas A. & Clemmie    P. J.W.E. & Nellie
Oc. Farmer    M. W. D. Sharp

Date: 5-12-1909
Ezra Wylie Sarver    Maggie Dehart
A. 26 S. Bland    A. 21 S. Bland
P. C. M. & Martha    P. I. F. & Semphronia
Oc. Farmer    M. J. T. Taylor

Date: 5-28-1909
William Clark    Maud J. Bailey
A. 22 S. Bland    A. 16 S. Giles
P. J. W. & Martha A.    P. R. C. & Catherine
Oc. Farmer    M. W. A. Warner

Date: 6-9-1909
Wm. Riley Richardson    Edna Earl Gibson
A. 23 S. Bland    A. 18 S. Bland
P. A. R. & S. V.    P. Jas V. & Caroline V.
Oc. Farmer    M. N. B. Phillips

Date: 6-17-1909
Jos M. Hare    Mary Jane Radford
A. 26 S. Giles    A. 16 S. Bland
P. R. F. & S. E.    P. F. M. & S. L
Oc. Laborer    M. Geo T. Jordan

Date: 6-16-1909
John Lewis Stafford    Carrie Jane Wynn
A. 48 W. Bland    A. 31 S. Bland
P. Edward & Minerva    P. Jos & Kate
Oc. Carpenter    M. N. B. Phillips

Date: 6-19-1909
Willie F. Blankenship    Lillie Clark
A. 22 S. Mercer, WV    A. 17 S. Bland
P. Henry Blankenship    P. Geo & Margaret
Oc. Laborer    M. W. A. Warner

Date: 6-19-1909
Saunders Helton Hancock    Carrie Nellie Louisa Hancock
A. 18 S. Bland    A. 16 S. Bland
P. M. L. & Jennie    P. W. L. & Mary C.
Oc. Farmer    M. W. D. Sharp

Date: 7-4-1909
Jas C. Collins    Elizabeth Anderson
A. 60 W. Wisconsin    A. 60 W. Bland
P. Ed. & Bettie    P.
Oc. Farmer    M. L. N. Burris

Date: 7-16-1909
Arista Clarence    Thompson Effie Rose Pauley
A. 22 S. Bland    A. 16 S. Bland
P. J. E. & Rachel    P. Newton I. & Martha A.
Oc. Laborer    M. J. E. Bruce

Date: 8-18-1909
James Monroe Peck    Martha Jane Munsey
A. 41 W. Giles    A. 32 S. Bland
P. J. H. & Louisa    P. Davis H. & Julia Ann

Oc. Farmer    M. W.D. Sharp

Date: 8-25-1909
John Madison Allen    Maud Jane Fanning
A. 28 S. Bland    A. 27 S. Bland
P. Jno Poage &    P. Geo. W. & Matilda H.
Fannie R. Bane
Oc. Farmer    M. Geo T. Jordan

Date: 8-23-1909
Willie Johnson French     Annie L. Pruett
A. 28 S. Bland            A. 22 S. Bland
P. Wm. H. & Isabelle      P. D. H. & Lucy
Oc. Railroading           M. W. D. Sharp

Date: 9-8-1909
David Spencer Owen        Maggie Johnson Britts
A. 25 S. Pulaski          A. 23 S. Bland
P. J. D. & E.E.           P. Ch H. & M. D.
Oc. Farmer                M. C. G. Pangle

Date: 9-15-1909
Allen Taylor Newberry,Jr  Maud Ellen Stuart
A. 24 S. Bland            A. 22 S. Bland
P. Allen Taylor &         P. Wm. Buchanan &
Nannie E. Gross           Sarah mariah Mustard
Oc. Farmer                M. Geo T. Jordan

Date: 9-26-1909
Hayes Gordon Saddler      Nellie Gray Hancock
A. 25 S. Bland            A. 17 S. Bland
P. G. S. & Belle          P. N. B. & Maggie
Oc. Farmer                M. W.D. Sharp

Date: 10-13-1909
Wm. Thos. Neel            Josie Edith Umbarger
A. 19 S. Bland            A. 19 S. Bland
P. Alex & Mollie          P. Henry & Jane

Oc. Farmer                M. James Mahood

Date: 11-3-1909
Chas. J. Bailey           Maud Naff Dunagan
A. 32 W. Giles            A. 25 S. Bland
P. __?__Bailey            P. Wm. & Mary M.
Oc. Laborer               M. S.V. Morris

Date: 11-17-1909
Chas. Dan'l Wells         Dora Blankenship
A. 20 S. Mercer, WV       A. 22 S. Bland
P. Dan'l & Dorcas         P. B. & Ardelia
Oc. Farmer                M. F. F. Repass

Date: 12-22-1909
Wm. Frazier Kidd          Louisa Victoria Looney
A. 22 S. Bland            A. 19 S. Bland
P. F. W. & Rosa A.        P. Henry & Frances
Oc. Farmer                M. W.K. Neel

Date: 9-2-1909
Floyd Anderson Walker     Lizzie Brown
A. 27 S. Tazewell         A. 18 S. Bland
P. J. L. & Araminta       P. J. J. & Missouri
Oc. Miller                M. James Mahood

Date: 9-15-1909
Kelly Orsen Hamilton      Josie Collins
A. 19 S. Bland            A. 17 S. Bland
P. Elizabeth Hamilton     P. Jas & Lizzie
Oc. Laborer               M. Geo W. Penley

Date: 9-15-1909
John David Horne          Kate Muncy
A. 57 W. Smyth            A. 36 S. Bland
P. Henry & Elizabeth      P. Davis H. & Julia Ann

Oc. Farmer                M. W. D. Sharp

Date: 10-7-1909
Wm. Gray (B)              Lettie Wagner (B)
A. 40 W. Franklin         A. 44 W. Pulaski
P. Henry & Octavia        P. M.adison & Dilsey Miller
Oc. Farmer                M. R. W. Hill?

Date: 10-13-1909
Arthur W. Price           Minnie L. Miller
A. 27 S. Bland            A. 17 S. Bland
P. Isaiah & Ellen         P. Rev. Will Rice &
                          Emma Jane Morehead
Oc. Farmer                M. G. T. Jordan

Date: 11-10-1909
Archie Columbus Kidd      Ettie Carter
A. 27 S. Bland            A. 19 S. Tazewell
P. Ray & Charlotte        P. Mart. & Bert.?
Oc. Farmer                M. W. K. Neel

Date: 12-19-1909
Wm. Arthur Songer         Lottie Clark
A. 24 S. Giles            A. 19 S. Bland
P. ___?___Songer          P. Miller & Julia
Oc. Farmer                M. W. A. Warner

Date: 12-22-1909
Jas. Rayburn Burress      Cora Lou Kidd
A. 26 S. Bland            A. 17 S. Bland
P. Jno H. & J. A.         P. I. W. & Rosa A.
Oc. Farmer                M. W. K. Neel

Date: 12-23-1909  
Henry Robinett                Bertie May Clark  
A. 26 S. Bland                A. 17 S. Bland  
P. Chas & N. V.               P. Kerrie & Minnie  
Oc. Farmer                    M. S. V. Morris  

Date: 12-23-1909  
Miller Allen Dillow           Mary Hester Davis  
A. 20 S. Bland                A. 23 S. Bland  
P. Lafayette F. &             P. Jno David & Margaret  
Mackie Mattie Burress         Elizabeth Bogle  
Oc. Farmer                    M. W. D. Sharp  

Date: 1-6-1910  
Harvey Levi Dillman           Fannie Edwards  
A. 26 S. Bland                A. 19 S. Bland  
P. Jno. D. & Amanda           P. Chas & Rebecca  
Oc. Farmer                    M. James Mahood  

Date: 1-19-1910  
Davis H. Munsey               Mary Grey Suiter  
A. 60 W. Bland                A. 54 W. Giles  
P. Jacob & Martha             P. Albert Galatin &  
Detimore                      Mary Agnes Updyke  
Oc. Farmer                    M. W. D. Shay  

Date: 1-26-1910  
Edgar Tolbert                 Mamie Guy  
A. 23 S. Bland                A. 20 S. Bland  
P. Jno B. & Maria J.          P. S. W. & Jeanette  
Oc. Farmer                    M. C. A. Pangle  

Date: 1-28-1910  
Geo W. French                 E. M. French  
A. 23 S. Bland                A. 17 S. Bland  
P. Wm H. & Sarah              P. J. D. & Virginia  
Oc. Railroad Fireman          M. C. A. Pangle  

Date: 2-28-1910  
John Henry Stevens? (B)       Lelia Lee Gray (B)  
A. 21 S. Mercer, WV           A 17 S. Bland  
P. Chas. C. & Grorgia         P. Wm. & Mary A.  
Oc. Railroading               M. Rev. R. W. Hill  

Date: 4-6-1910  
Harrison M. Lampert           Myrie F. Hounshell  
A. 21 S. Bland                A. 21 S. Bland  
P.W. W. & Rhoda E.            P. Jos & Margaret  
Oc. Farmer                    M. W.D. Shay  

Date: 12-29-1909  
Wm. H. Wheeler                Nora Lake Lambert  
A. 33 S. Bland                A. 22 S. Bland  
P. C. F. Wheeler              P. S. J. & L. E.  
Oc. Farmer                    M. C. A. Pangle  

Begin Page 55 of Original Book  
Date: 12-29-1909  
Junius Marcelis Updyke        Ada Lee Davis  
A. 46 S. Bland                A. 26 S. Bland  
P. Albert Galatin &           P. Arnold Edward  
Mary Agnes Updyke             & Sarilda Angela Dills  
Oc. Farmer                    M. J. G. Reveley  

Date: 1-6-1910  
Jos Parson Taylor             Virginia Margaret Thompson  
A. 20 S. Wythe                A. 16 S. Bland  
P. J. C. & Margaret A.        P. C. E. & Margaret  
Oc. Farmer                    M. J. G. Reveley  

Date: 1-26-1910  
Doc. Oxley                    Etta Missouri Munsey  
A. 31 S. Mercer, WV           A. 26 S. Bland  
P. Benj. H. & Nancy M.        P. Davis H. & Julia A.  

Oc. Painter                   M. J. G. Reveley  

Date: 1-26-1910  
John Crockett Mustard         Effie Bird Wagner  
A. 40 S. Bland                A. 25 S. Bland  
P. Jas Harvey & Marcia        P. Jacob A. & Josephine  
Oc. Farmer                    M. W. D. Sharp  

Date: 2-23-1910  
Arnold A. Umbarger            Ruth Baugh  
A. 20 S. Bland                A. 18 S. Bland  
P. R. M. & Eliza J.           P. D. M. & Nikcatie L.  
Oc. Farmer                    M. Geo T. Jordan  

Date: 3-30-1910  
Taylor W. Mustard             Victoria B. Mitchell  
A. 31 S. Bland                A. 29 S. Bland  
P. Jas H. & Hattie E.         P. Tim. E. & Ardelia  
Oc. Traveling Salesman        M. S. O. Hall  
Married in Tazewell  

Date: 4-17-1910  
Geo Wm King                   Eva Trottie Hancock  
A. 25 S. Bland                A. 17 S. Bland  
P. W. T. & Nancy L.           P. M. W. & Mahala  
Oc. Farmer                    M. L. M. Burris

Date: 4-29-1910
Columbia C. Clark     Belle Sarver
A. 24 S. Bland     A. 17 S. Bland
P.Kere. & Minnie     P. J. W. & Geneva
Oc. Farmer     M. S. V. Morris

Date: 5-5-1910
James Thos Lloyd     Gracie Ann Morris
A. 30 S. Roanoke     A. 17 S. Bland
P. Wm. & Jennie E.     P. E. B. & Julia E.
Oc. Teamster     M. S. V. Morris

Date: 5-18-1910
John Harrison Looney     Virgie Short
A. 20 S. Buchanan     A. 18 S. Buchanan
P. H. J. & Mary F.     P. Henry & Vicy

Oc. Farmer     M. W. K. Neel

Date: 7-1-1910
Newton Foy White     Eliza Ann Davis
A. 52 D. Pulaski     A. 25 S. Bland
P. J. W. & Martha M.     P. J. W. & Nancy J.
Oc. Farmer     M. L. M. Burris

Date: 6-8-1910
Chas Pearson Pauley     Barbara Lampert
A. 31 S. Bland     A. 21 S. Bland
P. H.S.C. & S.A.     P. Jno & Jane
Oc. Sawmilling     M. J. G. Reveley

Date: 6-24-1910
Earny Bailey     Lulu Clark
A. 18 S. Giles     A. 18 S. Bland
P. R. C. & Rozella     P. Geo & Maggie
Oc. Farmer     M. G. A. Pangle

Date: 8-28-1910
Thos Edgar Oney     Eserie May Pruett
A. 24 S. Tazewell     A. 16 S. Bland
P.Jeff & Mary     P. P. D. & Rhoda
Oc. Car Repairer     M. C A. Pangle

Date: 9-12-1910
Charles Arthur Scott     Mary Etta Pauley
A. 19 S. Giles     A. 17 S. Bland
P. J. A. & Mary S.     P. Gordon Paris &
    Sarah S. Thompson
Oc. Railroading     M. J. E. Bruce

Date: 4-30-1910
Luther Walter Comerford Della M.yrtle Pruett
A. 26 S. Bland     A 18 S. Bland
P. Wm. & Margaret     P. J. W. & Sarah
Oc. Car Repairer     M. C. A. Pangler

Date: 5-11-1910
Wm. Preston Hart     Minnie Viola Faulkner
A. 21 S. Bland     A. 19 S. Bland
P. W. R. & M.V.     P. Geo Alex & Laura Ellen
Oc. Farmer     M. S. V. Morris

Date: 5-18-1910
Rob't Frazier Compton     Kate Elizabeth Wohlford
A. 23 S. Bland     A. 24 S. Bland
P. J. B. & V. A.     P. Gordon &
    Matilda Ann Byrnes
Oc. Farmer     M. Geo T. Jordan

Date: 6-1-1910
Wm Shrader     Mary Lizzie Robinett
A. 25 S. Mercer, WV     A. 22 S. Bland
P. Green & Rebecca     P. R. A. & Lucy
Oc. Farmer     M. W. K. Neel

Date: 6-15-1910
James Logan     Amanda Lutheria Austin
A. 24 S. Bland     A. 36 S. Floyd
P. Jno W. Logan     P. W. G. & Elizabeth
Oc. Laborer     M. S. K. Byrd

Date: 8-3-1910
James Linkous     Alice Belle Stowers
A. 26 S. Bland     A. 17 S. Bland
P. Winton & Hester     P. Chas & Sallie
Oc. Railroading     M. C. A. Pangle

Date: 9-7-1910
Abner Webster Parsell     Elsie Vernon Hamblin
A. 1 S. Bland     A. 20 S. Bland
P. Calvin & Cynthia M.     P. J. S. & Sarah C.
Oc. Laborer     M. L. M. Burris

Date: 10-12-1910
Charles W. Britts     Minnie J. Looney
A. 2 1 S. Bland     A. 21 S. Buchanan
P. C. H. & M. E.     P. H. J. & M. F.

Oc. Farmer     M. W. K. Neel

Date: 10-19-1910
James Martin Kitts          Leota Jane Lampert
A.. 211 S. Bland            A. 14 S. Bland
P. Wm & Victoria           P. J. W. & Thyrza J.
Oc. Farmer                 M. Geo. T. Jordan

Date: 10-19-1910
Wm. Beverly Lester         Henrietta Elener French
A. 20 S.Tazewell           A. 19 S. Bland
P. Jno A. & Lou  J.        P. Jno  D. & Willie A.
Oc. Farmer                 M. H. B. Worley

Begin Page 56 of Original Book
Date: 11-2-1910
William Lowe Kitts          Myrtle Nehema Hancock
A. 23 S. Bland             A. 19 S. Bland
P. Breckenridge Harvey     P. Ollie Hancock
& Emma Caroline Bowles
Oc. Farmer                 M. J. W. Christian

Date: 11-9-1910
Sam. Patterson             Minnie French
A. 25 S. Giles            A. 21 S. Bland
P. Wm. & Eliza            P. Benj. & Mary M

Oc. Farmer                 M. W. A. Gose

Date: 11-16-1910
Jas. McNutt Grayson        Ida Saunders Newberry
A. 23 S. Bland            A. 21 S. Bland
P. Jas F. & Lucy A.       P. L. M. & Lou
Oc. Electrical Engineer    M. J. W. Christian

Date: 11-23-1910
Rees Winston               Araminta Clark
A. 50 W. Lomers, MS        A. 41 W. Bland
P. Rob't & Mary            P. W. P. & Elizabeth French
Oc. Farmer                 M. S. V. Morris

Date: 11-28-1910
Jas  Martin Nestor         Nannie Jane Pauley
A. 21 S. Carroll          A. 19 W. Carroll
P. Fielder & Mary         P. J. D. & Rebecca Kelly
Oc. Laborer                M. J. G. Reveley

Date: 12-14-1910
Jas. W. Bridges            Laura Bell Harner
A. 34 S.Bland             A. 21 S. Bland
P. M. S. & Mary           P. B. W. P. & Nancy
Oc. Farmer                 M. Geo T. Jordan

Date: 12-13-1910
Marcus Walker Hancock  Lizzie Akers
A. 55 W. Bland            A. 37 S. Bland
P. Geo W. & Julia         P. Moses & Sallie
Oc. Farmer                 M. J. E. Bruce

Date: 12-18-1910
Will Dyer Hunt             Loura Gray Dillow
A. 26 S. Wythe            A. 19 S. Bland
P. Geo & Nannie           P. Wm A. & Elizabeth
Oc. Laborer                M. J. W. Christian

Date: 12-29-1910
Buford Hedge               Mamie Farmer
A. 21 S. Pulaski          A. 18 S. Pulaski
P. J. C. & Lucy           P. Jno T. & Jennie
Oc. Farmer                 J. W. Christian

Date: 1-12-1911
Roy Edward Hall            Elizabeth Farmer
A. 20 S. Bland            A. 17 S. Bland
P. G. E. & O. B.          P. N. B. & Eugenia
Oc. Farmer                 M. J. W. Christian

Date: 1-18-1911
Howard Colby  Stowers      Bessie Lee Robinett
A. 23 S. Bland            A. 18 S. Bland
P. Geo W. & Sarah J.      P. R. B. & Liza
Oc. Farmer                 M. W. A. Gose

Date: 1-24-1911
Charlie C. Davis           Lucy  C. Davis
A. 23 S. Bland            A. 16 S. Bland
P. Jno T. & Mary D.       P. C. A. & N E.
Oc. Farmer                 M.  J. W. Christian

Date: 2-8-1911
James David Neel           Effie Gray Umbarger
A. 22 S. Bland            A. 26 S. Bland
P. Alex & Mary M          P. Henry & Jane
Oc. Farmer                 M. Geo. T. Jordan

Date: 2-8-1911
Levi Daniel  Crow          Margaret Elizabeth Hancock
A. 40 S. Bland            A. 24 S. Bland
P. J. M. & Christina      P. Thos & Louisa
Oc. Lumberman              M. Geo T. Jordan

Date: 2-28-1911
John Sam'l Kelly          Mattie Brook Dillow
A. 19 S. Carroll          A. 17 S. Bland
P. J. D. & Rebecca        P. L. F. & Mackie
Oc. Farmer                M. J. W. Christian

Date: 3-29-1911
Wm. Clarence Bowles       Poca Alice Coburn
A. 20 S. Bland            A. 25 S. Bland
P. C. W. & M. A.          P. T. G. & Cynthia M.
Oc. Farmer                M. J. W. Christian

Date: 4-5-1911
John C. Neel              Julia C. Kidd
A. 18 S Bland             A. 18 S. Bland
P. Alex & Mary M.         P. G. W. & M. C.

Oc. Farmer                M. W. K. Neel

Date: 4-12-1911
Chas Hoge Blankenship     Minnie Lavona Tickle
A. 27 S. Bland            A. 17 S. Bland
P. Wm Jackson &           P. Jackson Nye &
Loutheria Dillow          Mary Ann Waggoner
Oc. Farmer                M. J. E. Bruce

Date: 4-26-1911
Geo Crockett Crabtree     Mary Sophie Voight
A. 34 S. Bland            A. 29 S. Charleston, SC
P. J. H. & Susan          P. Geo & Anna C. A.
Oc. Farmer                M. M. L. Huddle

Date: 4-27-1911
Charlie Hicks (B)         Bessie Ann Hobbs (B)
A. 26 S. Giles            A. 19 S. Giles
P. Green & Rachel         P. Lewis & Cynthia
Oc. Farmer                M. W. R. Miller

Date: 5-4-1911
Adam S. Shannon           Margaret Barnes Neel
A. 25 S. Bland            A. 23 S. Tazewell
P. W. W. & S. J.          P. M. F. & Hattie
Oc.Farmer                 M. W. A. Gose

Date: 5-4-1911
Jos Edley Brown           Nannie Frances Dillow
A. 41 W. Wythe            A. 37 W. Bland
P. Nathan L. & Barbara    P. Thos G. & Annie K. Pauley
Oc. Farmer                M. J. G. Reveley

Date: 5-11-1911
Edward Fox                Vernie Dot Gregory
A. 21 S. Tazewell         A. 16 S. Bland
P. A. P. & Mary           P. T. E. & Lucy E.
Oc. Farmer                M. W. A. Gose

Date: 5-31-1911
Thos. F. Lawrence         Ida F. Lefew
A. 24 S. Smyth            A. 22 S. Bland
P. Leroy & Bettie         P. J. M. & Priscilla
Oc. Electrician           M. S. K. Byrd

Date: 5-31-1911
Rice G. Thomas            Mattie M. Woods
A. 60 W. Bland            A. 44 S. Bland
P. Jno & Katie            P. Moses & Drusilla
Oc. Plasterer             M. J. G. Reveley

Date: 6-13-1911
Woodson Morris            Virgie Smith
A. 31 S. Giies            A. 25 S. Bland
P. Sam'l & Octavia        P. Jno D. & Gilly
Oc. Farmer                M. W. A. Gose

Date: 6-7-1911
Jas. Pierce Wagner        Lelia Myrtle Tieche
A. 23 S. Tazewell         A. 26 S. Bland
P. E. G. & Martha A.      P. A. W. & A. L
Oc. Farmer                M. W. N. Wagner

Date: 6-15-1911
Raleigh C. Fox            Mary M. Robinett
A. 21 S. Bland            A. 23 S. Bland
P. G. C. & R. J.          P. R. B. & L. J.
Oc. Farmer                M. W. K. Neel

Date: 6-24-1911
John S. Wohlford          Nannie May Sheppard
A. 45 S. Bland            A. 26 S. Bland
P. Geo & Jane             P. Harman E. & Bessie
Oc. Merchant              M. S. K. Byrd

Date: 7-10-1911
Ira Nelson                Viciea Hull
A. 24 S. Bland            A. 19 S. Bland
P. R. B. & Lizzie         P. J. R. & Ida
Oc. Farmer                M. W. A. Gose

Begin Page 57 of Original Book

Date:8-2-1911
Gordon Kelly Kitts          Grace Myrtle Tolbert
A. 21 S. Bland              A. 16 S. Bland
P.Geo Floyd &               P. J. T. & Laura
Martha Ann Dillman
Oc. Farmer                  M. Geo T. Jordan

Date: 8-9-1911
Harvey E. Duncan            Missouri Kitts
A. 36 D. Floyd              A. 39 S. Bland
P. Allen Taylor             P. Jacob & Matilda
& Rebecca Ann Woods
Oc. Carpenter               M. M. D. Huddle

Date: 8-16-1911
Jos Watson Shrader          Bessie Alderman
A. 26 Bland                 A. 16 S. Giles
P. J. M. & Emily            P. G.W. & Carrie
Oc. Merchant                M. W. A. Gose

Date: 9-6-1911
Wm. Oscar Saunders          Myrtle French
A. 21 S. Mercer, WV         A. 17 S. Bland
P. Riley & Nancy P.         P. T. M. & Eliza J.
Oc. Farmer                  M. S. V. Morris

Date: 9-27-1911
Robt. French Dillow         Incie Emma. Davis
A. 23 S. Bland              A. 26 S. Bland
P. L. F. & Mackie           P. David & Margaret

Oc. Farmer                  M. J. W. & Christian

Date: 10-21-1911
Henry Ellis Hardy           Lillie Kitts
A. 36 S. Carroll            A. 25 W. Bland
P. Henry & Jestin           P. Wm & Ollie Hamblin
Oc. Farmer                  M. J. W. Christian

Date: 11-16-1911
Truby Corner                Permelia Dalton
A. 21 S. Bland              A. 17 Carroll
P. Mintie Corner            P. Ballard & Lucy A.
Oc. Farmer                  M. S. K. Byrd

Date: 12-6-1911
James  Conrad Tuggle        Rosalie Shell Mustard
A. 29 S. Bland              A. 28 S. Bland
P.J. M. & Matilda J.        P. W. N. & Caroline
Oc. Farmer                  M. J. G. Reveley

Date: 8-9-1911
Estle Crabtree              Hattie Tilson
A. 30 S. Bland              A. 20 S. Payson City, Utah
P. Reese & Polly            P.  Jas P. & C. V.

Oc. Farmer                  M. Geo H. Rhodes

Date: 8-9-1911
Columbus Milton Hollyfield  Maud  Mitchell Davis
A. 26 Surry, NC             A. 27 S. Bland
P. Jno. & Alice             P. Sam'l & Sallie

Oc. Locomotiva Engineer M. Geo T. Jordan

Date: 8-24-1911
Thos Maiden Stowers         Cannie May Perkey
A. 24 S. Bland              A. 21 S. Bland
P. E. S. & Ludemia          P. P.W. & E. M.
Oc. Farmer                  M. J. G. Reveley

Date: 9-3-1911
Philip Crockett Baugh       Pauline Turly
A. 25 S. Tazewell           A. 27 S. Tazewell
P. D. M. & Nickitie         P. R. T. & Margaret
Oc. Farmer                  M. Geo T. Jordan

Date: 9-27-1911
Allen Lanz Duncan           Jessie Clotho Kitts
A. 24 S. Giles              A. 18 S. Bland
P. Allen Taylor &           P. Newton Montgomery &
Rebecca Ann Woods           Eliz Angeline Williams
Oc. Carpenter               M. M. D. Huddle

Date: 10-25-1911
Wirt Carrington Williams    Hattie Josephine Allen
A. 23 S. Single             A. 21 S. Bland
P. Sam'l W. & Maggie        P. Miller B. & Shan.
Oc. Merchant                M. J. G. Reveley

Date: 11-29-1911
Albert Henderson Lambert    Annie May Andrews
A. 22 S. Tazewell           A. 16 S. Bland
P. Geo & Jennie             P. Robt. & Laura E.
Oc. Farmer                  M.  J. W. Stewart

Date: 12-20-1911
Kent Cooper Foglesong       Abbie Davis Kimberling
A. 25 S. Bland              A. 21 S. Bland
P. Chris & Mollie           P. E. H. & Louisa C.
Oc. Farmer                  M. Geo T. Jordan

121

Date: 12-19-1911
Houston Damerl (B)    Effie Damerl (B)
A. 28 W. Bland    A. 21 W. Bland
P. Sam & Eliza    P. Ross & Eva Henderson
Oc. Laborer    M. S. K. Bird

Date: 12-21-1911
Meek Clark    Della Myers
A. 23 S. Bland    A. 19 S. Bland
P. Kere & Araminta    P. W. G. & Laura
Oc. Farmer    M. W. R. Miller

Begin Page 58 of Original Book
Date: 2-7-1912
Daniel Crockett Pauley    Bertha Hancock
A. 23 S. Bland    A. 16 S. Bland
P. Gratton Crocket &    P. Ollie Hancock
Mary Geneva Kitts
Oc. Farme r    M. J. E. Bruce

Date: 3-13-1912
C. B. Lambert    Laura Willis
A. 19 S. Bland    A. 22 S. Bland
P. Alex & Sallie    P. W. A. & Rebecca
Oc. Stone mason    M. J. W. Stewart

Date: 3-20-1912
Jackson Hiram Tabor    Minnie Ailsie Miller
A. 20 S Mercer, WV    A. 17 S. Bland
P. F. J. & Amanda R.    P. Chas. W. & Mary L. Ramsey
Oc. Farmer    M. W. R. Miller

Date: 3-27-1912
James Clarence Jones    Lucy Ann Steel
A. 25 S. Tazewell    A. 17 S. Bland
P. W. D. & Annie E.    P. J. F. & G. E.
Oc. Farmer    M. W. K. Neel

Date: 4-8-1912
John Cooper    Ella Shrader
A. 28 S. Giles    A. 23 S. Bland
P. Jos Cooper    P. S. G. & Nickitie
Oc. Brakeman    M. J. W. Stewart

Date: 4-23-1912
Preston Farmer    Emma Clark
A. 25 S. Mercer, WV    A. 19 S. Bland
P. Jno & Millie    P. Kere & Araminta
Oc. Laborer    M. S. V. Morris

Date: 5-8-1912
Jas Peter Tolbert    Ollie Martin
A. 21 S. Bland    A. 19 S. Bland
P. J. B. & Mariah J.    P. Rutha Willis

Oc. Farmer    M. J. W. Stewart

Date: 12-22-1912 **
Chas Lee Morehead    Dora May Walker
A. 25 S. Bland    A. 21 S. Bland
P. Jas. Magruder &    P. Howard Franklin &
Melinda Jane Shrader    Nina Victoria Hicks
Oc. Farmer    M. J. W. Stewart

Date: 5-23-1912
Sherman Nowlin    Virgie Matilda Radford
A. 30 W. Franklin    A. 21 S. Bland
P. Jas. & Nancy    P. F. M. & E. L.
Oc. Farmer    M. S. V. Morris

Date: 5-27-1912
Geo. Edmondson (B)    Cynthia Mary Green (B)
A. 24 S. Pulaski    A. 19 S. Bland
P. Rob't & Mary    P. Claiborne & Viney
Oc. Laborer    M. Walter Hodge

Date: 5-27-1912
Wm. Thos. Umbarger    Pearl Powers
A. 26 S. Bland    A. 18 S. Bland
P. Jonas & Barbara E.    P. J. J. & Jennie
Oc. Plasterer & Carpenter M. S.K. Byrd

Date: 6-7-1912
Arthur Farmer    Mandie French
A. 22 S. Mercer, WV    A. 16 S. Bland
P. Henry & Dora    P. J. M. & Cora
Oc. Laborer    M. F. M. Radford

Date: 6-10-1912
Noah Becklehimer    Nannie French
A. 21 S. Mercer, WV    A. 16 S. Bland
P. General & Rhoda    P. Miller & Allie

Oc. Laborer    M. F. M. Radford

Date: 6-19-1912
Wm. Ed. "Boss" Gusler    Sarah Ethel Morehead
A. 20 S. Giles    A. 22 S. Bland
P. Jas A. & Ollie    P. Gordon Andrew &
    Tacy Adaline Pruett
Oc. Farmer    M. S. K. Byrd

Date: 6-19-1912
Charles White Stanley | Lillie Ellen Dalton
A. 22 S. Franklin | A. wo S. Carroll
P. Harvey & Virginia | P. Bal. & Lucy A.
Oc. Farmer | M. F. F. Repass

Date: 6-23? 1912
Allen Waddle | Ina Gertrude Waddle
A. 24 S. Bland | A. 16 S. Bland
P. Price W. & Charity C. | P. J. D. & Laura
Oc. Farmer | M. Geo T. Jordan

Date: 6-26-1912
Ellis Miller Brown | Flora Fortner
A. 22 S. Bland | A. 18 S. Bland
P. J. J. & Missouri M. | P. John & Kate L.
Oc. Farmer | M. M. D. Huddle

Date: 7-17-1912
Allen Wesley Stowers | Mary Eliz. Comaford
A. 21 S. Bland | A. 17 S. Bluefield, WV
P. Allen & Victoria | P. J. D. & Ellen
Oc. Brakeman | M. C. A. Miller?

Date: 7-24-1912
Sam'l Grayson Stephens | Mary Josephine Kitts
A. 33 S. Giles | A. 21 S. Bland
P. Solomon I. & | P. Breckenridge Harvey &
Elizabeth | Emma Caroline Bowles
Oc. Farmer | M. S. K. Byrd?

Date: 7-22-1912
Tona Londa | Allie Meadows Akers
A. 23 S. Italy | A. 26 W. Bland
P. Peitro & Marie | P. Frank A. Meadows

Oc. Laborer | M. C. A. Miller

Date: 8-14-1912
Luther Comerford | Stella Lambert
A. 28 S. Bland | A. 18 S. Bland
P. Wm. & Margaret | P. S. J. & L. E.
Oc. Sawmilling | M. Walter Hodge

Date: 8-21-1912
Charles Claude McClellan | Ada Florence Winesett
A. 20 S. Smyth | A. 19 S. Bland
P. Wm. & Josie | P. N. E. & Susan
Oc. Farmer | M. Geo T. Jordan

Date: 9-11-1912
Leonard Fugit Duncan | Louise Caroline Hanshew
A. 29 D. Floyd | A. 46 W. Smyth
P. Allen Taylor Duncan | P. Peter Hayton
Oc. Carpenter | M. M. D. Huddle

Date: 9-15-1912
Wm. M. Horton | Malinda B. Brown
A. 73 W. Russell | A. 62 W. Tazewell
P. Dan'l & Patience | P. Duncan & Margaret Cameron
Oc. Farmer | M. S.W. Good

Date: 10-23-1912
Asa Caldwell | Myra Gracie Hager
A. 24 S. Bland | A. 18 S. Bland
P. N. N. & Sarah | P. W. A. & S. A.
Oc. Farmer | M. C. A. Miller

Date: 10-30-1912
Wm. Thos. Nunn | Sarah Gregory
A. 43 W. Bland | A. 31 W. Bland
P. B. L. & M. E. | P. Ralph & Sevaniah Wyrick
Oc. Farmer | M. S. K. Byrd?

Date: 10-30-1912
Rob't Naff Brown | Annie Mary Bird
A. 27 S. Bland | A. 20 S. Bland
P. Ballard Preston & | P. Geo Thos.& Carrie
Lucinda Robinett | Louise Burton
Oc. Farmer | M. Walter Hodge

Date: 11-7-1912
John AndrewThompson | Minnie Nora May Morehead
A. 28 S. Giles | A. 21 S. Bland
P. Saunders & Belle | P. Gordon Andrew &
 | Tacy Adaline Pruett
Oc. Farmer | M. F. M. Radford

Date: 10-30-1912
Lucian Gleaves Yonce | Sallie Augusta Dillow
A. 35 W. Wythe | A. 29 S. Bland
P. Thos. & Alice | P. W. A. & Elizabeth
Oc. Farmer | M. Walter Hodge

Date: 11-27-1912
Jas. Franklin Blessing | Mary Loretta Umbarger
A. 43 S. Bland | A. 24 S. Bland
P. J. A. & Eliza J. | P. Jonas & Barbara E.
Oc. Mason | M. Geo T. Jordan

Date: 12-10-1912
Harvey Martin
A. 21 S. Giles
P. Sam'l & Mollie
Oc. Farmer

Bessie Meadows
A. 20 S. Bland
P. Frank Meadows
M. Walter Hodge

Date: 12-18-1912
Samuel Rider
A. 21 S. Bland
P. T. A. & Jennie
Oc. Farmer

Ella Sublett
A. 17 S. Bland
P. Jas & Minnie
M. W. K. Byrd

Date: 12-18-1912
Wm. Harrison Richardson
A. 28 S. Bland
P. C. W. & Bettie
Oc. Farmer

Addie Coburn
A. 27 S. Bland
P. T. G. & Maggie
M. Walter Hodge

Date: 12-19-1912
Henry C. Barlow
A. 69 W. Massachusetts
P. Ira & Clarissa
Oc. Carpenter

Nannie A. Howard
A. 55 W. Bland
P. J. H. & Janie Hoilman
M. W. R. Miller

Date: 12-22-1912
Estelle Ward Sands
A. 23 S. Giles
P. W. H. & Mary L.

Oc. Farmer

Mary Hare Bird
A. 20 S. Mercer, WV
P. Austin Letchel &
Geneva J. Miller
M. S. K. Byrd

Date: 12-18-1912
Charles Lawrence Leslie
A. 47 W. Wythe
P. Jas & Margaret

Oc. Farmer

Lizzie Davis Townley
A. 33 S. Bland
P. Jno W. S. & Mary
Catherine Harman
M. Walter Hodge

Begin Page 59 of Original Book
Date: 2-5-1913
Chas. R. Helvey
A. 43 W. Bland
P. Wm. Baltzer &
Elizabeth J. Wheeler
Oc. Harness maker

Lavena McNeil
A. 35 S. Bland
P. Jacob & Delilah

M. S. K. Byrd

Date: 12-26-1912
Jas Lawrence Miller
A. 22 S. Oakvale,WV
P. Ran. & Annie

Oc. Sawmilling

Latha Wall
A. 18 S. Phlegar, WV
P. John & Jennie

M. C. A. Miller

Date: 2-16-1913
David W. Clemons
A. 23 S. Wythe
P. Chas & Susan
Oc. Farmer

Mary E. Bowles
A. 19 S. Bland
P. C. W. & M. A.
M. C. A. Miller

Date: 2-19-1913
L. D. Mc Farland
A. 35 D. Tazewell
P. L. D. & Jane
Oc. Farmer

Rosa M. King
A. 26 S. Bland
P. W. P. & Ellen
M. Geo T. Jordan

Date: 3-10-1913
Bowman Munsey
A. 26 S. Bland
P. Harvey J. & Catherine
Oc. Farmer

Fanny Duncan
A. 26 S. Bland
P. Ananias & Adaline
M. Walter Hodge

Date: 3-13-1913
James E. Brown
A. 25 S. Smyth
P. J. T. & Margaret E.
Oc. Farmer

Ada Lampert
A. 21 S. Bland
P. Henry T. & Mary E.
M. Geo T. Jordan

Date: 3-18-1913
Henry Six
A. 21 S. Wythe
P.Stuart & Ida
Oc. Car Repairer

Julia Shuler Dehart
A. 18 S. Bland
P. I. F. & Mary
M. S. K. Byrd

Date: 3-19-1913
Walter Eli Bailey
A. 23 S. Mercer, WV
P. James & Jennie
Oc. Carpenter

Sheffey Hamilton
A. 25 S. Bland
P. S. M. & Sallie
M. S. K. Byrd

Date: 3-26-1913
Edward R. S. Gregory
A. 26 S. Bland
P. T. E. & Martha
Oc. Farmer

Lucy J. Bird
A. 17 S. Bland
P. J. B. & L. V.
M. J. W. Stewart

Date: 4-5-1913
Wm Cecil St.Clair
A. 26 S. Giles
P. P. F. & Loura
Oc. Farmer

Nannie Belle Tuggle Hale
A. 23 D. Bland
P. J. M. & Matilda Tuggle
M. Returned, not used.

Date: 4-10-1913
John Rider
A. 22 S. Bland
P. T. A. & Jennie
Oc. Miner

Myrtle Hall
A. 23 S. KY
P. W. H. & Mary
M. W. R. Miller

Date: 4-28-1913
C. N. Wilson
A. 22 S. Bland
P. C. H. & E.iza E.
Oc. Farmer

Mary Pruett
A. 20 S. Bland
P. W. H. & Lucy J.
M. J. W. Stewart

Date: 5-2-1913
Ben Bedwell
A. 18 S. Wyoming, WV
P. Lee & Mary
Oc. Tile setter

Mary Taylor
A. 17 S. Bland
P. Lucy J. Taylor
M. S. K. Byrd

DateP 5-28-1913
Alpheus Madison Cox
A. 68 W. Goochland
P. Henry & Nancy M.
Oc. Farmer

Matilda Tibbs
A. 58 W. Bland
P. Jno A. & Kate Brown
M. M. D. Huddle

Date: 6-7-1913
Robert Jackson (B)
A. 21 S. Bland
P. Wint. & Hulda
Oc. Laborer

Nannie Johnston (B)
A. 23 S. Bland
P. Bud & Matilda
M. Walter Hodge

Date: 6-11-1913
R. W. Robison
A. 24 S. Missouri
P.
Oc. Electrician

Maria Elizabeth Allen
A. 24 S. Bland
P. B. & Shan. J.
M. J. G. Reveley

Date: 6-18-1913
Harvey E. Brewster
A. 53 W. McDowell, WV
P. Arch. & Catherine J.
Oc. Farmer

Ida Missouri Kinder
A. 37 S. Bland
P. Jos M. & Sophia
M. Geo T. Jordan

Date: 6-11-1913
Allen French Eaton
A. 27 S. Giles
P. Geo Brown & Mattie Eaton
Oc. Farmer

Drusa May Faulkner
A. 19 S. Bland
P. Geo A. & Ella
M. D. T. Miles?

Date: 6-19-1913
Robt Jennings Reveley
A. 26 S. Rockbridge
P. David R. & Rachel A.

Oc. Teacher

Margurite Emily Grayson
A. 22 S. Bland
P. Jas Floyd &
Lucy Ann McNutt
M. J. G. Reveley

Date: 6-25-1913
William Smith Penley
A. 36 S. Bland
P. Braxton H. &
Adaline Robinett
Oc. Mechanic

Lena Estelle Bernard
A. 26 S. Bland
P. Samuel H. &
Elizabeth Pelter
M. Walter Hodge

Date: 7-9-1913
Sephen S. Tibbs
A. 20 S. wythe
P. Chas. M. & Mary
Oc. Laborer

Dora O'Dell
A. 22 S. Grayson
P. Patrick & Addie
M. Geo T. Jordan

Date: 7-23-1913
Estill Paris Thompson
A. 24 S. Bland
P. Comey & Mag.
Oc. Laborer

Nannie E. Lillie
A. 21 S. Bland
P.
M. J. W. Stewart

Date: 8-6-1913
Frank Bailey Duncan
A. 19 S. Giles
P. Allen Taylor &
Rebecca Ann Woods
Oc. Carpenter

Estelle Elvira Harner
A. 19 S. Bland
P. W. T. & Elvira

M. Geo T. Jordan

Date: 8-6-1913
Oll Danielley?
A. 26 S. Mercer, WV
P. H. A. &. & J. A.

Oc. Farmer

Ether Esther Rudder
A. 24 S. Bland
P. Charles Martin &
Louisa Jerusha Mustard
M. Walter Hodge

Date: 9-10-1913
John Henry Hart
A. 21 S. Bland
P. W.R. & M. V.
Oc. Farmer

Lena May Sarver
A. 21 S. Bland
P. S. E. & Maggie
M. F. F. Repass

Date: 1-17-1913
Robt. Kelley Brunk
A. 26 S. Pulaski
P. W. S. & Eliza
Oc. Farmer

Effie Ethel Davis
A. 21 S. Pulaski
P. Chas W. & Louoisa V.
M. W. R. Miller

125

Date: 9-17-1913
Kelly Foster Tickle          Nannie Miller Burton
A. 23 S. Bland               A. 24 S. Bland
P. Jackson Nye &             P. Giles Henderson &
Mary Ann Waggoner            Callie Dixie Burton
Oc. Farmer                   M. Walter Hodge

Date: 9-17-1913
Lorenzo Naff Ramsey          Leona Miller
A. 28 S. Bland               A. 26 S. Bland
P.C. B. & W. A.              P. Chas E. & S. E.
Oc. Farmer                   M. S. V. Morris

Date: 10-1-1913
Arthur A. Spence             Vicie Dillow
A. 32 S. Grayson             A. 25 S. Bland
P. Richard & Melvina?        P. W. A. & Mary Eliz. Waddle
Oc. Painter                  M. J. E. Bruce

Date: 10-19-1913
Guy Moore                    Bertha Va. Burrass
A. 21 S. Pulaski             A. 16 S. Bland
P. Thos. & Elizabeth         P. R. R. & Margaret C.
Oc. Laborer                  M. J. W. Stewart

Date: 11-26-1913
Wise L. Davis                Martha Parcell
A. 26 S. Bland               A. 17 S. Bland
P. J. E. & Ollie E.          P. Calvin & Maggie
Oc. Farmer                   M. W. R. Miller

Date: 12-3-1913
Grover Cleveland Wright Nellie Rosetta Nunn
A. 20 S. Bland               A. 18 S. Bland
P. Doc. Wm. McComas & P. Doc. Lee &
Sarah Ann Bruce              Cynthia Rosetta Miller
Oc. Farmer                   M. James Mahood

Date: 12-13-1913
Elmer Blankenship            Clara Clark
A. 24 S. Bland               A. 17 S. Bland
P. Berry & Ardelia           P. Cary & Minnie
Oc. ?                        M. F. M. Radford

Date: 12-24-1913
Wm. E. Stowers               Cora Wiley
A. 21 S. Bland               A. 20 S. Bland
P. Sim & Lizzie              P. N.J. & Ollie C.

Oc. Railroading              M. J. W. Stewart

Date: 9-17-1913
Wm. Trigg Farmer             Myrthel Patton
A. 36 W. Wythe               A. 22 S. Bland
P. S. M. & Fannie            P.

Oc. Farmer                   M. J. E. K?

Date: 10-1-1913
Charles Gibson               Cora Thompson
A. 24 S. Bland               A. 21 S. Bland
P. J. V. & Caroline          P. M. A. & M. J.
Oc. Carpenter                M. C. A. Miller

Date: 10-9-1913
Jacob Smith                  Ettie Meadows
A. 29 S. Carter, KY          A. 14 S. Bland
P. W. A. & Jane              P. F. A. & Eliza V.
Oc. Coal miner               M. C. A. Miller

Date: 11-3-1913
James C. Price (B)           Wanetia M. Hogan (B)
A. 24 S. Floyd               A. 18 S. Bland
P. Jas & Rosie               P. Humphery H. & Maud M.
Oc. Laborer                  M. J. W. Stewart

Date: 11-26-1913
Thomas King                  Lillian Victoria Atwell
A. 22 S. Bland               A. 21 S. Bland
P. Wm. P. & M. E.            P. J. E. & L. J.
Oc. Farmer                   M. James Mahood

Date: 12-11-1913
Wm. A. Lampert               Minnie Clark
A. 27 S. Bland               A. 19 S. Bland
P. Lindsey & Lizzy           P. Alex & Jane

Oc. Farmer                   M. Walter Hodge

Date: 12-17-1913
Mason Robinett               Mellie E.Davis
A. 20 S. Bland               A. 17 S. Tazewell
P. Rob't. H. & Lucy          P. Isaac J. & Rhoda C.
Oc. Farmer                   M. J. W. Stewart

Begin Page 60 of Original Book
Date: 12-24-1913
Lorenza Dell Burton          Ada Hutsell Tickle
A. 22 S. Bland               A. 22 S. Bland
P. Giles Henderson          P. Ira Lozier &
& Callie Dixie Kitts         Mary Elizabeth Flora Hutsell
Oc. Farmer                   M. Walter Hodge

126

Date: 12-24-1913
Barnett Anderson Neal
A. 27 S. Bland
P.Chas M. &
Isabell A. Tickle
Oc. Brakeman

Nellie Gray Tickle
A. 18 S. Bland
P. Barnitz Lemuel &
Rose Mariam Kitts
M. Walter Hodge

Date: 12-24-1913
Dall Wisley Stowers
A. 32 S. Bland
P. E. S. & L. D.

Oc. Farmer

Maud Victoria Gearing
A. 24 S. Bland
P. F. G. & Ibbie

M. Walter Hodge

Date: 12-21-1913
Alexander Rose
A. 22 S. Bland
P.
Oc Railroading

Julia Thompson
A. 18 S. Bland
P. Jas & Mary
M. J. W. Stewart

Date: 12-31-1913
S. Walt. Neel
A. 59 D. Tazewell
P. Robt & Nancy
Oc. Farmer

Lucy J. Robinett
A. 49 W. Bland
P. Henry Pruett
M. D. A. Leffel

Date: 12-31-1913
Ira Kelley Thompson
A. 23 S. Bland
P. J. E. & Rachel
Oc. Farmer

Eliza Agnes King
A. 16 S. Wythe
P. H. N. & Susan E.
M. J. E. Guthrie

Date: 1-16-1914
Arthur Fanning
A. 21 S. Bland
P. Geo & M. J.
Oc. Laborer

Nannie Stowers
A. 27 S. Bland
P. Grayson & Lucinda
M. S. V. Morris

Date: 1-21-1914
John Gordon Patton
A. 23 S. Bland
P. Robt & Mary
Oc. Farmer

Conie? Havens
A. 21 S. Bland
P. Wylie & Victoria
M. Walter Hodge

Date: 1-28-1914
Jno Wesley Linkous
A. 21 S. Bland
P. John & Izzie V.
Oc. Laborer

Bessie Belle Wiley
A. 22 S. Bland
P. R. S. & Mary
M. C. A. Miller

Date: 2-4-1914
Alvey Edson Tabor
A. 17 S. Bland
P. Frank & Helen
Oc. Farmer

Fanny Gray Neece
A. 16 S. Bland
P. A. T.? & Mollie
M. C. A. Miller

Date: 2-8-1914
James Kelley Lambert
A. 26 S. Tazewell
P. S. J. & Ella
Oc. Laborer

Lola Dangerfield
A. 27 S. Bland
P. Green & Mittie D.
M. C. A. Miller

Date: 2-7-1914
Fred A. Jackson
A. 21 S. Washington
P.G. M. & M. L.
Oc. Stenographer

Martha Washington Mills
A. 22 S. Washington
P. J. B. & M. J.
M. Walter Hodge

Date; 2-9-1914
James Daniel Carver
A. 20 S. Washington
P. Samuel D. & Martha J.
Oc. Laborer

Lillian Dunn Wynn
A. 26 S. Bland
P. Andy & Julia
M. Walter Hodge

Date: 2-22-1914
Chas. R. Blankenship
A. 37 W. Bland
P. Wash. & Julia
Oc. Farmer

Flora Gray Ramsey
A. 20 S. Bland
P. W. W. & Ida V.
M. W. V. Morris

Date 3-22-1914
Haven Howard Farmer
A. 26 S. Pulaski
P. Jno T. & Jennie
Oc. Carrepairer

Ada Belle Shufflebarger
A. 23 S. Bland
P. A. J. & Mary
M. J. E. Guthrie

Date: 4-1-1914
Charles Walls
A. 22 S. Mercer, WV
P. Jas E. & Jennie
Oc. Miner

Bertha Lambert
A. 19 S. Giles
P. C. F. Lampert
M. J. W. Stewart

Date: 4-10-1914
Richard Mark Hager
A. 24 S. Bland
P. R. L. & Matilda M.
Oc. Stenographer

Mary B. Radford
A. 18 S. Bland
P. F.M. & Sarah E L
M. J. H. Umbarger

Date: 4-14-1914
Mack Evans (B)               Bertie Charlton (B)
A. 28 S. Georgia             A. 21 S. Bland
P. Sam'l & Maggie            P. Noah & Sarah
Oc. Farmer                   M. J. W. Stewart

Date: 4-22-1914
Chas. Hicks Morris           Roxie Annie Sexton
A. 23 S. Pulaski             A. 18 S. Bland
P. E. J. & Martha E.         P. O. B. & Josie
Oc. Farmer                   M. J. G. Umbarger

Date: 5-28-1914
Wm. Franklin McColgan, Jr.   Lois Fern Walker
A. 24 S. Bland               A. 18 S. Bland
P. W. F. & Mary G.           P. H. F. & Nina H.
Oc. Electrician              M. Walter Hodge

Date: 8-6-1914
Layman Richard Bird          Nannie May Thomas
A. 21 S. Bland               A. 18 S. Bland
P. C. R. & S. E.             P. C. C. & N. V.

Oc. Farmer                   M. Walter Hodge

Date: 9-2-1914
Basil Marvin Crabtree        Ethel Verna Hardison
A. 28 S. Bland               A. 23 W. Carroll
P.J. N. & Susan              P. Albert & Sarah Ward?
Oc. Teacher & Farmer         M. S. K. Byrd

Date: 9-2-1914
Claude Hicks Wagner          Pearl Edwina Mustard
A. 24 S. Tazewell            A. 27 S. Tazewell
P. E. G. & Alice             P. Newt. Shell & Ella Crockett
Oc. Farmer                   M. James ? Umbarger

Date: 9-2-1914
Chas Henry Bird              Sally Walls
A. 21 S. Bland               A. 21 S. Bland
P. J. H. & M. J.             P. Sam & Nannie
Oc. Farmer                   M. J. W. Stewart

Begin Page 61 of Original Book
Date: 9-16-1914
Harman Wagner Pauley         Myrtle Nehema Hancock Kitts
A. 22 S. Bland               A. 23 W. Bland
P. Graton Crockett &         P. Ollie Hancock
Mary Geneva Kitts
Oc. Farme r                  M. J. E. Bruce

Date: 4-15-1914
Crockett Looney              Pricie Jane Childress
A. 24 S. Buchanan            A. 19 S. Buchanan
P. Hick & Vicie              P. J. S. & S. M.
Oc. Farmer                   M. W. K. Neel

Date: 4-30-1914
James Henry Howard Taylor (B)  Helen Stone (B)
A. 49 W? Bath                A. 21 S. Roanoke City
P. Perry & Louisa            P. Rob't & Frannie
Oc. Laborer                  M. J. W. Stewart

Date: 6-25-1914
Paul Martin Campbell         Estelle Bruce
A. 21 S. Tazewell            A. 19 S. Tazewell
P. Jas. C. & Sarah E.        P.G. D. & Nannie
Oc. Cashier for APC          M. J. Earl Guthrie

Date: 8-5-1914
James Sam'l Ashworth         Angie Louisa Bird
A. 40 S. Bland               A. 24 S. Bland
P. Wm.B. & Martha E.         P. Wm. Washington &
                             Nannie L. Burton
Oc. Farmer                   M. Walter Hodge

Date: 8-30-1914
John Vance Neel              Hassie Rose Atkins
A. 23 S. Tazewell            A. 21 S. Bland
P. Andy & Sallie             P. Wiley & Edna
Oc. Farmer                   M. W. K. Neel

Date: 9-2-2914
Jas David Ratliff            Belle Pauley
A. 25 W. Wythe               A. 19 S. Bland
P. Jennie Ratliff            P. G. P. & Sallie
Oc. Laborer                  M. J. Earl Guthrie

Date: 9-8-1914
John Perdue                  Katie J. Clark
A. 24 S. Giles               A. 18 S. Bland
P. Perrell & Tishia          P. Geo & Maggie M.
Oc. ??                       M. J. W. Stewart

Date: 9-19-1914
Early Pierce Neel            Katie Atkins
A. 26 S. Tazewell            A. 19 S. Bland
P. A. B. & Sallie            P. H. W. & Edna
Oc. Farmer                   M. W. K. Neel

128

Date: 9-29-1914
Moses M. Starling     Laura L. Comaford
A. 22 S. Bland     A. 18 S. Mercer, WV
P.Ben & Sarah     P. J. D. & Ella
Oc. Laborer     M. J. W. Stewart

Date: 10-29-1914
Elmer Myers     Minnie Hamilton
A. 20 S. Bland     A. 19 S. Bland
P. Gordon & Laura     P. S. H. & Ada
Oc. Farmer     M. W. R. Miller

Date: 10-29-1914
Chas Edward Martin     Annie Patton
A. 22 S. Franklin     A. 18 S. Bland
P. Frank & Margaret     P. J. M. & Thula
Oc. Laborer     M. J. E. Guthrie

Date: 11-1-1914
Robt Edward Dunn     Camilla Bird
A. 26 S. Bland     A. 18 S. Bland
P. Wythe G. &     P. Austin Letchel &
Sarah Jane Bowles     Geneva J. Miller
Oc. Farmer     M. Walter Hodge

Date: 11-15-1914
Henry Ratcliff     Cora Pruett
A. 19 S. Bland     A. 24 S. Bland
P.Chas. F. & Netta     P. Isaac & Lucinda
Oc. Farmer     M. C. A. Miller

Date: 12-23-1914
W. R. Spangler     Lena Ramsey
A. 21 S. Mercer, WV     A. 16 S. Bland
P. Rob't & Nannie     P. T. R. & Caroline
Oc. Farmer     M. W. R. Miller

Date: 1-13-1915
Jos. H. Burton     Fanny K. Clark
A. 26 S. Bland     A. 18 S. Bland
P. Travis & Mary     P. R. M. & Mary J.
Oc. Farmer     M. C. A. Miller

Date: 1-20-1915
Luther Dunford     Louisa French
A. 28 S. Giles     A. 16 S. Bland
P. Isaac Dunford     P. M. L. & Allie Belle
Oc. Farmer     M. F. M. Radford

Date: 10-9-1914
Wiley L. French     Mary Ettie Pruett
A. 29 S. Bland     A. 22 S. Bland
P. Wm. H. & Isabella     P. P. D. & Rhoda
Oc. Farmer     M. C. A. Miller

Date: 10-28-1914
Dorsey W. Wheeler     Pearl B. Lambert
A. 24 S. Washington, PA     A. 24 S. Tazewell
P. Wm. H. & Lucinda     P. Sam J. & Ella
Oc. Laborer     M. J. W. Stewart

Date: 11-1-1914
Frank E. Conner     Ada B. Pruett
A. 23 S. Monroe, WV     A. 18 S. Bland
P. Sam'l & Mary     P.J. W. & Sarah
Oc. Farmer     M. C. A. Miller

Date: 11-18-1914
P. Curtis Banner     Clara Ethel Davis
A. 29 S. Lee     A. 26 S. Wythe
P. V. S. & Mattie H.     P. Henry E. & Va. E.

Oc. Traveling Salesman     M. J. Earl Guthrie

Date: 11-25-1914
Oley Muncy Thompson     Va. Kyle Coburn
A. 22 S. Bland     A. 18 S. Bland
P. M. A. & Jane     P. G. C. & Alice
Oc. Farmer     M. C. A. Miller

Date: 12-23-1914
David F. Clark     Viola O. French
A. 25 S. Bland     A. 18 S. Bland
P. Jno W. & Martha     P. Ballard P. & Ollie R.
Oc.Farmer     M. C. A. Miller

Date: 1-13-1915
Kent Williams     Mary Lela Cox
A. 26 S. Bland     A. 18 S. Bland
P. Jack. A. & Matilda     P. L. M. & Susan
Oc. Farmer     M. S. K. Bird

Date: 2-3-1915
Chas. Kemper Bowles     Ona Havens
A. 22 S. Bland     A. 18 S. Bland
P. C. W. & Mahulda     P. W. T. & Elvira
Oc. Farmer     M. J. E. Guthrie

Date: 2-17-1915
Chas Clark | Dadie? Elizabeth Myers
A. 22 S. Bland | A. 18 S. Bland
P. R. M. & Mary Jane | P. W.G. & Laura
Oc. Farmer | M. S. V. Morris

Date: 3-23-191 5
Andy Wm Davis | Mary Frances Parcell
A. 21 S. Pulaski | A. 21 S. Bland
P. Chas W. & Virginia | P. Calvin V. & Cynthia M.
Oc. Farmer | M. T. D. Strader

Date: 4-14-1915
John Roman Gordon | Virginia Alice Mustard
A. 25 S. Bland | A. 26 S. Bland
P. Marion & Ellen | P. Charlie L. & Henrietta
Oc. Carpenter | M. Walter Hodge

Date: 6-4-1915
Martin Akers | Lila Mae Harington
A, 21 S. Bland | A. 16 S. Bland
P. C. K. & Elizabeth | P. C. L. & Jennie
Oc. | Returned, not used

Date: 6-10-1915
Albert Martin Kitts | Ethel Kate Bird
A. 22 S. Bland | A. 21 S. Bland
P. Ballard Graham & | P. Austin Letchel &
Ollie Norabell Harman | Geneva J. Miller
Oc. Laborer | M. Walter Hodge

Date: 7-6-1915
Verner Clyde Lindamood Ada Texas Perkey
A. 21 S. Wythe | A. 22 S. Bland
P. W. G. & M. B. | P. P. W. & E. M.
Oc. Farmer | M. M. F. Marsh

Date: 7-11-1915
Edwin Gray Repass | Sena E. Linkous
A. 27 S. Bland | A. 19 S. Bland
P. Sam'l L. & Lucinda | P. Jas & Nannie
Oc. Farmer | M. J. Earl Guthrie

Date: 9-1-1915
Millard Newton Starling | Rosie Comaford
A. 20 S. Bland | A. 17 S. Bland
P. B. F. & Sarah C. | P. J. D. & Ellen
Oc. Farmer | M. C. A. Miller

Date: 3-4-1914
Jas Larkin Corder | Mary Elizabeth Hancock
A. 56 W. Bland | A. 24 S. Bland
P. B. F. & Julia A. | P. G. W. & Belle
Oc. Carpenter | M. Walter Hodge

Date: 3-24-1915
Ballard Woodson Miller | Esther Lourina Finley
A. 46 W. Bland | A. 37 S. Bland
P. Abram W. & Alsie Munsey | P. J. W. & Nannie
Oc. Farmer | M. Jas H. Umbarger

Date: 5-9-1915
Charlie Brewer | Virgie E. Pruett
A. 21 S. Mingo, WV | A. 18 S. Bland
P.Jno & Elizabeth | P. Paris D. & Rhoda
Oc. | M. C. A. Miller

Date: 6-9-1915
Claude Glenn Anderson | Mabel A. Dangerfield
A. 21 S. Lee | A. 15 S. Bland
P. Lee & Alice | P. Greeen & Mittie
Oc. Sawmilling | M. A. H. Towe

Date: 6-30-1915
Rob't Mont. Miller | Mary Elizabeth Miller
A. 22 S. Bland | A. 21 S. Bland
P. L. M. & R. M. | P. Ballard Woodson &
 | Roxie Belle Pruett
Oc. Farmer | M. W. R. Miller

Date: 7-7-1915
Linkous Looney | Mollie Igo
A. 21 S. Buchanan | A. 18 S. Tazewell
P. Hick & Vicie | P. James & Mary
Oc. Farmer | M. W. K. Neel

Begin Page 62 of Original Book
Date: 7-28-1915
Mathias Scaggs Harmon | Bula Josephine Cox
A. 35 S. Tazewell | A. 16 S. Smyth
P. Wm. & Derinda | P. Henry I. & Sarah
Oc. Farmer | M. S.K. Byrd

Date: 9-1-1915
Clifford Grayson Tolbert | Cecil Edith Gibson
A. 22 S. Bland | A. 18 S. Bland
P. C. F. & N.E. | P. J. V. & C. V.
Oc. Car Repairer | M. C. A. Miller

Date: 9-5-1915
Sam'l Maylon          Alice Creger
Damewood
A. 68 W. Union, TN    A. 55 W. Bland
P. Isaac & Milsie     P. Ganam & Abigal Ann Kitts
Oc. Farmer            M. Walter Hodge

Date: 9-15-1915
W. J. Blankenship     Martha B. Johnston
A. 54 W. Bland        A. 41 W. Bland
P. Daniel & Mary      P. James & Lucy Brown
Oc. Farmer            M. Walter Hodge

Date: 9-26-1915
Areen Smith           Nora Ethel French
A. 22 S. Bland        A. 17 S. Bland
P. Taylor & Mary      P. G. E. & Cora Alice
Oc. Farmer            M. A. H. Towe

Date: 10-14-1915
Stewart Gleeves Painter   Alice Arabelle Burton
A. 29 W. Bland        A. 29 S. Bland
P. Geo Dabney &       P. Giles Henderson &
Elizabeth Nancy Tickle   Callie Dixie Kitts
Oc. Sawmilling        M. Walter Hodge

Date: 10-20-1915
Floyd Starling        Lucy Lockie Thompson
A. 37 S. Bland        A. 22 S. Bland
P. Jno & Sarah        P. Catherine Neel
Oc. Farmer            M. A. H. Towe

Date: 10-28-1915
Hatcher Giles Thompson   Virginia Gray Patterson
A. 24 S. Bland        A. 17 S. Bland
P. J. E. & Rachel     P.W. E. & Alice
Oc. Laborer           M. Walter Hodge

Date: 11-10-1915
Isaac Dalton          Sarah Delphia Dalton
A. 23 S. Carroll      A. 17 S. Carroll
P. J. S. Dalton       P. B. & Lucy A.
Oc. Farming           M. W. M. Ellis

Date: 11-25-1915
Albert Terry Meadows   Laura Emily Millirons
A. 20 S. Bland        A. 17 S. Bland
P. J. W. & Ida B.     P. R. L. & Anna K.
Oc. Farming           M. T. D. Strader

Date: 9-12-1915
Wm. Archie Helvey     Nomia K. Shufflebarger
A. 30 S. Bland        A. 24 S. Bland
P. Sam'l Houston. &   P. Harvey Boston
Nickitie Miller       & Maggie
Oc. Farmer            M. Will Rice Miller

Date: 9-22-1915
Dick Albert (B)       Mary Henderson (B)
A. 21 S. Giles        A. 15 S. Giles
P.                    P. Eva Henderson
Oc. Laborer           M. Jas H. Umbarger

Date: 10-13-1915
Geo. Gillian Trent    Ina Tarter Kitts
A. 39 S. Campbell     A. 23 S. Bland
P. Thos H. & Caroline S.   P. Miller & Ida V. Kitts
Oc. Blacksmith        M. Walter Hodge

Date: 10-20-1915
Luther Jefferson Lambert   Lela May Harrington
A. 22 S. Tazewell     A. 16 S. Grayson
P. S. J. & Ella       P. Colby Harrington

Oc. Sawmilling        M. A. H. Towe

Date: 10-27-1915
James Walter Tolbert   Mary Goldie Lawrence
A. 25 S. Bland        A. 19 S. Bland
P. C. F. & Nancy      P. Bud & Martha
Oc. Farmer            M. A. H. Towe

Date: 11-11-1915
Fonnie Crawford       Pearl Cassell
A. 20 S. Bland        A. 18 S. WV
P. Howe & Sallie      P. Con. & Effie
Oc. Sawmilling        M. Fulton Blankenship

Date: 11-24-1915
Rob't Neel Havens     Lennie Mae Towe
A. 25 S. Lincoln, Neb.   A. 20 S. Evansville, TN
P. W. M. & Victoria   P. M/M A. H. Towe
Oc. Minister          M. A. H. Towe

Date: 11-17-1015
Robert Lee Groseclose   Edna Hester Waddle
A. 35 S. Bland        A. 28 S. Bland
P. Henry & Mary Devor   P. Rich & Dillie (Kegley)
Oc. Farming           M. J. R. Walker

Date: 11-24-1915
Chas Crockett Harden    Lena Delilah Turley
A. 21 S. Bland    A. 24 S. Tazewell
P. Sam & Fannie    P. Jno & Margaret
Oc. Farming    M. J. R. Walker

Date: 11-25-1915
Jas Edward Meadows    Ida Brook Bowles
A. 27 S. Bland    A. 17 S. Bland
P. Frank & Eliza    P. Chas W. & Mary A.
Oc. Railroading    M. W. C. Crockett

Date: 11-29-1915
Harry Scott Shanklin    Margaret Eugenia Sheppard
A. 23 S. Montgomery    A. 23 S. Bland
P. Sam'l J. & Alice R.    P. Harman E. & Hester E.
Oc. Timekeeper    M. W. C. Crockett

Date: 12-16-1915
Harve Farmer    Lou Perkey
A. 20 S. Bland    A. 19 S. Bland
P. Rachel Pugh    P. P. W. & Eliza
Oc. Laborer    M. W. C. Crockett

Date: 12-25-1915
Roger Arten Repass    Eula Elvira Kitts
A. 24 S. Bland    A. 19 S. Bland
P. L. D.& Ardelia B.    P. S. L. & Amanda E.
Oc. Farmer    M. Jas. F. Deal

Date: 12-29-1915
Richard Floyd Davis    Vernie Eliza Brunk
A. 29 S. Bland    A. 25 S. Bland
P. J. W. & Nancy L.    P. W. S. & Eliza
Oc. Farmer    M. Tyler D. Strader

Date: 12-29-1915
Jno Thomas Dillman    Mollie Umbarger
A. 48 W. Bland    A.33 S. Bland
P. John D. & Barbara A.    P. Henry & Mary J.
Oc. Farmer    M. Jas. F. Deal

Date: 12-29-1915
Mason Wiley    Connie Belle Dillow
A. 22 S. Bland    A. 16 S. Bland
P. Rob't & Mary    P. J. F. & L. B.
Oc. Farmer    M. A. H. Towe

Begin Page 63 of Original Book
Date: 1-4-1916
C.C. Hager    Emma Zella Hager
A. 23 S. Bland    A. 18 S. Bland
P. Bishop & Lizzie    P. R. L. & Matilda
Oc. Miner    M. S.V. Morris

Date: 12-29-1915
Paris Miller Hall    Lou Kate Wynn
A. 27 S. Bland    A. 27 S. Bland
P. S. H. & Susan    P. Jos & Kate
Oc. Laborer    M. Jas F. Deal

Date: 1-12-1916
Allen Taylor Duncan    Virginia Kitts
A. 60 W. Floyd    A. 40 S. Bland
P. Geo Reed & Nancy    P. David N. &
Maria Boothe    Molly Adaline Tickle
Oc. Carpenter    M. W. C. Crockett

Date: 2-9-1916
Jas. Bishop Akers    Lula E. Lambert
A. 21 W. Bland    A. 16 S. Bland
P. Jas. L. & Jane W.    P. S. J. & Ella

Oc. Farmer    M. A. H. Lowe

Date: 2-23-1916
Jas. Wm. Davis    Annette Christian
A. 27 S. Bland    A. 25 S. Tazewell
P. Ed. & Zarilda    P. Martin T. & Cosbie C.
Oc. Farmer    M. A. H. Towe

Date: 4-26-1916
James Hayden (B)    Emma Bullard (B)
A. 26 S. Bland    A. 23 S. Bland
P. Dan'l & Callie    P. Ransom & Causby
Oc. Miner    M. W. C. Crockett

Date: 4-29-1916
Allen T. Buchanan    Berte Newberry
A. 31 S. Tazewell    A. 33 S. Bland
P. Harold & Carrie    P. Henry & Laura M.
   Porter
Oc. Mail Clerk on RY    M. U. G. Foote
Married in Roanoke City

Date: 4-29-1916
Geo. Thos Thompson    Nan Evans Newberry
A. 24 S. Bland    A. 22 S. Bland
P. Geo Wash.&    P. Henry & Laura M.
Mattie Fox    Porter
Oc. Merchant    M. U. G. Foote
Married in Roanoke City

Date: 5-3-1916
Virgil Baldwin — Mary Mullins
A. 18 S. Tazewell — A. 17 S. TN
P. Jas & Marcelle — P. Frank & Dee

Oc. Farmer — M. Jas. F. Deal

Date: 5-6-1916
Gilbert Raymond Repass — Hazel Edna Bruce
A. 23 S. Bland — A. 17 S. Mercer, WV
P. Raymond C. & — P. J. E. & Edna H.
Juliet E. Kitts
Oc. Deputy Clerk — M. W. C. Crockett

Date: 5-10-1916
Jos Ernest Wheeler — Mary Ann Starling
A. 18 S. Bland — A. 17 S. Mercer, WV
P. W. H. & Emma — P. Ben F. & Sarah C.
Oc. Farmer — M. A. H. Lowe

Date: 5-10-1916
Henry Thos Daugherty — Hattie Shrader
A. 23 S. Monroe, WV — A. 18 S. Bland
P. W. G. & T. G. — P. J. E. & Nona E.
Oc. Veterinary Surgeon — M. Z. D. Holbrock

Date: 5-31-1916
Clarence Walls — Clydie Gibson
A. 22 S. Giles — A. 22 S. Bland
P. John & Jennie — P. J. V. & Caroline
Oc. Laborer — M. A. H. Towe

Date: 6-7-1916
Sam'l R. Ashworth — Laura Louisa Stinson
A. 37 W. Bland — A. 33 S. Tazewell
P. J. M. Ashworth — P. Sam'l E. & Mollie
Oc. Farmer — M. S. W. Bourne

Date: 6-7-1916
John D. Davis — Rose Eva Stinson
A. 26 S. Bland — A. 26 S. Bland
P. Edward A. & Zarilda — P. S.am'l E. & Mollie
Oc. Farmer — M. S. W. Bourne

Date: 5-31-1916
Kent Henry Robertson — Ina Elizabeth Pruett
A. 26 S. Bland — A. 19 S. Bland
P. W. T. & Mary E. — P. J. M. & Cora L. Helvey
Oc. Farmer — M. W. C. Crockett

Date: 6-18-1916
Jno R. Miller — Mattie Dora Dangerfield
A. 55 W. Mercer, WV — A. 49 W. Bland
P. Richard A. & Rebbea J.? P. Alfred J. & Francis Keeling
Oc. Blacksmith — M. J. E. Pannell

Date: 6-20-1916
Kemper Radford — Lithie Nelson
A. 21 S. Floyd — A. 20 S. Bland
P. Fayette & Delia — P. R. R. & Lizzie
Oc. Laborer — M. J. E. Pannell

Date: 6-26-1916
Oscar Wiley Caldwell — Sallie Hall
A. 37 S. Mercer, WV — A. 28 W. Bland
P. N. N. & Sarah — P. J. B. & Vicie
Oc. Farming — M. W. K. Neel

Date: 6-30-1916
Eugene Johnson (B) — Mollie Bullard (B)
A. 22 S. Bland — A. 22 S. Bland
P. Nannie Johnson — P. Ransom & Causby
Oc. Laborer — M. W. C. Crockett

Date: 9-10-1916
Jesse Reed Kirk — Mary Lelia Morehead
A. 20 S. Giles — A. 20 S. Bland
P. Webb & — P. Gord. Andrew &
Bertha Overstreet — Tacy Adaline Pruett
Oc. Farmer — M. M. M. Ellis

Date: 9-19-1916
Harman Carter — Minnie Lee Kidd
A. 34 S. Tazewell — A. 17 S. Bland

P. Mart. & D. B. — P. Henley H. & Ollie
Oc. Farmer — M. W. K. Neel

Date: 9-19-1916
Wm. Donathan — Lula E. Richardson
A. 23 S. Bath, KY — A. 16 S. Bland
P. Jas . & Lucy — P. H. W. & V. V.
Oc. Laborer — M. Allen Jones, Sr.

Date: 9-27-1916
Wylie Hicks Stowers — Clara May Walters
A. 25 S. Bland — A. 19 S. Bland
P. W. H. & S. C. — P. J. W. & Sallie B.
Oc. Farmer — M. W. C. Crockett

Date: 10-1-1916
Jas. Henry Lambert        Ora Myers
A. 31 S. Tazewell         A. 27 S. Bland
P. J. C. & Catherine      P. Gordon & Rhoda
Oc. Sawmilling            M. F. M. Radford

Date: 10-25-1916
Jno. W. Nunn              Cleo Gibson
A. 22 S. Bland            A. 20 S. Bland
P. W. T. & Ella           P. J. V. & Caroline
Oc. Laborer               M. A. H. Gentry

Date: 11-15-1916
Walter Howe Taylor        Ossie Myrtle Gusler
A. 22 S. Giles            A. 22 S. Bland
P. Green & Lucy J.        P. Jacob S. & Maggie L.
Oc. Farmer                M. W. M. Ellis

Date: 12-20-1916
Walter Hugh Kitts         Stella Mae Kimberlin
A. 27 S. Bland            A. 24 S. Bland
P. N. M. & Eliza A.       P. E. H. & Louisa
Oc. Farmer                M. Jas. F. Deal

Date: 12-25-1916
Harry Allen Murrell       Ocie Jane Wall
A. 26 S. East Radford     A.19 S. Groseclose
P. R. N. & Virginia C.    P. Z. A. & Lizzie
Oc. Forman Ford
Motor Co.                 M. Jas. F. Deal

Date: 12-17-1916
Eugene Mortimer           Sallie Elizabeth Jarrell
Davidson
A. 30 S. Bland            A. 21 S. Bland
P. Jno A. & Mattie J.     P. Chas & Mary
Oc. Civil Engineer        M. Albert H. Gentry

Date: 1-4-1917
Floyd Ramsey              Dallis Havens
A. 22 S. Bland            A. 22 S. Bland
P. Dock & Caroline        P. W. H. & Victoria
Oc. Farmer                M. W. C. Crockett

Date: 2-3-1917
Willie Peery Tibbs        Elie May Kitts
A. 21 S. Bland            A. 18 S. Bland
P. Jno & Matilda          P. Henry Hiram &
                          Lucinda McFarland
Oc. Farmer                M. Jas. F. Deal

Date: 10-13-1916
Millard Fillmore Blankenship  Bessie Isora Radford
A. 35 S. Bland            A. 27 S. Bland
P. Berry & Ardelia        P. F. M. & Sarah E. L.
Oc. Farmer                M. W. A. Warner

Date: 11-3-1916
Clarence Ezra Thomas      Virginia Nestor
A. 22 S. Giles            A. 30 D. Carroll
P. B. P. & Maggie         P. Rebecca Combs
Oc. R. R. Section Man.    M. C. A. Brown

12-6-1916
Jos Smith Childress       Lila Igo
A. 47 W. Buchanan         A. 31 S. Bland
P. Wm. & Nancy            P. J. W. & Mary
Oc. Farmer                M. W. K. Neel

Date: 12-20-1916
John Thompson             Luticia Stowers
A. 21 S. Bland            A. 16 S. Bland
P. Jas A. & Mary E.       P. W. H. & Mollie A.
Oc. Famer                 M. Albert H. Gentry

Date: 12-27-1916
Authur Lluen? Hamilton    Ada Elizabeth Stinson
A. 35 S. Bland            A. 39 S. Bland
P. S. M. & Sallie A.      P. John & Hester
Oc. Mining                M. W. M. Ellis

Begin Page 64 of Original Book
Date: 1-4-1917
Riley Harrison Hancock    Stella Ernest Hancock

A. 27 S. Bland            A. 19 S. Bland
P. Jno A. & Barbara       P. Geo W. & Belle
Oc. Farmer                M. W. C. Crockett

Date: 1-10-1917
Wylie Preston Clark       Annie Belver Myers
A. 30 S. Bland            A. 16 S. Bland
P. R. M. & M. J.          P. Wm G. & Laura
Oc. Farmer                M. F. M. Radford

Date: 2-12-1917
Walter Wirt Hall          Emily J. Davis
A. 20 S. Bland            A. 21 S. Bland
P. G. E. & O. B.          P. C A. & Nannie

Oc. Farmer                M. T. D. Strader

Date: 2-14-1917
Robt Sydney Neel
A. 22 S. Bland
P. Robert Lee &
Sara Ellen Umbarger
Oc. Farmer

Ollie Mae Crow
A. 20 S. Bland
P. D. A. & Mary C.

M.  Allen Jones, Sr.

Date: 3-21-1917
Kelley Marvin Kidd
A. 20 S. Bland
P. S. S. & Cynthia L.

Oc. Farmer

Sallie Belle Wolf
A. 17 S. Tazewell
P. D. S. & A. D.

M.  W. K. Neel

Date: 4-11-1917
Dan'l T. Carver
A. 42 S. Tazewell
P. Dan'l & Martha C.
Oc. La;borer

Lucy Kate Carver
A. 15 S. Washington
P. W. W. & M. A.
M.  A. H. Gentry

Date: 4-9-1917
Graham Hager
A. 21 S. Bland
P. Robt & Matilda
Oc. Farmer

Lena G. Pruett
A. 16 S. Bland
P. P. D. & Rhoda
M.  A. H. Gentry

Date: 4-11-1917
Jno Patrick Turley
A. 35 S. Bland
P. Reese T. &
Margaret Alice Hilt
Oc. Farmer

Ada Gray Kitts
A. 24 S. Bland
P. Harvey John &
Sarah Elizabeth Williams
M.  Z. A. Wall

Date: 4-19-1917
John Preston Stowers
A. 51 W. Bland
P. Geo W. & Mary A.

Oc. Farmer

Nannie Eveline Kidd
A. 45 S. Bland
P. Elbert S. & Clara

M.  W. C. Crockett

Date: 5-16-1917
Wylie Barnes Compton
A. 25 S. Bland
P. J. B. & Jennie
Oc. Farmer

Ruth Bernie Palmer
A. 21 S. Giles
P. S. R. & Amanda
M.  J. F. Jones

Date: 5-22-1917
Stephen Greever Lampert
A. 23 S. Bland
P. Jas A. & Clemmie
Oc. Farmer

Dorsie Della Harden
A. 19 S. Bland
P. Sam'l H. & Farnie V.
M.  Z. A. Wall

Date: 5-30-1917
Robt. Sam'l Newberry
A. 21 S. Bland
P. Samuel  Price &
Malissa Rose Miller
Oc. Farmer

Zella Eileen Burton
A. 21 S. Bland
P. John W. &
Madella J. Repass
M.  H. W. Leslie

Date: 6-1-1917
Wm. Jonathan Tracy
A. 30 S. Bland
P. E. G. & Jane Boling

Oc. Farmer

Mrs. Wilma Cooley
A. 34 W. Carroll
P. Armstead & Pearlie
Virginia Mathews
M.  F. M. Radford

Date: 6-6-1917
Chas. Rob't Patton
A. 19 S. Bland
P. M. M. & Poca
Oc. Farmer

Sadie May Thompson
A. 18 S. Giles
P. W M. Thompson
M.W. C. Crockett

Date: 7-18-1917
Robert Davis
A. 29 D. Tazewell
P. John & Sallie
Oc. Railroad worker

Nettie Maud  Richardson
A. 19 S. Bland
P. A. R. & S. V.
M.

Date: 7-18-1917
Edward Cooper Creger
A. 22 S. Smyth
P. Miller & Minnie
Oc. Farmer
Written in book, 6-6-1914

Maggie Missouri Kitts
A. 25 S. Bland
P. Henry H. & Lucinda McF.
M.  Z. A. Wall

Date: 8-5-1917
James H. Earles
A. 21 S. Tazewell
P. James & Mary
Oc. Farmer

Lucy A. King
A. 16 S. Bland
P. E. T. & Mary
M.  A. H. Gentry

Date: 8-25-1917 (Married in Princeton)
Dave Newton Shufflebarger Elizabeth Starks Bruce
A. 24 S. Bland         A. 19 S. Bland
P. Harvey B. & Margaret P. W. J. & Elvira
Oc. Farmer         M. C. N. Williams

Date: 9-16-1917
Wiley Hicks Burress
A. 21 S. Bland
P. W. W. & Julia
Oc. Farmer

Maggie Lillian Bailey
A. 26 W. Bluefield, WV
P. D. C. & Pauline Akers
M. F. M. Radford

Date: 9-14-1917
Walter Carlos French    Sallie Belle Hager
A. 19 S. Bland    A. 16 S. Bland
P. Wm. A. & Leona    P. I. M. & Cora
Oc. Farmer    M. W. C. Crockett

Date: 9-20-1917
Chas. Martin Rudder, Jr    Ola Louise Mitchell
A. 33 S. Bland    A. 22 S. Bland
P. Chas Martin, Sr. &    P. C. A. & Minnie Dulaney
Louvicia Jerusha Mustard
Oc. Banker    M. W. M. Ellis

Date: 10-17-1917
Wm. Jas Bond    Bertha Hester Terry
A. 21 S. Pulaski    A. 18 S. Bland
P. James & Martha    P. Wm. E. & Eugenia T.

Oc. Sawmilling    M. W. C. Crockett

Date: 10-31-1917
Henderson Monroe    Bessie Elizabeth
Gusler    Morehead
A. 22 S. Giles    A. 18 S. Bland
P. J. A. & Ollie G.    P. Gordon Andrew &
   Tacy Adaline Pruett
Oc. Farmer    M. S. V. Morris

Date: 11-14-1917
Geo Stuart Corner    Josie Thompson
A. 50 W. Bland    A. 45 W. Bland
P. Geo & Nancy    P. Blankenship
Oc. Farmer    M. W. M. Ellis

Date: 11-28-1917
Robt Hicks Christian    Virgie Tolbert
A. 23 S. Tazewell    A. 16 S. Bland
P. M. T. & Causby C.    P. J. B. & Maria J.

Oc. Farmer    M. S. D. Lambert

Date: 1-23-1918
Robt Glenn Fanning    Grace Havens
A. 18 S. Bland    A. 16 S. Bland
P. Jas Mathew &    P. Earsten Sheppard &
Nannie Jane Mustard    Lillie Woods
Oc. Farmer    M. W. C. Crockett


Date: 9-20-1917
Everett Vance Dunn    Nora Belle Hylton
A. 21 S. Bland    A. 25 S. Giles
P. W. G. & Jane    P. H. P. & Sallie
Oc. Patrolman    M. Returned, not used
Married in Welch, WV

Date: 9-26-1917
Houston Neel Brunk    Genoa Agnes Davis
A. 21 S. Bland    A. 16 S. Giles
P. Wm. & Nancy    P. Has. W. & Louisa Va.

Oc. Farmer    M. Allen Jones, Sr.

Date: 10-27-1917
Miller Shannon Allen    Delia May Mustard
A. 23 S. Bland    A. 22 S. Bland
P. M. B. & Shannon    P. Newton Shell &
   Ella Ancel Crockett
Oc. Farmer    M. T. A. Smoot
Married in Richmond

Date: 10-31-1917
Roma Lee Hager    Pearl Hart

A. 21 S. Bland    A. 31 W. Bland
P. Mandona Hager    P. Berry & Ardelia
   Blankenship
Oc. Farmer    M. Fulton Blankenship

Date: 11-24-1917
Arthur Barlow    Nancy J. Pridemore
A. 28 S. N. C.    A. 20 S. TN
P. Mike & Nancy    P. Geo & Lucinda
Oc. Farmer    M. H. S. Johnston

Begin Page 65 of Original Book
Date: 1-6-1918
Everett G. Walters    Fannie Lee Kimberling
A. 21 S. Wythe    A. 17 S. Bland
P. Kelly Repass &    P. Jennie Bane
Poca Geneva Walters
Oc. Farmer    M. W. C. Crockett

Date: 1-23-1918
Jesse Ingram    Ossie Bruce
A. 20 S. Bland    A. 17 S. Bland
P. Sam V. & Ettie    P. Ella Bruce Clemons

Oc. Laborer    M. W. C. Crockett

Date: 1-30-1918
Howard H. Saunders       Dora Lee Sarver
A. 19 S. Mercer, WV      A. 21 S. Bland
P. J. R. & N. A.         P. J. W. & Geneva
Oc. Farmer               M. T. R. Darr

Date: 3-9-1918
Milton Bivens            Mona Perdue
A. 17 Giles              A. 18 S. Giles
P. L. C. & Della         P. Burl & Tishie
Oc. Farmer               M. T. R. Darr

Date: 4-27-1918
Davis Hicks Cassell      Pearl Lucile Cox
A. 28 S. Smyth           A. 22 S. Bland
P. H. J. & M. J.         P. L. M. & Susan

Oc. Farmer               M. H. S. Johnston

Date: 5-22-1918
Geo Wesley Lampert       Stella Annie Jane Pauley
A. 20 S. Bland           A. 15 S. Bland
P. J. I. & B. D.         P. J. Roach &. Molly M.
Oc. Farmer               M. R. Homer Anderson

Date: 5-26-1918
Otto Pruett              Rosa Ashworth
A. 41 S. Bland           A. 32 S. Bland
P. J. M. & Elizabeth     P. W. B. & Martha
Oc. Farmer               M. S. V. Morris

Date: 5-30-1918
John Jesse Meadows       Mary Alberta Davis
A. 28 S. Bland           A. 21 S. Bland
P. J. W. & Ida B.        P. H. N. & E. C.
Oc. Farmer               M. Allen Jones, Sr.

Date: 7-24-1918
Monte Hare               Maggie Akers
A. 40 W. Giles           A. 35 W. Bland
P.                       P.
Oc. Sawmilling           M. C. W. Stone

Date: 7-25-1918
W. R. Neel               Sallie Pruett
A. 41 W. Tazewell        A. 47 W. Bland
P. S. W. Neel            P. R. A. & Nancy Walters
Oc. Railroading          M. S. D. Lambert

Date: 2-11-1918
Albert Jackson Davis     Nannie Virginia Davis
A. 19 S. Bland           A. 18 S. Bland
P. C. A. & Nannie        P. Jas W. & Nancy J.
Oc. Farmer               M. W. C. Crockett

Date: 4-4-1918
John Smith               Sarah Stowers
A. 18 S. Bland           A. 16 S. Bland
P. G. L. & Belle         P. G. H. & Julia A.
Oc. Farmer               M. S. D. Lambert

Date: 5-5-1918
Robt Lee Gusler          Ella Sue Morehead
A. 26 S. Giles           A. 22 S. Bland
P. John & Lizzie         P. John Marshall
                         & Sallie J. Shufflebarger
Oc. Farmer               M. W. M. Ellis

Date: 5-26-1918
Millard F. Russell       Gussie A. French
A. 33 W. TN              A. 18 S. Bland
P. H. J. & Sarah         P. T. E. & Alice
Oc. Ralilroading         M. T. R. Darr

Date: 5-29-1918
Luther Burton            Annie Smith
A. 18 S. Bland           A. 16 S. Bland
P. Pauline Burton        P. G. L. & Belle
Oc. Farmer               M. S. D. Lambert

Date: 7-14-1918
James Frank Hancock      Madie Maxwell Hanshew
A. 29 S. Bland           A. 23 S. Bland
P. N. B. & Margaret E.   P. C. W. & Maud
Oc. Farmer               M. H. S. Johnston

Date: 7-25-1918
Wm. McKinley Devor       Effie Burress
A. 21 S. Bland           A. 21 S. Bland
P. H. P. & Delvia        P. Rob't & Maggie
Oc. Laborer              M. W. C. Crockett

Date: 8-1-1918
Wm Linthicum             Emma Dunnagan
A. 50 W. Mercer, WV      A. 40 S. Bland
P. C. & Polly            P. R. B. & L. V. Wyrick
Oc. Lumberman            M. Allen Jones, Sr.

Date: 9-11-1918
Wm. Easten Havens          Effie Nunn
A. 22 S. Bland             A. 19 S. Bland
P. W. H. & Victoria        P. D. L. & Cynthia

Oc. Farmer                 M. W. M. Ellis

Date: 9-25-1918
Marvi n Cecil Havens       Louisa J. Fanning
A. 22 S. Bland             A. 17 S. Bland
P. Shep & Lizzie           P. J. M. & Nannie
Oc. Farmer                 M. W. C. Crockett

Date: 10-19-1918
Ballard Randolph Thomas Ella  Smith
A. 19 S. Giles             A. 21 S. Bland
P. B. P. & Maggie          P. J. D. & Mary G. Shrader
Oc. Sectionhand on R.R.    M. Allen Jones, Sr.

Date: 10-21-1918
Geo Floyd Stafford         Lauretta Jane Robertson
A. 23 S. Giles             A. 26 S. Bland
P. Will & Avis             P. W. T. & Ettie
Oc. Farmer                 M. W. M. Ellis

Begin Page 66 of Original Book
Date: 1-3-1919
Floyd Montague Jones       Matilda Jane Harris
A. 21 S.                   A. 22 S. Radford
P.Rufus & Lucy             P. Giles & Sina
Oc. Farmer                 M. S. D. Lambert

Date: 1-11-1919
Roy Scott Lambert          Missouri Clark
A. 24 S. Bland             A. 19 S. Bland
P. Kelley & Nannie B.      P. Kere & Minnie
Oc. Miner                  M. F. M. Radford

Date: 2-7-1919
James Adam Lesley          Fannie Marie Davis
A. 26 S. Tusclossa, AL     A. 19 S. Bland
P. John & Mary             P. Harry E. & Virginia
Oc. Farmer                 M. Allen Jones, Sr.

Date: 3-2-1919
Jacob Leech Rhudy          Nellie Bertha Hanshew
A. 24 S. Tazewell          A. 22 S. Bland
P. Jno C. & Rebecca J.     P. C. W. & Maud
Oc. Farmer                 M. H. S. Johnston

Date: 9-15-1918
James Andrew Kitts         Louvenia Eliz. Sarver
A. A. 33 S. Bland          A. 24 S. Bland
P. Wm. Ray &               P. S. E. & Margaret
Nannie Edith Burton
Oc. Farmer                 M. W. C. Crockett

Date: 10-3-1918
Sam. Webb (B)              Eddith Ramsey (B)
A. 38 S. Franklin          A. 22 S. Bland
P. Dan & Zo.               P. Green & Huldy
Oc. Farmer                 M. W. C. Crockett

Date: 10-23-1918
John C. Strock             Rosie Dalton
A. 22 S. Bland             A. 22 S. Giles
P. Sam Strock              P. Ballard Dalton
Oc. Farmer                 M.

Date: 12-24-1918
Wm. Arthur Hounshell       Clara Alberta Thompson
A. 27 S. Bland             A. 23 S. Bland
P. Joe & Maggie            P. Frank & Ibbie
Oc. Farmer                 M. W. C. Crockett

Date: 1-8-1919
Edward Hicks Stowers       Laura Texas Igo
A. 25 S. Bland             A. 23 S. Bland
P. M. F. & Susie           P. James & Mary
Oc. Farmer                 M. S. D. Lambert

Date: 2-5-1919
LeRoy Blaine Thompson      Annie M. Bruce
A. 24 S. Bland             A. 31 S. Bland
P. G. W. & Mattie L.       P. W. J. & Amanda E.
Oc. Farmer                 M. C. A. Brown
Married in Giles

Date: 2-16-1919
Kelley Robert Wall         Pearl Mae Hager
A. 28 S. bland             A. 18 S. Bland
P. Sam S. & Naomie S.      P. R. L. & T M.
Oc. Farmer                 M. C. W. Stone

Date: 3-11-1919
Guy Stafford               Beatrice Clark
A. 23 S. Mercer, WV        A. 22 S. Bland
P. Dock & Annie            P. Miller & Julia
Oc. Sawmilling             M. H. G. Gearhart
Married in Giles

Date: 4-11-1919
China Winton Lampert    Sarah L. Bane
A. 46 W. Bland    A. 48 S. Bland
P. G. W. & Sarah A.    P. J. S. C. & Margaret
Oc. Carpenter    M. H. S. Johnston

Date: 4-22-1919
Victor C. Nestor    Sara J. Neece
A. 18 S. Bland    A. 17 S. Bland
P. J. H. & Virginia    P. Bane & Lena
Oc. Sawmilling    M. Allen Jones, Sr.

Date: 5-1-1919
John H. French    Bertha Wall
A. 26 S. Bland    A. 23 W. Giles
P. W. A. & Laura    P. Lum. & Ellen Lambert
Oc. Farmer    M. Allen Jones, Sr.

Date: 5-23-1919
Edward Lee Kitts    Mary Florlence Nestor
A. 22 S. Bland    A. 16 S. Bland
P. Ballard Graham &    P. J. H. &
Ollie Norabelle Harman    Virginia E. Combs
Oc. Laborer    M. Allen Jones, Sr.

Date: 6-25-1919
Geo A. Allen    Ethel L. Newberry
A. 25 S. Bland    A. 22 S. Bland
P. W. B. & Maggie T.    P. L. M. & Lou
Oc. Farmer    M. W. C. Crockett

Date: 7-9-1919
Sam'l White Burton    Nellie Wayne Robinett
A. 25 S. Bland    A. 19 S. Bland
P. Jas Wm &    P. S. B. & Nellie
Lola Orga Painter
Oc. Printer    M. W. C. Crockett

Date: 7-16-1919
A. M. Parsell    Minnie P. Stinson
A. 29 S. Bland    A. 33 S. Bland
P. C. L. & Martha    P. John & Hester
Oc. Carpenter    M. W. M. Ellis

Date: 7-23-1919
H. Kent Hall    Mary Ann Neel
A. 24 S. Bland    A. 24 S. Bland
P. Greg. E. & O. B.    P. Allen J. Neel &
    Nancy Elizabeth Tibbs
Oc. Farmer    M. Allen Jones, Sr.

Date: 4-11-1919
Curtis Joseph Tade    Mary E. Tolbert
A.23 S. Bland    A. 22 S. N. C.
P. Jos & Mattie    P. C. F. & Nancy
Oc. Railroading    M. C. W. Stone

Date: 4-30-1919
Sam C. Thompson    Ella Burnes Patton
A. 22 S. Giles    A. 17 S. Bland
P. W. M. & Mary A.    P. W. M. & Poca
Oc. Farmer    M. W. C. Crockett

Date: 5-18-1919
Chas C. Melvin    Carrie Price
A. 43 S. Bland    A. 38 S. Bland
P. E. M. & Sarah M.    P. Isaiah K. & Ellen
Oc. Farmer    M. W. R. Miller

Date: 6-18-1919
Archie Arnold Wimmer    Zadie Pearl Kidd
A. 17 S. Giles    A. 19 S. Bland
P. H. K. & Cordella    P. Franklin Stuart &
    Dora Sweeney
Oc. Sawmilling    M. Allen Jones, Sr.

Date: 7-3-1919
Elias Conley    Edna M. Thompson
A. 41 S. Giles    A. 34 S. Bland
P. Emma Conley    P. J. A. & Mary
Oc. Sawmilling    M. S. D. Lambert

Date: 7-19-1919
Arthur B. Robinett    Lucy Kimberling
A. 22 S. Bland    A. 19 S. Bland
P. R. A. & Lucy    P. W. D. & Blanche
Oc. Farmer    M. C. W. Stone

Date: 7-20-1919
H. T. Anderson    Minnie Hayton
A. 60 W. Smyth    A. 50 S. Bland
P. J. H. & Jennie    P. Thos & Ann
Oc. Farmer    M. H. S. Johnston
Married in Smyth

Date: 7-23-1919
Clarence E. Stowers    Mary C. Barger
A. 22 S. Bland    A. 21 S. Bland
P. F. S. & Belle    P. G. W. & Ann
Oc. Farmer    M. H. S. Johnston

Date: 7-23-1919
Edgar Carpenter | Alice Davis
A. 21 S. Carroll | A. 22 S. Bland
P. Wm. & Laura | P. C. A. & Nannie

Oc. Sawmilling | M. Allen Jones, Sr.

Date: 8-14-1919
Robt. P. Saunders | Genoa A. Bogle

A. 52 S. Giles | A. 48 S. Bland
P. R. T. & R. J. | P. Jno L. & Julia A.
Oc. Farmer | M. W. M. Ellis

Date: 8-22-1919
Clarence Sarver | Dora M. French
A. 21 S. Bland | A. 18 S. Bland
P. J. W. & Geneva | P. W. S. & Gillie
Oc. Farmer | M. S. V. Morris

Date: 9-10-1919
Paris Looney | Lena O. Kidd
A. 21 S. Buchanan | A. 20 S. Bland
P. Hick & Vicie | P. S. S. & L. C.

Oc. Farmer | M. W. K. Neel

Date: 9-17-1919
Elliott W. Williams | Ella Davis
A. 28 S. Carroll | A. 28 S. Bland
P. Albert & Rena | P. H. N. & Lizzie
Oc. Sawmilling | M. Allen Jones, Sr.

Date: 10-8-1919
Ballard Burton | Luticia Thompson
A. 21 S. Bland | A. 19 W. Bland
P. Pauline Burton | P. J. H. & Martha Stowers
Oc. Farmer | M. C. W. Stone

Date: 10-19-1919
John B. Wiley | Viola Tinkey
A. 28 S. Giles | A. 21 S. Somerset, PA
P. Lewis & Sallie | P. Sam & Ida
Oc. Engineer | M. S. V. Morris

Date: 10-21-1919
John GrahamKitts | Ona Nellie Ramsey
A. 19 S. Bland | A. 20 S. Bland
P. Ballard Graham & | P. W. W. & Ida V.
Ollie Norabelle Harman
Oc. Sawmilling | M. W. R. Miller

Date: 8-13-1919
Wm. Clinton Dillow | Mary Kordelila Hanshew
A. 25 S. Bland | A. 17 S. Smyth
P. Wm. Addison & | P. H. F. & N. J.
Nancy Elizabeth Waddle
Oc. Farmer | M. W. C. Crockett

Date: 8-16-1919
Marion Martin Minor | Augustus Elizabeth "Bess"
Muncy | Repass
A. 27 S. Bland | A. 24 S. Bland
P. Chas P. & Mary E. | P. Raymond C. & Juliet K.
Oc. Farmer | M. Allen Jones, Sr.

Date: 8-21-1919
Walter A. Blessing | Georgia T. Trinckle
A. 26 S. Bland | A. 19 S. Smyth
P. E. F. & L. B. | P. W. C. & Virginia
Oc. Mason | M. Allen Jones, Sr.

Date: 9-12-1919
Hugh D. Hamblin | Ethel S. Kitts
A. 27 S. Bland | A. 18 S. Bland
P. J. S. & S. C. | P. Breckenridge Harvey &
| Emma Caroline Bowles
Oc. Truck Driver | M. Allen Jones, Sr.

Date: 10-1-1919
Geo E. Hailey | Mayme H. Thornton
A. 21 S. Carroll | A. 19 S. Giles
P. A. J. & Lucy | P. J. T. & L. A.
Oc. Plumber | M. W. C. Crockett

Date: 10-9-1919
Andrew M. Cox | Lourena M. Neece
A. 24 S. Bland | A. 16 S. Bland
P. G. W. & M. T. | P. Bane & Laura
Oc. Sawmilling | M. Allen Jones, Sr.

Date: 10-20-1919
Thos W. Ogle | Berta M. Collins
A. 64 D. Carroll | A. 19 S. Bland
P. John & Sarah C. | P. J. H. & Gillie B.
Oc. Farming | M. Jacob Smith

Date: 10-21-1919
Allen D. Neece | Cassie E. Thompson
A. 19 S. Bland | A. 18 S. Tazewell
P. Bane & Lena | P. Chas & Nan.

Oc. Sawmilling | M. Allen Jones, Sr.

Begin Page 67 of Original Book

Date: 10-22-1919
Otho Ramsey — Annie Sarver
A. 20 S. Bland — A. 21 S. Bland
P. C. H. & Almeda — P. S. E. & Maggie
Oc. Sawmilling — M. W. M. Ellis

Date: 10-28-1919
S. A. Gusler — Eula L. Ramsey
A. 20 S. Giles — A. 17 S. Bland
P. J. A. & Ollie — P. Jno & Emma
Oc. Clerk in Store — M. W. M. Ellis

Date: 10-29-1919
Chas W. Davis — Sarah L. Millirons
A. 54 W. Bland — A. 19 S. Bland
P. S. C. & Liza A. — P. R. L. & Annie K.
Oc. Farming — M. Allen Jones, Sr.

Date: 11-11-1919
Martin Luther Greever — Mary A. Newberry
A. 30 S. Tazewell — A. 26 S. Bland
P. John H. & — P. Lafayette M. &
Letitia C. Peery — Mary Louise Bird
Oc. Farming — M. J. W. Morris

Date: 11-12-1919
Edgar Palmer King — Texie Miller Davis
A. 24 S. Pulaski — A. 20 S. Bland
P. H. N. & Susan — P. H. N. & Eliz.. C.
Oc. Farmer — M. J. W. Morris

Date: 11-19-1919
Lawrence Lafay. Harner — Lute Burton
A. 28 S. Bland — A. 23 S. Bland
P. Wm Thos & — P. James Wm. &
Elvira R. Neal — Lola Orga Painter
Oc. Lumberman — M. W. N. Baker

Date: 12-6-1919
Theo. Mosci Townley — Nella L. Dunnagan
A. 34 S. Bland — A. 26 S. Bland
P. Jno W. S. & Mary K. — P. Enoch & Ella
Oc. Farmer — M. Allen Jones, Sr.

Date: 12-23-1919
James Harvey French — Nannie M. Ramsey
A. 42 S. Giles — A. 23 S. Bland
P. Hugh & Susan — P. T. R. & Caroline K.
Oc. Farmer — M. F. M. Radford

Date: 10-22-1919
Wm. L. Hamilton — Ida Sarver
A. 19 S. Bland — A. 21 S. Bland
P. Samuel & Ada — P. S. E. & Maggie
Oc. Engineer — M. W. C. Crockett

Date: 10-29-1919
Robt. R. Davis — Virginia Dalton
A. 18 S. Carroll — A. 22 S. WV
P. T. F. & Minnie — P. J. S. Dalton
Oc. Sawmill worker — M. S. V. Morris

Date: 11-12-1919
Jas P. Shewey — Luella Farmer
A. 26 S. Smyth — A. 23 W. Bland
P. John & Florence — P. P. W. & Eliza Perkey
Oc. Farming — M. I. L. Cox

Date: 11-13-1919
Jas W. Lucas — Cora E. Britts
A. 31 W. Lexington — A. 27 S. Bland

P. J. W. & Nannie Tyler — P. C. H. & M. E.
Oc. Soldier — M. J. W. Morris

Date: 11-20-1919
Edgar H. Millirons — Cecil T. Davis
A. 23 S. Pulaski — A. 20 S. Bland
P. R. L. & A. K. — P. C. C. & Willie F.
Oc. Surveying — M. W. D. Larrowe

Date: 11-26-1919
Miller Shannon Allen — Ethel K. Bird
A. 25 W. Bland — A. 21 S. Bland
P. M. B. & Shan. H. — P. Geo. Thomas Bird
— Carrie Louise Burton
Oc. Farmer — M. J. W. Morris

Date: 12-17-1919
H. W. Suiter — Laura Lester Finley
A. 37 S. Bland — A. 21 S. Bland
P. F. I. & M. G. — P. T. N. & Laura
O. Supt.of timber lands — M. D. H. Kern
Married in Roanoke

Date: 12-24-1919
Wm. R. Sarver — Della Mae Williams
A. 20 S. Mercer, WV — A. 16 S. Mercer, WV
P. J. B. & Lena M. — P. Eugene & Pet
Oc. Farmer — M. W. N. Baker

Date: 12-25-1919
Kelley P. Williams            Frankie A. Atwell
A. 25 S. Bland                A. 22 S. Bland
P. A. J. & M. L.              P. G. S. & Essie A.
Oc. Farmer                    M. H. S. Johnston

Date: 12-26-1919
James C. Baker                Flora B. Thompson
A. 22 S. Bland                A. 25 S. Bland
P. J. W. & Nellie             P. J. E. & Rachel
Oc. Laborer                   M. J. W. Morris

Date: 12-26-1919
Wm. W. Waddle                 Nellie G. Davis
A. 24 S. Bland                A. 23 S. Bland
P. W. G. & Bettie             P. S. S. & Sallie
Oc. Farmer                    M. Allen Jones, Sr.

Date: 12-31-1919
James L. Garvin               Bettie M. Fanning
A. 41 W. Monroe, WV           A. 30 S. Bland
P. Saml. & Martha R.          P. Geo W. & Matilda H. D.
Oc. Farmer                    M. W. N. Baker

Date: 2-12-1920
Rob't L. Wright               Nellie French
A. 18 S. Bland                A. 19 S. Bland
P.L. J. & Matilda             P. T. M. & Eliza Jane

Oc. Farmer                    M. F. M. Radford

Date: 2-18-1920
Geo H. Pauley                 Dora L. Fortner
A. 21 S. Bland                A. 18 S. Bland
P. G. P. & Sallie S.          P. John & Sylvia
Oc. Farmer                    M. J. W. Morris

Date: 2-26-1920
E. Hampton Dillon             Nora Mills
A. 21 S. Monroe, WV           A. 18 S. Monroe, WV
P. Walter & Alice             P. W. H. & Minnie
Oc. Farmer                    M. S. V. Morris

Date: 4-7-1920
Horace Lingenfelt             Linnie Leslie
A. 23 S. Lincoln, NC          A. 24 S. Wythe
P. B. P. & Eliza              P. Chas L. & Dora
Oc. Factory worker            M. Allen Jones, Sr.

Date: 12-24-1919
Chas G. Pauley                Gertrude Baker
A. 26 S. Bland                A. 21 S. Bland
P. G. P. & Sallie S.          P. J. W. & Nellie
Oc. Laborer                   M. Allen Jones, Sr.

Date: 12-30-1919
Luther Dickenson (B)          Elizabeth Hobbs (B)
A. 21 S. Tazewell             A. 17 S Bland
P. A. & Loursa?               P. Lewis A. & Cynthia
Oc. Laborer                   M. W. N. Baker

Begin Page 68 of Original Book
Date: 1-14-1920
John E. Carr                  Etta F. Repass
A. 56 W. Bland                A. 38 W. Bland
P. Wm. & Matilda              P. M. F. & Hester Lampert
Oc. Farmer                    M. J. W. Morris

Date 2-18-1920
Roney Lee Nunn                Sallie Vennia Morehead
A. 25 S. Bland                A. 19 S. Bland
P.Doc Lee & Cynthia           P. Jno Marshall
Rosetta Miller                Sallie Shufflebarger
Oc. Farmer                    M. W. N. Baker

Date: 2-26-1920
Claude Robert Scott           Lute Finley
A. 23 S. Nansemond            A. 29 S. Bland
P. R. G. & Susie P.           P. T. N. & Loura?
Oc. Farmer                    M. J. W. Morris

Date: 3-24-1920
Roy Alva Neel                 Louisa Hounshell
A. 21 S. Tazewell             A. 24 S. Bland
P. L. F. & Ella               P. Wm. Hounshell
Oc. Sawmilling                M. H. S. Johnston

Date: 4-29-1920
Stanley L. Tibbs              Nellie Lampert
A.24 Smyth                    A. 23 S. Bland
P. Martin J. & Lula I.        P. J. A. & Clemmie
Oc. Farmer                    M. S. W. Hahn
Married in Tazewell

Date: 5-3-1920
Zebulon Lamont Painter   Ola Kate Burton
A. 27 S. Bland          A. 22 S. Bland
P. Geo, Dabney &        P. Giles Henderson
Elizabeth Nancy Tickle  & Callie Dixie Kitts
Oc. Postmaster          M. J. W. Morris

Date: 5-23-1920
Dotson Clark            Bessie Bivens
A.20 S. Bland           A. 17 S. Giles
P. J. W. & Martha       P. L. C. & Della
Oc. Farmer              M. T. R. Darr

Date: 5-31-1920
Wm. Emmett Leavitt      Laura Kidd
A. 24 S. Giles          A. 27 S. Bland
P. Oscar & Mollie       P. Geo & Causby
Oc. Farmer              M. Geo H. Gilmer

Date: 6-4-1920
Gilbert Percival Hubble  Cora Lee Crabtree
A. 21 S. Wythe          A. A. 21 S. Bland
P. T. D. & Ossie        P. C. A. & Allie Fonlesong
Oc. Farmer              M. J. Luther Sieber
Married in Roanoke

Date: 6-1-1920
Joseph Arthur Thomas    Annie Elizabeth Walker
A. 32 S. Princeton,WV   A. 25 S. Newcastle
P. R. G. & Susan V.     P. J. B. & Jane
Oc. Farmer              M. J. W. Morris

Date: 6-16-1920
James Frazier Kidd      Mamie Belle Smith
A. 22 S. Raliegh, WV    A. 16 S. Bland
P. F. S. & Dora         P. J. D. & Gillie
Oc. Farmer              M. J. W. Morris

Date: 6-30-1920
Harrison Gordon Bird    Bertie Rementa Burton
A. 36 S. Mercer, WV     A. 22 S. Bland
P. J. S. H. & E. S.     P. Jas Wm &
                        Lola Orga Painter
Oc. Carpenter           M. J. W. Morris

Date: 8-11-1920
Floyd H. Sarver         Rosela Grace Tabor
A. 20 S. Bland          A. 18 S. Bland
P. J. W. & Geneva       P. F. G. & Helen
Oc. Laborer             M. C. W. Stone

Date: 5-16-1920
Robt. B. Stalmaker      Eva Pauley
A. 40 W. Elkins,WV      A. 21 S. Bland

P. T. J. & Mary         P. Newton T. & Martha
Oc. Farmer              M. R. L. Parks

Date: 5-26-1920
Stephen Edward Peery    Nina Marian Pruett
A. 32 S. Bland          A. 23 S. Bland
P. J. G. & Mary J.      P. J. M. & Cora L.
Oc. Farmer              M. J. W. Morris

Date: 6-1-1920 (Married in Wythe)
Wm. L. Havens           Rosa M. Townley
A. 55 W. Bland          A. 37 S. Bland
P. Jno & Jane Harman    P. Jno W. S. & Mary Kath.
Oc. Farmer              M. Rev. Oliver Shanks

Date: 6-2-1920
Chas Floy Hancock       Clare Elizabeth Davis
A. 25 S. Bland          A. 27 S. Bland
P. N. B. & Maggie       P. S. S. & Sallie
Oc. Farmer              M. John Williams Rader
Married in Wythe

Date: 6-10-1920
Wm. Henderson Pauley    Lula Elizabeth Clark
A. 25 S. Bland          A. 23 A. Wythe
P. Julia A. Pauley      P. J. A. Jane
Oc. Farmer              M. W. D. Larrowe
Married in Wythe

Date: 6-16-1920
Albert T. Davis         Annie K. King
A. 35 W. Bland          A. 24 S. Bland
P. J. T. & Mary D.      P. Jos & Emma E.
Oc. Farmer              M. J. W. Morris

Date: 7-3-1920
Wm. Hearn Newberry      Bertha Lee Thompson
A. 30 S. Bland          A. 21 S. Bland
P. Dunn Bogle &         P. Miller Hoge &
Victoria Harman         Mollie Kate Ashworth
Oc. Comm. Of Revenue    M. J. W. Morris

Date: 8-11-1920
Chas. L. Mustard        Mary J. Patton
A. 54 W. Bland          A. 45 S. Bland
P. Henry P. & Franzenia  P. Robt. & Mary M.
Oc. Farmer              M. S. V. Morris

Date: 8-11-1920
Peery D. Bruce     Cordie Jane Stafford
A. 37 S. Bland     A. 26 S. Bland
P. J. W. & Lizzie     P. Ralph Montgomery &
        Mary Elizabeth Crawford
Oc. Farmer     M. J. W. Morris

Date: 9-10-1920
Geo Albert Williams   Lena Byrnes Stafford
A. A. 27 S. Hazelton, PA   A. 29 S. Bland
P. A. E. & Mary E.    P. John W. & Flora W.
Oc. Teacher     M. A. E. Williams

Date: 9-15-1920
Oscar Davis King    Lillie May Sutphin
A. 27 S. Pulaski    A. 23 D. Floyd
P. W. D. & Ollie V.    P. M. F. & Luella
Oc. Lumberman    M. J. W. Morris

Date: 10-6-1920
Kyle Thompson    Opal Burton
A. 23 S. Grayson    A. 22 S. Bland
P. Geo & Marilda    P. Giles H. & Dixie
Oc. Minning     M. J. W. Morris

Date: 10-21-1920    (Married in Tazewell)
Samuel Yost     Evelyn Levitt
A. 27 S. Tazewell    A. 20 S. Giles
P. Preston & Mollie    P. Oscar & Mollie C.

Oc. Farmer     M. W. K. Neel

Date: 10-27-1920    (Married in Wythe)
Cloyd W. Lefler    Ina Davis
A. 20 S. Wythe    A. 18 S. Bland
P. T. R. & M. J.    P. C. W. & Louisa
Oc. Farmer     M. W. D. Larrowe

Date: 11-29-1920    (Married in Giles)
G. L. Montgomery (B)   Nannie Gordon (B)
A. 27 S. Giles     A. 24 S. Bland
P. Will & Mary C.    P. Arthur & Lav. H.
Oc. Farmer     M.

Date: 12-15-1920
Jas Walker Kitts    Ethel May Kidd
A. 22 S. Bland     A. 24 S. Raliegh, WV
P. Ballard Graham &   P. Franklin Stuart
Ollie Norabell Harman   & Dora Sweeny
Oc. Sawmilling    M. C. W. Stone

Date: 9-1-1920
Chas. Newton Richardson   Alice Virginia Burton
A. 33 S. Bland     A. 20 S. Bland
P. Chas. W. &     P. Jas. Wm. &
Elizabeth Bowles    Lola Orga Painter
Oc. Sawmilling    M. J. W. Morris

Date: 9-6-1920
Willie Montgomery (B)   Jessie Bullard (B)
A. 24 S. California    A. 21 S. Bland
P. Victoria Hurt    P. Ranson & Causby
Oc. Electrician    M. Allen Jones, Sr.

Date: 9-9-1920     (Married in Pearisburg)
Bruce Kelley Noble    Lora? E. Nestor
A. 21 S. Mercer, WV   A. 16 S. Bland
P. Henry & Valera?   P. J. H. & Virginia Thomas
Oc. Farmer     M. Geo. W. Ferrell

Date: 10-18-1920
Chas Switzer Thomas   Elizabeth Jane Flick
A. 27 S. Bland     A. 26 S. Bland
P. R. G. & Sue V.    P. C. M. & M. E.
Oc. Farmer     M. W. N. Baker

Date: 10-31-1920
Wm. McKinley Croy   Lillie Elsie Morehead
A. 24 S. Bland     A. 28 S. Bland
P. John & Benia    P. Lee Kyle &
        Emma Catherine Miller
Oc. Laborer     M. W. N. Baker

Date: 11-26-1920
Joshua D. Blankenship   Lula M. Burton
A. 40 S. Bland     A. 18 S. Bland
P. Berry & Ardelia    P. Bud & Lona
Oc. Sawmilling    M. J. M. Morris

Date: 12-8-1920
Tarter Neese     Nannie J. Tabor
A. 25 S. Bland     A. 17 S. Bland
P. A. T. & Mollie Repass   P. Frank & Helen Wolfe
Oc. Farmer     M. J. D. Spitzer

Begin Page 69 of Original Bo
Date: 12-17-1920
Hezzy C. Underwood   Daisy Lambert
A. 30 S. Mercer, WV   A. 19 S. Bland

P. Creed & Ruth    P. Alex. & Sallie
Oc. Sawmilling    M. C. W. Stone

Date: 12-21-1920  
Wm. Elijah Lambert     Rosa Thompson  
A. 32 S. Bland     A. 21 S. Bland  
P. Henry & Mary     P. Jas & Mary  

Oc. Laborer     M. J. D. Spitser  

Date: 12-18-1920  
Robt Peel Harmon     Bessie L. Muncy  
A. 26 S. McDowell, WV     A. 21 S. Bluefield, WV  
P. Peel & Mary A.     P. John Gordon &  
    Julia Missouri Havens  
Oc. Farmer     M. J. W. Morris  

Date: 12-23-1920  
Grover Hamilton     Carrie L. Bailey  
A. 21 S. Bland     A. 17 S. Bland  
P. Sam & Ada B.     P. Wm. H.. & Laura E.  
Oc. Laborer     M. S. V. Morris  

Date: 12-23-1920  
Dan Starling     Florie Pauley  
A. 34 D. Bland     A. 26 S. Tazewell  
P. John & Sallie     P. Creed F. & Martelia Kitts  
Oc. Laborer     M. J. W. Morris  

Date: 12-23-1920  
McKinley Spangler     Viola Payne  
A. 22 S. Giles     A. 18 S. Monroe, WV  
P. Jas & Leona     P. Jos & Fannie  
Oc. Farmer     M. S. V. Morris  

Date: 12-23-1920  
Dana Mise     Littie Hubbard  
A. 19 S. Hancock, TN     A. 16 S. Wythe  
P. Henry & Emily     P. Thos & Risie  
Oc. Laborer     M. J. W. Morris  

Date: 12-25-1920  
Fred M. Houdashell     Tess Cox  
A. 20 S. Smyth     A. 20 S. Bland  
P. John & Mary     P. L. M. & S. M.  

Oc. Chauffeur     M. I. N. Munsey  

Date: 12-25-1920  
Grady Hampton Miller     Nellie Hoge Mustard  
A. 26 S. Bland     A. 23 S. Bland  
P. L. M. & Rebecca M.     P. Thos Harvey & Maggie  
    Caroline Newberry  
Oc. Salesman     M. W. N. Baker  

Date: 12-29-1920  
Marion Robert Peck     Mary J. Davis  
A. 28 S. Tazewell     A. 22 S. Bland  
P. T. J. & L. V.     P. R. M. & E. F.  
Oc. Farmer     M. I. L. Cox  

Date: 1-6-1921  
Edward M. Lambert     Laura Rebecca May Pauley  
A. 24 S. Bland     A. 17 S. Bland  
P. H. T. & Mary E.     P. Jno W. & Polly A.  
Oc. Farmer     M. I. N. Munsey  

Date: 1-12-1921  
Glenn Shuler Harman     India Effel Munsey  
A. 27 S. Bland     A. 27 S. Bland  
P. Orsova Cecil &     P. Jos. Wm. Patton &  
Mary Ann Robinson     Emily Florence Kitts  
Oc. Farme r     M. J. W. Morris  

Date: 1-14-1921  
Brook L. Williams     Georgia King  
A. 24 S. Wythe     A. 21 D. Bland  
P. S. W. & Maggie     P. W. D. & Nannie Eagle  

Oc. Rural Letter Carrier     M. J. W. Morris  

Date: 2-1-1921  
Clarence Davis (B)     Virgie Ramsey (B)  
A. 22 S. Winston Salem, NC     A. 21 S. Bland  
P. John & Edna     P. Green & Hulda  
Oc. Laborer     M. J. W. Morris  

Date: 2-2-1921  
Wayne D. Hall     Mary A. Havens  
A. 21 S. Bland     A. 17 S. Bland  
P. G. E. & Beatrice     P. Shep & Lou  
Oc. Farmer     M. J. W. Morri  

Date: 2-25-1921  
Robt. C. Atkins     Rosa Waddle Lampert  
A. 63 W. Smyth     A. 20 D. Bland  
P. J. M. & Lydie E.     P. P. W. & Charity Waddle  
Oc. Farmer     M. I. N. Munsey  

Date: 3-2-1921  
Jos S. Gibson     Cora W. Dunagan  
A. 22 S. Bland     A. 22 S. Bland  
P. J. V. & C. V.     P. Martin Dunagan  
Oc. Farmer     M. C. W. Stone

Date: 3-11-1921
Johnson French  Lathy Clark
A. 23 S. Giles  A. 16 S. Bland
P. Jas & Alice  P. Miller & Julia

Oc. Railroading  M. C. W. Stone

Date : 3-27-1921
Geo Winton Flick  Flossie J. Morehead
A. 26 S. Bland  A. 24 S. Bland
P. C. M. & Mary E.  P. Jno Marshall &
 Sally J. Shufflebarger
Oc. Farmer  M. W. N. Baker

Date: 3-23-1921
Wm. Sherill McNutt  Beulah Umbarger
A. 26 S. Bland  A. 17 S. Bland
P. W. T. & N. M.  P. R. M. & E. J.

Oc. Farming  M. D. P. Hurley

Date: 4-10-1921
Lorenza Dunn McFarlane Mattie Brook King
A. 43 W. Bland  A. 27 S. Bland
P. Ranze & Jane M.  P. W. P. & Ellen
Oc. Farming  M. I. N. Munsey

Date: 4-16-1921
Arthur Carlton Bruce  Ella Jane Harman
A. 28 S. Bland  A. 18 S. Bland
P. Wm Johnson &  P. Jas Wesley Hoge
Amanda Elvira Starks  & Mary Va. Kitts
Oc. Sawmilling  M. J. W. Morris

Date: 4-14-1921
John Adams Powers  Marie E. Baker
A. 30 S. Bland  A. 24 S. Wise
P. J. J. & Jennie  P. W. H. & Hannah J.
Oc. Jitney Driver  M. W. N. Baker

Date: 4-16-1921
Hubert Pearce Waller  Rosa Pauley
A. 19 S. Wythe  A. 20 S. Bland
P. Geo & Nora Hale  P. Roach & Mollie
Oc. Sawmilling  M. J. W. Morris

Date: 5-11-1921
Enoch Taylor  Della Baker
A. 20 S. Grayson  A. 19 S. Bland
P. Jesse & Addie  P. J. E. & Nellie
Oc. Laborer  M. J. W. Morris

Date: 3-13-1921
Thomas B. Townley  Dora R. Hamblin
A. 40 S. Bland  A. 37 S. Bland
P. Jno W. S. & Mary  P. John & Sarah C.
Catherine Harman
Oc. Farmer  M. W. D. Larrowe

Date: 3-21-1921
Wm. Frasier Kidd  Effie Devor
A. 27 W. Bland  A. 21 W. Bland
P. I. W. & Mary Ann  P. Robert & Maggie Burress

Oc. Railroading  M. J. W. Morris

Date: 4-3-1921
Zeyn Repass  Okie Marie Kitts
A. 26 S. Bland  A. 24 S. Bland
P. Lafayette Digby &  P. Newton Montgomery &
Adelia Delzora Baumgardner Eliza Angeline Williams
Oc. Merchant  M. I. N. Munsey

Date: 4-11-1921
Sam Addington Davis  Hattie Catherine Winesett
A. 22 S. Bland  A. 16 S. Carroll
P. S. S. & Sallie A.  P. H. M. & R. E.
Oc. Farming  M. J. W. Morris

Date: 4-13-1921
John Sam'l Smith  Tamsy Opal Davis
A. 19 S. Wythe  A. 17 S. Bland

P. S. A. & Mary M.  P. Jno A. & Kate
Oc. Sawmilling  M. J. W. Morris

Date: 4-16-1921
Gentry Smith  Danewood Dunagan
A. 24 S. Jackson, KY  A. 23 S. Bland
P. Noah & Catherine  P. Martin & Cynthia
Oc. Sawmilling  M. C. W. Stone

Date: 4-16-1921
Geo Elves Jones  Annie Myrtle Umbarger
A. 22 S. Tazewell  A. 20 S. Bland
P. M. C. & Nannie  P. J. J. & Laura C.
Oc. Clerk  M. L. M. Burris

Date: 5-12-1921
Chas Edward Sutphin  Ola Gray Lampert
A. 19 S. Floyd  A. 16 S. Smyth
P. F. M. & Louella  P. P. G. & Louemma
Oc. Lumberman  M. J. W. Morris

Date: 6-2-1921
Eugene Mortimer Davidson     Princie Ethel Johnston
A. 34 W. Bland     A. 28 S. Bland
P. Jno A. & Mattie J.     P. J. Newton. & Bertha B.

Oc. Farmer     License not used, married in W. Va.

Begin Page 70 of Original Book
Date: 6-8-1921
Johnson J. Shrader     Rosa Neece
A. 19 S. Giles     A. 17 S. Bland
P. L. A. & Effie     P. W. W. & Blanche

Oc. Farmer     M. C. W. Stone

Date: 6-15-1921
Wm. Gratton Baugh     Jessie Lucille Cassell
A. 27 S. Tazewell     A. 21 S. Bland
P. Phillip G. & Mary A.     P. Jas. F. & Mary E.

Oc. Bank Clerk     M. W. R. Brown

Date: 8-3-1921
Joseph Kinder     Daisy Belle Peak
A. 23 S. Tazewell     A. 19 S. Bland
P. Jacob & Allen     P. Lee & India

Oc. Farmer     M. S. W. Hahn
Married in Tazewell

Date: 8-28-1921
Sam'l Stuart Richardson     Artie E. King
A. 20 S. Bland     A. 21 S. Wythe
P. C. A. J. & Alice     P. Painter & Fannie
Oc. Salesman     M. J. W. Morris

Date: 9-7-1921
Irvin Renn Gordon     Jennie Grace Stuart
A. 29 S. Bland     A. 30 S. Bland
P. F. M. & Ella     P. W. B. & Sallie
Oc. Merchant     M. H. M. Linkous

Date: 9-7-1921
Henry Wysor Stowers     Cora Mae Stowers
A. 27 S. Tazewell     A. 21 S. Bland
P. W. H. & Sarah C.     P. S. F. & Mary E.
Oc. Farmer     M. J. W. Morris

Date: 6-8-1921
Ellis Hunter Newberry     Thelma Kathleen Wohlford
A. 26 S. Bland     A. 15 S. Bland
P. Sam'l Price     P. Chas. Byrnes &
Malissa Rose Miller     Maud Eliz. Kegley
Oc. Farmer     M. W. N. Baker

Date: 6-9-1921
Benjamin Trigg Tickle     Nellie Alberta King
A. 28 S. Bland     A. 21 S. Wythe
P. Geo Lee Roy     P. John Henry &
Ellen Smith Pegram     Frances Lou Martin
Oc. Chauffeur     M. J. V. Hall
Married in Wythe

Date: 7-4-1921
Chas. Henderson Kitts     Stella Sue Burton
A. 33 S. Bland     A. 20 S. Bland
P. Wm. Ray &     P. James Andrew &
Nannie Edith Burton     Core Ethel Corder
Oc. Farmer     M. J. W. Morris

Date: 8-10-1921
Fredrick T. Gordon     Goldie Jane Hamilton
A. 26 S. Bland     A. 20 S. Bland
P. F. M. & Ella     P. Saunders M. &
    Sally Ann Mustard
Oc. Clerk in Store     M. A. B. Moore

Date: 8-28-1921
Chas H. Wright     Hattie Lawrence
A. 23 S. Bland     A. 21 S. Bland
P. L. J. & Matilda     P. W.L. & Julia
Oc. Machinist     M. J. W. Morris

Date: 9-7-1921
Ward Dunn Stowers     Ollie Mae Shrader
A. 24 S. Bland     A. 17 S. Bland
P. S. F. & Mary E.     P. T. L. & Susie
Oc. Farmer     M. J. W. Morris

Date: 9-14-1921
John H. Barton     Mary Elizabeth King
A. 31 W. Pulaski     A. 17 S. Bland
P. John & Jennie     P. E. T. & Mary E.
Oc. Painter     M. J.D. Spitser

Date: 9-18-1921
Edgar Herman Sadler    Mabel Umbarger
A. 25 S. Bland    A. 19 S. Bland
P. G. S. & Isabelle    P. R. M. & Eliza
Oc. Farmer    M. John Moore Crowe
Married in Wytheville

Date: 9-21-1921
Dewey Glen Spangler    Ida French
A. 20 S. Bland    A. 16 S. Bland
P. J. H. & Bertha M.    P. T. M. & E. L. J.
Oc. Farmer    M. S. V. Morris

Date: 10-5-1921
Andrew Nicewander    Lelia Blanche Thompson
A. 24 S. Bland    A. 16 S. Giles
P. E. L. & Bessie    P. Wm. & Mary
Oc. Farmer    M. J. W. Morris

Date: 11-3-1921
Robt Garfield Ory    Sarah M. Neal
A. 27 S. Giles    A. 16 S. Giles
P. Will & Josie    P. Silas & Sadie
Oc. Farmer    M. J. M. Morris

Date: 12-8-1921
Harman Dillman    Maggie May Thompson
A. 40 W. Bland    A. 23 S. Bland
P. Geo W. & Lucinda    P. J. F. & I. F.

Oc. Farming    M. J. W. Morris

Date: 1-8-1922
Carl Conrad Kidd    Bertie May Barger
A. 23 S. Bland    A. 17 S. Bland
P. Jno W. & Lizzie    P. Geo W. & Annie B.
Oc. Farmer    M. I. N. Munsey

Date: 2-8-1922
David Dewey Hanshew    Louvina Myrtle Richardson
A. 23 D. Smyth    A. 23 S. Wythe
P. H. F. & N. A.    P. C. A. J. & Alice
Oc. Mechanic    M. J. W. Morris

Date: 3-30-1922
Gratton Harvey Mustard    Ora Webb Stafford
A. 36 S. Tazewell    A. 37 S. Bland
P. Newton Shell &    P. Ralph Montgomery &
Ella Ancel Crockett    Mary Elizabeth Crawford
Oc. Miller    M. H. M. Linkous

Date: 9-21-1921
Lester Marvin Sarver    Ethel Emmajean Saunders
A. 20 S. Bland    A. 16 S. Bland
P. S. E. & M. B.    P. W. V. & M. B.
Oc. Farmer    M. S. V. Morris

Date: 9-28-1921
Geo Rob't Worrell    Icy? Snow Lambert
A. 25 S. Mercer, WV    A. 18 S. Bland
P. F. A. & M. E.    P. P. H. & M. V.
Oc. Sawmilling    M. J. W. Morris

Date: 10-20-1921
Chas Lee Meadows    Bessie Kathleen Ramsey
A. 27 S. Monroe, WV    A.21 S. Bland
P. Wm. & Fannie    P. Harman & Dora L.
Oc. Sawmilling    M. S. V. Morris

Date: 12-5-1921
Wm. Hoge Hamilton    Emma Bralley Stinson
A. 37 S. Bland    A. 27 S. Bland
P. S. M. & Sallie A.    P. John & Hester
Oc. Farmer    Not used, Married in W.Va.

Date:12-23-1921
Gratton Mustard Muncy    Mary Elizabeth McNutt
A. 23 S. Bland    A. 23 S. Bland
P. Chas Peery &    P. W. T. & Nannie
Mary Ella Mustard
Oc. Merchant    M. E. H. Copenhaver

Date: 1-9-1922
Isaac Nestor    Rosa Dalton
A. 42 D. Carroll    A. 25 S. Carroll
P. J. C. & Sarah    P. Ballard & Lucy
Oc. Farmer    M. J. W. Morris

Date: 3-10-1922
Hugh Lagner Millirons    May Tarter Lambert
A. 34 D. Pulaski    A. 27 S. Bland
P. Wm. & Julia    P. Jas E. & Cynthia
Oc. Sawyer    M. J. W. Morris

Date: 3-29-1022
Arland DuPrie Burton    May Sarver
A. 28 S. Bland    A. 25 S. WV
P. J. W. & Madella J.    P. John & Lena M.

Oc. Farmer    M. W. N. Baker

Date: 4-6-1922  
Ellis Haymore — Mary Nelson  
A. 23 S. NC — A. 14 S. Bland  
P. John & Catherine — P. John & Ada  
Oc. Farmer — M. C. W. Stone

Date: 5-15-1922  
DeMoyer Gillespie — Nina Lee Wall  
A. 24 S. Mercer, WV — A. 18 S. Bland  
P. Ed. & Kensalia — P. Chas & Dolly  
Oc. Miner — M. J. W. Morris

Date: 6-8-1922  
Thaddeus O. Umbarger — Nellie B. Crabtree  
A. 22 S. Bland — A. 25 S. Bland  
P. H. F. & Ida M. — P. C. A. & Allie  
Oc. Farmer — M. W. R. Brown.

Date: 7-5-1922  
Jos E.Young — Lula V. Williams  
A. 36 S. Smyth — A. 26 S. Bland  
P. Jos P. & Mary E. — P. A. J. & Matilda  
Oc. Farmer — M. J. W. Morris

Date: 7-18-1922  
Jethro A. Hogans (B) — Gertrude Black (B)  
A. 22 S. Bland — A. 17 S. Bland  
P. H. H. & M.M — P. J. S. & M. C.  
Oc. Farmer — M. C. W. Stone

Date: 8-2-1922  
Wm. Edward Corder — Lula Ann Brunk  
A. 22 S. Mercer, WV — A. 25 S. Bland  
P. B. L. & F. B. — P. Wm. & Nannie  
Oc. Carpenter — M. J. W. Morris

Date: 9-3-1922  
Wm. Ray Harner — Floy Gilvia Repass  
A. 23 S. Bland — A. 19 S. Bland  
P. B.W.P. & Nancy — P. L. D. & Ardelia B.  
Oc. Farmer — M. I. N. Munsey

Date: 9-6-1922  
Isaac Newton Tickle — Anna Dillon Lambert  
A. 23 S. Bland — A. 20 S. Bland  
P. Geo Lee Roy & — P. James Edward &  
Ellen Smith Pegram — Cynthia E. Stowers  
Oc. Farmer — M. Jas W. Morris

Date: 5-9-1922  
Everett Testament — Minnie Pauley  
A. 21 S. NC — A. 16 S. Bland  
P. Roby & Polly — P. Ed. J. & Nannie  
Oc. Laborer — M. J. W. Morris

Date: 5-21-1922  
Robt Lee Lambert — Fannie Terry  
A. 22 S. Wythe — A. 16 S. Bland  
P. Mary Lambert — P. Ben & May  
Oc. Farmer — M. Will Rice Miller

Begin Page 71 of Original Book  
Date: 6-7-1922  
Bruce Cox — Ruby Pearl Beavers  
A. 25 S. Carroll — A. 21 S. Bland  
P. Jas P. & Emma — P. Geo F. & Vira  
Oc. Lineman — M. J. W. Morris

Date: 7-12-1922  
Denzil Lenton Atwell — Cleo Earsley Kitts  
A. 26 D. Bland — A. 19 S. Bland  
P. J. E. & Laura J. — P. Newton Montgomery &  
— Eliza Angeline Williams  
Oc. Merchant — M. I. N. Muncy

Date: 7-27-1922  
Bennett Felton Adair — Gay Peery Hudson  
A. 27 S. Giles — A. 27 S. Bland  
P. Jno A. & Fannie W. — P. Jno M. & Florence  
Oc. Salesman — M. W. E. Hudson

Date: 8-12-1922  
Raymond Anderson Coffey — Josephine Powers  
A. 21 S. Louisa — A. 21 S. Bland  
P. H. D. & Lydia — P. Harvey Crow & Rose  
Oc. Dry Cleaner — M. J. W. Morris

Date: 9-4-1922  
Eugene Miller Morehead — Annie Charlotte Harman  
A. 24 S. Bland — A. 19 S. Bland  
P. Lee Kyle & — P. Otto Verona &  
Emmarilla Catherine Miller — Katherine Eve Bogle  
Oc. Carpenter — M. J. W. Morris

Date: 10-16-1922  
Jesse Adington Lambert — Mary Belle Owens  
A. 21 S. Bland — A. 16 S. Pulaski  
P. P. G. & L. E. — P. Frank & Lauara M.  
Oc. Sawmilling — M. J. W. Morris

149

Date: 11-27-1922
John Lewis Hayton  Ollie Estella Hanshew
A. 53 S. Bland  A. 30 S. Bland
P. Thos & Louisa Ann  P. Sam'l S. & Markum V.
Oc. Miller  M. J. D. Spitser

Date: 1-16-1923
Bill Joe French  Gertrude Blankenship
A. 31 S. Bland  A. 16 S. Bland
P. B. P. & Ollie  P. Walter & Bell
Oc. Sawmilling  M. T. R. Darr

Date: 2-20-1923
Clarence Hall  Effie Starling
A. 22 S. Tazewell  A. 16 S. Bland
P. Thos M. & Martha  P. B. F. & S. C.
Oc. Farmer  M. I. B. Underwood

Date: 2-28-1923
John Paris Neel  Susie Elvira Shrader
A. 46 S. Tazewell  A. 36 W. Bland
P. Rob't R. & Mary E.  P. M. A. & Mary J. Thompson
Oc. Farmer  M. C. W. Stone

Date: 3-8-1923
Wm. Jos. Patton Munsey  Willie Sue Morehead

A. 49 W. Bland  A. 31 S. Bland
P. Jas. H. &  P. Leonard Franklin &
Margaret Hutsell  Emma Louise Robinett
Oc. Farmer  M. J. W. Morris

Date: 4-8-1923
G. E. Richardson  Bernice Underwood
A. 22 S. Bland  A. 17 S. Bland
P. J. T. & Delia  P. R. R. & Maude

Oc. Plumber  M. C. W. Stone

Date: 4-10-1923
Martin Luther  Isabell Powers
Nicewander
A. 40 S. Bland  A. 55 W. Bland
P. H. F. & Rhoda  P. _____ Corner
Oc. Farmer  M. J. W. Morris

Date: 12-26-1922
A. L. Hobbs (B)  Mandy Woods (B)
A. 56 W. Bland  A. 68 W. Franklin
P. Thos & Julia  P. Thos Edwards &
  Pauline Palmer
Oc. Laborer  M. C. W. Stone

Date: 2-11-1923
Roy G. Durmon  Lena P. Kitts
A. 22 S. Pulaski  A. 21 S. Bland
P. J. D. & Laura  P. Lee & Sultana
Oc. Carpenter  M. W. E. Balderson
Married in Pulaski

Date: 2-22-1923
Luther Fulton Stump  Ethel Mary Neel
A. 26 W. Washington  A. 21 S. Bland
P. H. N. & Emma C.  P. L. F. & Ella
Oc. Sawmilling  M. J. W. Morris
Married in Tazewell

Date: 3-7-1923
Silvey Mason Burress  Sallie Mamie Kidd
A. 21 S. Bland  A. 21 S. Bland
P. Rob't & Maggie  P. Henley H. & Ollie M.
Oc. Farmer  M. W. K. Neel
Married in Tazewell

Date: 3-14-1923
Oker Atkins  Ethel Mary King

A. 23 S. Bland  A. 18 S. Bland
P. H. W. & Edna  P. E. J. & Mary E.

Oc. Miller  M. W. K. Neel

Date: 4-9-1923
Louis P. Lagorio  Maria Newberry Stone
A. 33 W. San Francisco, CA  A. 22 D. Bland
P. Lewis Wm.  P. Wm Allen Taylor
& Mary J. Roche  Lucy Virginia Kidd
Oc. Musician  M. J. W. Morris

Date: 5-23-1923
Walter Albert Newman  Laura Belle Willis

A. 23 S. Wythe  A. 18 S. Bland
P. Rob't & Jane  P. J. T. & Hattie
Oc. Laborer  M. I. B. Underwood

Date: 6-1-1923
Chas. Alfred Crabtree          Ruth Harman Tilson
A. 27 S. Bland                 A. 30 S. Tuscon, Utah
P. Chas A. & Susan A.          P. Jas P. & Clotilda Augustus

Oc. Farmer                     M. G. A. Wilson, Jr.
Married in Smyth

Date: 8-22-1923
Jesse Moore Karr               Mary Lynwood Stafford
A. 32 S. Tazewell              A. 29 S. Bland
P. Giles R. & Octavia Moore    P. J. W. & Flora W.
Oc. Car Inspector N&W RR       M. P. P. Hasselvander

Date: 8-29-1923
Luther Oscar Clark             Virginia Ethel Day
A. 27 S. Bland                 A. 19 S. Bland
P. Jno W. & Martha             P. Miller F. & Pearl
Oc. Railroading                M. F. M. Radford

Begin Page 72 of Original Book
Date: 9-8-1923
Wallace Crockett Bane          Effie Clemons
A. 20 S. Bland                 A. 15 S. Bland
P. Henry & Virginia            P. Chas & Ella
Oc. Farmer                     M. J. W. Morris

Date: 9-29-1923
W. Neel Wilson                 Mabel Margaret Hubble
A. 27 S. Bland                 A. 27 S. Smyth
P. B. F. & Ellen S.            P. C. H. & Minerva B

Oc. Carpenter N&W RR           M. Walter Hodge
Married in Tazewell

Date: 10-3-1923
Jesse Ernest Kitts             Lola Maud Tickle
A. 37 S. Bland                 A. 20 S. Bland
P. Harvey John &               P. Geo. Lee Roy &
Sarah Eliz. Williams           Ellen Smith Pegram
Oc. Sawmilling                 M. J. W. Morris

Date: 10-24-1923
Ernest S. Kidd                 Edna May Heileman
A. 21 S. Bland                 A. 16 S. McDowell, WV
P. Geo W. & Margaret C.        P. Fred W. & Fanny

Oc. Farmer                     M. D. A. Leffel

Date: 7-1-1923
Augustus Davis Repass          Mamie Melissa Tickle
A. 23 S. Bland                 A. 23 S. Bland
P. Sam'l L. & Lucinda          P. Ulysses Grant &
                               Lottie Virginia Tickle
Oc. Garage worker              M. J. W. Morris

Date: 8-18-1923
Clay Jackson Rucker            Eva Ollie Pulliam
A. 22 S. Carroll               A. 19 S. Giles
P. D. W. & Annie               P. J. B. & Rose
Oc. Farming                    M. J. W. Morris

Date: 9-2-1923
Cecil Repass                   Elva Tibbs
A. 22 S. Tazewell              A. 23 S. Bland
P. Arrington & Laura           P. S. F. & D. I.
Oc. Sawmilling                 M. J. D. Spitser

Date: 9-12-1923
Estill B. Hounshell            Mary V. Harden
A. 34 S. Bland                 A. 18 S. Bland
P. L. J. Hounshell             P. Morgan & Mary T.
Oc. Farmer                     M. J. W. Morris

Date: 10-3-1923
Lorenzo James Helvey           Emma Clara Morehead
A. 26 S. Bland                 A. 23 S. Bland
P. Sam'l Houston &             P. Leonard Franklin &
Nickatie Kinzer Miller         Emma Louise Robinette
Oc. Farmer                     M. W. N. Baker

Date: 10-7-1923
Wylie Mason Stowers            Beulah Cleo Lambert
A. 25 S. Nelson, Nebr.         A. 19 S. Bland
P. Jno P. & Nannie             P. A. A. & Lillie R.

Oc. Railroading                M. C. W. Stone

Date: 10-27-1923
Peter Harrison Morehead        Mary Zelda Patton
A. 23 S. Bland                 A. 18 S. Bland
P. Gordon Andrew &             P. Wm. Miller &
Tacy Adaline Pruett            Poca Dallas Pauley
Oc. Farmer                     M. J. L. Scott

Date: 11-17-1923
Grady Wright Thompson Jessie Katherine Davidson
A. 20 S. Bland             A. 18 S. Bland
P. G. W. & Mattie          P. Wm A. & Nannie
Oc. Clerk in store         M. J. L. Scott

Date: 11-28-1923
Sam'l Joseph Yonce         Eliza Millirons
A. 42 S. Wythe             A. 30 S. Pulaski
P. John & Ellen            P. W. M. & Julia
Oc. Carpenter & Farmer     M. J. L. Scott

Date: 12-26-1923
Jas. Harvey Williams       Myrtle Clara Wright
A. 19 S. Bland             A. 18 S. Bland
P. Eugene & Pet.           P. J. B. & Lila
Oc. Sawmilling             M. K. G. Munsey

Date: 1-10-1924
Brady Monroe Thompson Edith Rhoda Lampert
A. 21 S. Bland             A. 15 S. Bland
P. J. F. & Ibbie           P. D. G. & Corsie V.
Oc. Laborer                M.   J. L. Scott

Date: 2-8-1924
Hubert Nello Harden        Georgie Myrtle Tickle
A. 21 S. Bland             A. 18 S. Bland
P. David Morgan &          P. Geo. Lee Roy &
Mary Texas Neel            Ellen Smith Pegram
Oc. Sawmilling             M.   J. L. Scott

Date: 2-25-1924
Wm. Frank Townley          Iva May  Robinett
A. 24 S. Bland             A. 21 S. Bland
P. Samuel Mellicue Irvin P. R. F. & Fannie
Rebecca Alice Duncan
Oc. Silkmill worker        M.   J. L. Scott

Date: 3-10-1924
Clyde Hager                Ruth Hare
A. 21 S. Bland             A. 17 S. Bland
P. Dock & Cora             P. Rob't Hare
Oc. Sawmilling             M. H. L. Hanshew

Date: 3-28-1924
F. L. Francisco            Mary Clark
A. 30 S. Craig             A. 20 S. Bland
P. J. R. & Hattie          P. Cary & Minnie
Oc. Farmer                 M. F. M. Radford

Date: 11-26-1923
John Wylie Blessing        Ruby Eula Christian
A. 23 S. Bland             A. 21 S. Bland
P. J. H. & Stella          P. H. & Anna
Oc. Laborer                M. J. L. Scott

Date: 12-26-1923
Alvis Martin Christian     Gladys Irene Walters
A. 20 S. Bland             A. 21 S. Bland
P. M. T. & Causby C.       P. J. W. & Sallie
Oc. Farmer                 M. H. L. Hanshew

Date: 12-25-1923
Scott McKinley Harman      Dora Josephine Burton
A. 21 S. Bluefield, WV     A. 18 S. Bland
P. F. A. & Mary            P. J. H. & Daisy
Oc. Contractor             M. J. L. Scott

Date: 1-22-1924
Lilburn David Musser       Macia Mae Houdashell
A. 41 W. Bland             A. 35 S. Wythe
P. Wash. & Lavinia         P. Jas E. & Louisa Hanshew
Oc. Mechanic               M. A. G. Riddle
Married in Smyth

Date: 2-13-1924
Jesse Frank Lambert        Ollie Catherine Lambert
A. 26 S. Bland             A. 21 S. Bland
P. J. M. & Thirza          P. Jas A. & Clemmie

Oc. Farmer                 M. E. L. Bowyer
Married in Wythe

Date: 2-23-1924
W. Henry Hare              Lillie Pruett
A. 41 S. Giles             A. 36 S. Bland
P. _____ Hare              P. P. D. & Rhoda

Oc. Laborer                M. F. M. Radford

Date: 3-19-1924
John Walker Neel           Katie May Stowers
A. 21 S. Tazewell          A. 23 S. Bland
P. Clark W. & Ella L.      P. Geo H. & Julia
Oc. Farmer                 M. H. L. Hanshew

Date: 3-31-1924
Lodie Leon Prescott        Elsie Kaldier? Burton
A. 43 S. Maine?            A. 24 S. Bland
P. J. Lewis & Etta M.      P. Jas H. & Daisy
Oc. Mechanic               M. J. L. Scott

Date: 4-16-1924
Fred H. Boothe — Margaret Hare
A. 21 S. Peterstown, WV — A. 21 S. Giles
P. H. C. & Cora Lee — P. Mont. & Willie
Oc. Laborer — M. I. B. Underwood

Date: 5-25-1924
Cladius Lambert — Lennie Jane Clark
A. 21 S. Bland — A. 21 S. Bland
P. D.L.G. & Mary S. — P. Jno W. & Roberta
Oc. Miner — M. H. L. Hanshew

Date: 5-25-1924
Wm. Andrew Hubble — Mary Va. Umbarger
A. 22 S. Tacewell — A. 16 S. Bland
P. John & Minnie — P. Jas & Laura
Oc. Farmer — M. J. D. Spitzer

Date: 6-18-1924
Noah Charlton (B) — Ruth Clayborn (B)
A. 54 W. Tazewell — A. 28 S. Bluefield
P. Noah & Mary — P. Sam & Ruth Clayton?
Oc. Farmer — M. H. L. Hanshew

Date: 7-1-1924
Emory Oscar Lambert — Beula Bell Lambert
A. 30 S. Bland — A. 20 S. Bland
P. Jas A. & Clemmie — P. Walker & Emma
Oc. Farmer — M. E. L. Bowyer
Married in Wythe

Date: 7-3-1924
James Marvin Spangler — Elizabeth Alice Sarver
A. 19 S. Bland — A. 19 S. Bland
P.J. H. & Bertha M. — P. J. B. & Lena
Oc. Laborer — M. J. L. Scott

Date: 7-23-1924
Okey Corner — Gracie Ory
A. 20 S. Bland — A. 20 S. Bland
P. Tobe Neese & — P. Wm & Josie
Mintie Corner
Oc. Farmer — M. K. G. Munsey

Date: 7-31-1924
Dan Starling — Mary E. Richardson
A. 48 W. Bland — A. 47 W. Wythe
P. John & Sallie — P. John F. & Sarah
Oc. Laborer — M. J. L. Scott

Date: 5-1-1924
John Edd Levitt — Annie Thompson
A. 17 S. Bland — A. 18 S. Tazewell
P. R. E. & Sarah — P. W. B. & Sallie
Oc. Farmer — M. D. A. Loeffel
Married in Tazewell

Date: 5-25-1924
Wirt R. Bailey — Sadie E. Shrader
A. 21 S. Bland — A. 19 S. Bland
P. W. W. & M A. — P. D. W. & Allie
Oc. Miner — M. H. L. Hanshew

Date: 6-6-1924
Thos Isaac Whorley — Eula Gray Starling
A. 23 S. Patrick — A. 16 S. Bland
P. Thos & Rosa B. — P. B. F. & S. C.
Oc. Farmer — M. I. B. Underwood

Date: 6-25-1924
Dorse Davidson Burton — Minnie Madeline Patton
A. 21 S. Bland — A. 17 S. Bland
P. Jas H. & Daisy — P. Arnold & Ida
Oc. Sawmilling — M. J. L. Scott

Begin Page 73 of Original Book
Date: 6-30-1924
Cecil Wagner Townley — Elvira Kirby Davis
A. 22 S. Bland — A. 22 S. Bland
P. M. S. & Alice R. — P. C. N. & Lou Kirby
Oc. Farmer — M. F. R. Snaveley
(Adopted legally by Elvira T. Davis)

Date: 7-19-1924
James C. Repass — Zola B. Morehead
A. 20 S. Bland — A. 19 S. Bland
P. Ray. C. & Juliet E. — P. Lee Kyle & Emmarilla
Oc. Mechanic — M. J. L. Scott

Date: 7-21-1924
Sam'l Miller Hayton — Mintie Careen Hancock
A. 22 S. Bland — A. 25 S. Bland
P. A. J. & Mary D. — P. N. B. & Maggie

Oc. Farmer — M. J. D. Spitzer

Date: 8-16-1924
Robert Burton — Annie Clark
A. 23 S. Bland — A. 17 S. Bland
P. Bud. & Leona — P. Miller & Julia
Oc. Sawmilling — M. H. L. Hanshew

153

Date: 8-31-1924
W. E. Booth                    Lillie Richardson
A. 19 S. Monroe, WV            A. 18 S. Bland
P. H. C. & C.L.                P. J. T. & C. A.
Oc. Plumber                    M. T. R. Darr

Date: 9-7-1924
Wm. A. French                  Thelma V. Hager
A. 19 S. Bland                 A. 19 S. Bland
P. Wm A. & L. A.               P. R. B. & Nancy E.
Oc. Sawmilling                 M. H. L. Hanshew

Date: 9-10-1924
Wythe G. Kitts                 Missouri Kitts
A. 65 W. Bland                 A. 58 W. Bland
P. Ganam & Ann Steele          P. Jno & Evalier? Harden
Oc. Farmer                     M. J. D. Spitzer

Date: 9-24-1924
John Henry Prescott            Mabel Gray Akers
A. 30 S. Bland                 A. 21 S. Bland
P. D. H. & Lucy J.             P. W. D. & Maggie E.
Oc.Farmer                      M. W. A. Warner

Date: 10-12-1924
Martin Dunnagan                Sallie Lambert
A. 60 W. Surry, NC             A. 40 W. Bland
P. Louis & Nannie (Corder)P. John Sarver

Oc. Farmer                     M. F. M. Radford

Date: 11-19-1924
Dewey Meek Miller              Gladys Ruth Coleman
A. 24 S. Bland                 A. 23 D. Bland
P. Lorenzo Meek &              P. Thos Harvey Mustard &
Rebecca M. Finley              Maggie Caroline Newberry
Oc. Railroading                M. K. G. Munsey

Date: 12-3-1924
Floyd A. Walker                Bertie Sarver
A. 40 W. Tazewell              A. 21 S. Bland
P. John & Araminta A.          P. Wm. & Geneva

Oc. Miller                     M. F. M. Radford

Date: 12-21-1924
Fred Wyte Carroll              Willie Thomas
A. 20 S. Bland                 A. 16 S. Bland
P. Jacob & Mary                P. L. C. & Hattie
Oc. Farmer                     M. K. G. Munsey

Date: 9-3-1924
Albert Clayton Brookman Lena M. Bailey
A. 23 S. Bland                 A. 19 S. WV
P. Rob't & Emma                P. John & Minnie
Oc. Farmer                     M. J. L. Scott

Date: 9-7-1924
Arthur B. Hager                Alice C. French
A. 18 S. Bland                 A. 18 S. Bland
P. R. B. & Nancy E.            P. Wm A. & L. A.
P. Farmer                      M. H. L. Hanshew

Date: 9-15-1924
Bruce Banks  Bridges           Valerie Mae Cumiford
A. 23 S. Bland                 A. 19 S. Bland
P. M. S. & Georgia             P. J. D. & M. E.
Oc. Sawmilling                 M. J. L. Scott

Date: 10-1-1924
Rome Hancock                   Eunice Kitts
A. 21 S. Bland                 A. 18 S. Bland
P. C. E. & Mollie E.           P. R. H. & Bertha
Oc. Laborer                    M. C. B. Livesay
Married in Wythe

Date: 11-16-1924
Emory Morehead                 Nannie V. Burton
A. 36 W. Bland                 A. 25 S. Bland
P. Leonard Franklin &          P. Jas Andrew &
Emma Louise Robinett           Cora Ethel Corder
Oc. Farmer                     M. J. L. Scott

Date: 11-19-1924
Rob't Newton  King             Georgie Hancock
A. 25 S. Bland                 A. 18 S. Bland
P. J. S. & Emily P.            P. G. W. Hancock

Oc. Sawmilling                 M. J. L. Scott

Date: 12-16-1924
James W. Stone                 Nannie J. Fanning
A. 66 W. Pulaski               A. 53 W. Bland
P. Francis & Jemima            P. Wm. P. & Louisa
                               Mustard
Oc. Farmer                     M. ' J. L. Scott

Date: 12-23-1924             (Married in Roanoke)
John Ward Songer               Macie Catherine Waddell
A. 34 S. Bland                 A. 26 S. Bland
P. Ward & Carrie               P. Rich. & Dilla C.
Oc. Farmer                     M. Alfred C. Meadows

Date: 12-24-1924
Andrew Jackson Wynn  Nannie Dunnagan Wall
A. 61 W. Bland  A. 56 W. N. C.
P. Wm. & Millie  P. Lewis & Nancy Dunnagan
Oc. Farmer  M. C. W. Hancock

Date: 1-29-1925
Wm. Payne Tolbert  Violet Lee Jones
A. 27 S. Bland  A. 18 S. Monroe, WV
P. Jno B. & Mariah J.  P. D. A. & Mary M
Oc. Farmer  M. H. L. Hanshew

Date: 3-15-1925
Wm. Ramsey  Cora Lee Hubbard
A. 22 S. Bland  A. 18 S. Wythe
P. C. H. & Almedia  P. G. T. & Vicie
Oc. Laborer  M. F. M. Radford

Date: 4-4-1925
Jas Glenn Shufflebarger  Ettie Mabel Atwell
A. 21 S. Bland  A. 24 S. Bland
P. Harvey B. & Margaret  P. Jno H. & Carrie
Oc. Farmer  M. H. L. Hanshew

Date: 4-15-1925
Shular Bruce Kitts  Arlena Andrew Munsey
A. 31 S. Bland  A. 27 S. Bland
P. Miller White &  P. Wm. Jos. Patton &
Ida V. Kitts  Emily Florence Kitts
Oc. Farmer  M. J. L. Scott

Date: 7-1-1925
Jno Henry Blankenship  Maudie Ramsey
A. 20 S. Bland  A. 21 S. Bland
P. Waler B. & Jennie B.  P. Charley J. & Ida
Oc. Sawmilling  M. F. M. Radford

Date: 7-8-1925
David Davidson Carver  Sallie Belle Thompson
A. 22 S. Bland  A. 19 S. Bland
P. S. D. & Martha  P. Jas & Mary
Oc. Mail-carrier  M. J. L. Scott

Date: 7-22-1925
Estill C. Hamblin  Lena Davis
A. 31 S. Bland  A. 22 S. Bland
P. Jno S. & Sarah  P. Comy A. & Nannie E.
Oc. Farmer  M. J. L. Scott

Date: 12-25-1924
Chas Thos Ferguson  Una Myrtle Wright
A. 45 S. Floyd  A. 34 S. Bland
P. G. W. & Margeret Ellen  P. D. W. & S. A.
Oc. Farmer  M. J. L. Scott

Date: 3-4-1925
Tony Lee Ramsey  Viola Belle Ramsey
A. 24 S. Bland  A. 18 S. Bland
P. C. B. & Willie A.  P. A. D. & Allie
Oc. Farmer  M. K. G. Munsey

Date: 3-20-1925
Thos Kyle Shelton  Rosa Kate Hancock
A. 28 S. Grayson  A. 20 S. Bland
P. Nathan & Ettie  P. C. E. & Mollie
Oc. Miner  M. J. L. Scott

Date: 4-13-1925
James Fulton Patterson  Annie Miller Thompson
A. 21 S. Bland  A. 23 S. Bland
P. Wm E. & Alice  P. J. E. & Rachel
Oc. Sawmilling  M. F. M. Bushman?

Begin Page 74 of Original Book
Date: 5-23-1925
Geo. Lessie Kimberling  Lou Ella Ethel Wolfe
A. 21 S. Bland  A. 16 S. Bland
P. Wm. D. & Blanche  P. Wiley & Rosa

Oc. Farmer  M. H. L. Hanshew

Date: 7-8-1925
Geo Rob't Stinson  Zena G.ray Parsell
A. 26 S. Bland  A. 30 S. Bland
P. Jno & Hester A.  P. Chas & Martha J.
Oc. Railroading  M. J. L. Scott

Date: 7-15-1925
Sam'l Roosevelt Hancock  Annie Millirons
A. 22 S. Bland  A. 21 S. Bland
P. Geo W. & Belle  P. R. Lee & Kate
Oc. Farmer  M. J. L. Scott

Date: 7-26-1925
Jas Muncy Lambert  Linnie Allen Bivens
A. 31 S. Bland  A. 18 S. Bland
P. Thos A. & Clara  P. L. C. & Della
Oc. Farmer  M. H. L Hanshew

Date: 7-27-1925
Reese Sam'l Gillespie    Margaret Adaline Bane
A. 54 W. Tazewell    A. 39 S. Bland
P. Jno Gillespie    P. J. S. C. & M. M.
Oc. Farmer    M. F. M. Buhsman

Date: 8-12-1925
Edward Wright    Verrena Ramsey
A. 21 S. Bland    A. 16 S. Bland
P. L. J. & Matilda    P. Harman & Almeda
Oc. Laborer    M. Will Rice Miller

Date: 8-17-1925
Joe McGuire    Flora James Harman
A. 28 S. Montgomery    A. 19 S. Bland
P. Jos & Gay    P. Jas W. & Nettie
Oc. Railroading    M. K. G. Munsey

Date: 8-19-1925
Geo Franklin McDonald    Selma Lorena Kegley
A. 28 S. Smyth    A. 20 S. Bland
P. G. B. & Nannie    P. S. E. & Florence
Oc. Salesman    M. E. H. Copenhaver
Married in Smyth

Date: 9-1-1925
Terry Kimberlin    Alice McKinney
A. 30 S. Bland    A. 27 W. WV
P. W. D. & Blanche    P. (Oliff Clemons?)

Oc. Farmer    M. F. M. Radford

Date: 9-19-1925    (Married in Roanoke)
Francis Andrew Morehead    Mamie Edna Shrader
A. 21 S. Bland    A. 20 S. Bland
P. Jno. Marshall &    P. Wm L. &
Edna Kate Helvey    Annie Stowers
Oc. Spinner, Silk Mill    M. Chat. L. DeLong

Date: 9-16-1925
Robert Wright    Daisy Burton
A. 24 W. Bland    A. 16 S. Bland
P. L. J. & Matilda    P. Bob & Lula
Oc. Miner    M. W. R. Miller

Date: 9-27-1925    (Married in Pulaski)
Wm. Ellis Tickle    Beulah Elizabeth Morehead
A. 21 S. Bland    A. 19 S. Bland
P. Meek Bogle & Ella Palmyra P. Jno Marshall & Edna Kate
Oc. Farmer    M. L. D. Mayberry

Date: 10-12-1925
Adam Herbert Kidd    Bertie D. Kidd
A. 31 S. Bland    A. 29 S. Bland
P. S. S. & C. L.    P. G. W. & Causby
Oc. Farmer    M. J. L. Scott

Date: 10-25-1925
Watson Burton    Viola French
A. 23 S. Bland    A. 20 S. Bland
P. J. H. & Daisy    P. W. S. French
Oc. Farmer    M. F. M. Radford

Date: 11-2-1925    (Married in Pulaski)
John Gordon Leslie    Frances Catherine Brunk
A. 21 S. Wythe    A. 15 S. Pulaski
P. C. L. & Dora    P. W. H. & Nannie
Oc. Farmer    M. D. P. Hurley

Date: 12-16-1925
Roy Francis Repass    Mary Letitia Bruce
A. 24 S. Bland    A. 19 S. Bland
P. A.rthur G. & Maggie G. P. Riley W. & Dora M.
Oc. Farmer    M. V. M. Ross

Date: 12-23-1925
Thomas A. Andrews    Jessie B. Lampert
A. 46 S. Caldwell, NC    A. 22 S. Bland
P. Martha Epaline    P. William Lambert
Andrews    & Sarah Lampert
Oc. Lumberman    M. C. W. Hancock

Date: 1-25-1926
David Allen Hull    Sarah Jane Bailey
A. 17 S. Giles    A. 19 S. WV
P. Millard F. & Effie E.    P.Chas. R. & Delice G.

Oc. Farmer    M. F. M. Radford

Date: 3-5-1926
Robert Havens    Opal Hudson
A. 20 S. Bland    A. 20 S. WV
P. W. H. & Victoria    P. S. B. & Mattie
Oc. Sawmilling    M. C. W. Hancock

Date: 3-6-1926
Isaiah Bee Thomas    Lizzie Sheffey Dunagan
A. 31 S. Mercer, WV    A. 35 S. Bland
P. B. P. & Maggie    P. M. D. & Cynthia
Oc. Sawmilling    M. C. W. Hancock

Date: 3-18-1926
John Orey                  Flossie May Patton
A. 24 S. Giles             A. 17 S. Bland
P. Wm. & Josie             P. Jno W. & Susie Margaret
Oc. Farmer                 M. S. C. Weatherly

Date: 5-7-1926             (Married in Radford)
Jesse A.dams Rudder        Lucille Havens
A. 39 S. Bland             A. 28 S. Bland
P. Chas. Martin &          P. Thompson Crockett &
Louise Jerush Mustard      Emmer Penley
Oc. Mechanic               M. A. S. Thorn

Date: 6-9-1926
John Andrew White          Bertia Walker Tabor
A. 34 S. Mercer, WV        A. 18 S. Bland
P. R. C. & Martha R.       P. F. G. & Helen
Oc. Sawmilling             M. C. W. Hancock

Date: 6-30-1926
Eli Daily Kitts            Lula Clark Pauley
A. 53 D. Bland             A. 29 W. Bland
P. Ganam & Ann             P. Alex C. & Elizabeth Clark
Oc. Farmer                 M. S. C. Weatherly

Begin Page 75 of Original Book
Date: 8-19-1926
John Andrew Gusler         Gladys Neel Hoilman
A. 21 S. Giles             A. 16 S. Bland
P. Jas. A. & Ollie G.      P. Thos H. & Nettie
Oc. Farmer                 M. K. G. Munsey

Date: 9-4-1926
Montague S. Radford        Minnie Poff
A. 24 S. Bland             A. 20 S. Giles
P. F. M. & Lula            P. Wm. & Savannah

Oc. Farmer                 M. C. W. Hancock

Date: 9-12-1926
Trubie Bane Perkey         Carrie Edna Creger
A. 26 S. Bland             A. 18 S. Wythe
P. Ollie Perkey            P. S. E. & Winnie Bel
Oc. Farmer                 M. S. C. Weatherly

Date: 11-11-1926
John Tyler Carver          Ethel May Clemons
A. 21 S. Bland             A. 16 S. Bland
P. Sam D. & Martha J.      P. Jos. H. & Emma J.
Oc. Farmer                 M. C. W. Hancock

Date: 4-29-1926
Glenord C. Hamblin         Margaret Stephens
A. 21 S. Bland             A. 19 S. Giles
P. E. L. & Ollie           P. ___ Stephens
Oc. Farmer                 M. S. C. Weatherly

Date: 6-5-1926
Richard Emmett Hanshew     Georgia Wilson
A. 35 S. Bland             A. 29 S. Bland
P. H.F. & Nannie           P. A. P. L. & Grace

Oc. Farmer                 M. S. C. Weatherl

Date: 6-28-1926
Clarence Ezre Thomas       Bessie Gray Robbins
A. 32 D. Giles             A. 28 D. Giles
P. B. P.& Maggie           P. Jas S. & Ruth Bailey
Oc. Sawmilling             M. J. E. Graham

Date: 7-18-1926
Dewey Lee Clark            Straudie Miller
A. 28 D. Bland             A. 21 D. Giles
P. Miller & Julia &        P. Joe & Ida McCroskie
Oc. Section hand on RR      M. T.A. Darr

Date: 8-20-1926
Lessie Kimberling          Pinkie Thompson
A. 25 S. Bland             A. 26 S. Bland
P. Jno & Nancy C.          P. J. E. & Rachel
Oc. Laborer                M. S. C. Weatherly

Date: 9-7-1926             (Married in Pulaski)
John Kee                   Maude Elizabeth Frazier
A. 52 S. Gilmer, WV        A. 30 D. Montgomery
P. J. N. & Louisa J.       P. J. W. & Cora Hull
Simpkins
Oc. Attorney at Law        M. D. P. Hurley

Date: 9-25-1926
Ray Hill                   Viola Lawson
A. 23 S. Knoxville, TN     A. 20 S. Tazewell
P. J. R. & Willie B.       P. J. B. & Alice
Oc. Carpenter              M. S. C. Weatherly

Date: 11-17-1926
John Campbell Roope        Bertie Cree Hamblin
A. 42 W. Pulaski           A. 30 S. Bland
P. Geo & Cynthia Mary      P. Jno S. & Sarah C.
Oc. Laborer                M. Wm. N. Baker

157

Date: 11-25-1926 (Married in Pulaski)
Dewey B. Millirons    Clovia N. Kitts
A. 24 S. Bland    A. 22 S. Bland
P. Wm N. & Nannie    P. Rob't H. & Bertha
Oc. Farmer    M. P. P. Martin

Date: 1-5-1927 (Married in Roanoke)
Jas. Hobart Fanning    Fannie Blankenship
A. 30 S. Bland    A. 29 S. Bland
P. Jas M. & Nannie    P. Harvey & Mary
Nannie Jane Mustard
Oc. Silk Mill worker    M. John William Smith

Date: 1-30-1926
Dewey C. Thompson    Cassaline Carter
A. 27 S. Bland    A. 20 S. Bland
P. Den. & Julia    P. J. B. & Alice
Oc. Farmer    M. S. C. Weatherly

Date: 2-9-1927
Lundy Franklin Childress    Mildred Kate Kitts
A. 28 S. Buchanan    A. 22 S. Giles
P J. E. & Winnie    P. Ballard Graham &
   Ollie Norabelle Harman
Oc. Farmer    M. S. C. Weatherly

Date: 3-20-1927
Thos H. Booth    Clara Richardson
A. 18 S. Monroe, WV    A. 18 S. Bland
P. H. C. & C. L.    P. A. R. & S. V.
Oc. Laborer    M. I. B. Underwood

Date: 4-6-1927
John S. Dalton    Corrie A. L. Thompson
A. 67 W. Mercer, WV    A. 56 W. Bland
P. Alex & Millie    P. I. P. & Rebecca Pauley
Oc. Farmer    M. S. C. Weatherly

Date: 4-21-1927 (Married in Wythe)
J. C. Carr    Flossie Mitchell
A. 30 S. Giles    A. 21 S. Bland
P. G. W. & Sallie    P. Esca & Minnie
Oc. Farmer    M. L. E. Kilgore

Date: 5-12-1927
Sam Poff    Ruby Comeford
A. 27 S. Pulaski    A. 18 S. Bland
P. W. M. & S. J.    P. David & Ella
Oc. Sawmilling    M. C. W. Hancock

Date: 12-23-1926
Charley Lester    Blanche Neel
A. 25 S. Buchanan    A. 17 S. Bland
P. Elish. & Vicie    P. Lafayette & Ella
Oc. Farmer    M. S. C. Weatherly

Date: 1-29-1927
Early Burton    Jeannette Lambert
A. 20 S. Bland    A. 17 S. Bland
P. Luther & Ella    P. W. J. & Sarah
Oc. Laborer    M. J. E. Graham

Date: 1-14-1927
Lemuel Winesett    Alberta Chloe Harmon
A. 19 S. Carroll    A. 19 S. Bland
P. H. M. & Rhoda    P. S. T. & Macia
Oc. Farmer    M. S. C. Weatherly

Date: 2-12-1927
Theodore Caldwell    Bessie May Stump
A. 22 S. Mercer, WV    A. 19 S. Floyd
P. S. O. & Pearl G.    P. N. E. & Sallie
Oc. Farmer    M. S. C. Weatherly

Date: 4-3-1927
Frank Bane    Clara Elizabeth Harner
A. 30 S. Bland    A. 22 S. Bland
P. Sarah Bane    P. B. W. P. & Nancy
Oc. Mechanic    M. S. C. Weatherly

Date: 4-21-1927
William Lane    Minta Corner Hollins
A. 55 W. Pulaski    A. 56 D. Bland
P. Isaac & Margaret E.    P. James & Jane Corner
Oc. Farmer    M. K. G. Munsey

Date: 4-24-1927
Earl Stowers    Kathleen Neel
A. 24 S. Bland    A. 22 S. Bland
P. Milton & Susan    P. Alex & Minnie
Oc. Lineman    M. C. W. Hancock

Date: 5-14-1927 (Married in Wythe)
Elbert Cecil Durham    Eliza Harden
A. 23 D. Buchanan    A. 15 S. Bland
P. W. H. & Celina    P. W. M. & Lena
Oc. Sawmilling    M. L. E. Kilgore

Date: 6-1-1927
Guy Mannering Bruce       Cecil Irene Robinett
A. 26 S. Bland            A. 26 S. Bland
P. W. J. & Amanda E.      P. R. B. & Eliza
Oc. Carpenter             M. H. S. Coffey
Married in Roanoke

Date: 6-22-1927
Jas Thara Thompson        Ida Elizabeth Hounshell
A. 34 S. Bland            A. 22 S. Bland
P. Jas F. & Ibbie         P. Will & Minnie
Oc. Farmer                M. J. C. Spurlin

Date: 7-3-1927
Eugene Blake Williams     Lillian Pearl Wright
A. 21 S. Bland            A. 17 S. Bland
P. E. P. & Pet.           P. Wm G. & Mary
Oc. Farmer                M. C. W. Hancock

Date: 8-18-1927
Ballard Stowers           Eula Mae Smith
A. 20 S. Bland            A. 20 S. Bland
P. J. H. & Mollie A.      P. G. L. & Susie C.
Oc. Farmer                M. J.E. Graham

Date: 9-5-1927
Meek Hoge Bowen           Virginia J. Newberry
A. 22 S. Tazewell         A. 18 S. Bland
P. T. C. & Jane Hoge      P. W. A. & Lucy
Oc. Farming               M. J. C. Spurlin

Date: 9-17-1927
Hobart Johnson Lambert    Stella Gray Bailey
A. 24 S. Giles            A. 21 S. Bland
P. Estill & Della         P. Ernest & Lula
Oc. Farming               M. H. D. Coffey

Date: 9-24-1927
Lacy Mullens              Deloros Mae French
A. 22 S. Giles            A. 16 S. Bland
P. Jno Wm & Menervia      P. B. P. & Ollie R.
Oc. Sawmilling            M. J. E. Graham

Date: 10-1-1927
James Byrd                Zetta Clark
A. 22 S. Tazewell         A. 19 S. Bland
P. Jas O. & Mary          P. W. C. & Belle
Oc. Farmer                M. F. M. Radford

Date: 6-1-1927
Robert Lee Bounds         Jessie Catherine Muncy
A. 27 S. Wise             A. 26 S. Bland
P. W. B. & Margaret       P. J. A. & Josie
Oc. Civil Engineer        M. L. M. Burris
Married in Wythe

Date: 6-22-1927
Charlie Neal Brunk        Nellie Davis
A. 20 S. Pulaski          A. 23 S. Norchester
P. Walter & Nannie        P. S. P. & Ethel
Oc. Sawmill hand          M. J. C. Spurlier

Date: 8-14-1927
Ross Douglas Stowers      Emma Kate Ramsey
A. 20 S. Bland            A. 20 S. Bland
P. Mrs. Arthur Fanning    P. C. J. & Ida
Oc. Miner                 M. C. W. Hancock

Begin Page 76 of Original Book
Date: 9-3-1927
Wm. Olney Wright          Ollie Mae Falls
A. 32 S. Bland            A. 18 S. Giles
P. L. J. & Matilda E.     P. C. O. Falls
Oc. Sawmilling            M. C. W. Hancock

Date: 9-14-1927
Mitchell McK. French      Birdie Saunders
A. 21 S. Bland            A. 18 S. Mercer, WV
P. T. M. & E. L J.        P. Geo C. & Mollie
Oc. Farming               M. F. M. Radford

Date: 9-24-1927
Wm. Goebel Radford        Emma Sue Corner
A. 27 S. Bland            A. 22 S. Bland
P. E. M. & Lula           P. Geo S. & Matilda
Oc. Farming               M. R. L. Hager

Date: 9-25-1927
Sidney Earl Havens        Hattie V. Townley
A. 19 S. Bland            A. 23 S. Bland
P. Shep & Lillie          P. Sam & Alice
Oc. Farm Laborer          M. K. G. Munsey

Date: 10-5-1927          (Married in Roanoke)
Wm. Wallace Bruce         Bertha Mae Neel
A. 24 S. Bland            A. 22 S. Bland
P. W. J. & Amanda E.      P. L. F. & Ella
Oc. Carpenter             M. H. S. Coffey

Date: 10-12-1927
Vernie E. Wolfe      Willie K. Kirby
A. 20 S. Bland      A. 24 S. Bland
P. D. S. & Ada      P. C. N. & Lou
Oc. Farmer      M. Clarence W. Taylor

Date: 11-11-1927
Otis Windfield Gaskins      Mary Bobbie Pulliam
A. 47 S. Pitt, NC      A. 21 S. Bland
P. Chas P. & Louvenia H.      P. J. B. & Rosa
Oc. Insurance      M. J. E. Graham

Date: 11-14-1927
Wm. Ernest Riffey      Grace Belle Elkins
A. 23 S. Washington      A. 24 S. WV
P. J. F. & Blanche      P. J. N. & Irene
Oc. Farmer      M. Clarence W. Taylor

Date: 11-23-1927
Vance Blankenship      May Wright
A. 20 S. Bland      A. 18 S. Bland
P. C. R. & F. G.      P. J. B. & Lila
Oc. Farmer      M. C. W. Hancock

Date: 11-23-1927
Ernest Webb      Janie Willis
A. 20 S. Smyth      A. 18 S. Pulaski
P. W. A. & Susan      P. C. P. & Amanda
Oc. Laborer      M. Clarence W.Taylor

Date: 12-12-1927
Benton Stowers      Nannie Belle Smith
A. 20 S. Bland      A. 19 S. Bland
P. J. H. & Mollie      P. G. L. & Susie C.
Oc. Farmer      M. C. W. Hancock

Date: 12-26-1927
Orsen W. Chewning      Leona Hamblin
A. 24 S. Giles      A. 22 S. Bland
P. Ab. & Florence      P. Lizzie Hamblin
Oc. Farmer      M. W. N. Baker
Married in Wythe

Date: 12-28-1927
James Looney      Linnie Della Kidd
A. 22 S. Bland      A. 18 S. Bland
P. Hick & Vicie      P. H. H. & Ollie

Oc. Farmer      M. J. E. Graham

Date: 11-5-1927
Miller Cregger      Charlotte Willis
A. 22 S. Smyth      A. 16 S. Pulaski
P. Miller & Minnie      P. C. P & Amanda
Oc. Laborer      M. Clarence W. Taylor

Date: 11-12-1927
John Basley Fowler      Viola Kennedy Riffe
A. 37 W. Surrey, NC      A. 36 W. McDowell, WV
P. Henry & Martha      P. Wm. & Ellen Kennedy
Oc. Carpenter      M. Clarence W. Taylor

Date: 11-17-1927
Curtys A. Catron      Thelma Ann Sarver
A. 21 S. Bland      A. 18 S. Bland
P. John & Margaret      P. E. W. & Maggie
Oc. Farmer      M. F. M. Radford

Date: 11-23-1927
Wm. Stant Underwood      Masie Elvira Starling
A. 34 S. Floyd      A. 17 S. Bland
P. John & Retta      P. B. F. & Sarah C.
Oc. Miner      M. J. E. Graham

Date: 11-26-1927
Lonnie Maxfield      Belva Gladys Stump
A. 27 W. Russell      A. 18 S. Montgomery
P. Hugh & Annie      P. N. E. & Sallie
Oc. Farmer      M. Clarence W. Taylor

Date: 12-21-1927
Aubrey Wiley      Bessie Jones
A. 26 S. Bland      A. 22 S. Smyth
P. Rob't & Mary      P. John J. & Laura
Oc. Farmer      M. J. E. Graham

Date: 12-28-1927
Edd Stuart      Reba M. Melvin
A. 30 S. Pulaski      A. 22 S. WV
P. W. D. & Sallie M.      P. J. C. & Ella
Oc. Farmer      M. L. D. Mayberry
Married in Pulaski

Date: 2-1-1928
Robt Lee Harner      Henrietta Leona Harmon
A. 34 S. Bland      A. 24 S. Bland
P. B. W. P. Harner &      P. S. T. Harman &
Nancy Carr      Macie Groseclose
Oc. Farmer      M. J. W. Stewart

Date: 2-23-1928
Emanuel Peaco | Laura Hounshell
A. 23 S. Smyth | A. 24 S. Bland
P. James Peaco & | P. Wm. Hounshell &
Rhoda Thomas | Minnie Umbarger
Oc. Farmer | M. Clarence W. Taylor

Date: 3-13-1928
Clayton French | Minnie French
A. 19 S. Bland | A. 16 S. Bland
P. I. E. French | P. Dave French
& Alice Chapman | & Sallie Burton
Oc. Mechanic | M. J. E. Graham

Date: 3-14-1928
Charlie Cassell | Mandie Saunders
A. 21 S. Bland | A. 16 S. Bland
P. Chas A. Cassell | P. W. V. Saunders
& Nettie Saunders | & R. M. French
Oc. Mechanic | M. G. C. Looney

Date: 3-26-1928
Roy Shupe | Lucile King
A. 23 S. Smyth | A. 17 S. Wythe
P. Jas. Shupe | P. Robert King
& Lottie Cregger | & Eva Gullian
Oc. Farmer | M. J. W. Stewart

Date: 4-6-1928
Kent Henry Robertson | Gillie Frances Morehead
A. 39 W. Bland | A. 28 S. Bland
P. W. T. Robertson | P. Jas. Magruder
& Mary E. Henderson | & Melinda Jane Strader
Oc. Farmer | M. J. E. Graham

Date: 4-12-1928
Ernest Edward Clements | Lena Ruth Harman
A. 18 S. Maben, WV | A. 18 S. Bland
P. Ed. Clements | P. Jas Wesley Hoge
& Cindy Baker | & Mary Va. Kitts
Oc. Sawmilling | M. G. C. Looney

Begin Page 77 of Original Book
Date: 9-15-1928
Mark Price | Anna Belle Parks
A. 24 D. Montgomery | A. 16 S. Grayson
P. J. Floyd Price | P. J. W. Parks
& Nimmie M. Hurt | & Loura Combs
Oc. Farmer | M. R. L. Parks

Date: 9-22-1928
Jno Andy Walker Pauley | Mollie E. Hounshell
A. 24 S. Bland | A. 23 S. Bland
P. Creed F. Pauley | P. Chas M. Hounshell
& Martelia Ann Kitts | & Lillie Peak
Oc. Farmer | M. Otis C. Brown

Date: 9-28-1928
Cloyd Crockett Morris | Reba Jane Tibbs
A. 28 S. Giles | A. 20 S. Bland
P. S. V. Morris | P. Mazappe Cooly Tibbs
& Octavia Miller | & Margaret A. Groseclose
Oc. Farmer | M. J. W. Stewart

Date: 5-2-1928
Rob't Marvin Crabtree | Iva May Robinett
A. 35 S. Tazewell | A. 25 D. Bland
P. W. H. Crabtree | P. R. R. Robinett
& Mary E. Kinzer | & Fannie Stowers
Oc. Farmer | M. C. W. Hancock

Date: 5-5-1928
Henry Hugh Pruett | Eva Belle Williams
A. 20 S. Bland | A. 17 S. Bland
P. Hugh Pruett | P. Eugene Williams
& Pearlie Nunn | & Pet. Albert
Oc. Farmer | M. R. L. Parks

Date: 5-8-1928
Grover Wise Stowers | Nellie Alice Stowers
A. 21 S. Bland | A. 23 S. Bland
P. H. P. Stowers | P. Frank S. Stowers
& America Robinett | & Belle Wilson
Oc. Farmer | M. Otis C. Brown

Date: 5-15-1928
Wade Cox | Virgie Gibson
A. 21 S. Bland | A. 16 S. Bland
P. A. B. Cox | P. Willie H. Gibson
& Mary Brown | & Mollie Richardson
Oc. Farmer | M. C. W. Hancock

Date: 6-11-1928
Robert Craig Loeffel | Effie Marie Bird
A. 39 S. Tazewell | A. 22 S. Tazewell
P. Louis E. Loeffel | P. Geo Thos. Bird
& Julia A. Thornton | & Carrie Louise Burton
Oc. Banking | M. W. A. McCormack

Date: 6-13-1928  
Albert Lee Miller     Edna Ruth Dehart  
A. 22 S. Bland     A. 22 S. Bland  
P. Jas. L. Miller     P. Frank Dehart  
& Mellie Bird     & Kizzie Strock  
Oc. Farmer     M. C. A. Brown  
Married in Narrows

Date: 6-18-1928  
Doak Clinton Stowers     Elsie Ann Fox  
A. 22 S. Bland     A. 23 S. Bland  
P. H. Clint. Stowers     P. S. W. Fox  
& Ella Jones     & Hester Kidd  
Oc. Clerking     M. Otis C. Brown

Date: 6-27-1928  
Jas. Melvin Muffley     Rita Mays Hoilman  
A. 27 S. Nappone, Ind     A. 19 S. Bland  
P. James Muffley     P. T. G. Hoiliman  
& Margaret Helsol     & Jaynette Harman  
Oc. Lineman     M. R. L. Parks

Date: 7-14-1928  
Kelly Adams     Maude Nicewander  
A. 34 S. Wythe     A. 23 S. Bland  
P. Thos. Adams     P. Ed Nicewander  
& Esther Hudson     & Bessie Hughes  
Oc. Bricklayer     M. Otis C. Brown

Date: 8-17-1928  
Kerry Hubert Clemons     May Davis  
A. 25 S. Bland     A. 28 W. Buchanan  
P. J. H. Clemons     P. Jno. W. Davis  
& Emma Pugh     & Porbana? Cleverger  
Oc. Farmer     M. J. E. Graham

Date: 8-19-1928  
Eugene Walter Bowles     Nellie Kate Kimberlin  
A. 21 S. Bland     A. 25? S. Bland  
P. C. W. Bowles     P. W. D. Kimberlin  
& Mahulda Munsey     & Blanche Barnett  
Oc. Sawmilling     M. G. C. Looney

Date: 10-12-1928  
Raymond Douper Williams Elizabeth Clair Honaker  
A. 31 S. Pembroke     A. 21 S. Bland  
P. Jno Floyd Williams & P. Jas. Cline Honaker  
Alma Shelbourne Douper & Sallie Jarrell  
Oc. Postmaster/Merchant M. B. V. Twitzer  
Married in Roanoke

Date: 6-14-1928  
Samuel C. Bogle     Helen Dalton  
A. 55 W. Bland     A. 17 S. Bland  
P. Freeling Clay Bogle     P. Ballard Dalton  
& Martha Jane Bogle     & Lucy Hull  
Oc. Farmer     M. Otis C. Bown

Date: 6-27-1928  
Albert Thos Pauley     Ruby Hazel Tickle  
A. 25 S. Bland     S. 18 S. Bland  
P. Harve B. Pauley     P. Wm. N. Tickle  
& Julia Hancock     & Lizzie Hancock  
Oc. Farmer     M. J. E. Graham

Date: 7-7-1928  
Noah Perlie Stockner     Lois Lillian Bernard  
A. 30 S. Carroll     A. 15 S. Bland  
P. Jacob W. Stockner     P. John S. Bernard  
& Zilla Estelle Bramer     & Eula Lee Gordon  
Oc. Teacher     M. G. C. Looney

Date: 80801928  
Barger M. Shutt     Eva M. Smith  
A. 21 S. Rock, WV     A. 22 S. Buchanan  
P. Jefferson Shutt     P. John Smith  
& Mollie Bailey     & Gillie Shrader  
Oc. Soldier     M. Otis C. Brown

Date: 8-25-1928  
Giles Sarver     Nellie Clark  
A. 20 S. Bland     A. 17 S. Bland  
P. J. W. Sarver     P. W. J. Clark  
& Geneva Clark     & Maudie Bailey  
Oc. Farmer     M. C. W. Hancock

Date: 8-25-1928  
Ephiram Stacy     Minnie Wayne Pauley  
A. 30 W. Scott     A. 22 D. Bland  
P.     P. Ed. Pauley  
& Vine Stacy     & Nannie Kelley  
Oc. Logger     M. Otis C. Brown

Date: 10-8-1928  
Wayne Edwin Snow     Marie Updyke  
A. 21 S. Lambsburg     A. 20 S. Bland  
P. E. V. Snow     P. A. G. Updyke  
& Grace Wilburn     & Bertha Mustard  
Oc. Salesman     M. Clarence W. Taylor

Date: 10-1-1928
Raymond Earl Davis        Thelma Hamblin
A. 21 S. Northfork, WV    A. 18 S. Bland
P. Henry H. Davis         P. Edward Lee Hamblin
& Victoria A. Davis       & Ollie A. Millirons
Oc. Farmer                M. Clarence W. Taylor

Date: 10-13-1928
Jesse I. Perdue           Florence Beulah Clark
A. 19 S. Giles            A. 18 S. Bland
P. James Perdue           P. Andy Clark
& Isabelle Blankenship    & Izora Stowers
Oc. Farming               M. H. G. Gearhart

Date: 12-23-1928
Hubert Baker Hamilton     Argie Clark
A. 22 S. Bland            A. 16 S. Bland
P. S. H. Hamilton         P. Meek Clark
& Ada Chewning            & Della Morris
Oc. Timber cutter         M. C. L. Hancock

Date: 12-24-1928
Rufus Hubert Fizer        Eula Va. Clark
A. 28 S. Giles            A. 22 S. Bland
P. Estel Fizer            P. James Clark
& Elvira French           & Berte Burton
Oc. Farming               M. C. W. Hancock

Date: 12-25-1928
Wm. Patton French         Ada Glorice Myers
A. 22 S. Bland            A. 24 S. Bland
P. W. S. French           P. Gordon Myers
& Gillie Thompson         & Laura Blankenship
Oc. Farmer                M. Clarence W. Taylor

Begin Page 78 of Original Book
Date: 1-30-1929
Terry Chaffin Davis       Julia Rose Millirons
A. 28 S. Bland           A. 21 S. Bland
P. J. H. Davis            P. R. Lee Millirons
& Julie M. Akers          & Annie K. King
Oc. Tanner                M. Clarence W. Taylor

Date: 3-6-1929
John Davidson King        Willie Marie Kitts
A. 19 S. Bland           A. 16 S. Bland
P. H. N. King             P. Wm. Kitts
& Susan Gray              & Myrtle Hancock
Oc. Farmer                M. Clarence W. Taylor

Date: 10-20-1928
Otis Victor Estep         Kathleen Hall
A. 20 S. Scott            A. 18 S. Lee
P. Thomas Estep           P. John Hall
& Lou Owens               & Rebecca Salley
Oc. Sawmilling            M. G. S. Wagner

Date: 11-26-1928
Roosevelt Dalton          Etta Meadows
A. 21 S. Bland           A. 35 S. Bland
P. Ballard Dalton         P. Frank Meadows
& Lucy Hull               & Eliza Rhinehart
Oc. Farmer                M. C. W. Taylor

Date: 12-22-1928
Clarence Walter Presley   Elizabeth Cooper
A. 21 S. Russell          A. 21 S. Emorysville, TN
P. Arthur Presley         P. Wm. Cooper
& Nannie Music            & Dora Wilson
Oc. Lumber Inspector      M. Clarence W. Taylor

Date: 12-25-1928
James Annis Stephens      Gladys Orey
A. 20 S. Bland           A. 19 S. Bland
P. James Stephens         P. W. M. Orey
& Flora A. Flick          & Alice Day
Oc. Farmer                M. R. L. Parks

Date: 12-26-1928
Dale David Duncan         Mary Stacy
A. 21 S. Wathington       A. 22 S. Scott
P. Will Duncan            P. John Stacy
& Stella Webb             & Dora Rhoton
Oc. Logging               M. G. C. Looney

Date: 2-6-1929
Lennie Wm. Wagner         Clara Burton Stowers
A. 22 S. Bland           A. 24 S. Bland
P. Emory H. Wagner        P. J. M. Stowers
& Mollie E. Morehead      & Amanda McFarland
Oc. Mechanic              M. Clarence W. Taylor

Date: 1-13-1929
George Jones              Rita McKinney
A. 21 Union, WV          A. 21 S. Mercer
P. D. A. Jones            P. Elbert McKinney
& Mary Bivens             & Alice Clemons
Oc. Laborer               M. Clarence W. Taylor

Date: 3-23-1929
Clifford Combs
A. 24 S. Russell
P. Walter Combs
& Belle Ray
Oc. Lumberman

Lona Bailey
A. 25 S. Tazewell
P. John Bailey
& Jennie Strouth
M. Clarence W. Taylor

Date: 3-27-1929
Geo. Edward Lane
A. 21 S. Scott
P. Hop Lane
& Melissa Sluss
Oc. Lumberman

Amy Pearl Kitts
A. 14 S. Bland
P. J. M. Kitts
& Leona Lambert
M. Clarence W. Taylor

Date: 4-10-1929
Harvey Hiram Pauley
A. 43 S. Bland
P. G. C. Pauley
& Mary G. Kitts
Oc. Farmer

Rosa May Penley
A. 38 W. Bland
P. C. W. Miller
& Mary Lou Ramsey
M. G. C. Looney

Date: 4-19-1929
Frank Estel Collins
A. 23 S. Bland
P. John Collins
& Gillie Akers
Oc. Farmer

Rose Catherine Handcock
A. 19 S. Bland
P. S. H. Handcock
& Carrie Hancock
M. Otis C. Borwn

Date: 4-27-1929
Hurley Peery Anderson
A. 21 S. Wythe
P.
& Emma Lou Anderson
Oc. Teamster

Lillie Marie Perkey
A. 22 S. Bland
P. P. W. Perkey
& Eliza M. Lambert
M. Clarence W. Taylor

Date: 5-8-1929
Frank Chapplin Kidd
A. 22 S. Bland
P. H. H. Kidd
& Ollie V. Yost
Oc. Farmer

Ollie Ruth Blessing
A. 18 S. Bland
P. J. H. Blessing
& Stella Kidd
M. Otis C. Brown

Date: 5-21-1929
Zelia Shelton Harden
A. 26 S. Bland
P. David M. Harden
& Mary T. Neal
Oc. Farmer

Ida Kemp Dillow
A. 20 S. Bland
P. H. H. Dillow
& Nannie Pauley
M. Clarence W. Taylor

Date: 5-23-1929
Eugene Morris
A. 21 S. Pulaski
P. James W. Morris
& Lucy Morris
Oc. Lumberman

Mabel Marie Tibbs
A. 18 S. Bland
P. M. C. Tibbs
& Mararet A. Groseclose
M. Clarence W. Taylor

Date: 6-5-1929
Jno Troy Willis
A. 24 S. Pulaski
P. C. P. Willis
& Mandy Wright
Oc. Lumberman

Berthe Bill Cook
A. 22 S. Sparta, NC
P. Wm. R. Cook
& Rose Crouse
M. C. W. Hancock

Date: 6-17-1929
Rob't Franklin Baker
A. 21 S. Bland
P. J. W. E. Baker
& Nellie Kidd
Oc. Farmer

Virginia Rose Wiley
A. 19 S. Bland
P. Rob't S. Wylie
& Mary E. Hurt
M. F. M. Radford

Date: 6-19-1929
John Wiley Burress
A. 20 S. Bland
P. Rob't Burress
& Maggie Tabor
Oc. Farmer

Lettie Ethel Burress
A. 17 S. Bland
P. J. R. Burress
& Corrie L. Kidd
M. Clarence W. Taylor

Date: 6-29-1929
Claude McFarland
A. 21 S. Tazewell
P. Joe McFarland
& Susie Kinder
Oc. Farmer

Nellie Gray Neal
A. 17 S. Bland
P. E. F. Neal
& Minnie Atwell
M. F. M. Radford

Date: 6-29-1929
Jasper Ernest Thomas
A. 27 S. Giles
P. B. P. Thomas
& Margaret Jones
Oc. Sawmilling

Maggie Elizabeth Neal
A. 22 S. Bland
P. L. F. Neal
& Ellie Wynn
M. Clarence W. Taylor

Date: 7-4-1929
James Price Lambert
A. 19 S. Wythe
P. P. G. Lambert
& Lou Emma Cox
Oc. Truck Driver

Ruby Victoria Clark
A. 14 S. Bland
P. Meek Clark
& Della Myers
M. M. Quessenbury

Date: 8-6-1929
Benj. Franklin Roark          Ora May Pine
A. 39 D. Ashe, NC             A. 39 S. Giles
P.                            P. Jas R. Pine
&Rosa Roark                   & Louise White
Oc. Sawmilling                M. Clarence W. Taylor

Date: 8-12-1929
Paul James Thompson           Ledna Maye Davis
A. 23 S. Radford              A. 21 S. Zebulin, KY
P.                            P. R. M. Davis
& Poca Thompson               & Pearl McKee
Oc. Book keeper               M. Clarence W. Taylor

Date: 8-17-1929
Sam'l Garland Babb            Elsie Irene Kitts
A. 27 S. Russell              A. 25 S. Bland
P. Charley Bobb               P. G. W. Kitts
& Rebecca Parks               & Blanche Burton
Oc. Lineman                   M. Clarence W. Taylor

Date: 8-18-1929
Glen Kale Morehead            Fannie Lee Looney
A. 27 S. Bland                A. 18 S. Buchanan
P. Lee Kyle Morehead          P. Geo. W. Looney
& Emmarilla Catherine Miller  & May Neikirk
Oc. Merchant                  M. Clarence W. Taylor

Date: 8-19-1929
Walter English Mills          Grace Dexter Tabor
A. 22 S. Ashland, WV          A. 21 S. Boissevain
P. Billy T. Mills             P. Cleve Tabor
& Georgia Wingo               & Sally Mills
Oc. Miner                     M. Clarence W. Taylor

Date: 9-4-1929
Otis Calhoun Brown            Lela Seagle Mustard
A. 29 S. Pulaski              A. 28 S. Bland
P. Walter C. Brown            P. Newton Shell Mustard
& Mary J. Calhoun             & Ella A. Crockett
Oc. Minister                  M. Clyde J. Walsh

Date: 9-7-1929
Chas Ed. Gibson               Helen Maria Tabor
A. 20 S. Bland                A. 20 S. Bland
P. Wm. Gibson                 P. F. G. Tabor
& Mollie Richardson           & Helen Wolfe
Oc. Farmer                    M. Clarence W. Taylor

Date: 10-10-1929
Frank Gordon Tabor            Bertha Dora Lambert
A. 54 W. Mercer, WV           A. 47 W. Smyth
P. James Tabor                P. George Gilmer
& Virginia Campbell           & Lucinda Herron
Oc. Farmer                    M. Otis C. Brown

Date: 10-10-1929
Daniel Claude Huckabee        Myrtle Lena Harman
A. 32 D. Rockingham           A. 39 S.Bland
P. D. C. Huckabee             P. Newton E. Harman
& Martha A. Brewer            & Nancy J. Beard
Oc. Laborer                   M. C. L. Looney

Date: 10-28-1929
Jas. Richard Clayton          Julie Catherine Jones
A. 45 W. Scott                A. 28 W. Kanawha, WV
P. John Clayton               P. Maleties Dolin
& Lou Kindle                  & Almeda Fry
Oc. Mechanic                  M. Otis C. Brown

Date: 10-31-1929
Roby Grose                    Litha Hager
A. 22 S. McDowell, WV         A. 21 S. Mercer, WV
P. Henry H.Grose              P. Robert Hager
& Sadie Lambert               & Cora Bailey
Oc.Salesman                   M. Clarence W. Taylor

Date: 11-3-1929
Harry Clifford Harmon         Willie Douglas Hill
A. 22 S. McDowell, WV         A. 21 S. Tazewell
P. John B. Harmon             P. Thos. Hill
& Lou Tabor                   & Mary Hopkins
Oc. Miner                     M.

Date: 11-10-1929
Wm. Davidson Tuggle           Wanda May Wohlford
A. 42 S. Bland                A. 25 S. Bland
P. J. M. Tuggle               P. L. P. Wohlford
& Matilda Honaker             & Cannie Sheppard
Oc. Farmer                    M. Stanley H. Haynes
Married in Bluefield

Date: 11-23-1929
Theodore Tibbs                Georgie Brown
A. 24 S. Smythe               A. 17 S. Allaghaney, NC
P. Wm. V. Tibbs               P. James Brown
& Nellie Buchanan             & Emaline Blevins
Oc. Railroading               M. Clarence W. Taylor

Date: 11-28-1929
Carl Monroe DeHart     Dorothy J. Ramsey
A. 22 S. Bland     A. 18 S. Bland
P. John Stern DeHart     P. Chas. Jas. Ramsey
& Lillian Grace Wright     & Ida May Spangler
Oc. Farmer     M. Clarence W. Taylor

Date: 12-5-1929
Chas. Hubert Stowers     Daisy Mae Lawson
A. 33 S. Bland     A. 23 S. Mercer, WV
P. C. F. Stowers     P. Alex F. Lawson
& Rebecca Steele     & Jennie Bell Townley
Oc. Farmer     M. C. W. Hancock

Date: 12-21-1929
Elbert Nelson     Mollie Ethel Lambert
A. 18 S. Bland     A. 18 S. Bland
P. Ira Nelson     P. Alex Lambert
& Vina Hull     & Sallie Sarver
Oc. Farmer     M. C. W. Taylor

Date: 12-23-1929
Warren Glenn Gage     Mrs. Virginia Dalton Davis
A. 42 S. Bedford, PA     A. 36 W. Carroll
P. Joseph Gage     P. John Dalton
& Lucinda Holton     & Lucy Dalton
Oc. Attorney     M. W. H. Bowman
Married in Wytheville

Date: 12-23-1929
Henry Hampton Davis     Ida Augusta Parcell
A. 46 W. Bland     A. 38 S. Bland
P. Henry Davis     P. Chas. L. Parcell
& Margaret Fowler     & Martha Davis
Oc. Farmer     M. Clarence W. Taylor

Date: 12-24-1929
Eugene Wellington Wright     Minnie Edith Ramsey
A. 22 S. Bland     A. 20 S. Bland
P. Wm. G. Wright     P. A. D. Lawson
& Macie M. Spangler     & Ollie Thompson
Oc. Laborer     M. R. L. Parks

Date: 12-25-1929
Carl David Walker     Mary Maddolene Casell
A. 31 S. Bland     A. 22 Wasley, WV
P. H. F. Walker     P. J. S. Casell
& Nina Hicks     & Lily French
Oc. Farmer     M. G. C. Looney

Date: 12-25-1929
Minister Wyrick     Bertha French
A. 21 S. Giles     A. 16 S. Bland
P. H. A. Wyrick     P. W. S. French
& Louisa J. Hunter     & Gillie Thompson
Oc. Farmer     M. Clarence W. Taylor

Franklin, Sam. 31
Francisco, F. L. 153
French, A. 52-55
French, B. 64-150
French, C. 161
French, David 68
French, Estil 71
French, F.H. 96
French, G. W. 117
French, H. C. 8
French, I. E. 82
French, J.10-59-69-75-77-79-100-139-141-146
French, Josh. G. 75
French, M. 80-160
French, R. A. 13
French, Rufus 6
French, Tim. M. 71
French, W. 12-27- 60-116-129-136-154-164
Frey, Stephen V. 33
Fry, E. B. 110
Fry, Lafayette 69
Fugate, H.M. 92
Fulkenson, C.H.C. 16
Furguson, C.T. 155
Furgusson, W. M. 47
Gaskins, O.W. 160
Garvin, J. L. 142
Gearing, A. J. 2
Gearing, P. G. 46
Gibson, C. 126-166
Gibson, Geo. W. 30
Gibson, J. 36-145
Gibson, S.S. 108
Gibson, W. H. 113
Gillespie, D. 149
Gillespie, R.S. 68-156
Gilliam, E.B. 86
Gilliam, I.H. 97
Gills, J. 4-42
Gleason, J.W. 105
Glendy, And. 53
Goad, W.W. 90
Goff, Chas. 41
Gollehon, J. T. 21
Gollehon, W. H. 111
Goodwin, J.D. 101
Gordon, Arthur 66
Gordon, I. R. 147

Gordon, F. R. 147
Gordon, J. 100-130
Gordon, Taylor 69
Gravely, J. H. H. 52
Gray, W. 88-107-116 -144
Grayson, C.R. 88
Grayson, J. 48-119
Grayson, L. 93-114
Graves, B.D. 3
Green, C. 26
Green, Jackson 26
Green, J. W. 32
Green, Thos. A. 15
Green, W.D. 104
Greever, M. L. 141
Gregory, Jno B. 69
Gregory, J. C. 48
Gregory, E. R. 124
Gregory, T. E. 1
Grose, Roby 166
Groseclose, A. D. 19
Groseclose, C. S. 112
Groseclose, D. 50-84
Groseclose, G.W. 24
Groseclose, H. 40-108
Groseclose, Henry 12
Groseclose, J.A.T. 9
Groseclose, J. H. 20
Groseclose, J. 7-20-61-83
Groseclose, L. 19-107
Groseclos, R. L. 131
Groseclose, S. K. 74
Groseclose, T. H. 22
Groseclose, W.J. 101
Gross, E.S. 80
Gross, Jas. S. 60
Gross, J. M. 32
Grubb, C. A. 41
Gullian, J.W. 54
Gullion, W. W. 4
Gusler, H. M. 136
Gusler, J. A. 158
Gusler, R. L. 137
Gusler, S. A. 141
Guy, Geo. M. 51
Guy, Sam'l W. 57
Gylpin, J. F. 48
Haden, Dan. 51
Haga, W.C.

107
Hagan, C.A. 92
Hager, A.B. 154
Hager, C. 132-152
Hager, G. 135
Hager, I.M. 91
Hager, J.R. 25
Hager, Lewis 10
Hager, N. E. 58
Hager, R. 59-101-127-136
Hager, S. B. 51
Hager, Wm. A. 64
Hailey, G. E. 140
Hale, Wm. H. 28
Hall, A. G. 35
Hall, C. 99-114-150
Hall, G. E. 60
Hall, H. K. 139
Hall, J. 39-97
Hall, P. M. 132
Hall, R. 62- 63-77-119
Hall, S. 5- 15
Hall, T.M. 84
Hall, W. 134-145
Halsey, J. T. 65
Halsey, T.J. 49
Hamblin, E. C. 156
Hamblin, G. C. 157
Hamblin, H. 79-140
Hamilton, A. L. 134
Hamilton, G. 79-145
Hamilton, H. B. 164
Hamilton, J. M. 21
Hamilton, K.O. 116
Hamilton, S. M. 34
Hamilton, T.. B. 7
Hamilton, W. A. 78
Hamilton, W. 8-34-141-148
Hancock, C. 79-143
Hancock, E. 61-99
Hancock, Geo. 43-52
Hancock, J. H. 76-91
Hancock, J. 43-137
Hancock, M. 31-119
Hancock, N. B. 55
Hancock, P. T. 7-52
Hancock, R. 18-134-154
Hancock, S. 115-156

Hancock, W.L. 45
Hankala, W. C. 105
Hanks, C. T.? 51
Hannah, A. L. 6
Hanshew, D. 38-148
Hanshew, E.W. 66
Hanshew, R. E. 157
Hanshew, H. 59-62-106
Hanshew, T. J. 33
Harden, C.C. 132
Harden, H. 112-152
Harden, S. 22 -108
Harden, W. M. 113
Harden, Z. S. 165
Hardy, H. E. 121
Hare, J.M. 115
Hare, Monte 137
Hare, W. H. 152
Harley, Phlegar 33
Harman, A. 21-80
Harman, B. B. 37
Harman, C. 39-41
Harman, D. L. 2-84
Harman, G. 67-145
Harman, H. C. 166
Harman, Jas. 32
Harman, John H. 59
Harman, J. W. 17-65
Harman, Newt.E. 54
Harman, O.V. 95
Harman, P. 14-36
Harman, R. 33
Harman, S. M. 152
Harman, T.T. 95
Harman, W. 31-76-109
Harman, Wm. N. 36
Hamon, R. 145
Harmon, M. S. 130
Harner, E. 113
Harner, L. L. 141
Harner, R.L. 161
Harner, W. R. 149
Hart, G. N. 108
Hart, J.H. 125
Hart, W.P. 118
Hatch, John 37
Havens, G. D. 12
Havens, H. J. 11
Havens, M. C. 138

4

| | | | |
|---|---|---|---|
| Havens, N. M. 7 | Hobbs, A. L. 150 | Ingram, S. V. 95 | Kidd, K. M. 135 |
| Havens, J. 7-18-45 | Hobbs, W. 95 | Irvin, N. A. 40 | Kidd, R.C. 81 |
| Havens, R. 131-157 | Hogans, J. A. 149 | Jackson, E. 80-94 | Kidd, S. 29-97 |
| Havens, T.C. 80 | Hoge, Wm. . 51-74 | Jackson, F. 127 | Kidd, Sam. S. 69 |
| Havens, S. 77-81-92-160 | Hoilman, T.H. 110 | Jackson, J.R. 103 | Kidd, W.44-109-116-146 |
| Havens, W. 71-138-143 | Holland, Amos 68 | Jackson, R. 125 | |
| | Hollins, J. 106 | Janney, W.B. 65 | Kimbelton, C.N. 100 |
| Hayden, J. 132 | Hollyfield, C.M. 121 | Jarrell, Chas. L. 78 | Kimberlin, J. J. 77 |
| Haymore, E. 149 | Honaker, A. B. 22 | Jarrett, A.B. 113 | Kimberlin, T. 156 |
| Haynes, A. F. 33 | Honaker, J.17-25-103 | Jessup, J.F. 53 | Kimberling, A.A. 69 |
| Hayton, A.J. 87 | Honaker, Wm. C. 2 | Jonhson, E. 133 | Kimberling, E. H. 38 |
| Hayton, Chas. 101 | Horne, J.D. 116 | Johnson, F. 103 | Kimberling, J. 18-48 |
| Hayton, J. L. 150 | Hornbarger, M. L 76 | Johnson, G. M. 64 | Kimberling, L. 158 |
| Hayton, S. M. 154 | Horton, W.M. 123 | Johnson, I. L. 27 | Kimberling, S.S. 13 |
| Hearn, H. C. 2 | Houdashell, F. 145 | Johnson, John 3-28 | Kimberling, G. 155 |
| Hearn, Wm. S. 7 | Houdashell, Jas. 27 | Johnston, B. W. 37 | Kimberling, Wm. 4 |
| Heart, W.R. 52 | Hounshell, C.M. 97 | Johnston, J. N. 61 | Kimberling, W.D 77 |
| Heath, G.W. 103 | Hounshell, E. B. 151 | Johnston, J. C. 36 | Kinder, C. L. 90 |
| Hedge, B. 119 | Hounshell, H. 14 | Jones, C. 76-85-89 | Kinder, J. M. 6 |
| Hedrick, J. 30-63 | Hounshell, Jos. 44 | Jones, F. 4-138 | Kinder, J. 10-23-147 |
| Hedrick, W. C. 47-70 | Hounshell, W.40-74-138 | Jones, G. 82-146-164 | Kinder, W.P. 109 |
| Heileman, A.S. 109 | | Jones, H. W. 108 | King, Ben H. 76 |
| Heldridge, J. S.G. 8 | Howard, G.D. 98 | Jones, J. 15-27-50-122 | King, E. 22-86-108-141 |
| Hellens, Joseph 58 | Hubble, C.D. 99 | Jones, Thomas 2 | |
| Helmendollar, G. 49 | Hubble, J. 106 | Karr, J. M. 151 | King, G. 2-117 |
| Helmendollar, N. 40 | Hubble, G. 29-143 | Kee, John 158 | King, H. 102-111 |
| Hemger, J. A. 17 | Hubble, W. A. 153 | Keeling, Wm. B. 71 | King, J. 17-35-39-57-164 |
| Henderson, J. B. 3 | Huddle, F. G. 23 | Keen, J. 95-107 | |
| Henderson, Lewis 54 | Huddle, G. 26-143 | Keffer, Wm. H. 10 | King, O. D. 144 |
| Henderson, W. L. 59 | Huckabee, D. C. 166 | Kegley, Chas H. 64 | King, R. 84-154 |
| Helvey, C. R. 75-124 | Huddle, Jas A. 76 | Kegley, J. G. 22 | King, Solomon 6 |
| Helvey, G. 102 | Hudson, C. J. 3 | Kegley, J. J. 77 | King, T. 126 |
| Helvey, H. 108-109 | Hudson, John M. 56 | Keister, C.W. 56 | King, W. D. 40 |
| Helvey, J. 45-112 | Hudson, T. G. 17 | Keith, Jas E. 71 | King, W. I. 35 |
| Helvey, L. 22-151 | Hufford, G. R. 36 | Kellinger, J.P. 85 | King, W. P. 44 |
| Helvey, S. H. 51 | Hughes, Henry 49 | Kelly, H. 105 | Kinser, J. T. 30 |
| Helvey, W. A. 131 | Hughes, J.M. 101 | Kelly, J.S. 120 | Kinser, T.H. 105 |
| Helvey, Wm. B. 13 | Hull, D. A. 157 | Kelly, O.B. 93 | Kinzer, Geo. W. 23 |
| Hetherington, H. 94 | Humphreys, J. 104 | Kelly, R. K. 4 | Kinzer, J. N. 28 |
| Hetherington, J. 110 | Humphreys, S. D. 72 | Kelley, T.R. 98 | Kirby, C.N. 93 |
| Hicks, C. 120 | Hunt, John S. 73 | Kerr, J. F. 44 | Kirby, James M. 61 |
| Hicks, J.W. 31-42 | Hunter, John J. 6-16 | Kidd, A. 6-8-13-16-76-116-156 | Kirby, J. 11-94 |
| Hicks, Jno. P. 17 | Hurt, G. W. 11 | | Kirby, Monroe 72 |
| Higgenbotham, J. 41 | Hurt, W 101-119 | Kidd, C.C. 148 | Kirk, J. 133 |
| Hill, Max. 37 | Hushour, Wm. H. 75 | Kidd, E. 8-49-97-152 | Kitts, A. J. 6-17-44-13 |
| Hill, Ray 158 | Hutchins, J.R. 88 | Kidd, F. 76-165 | |
| Hilton, J.W. 84 | Hutchins, Wm. S. 23 | Kidd, Geo. 23-67 | Kitts, B. 45-45-70 |
| Hoback, D.P.R. 50 | Hutsell, J. C. 5 | Kidd, H. 86-89 | Kitts, C. 19-147 |
| Hoback, J. W. 43 | Igo, J. J. 85 | Kidd, I.W. 56-81 | Kitts, E. 139-157 |
| Hoback, S. S. 66 | Ingram, H. 82 | Kidd, J. 14-75-87-88-143 | Kitts, F. W. 32 |
| | Ingram, J. 136 | | Kitts, G. 18-121 |

6

| | | | |
|---|---|---|---|
| Morris, J. A. 53 | Neece, J. M. 11 | Nisewander, W.H. 67-77 | Patton, T. 110 |
| Morris, S. V. 30 | Neece, T.F. 112 | Noble, B. K. 144 | Pauley, A. T. 163 |
| Morris, W. 120 | Neece, W. 84-95 | Noonkester, E.E. 87-91 | Pauley, C. 41-118-142 |
| Muffley, J. M. 163 | Neel, A. J. 3-74-91-101 | Nowlin, S. 122 | Pauley, D. 112-122 |
| Muirhead, G. A. 50 | Neel, C 45-111 | Nunn, B. L. 5 | Pauley, E. J. 105 |
| Muirhead, G. B. 37 | Neel, C.W. 71 | Nunn, Chas. W. 71 | Pauley, G. 38-43-142 |
| Mullins, L. 160 | Neel, D. E. 17-39 | Nunn, D.H. 108 | Pauley, H. 27-128-165 |
| Mullins, J.H. 81-98 | Neel, Edward 12 | Nunn, H.B. 90 | Pauley, H.S.C. 29 |
| Mullins, S. 112 | Neel, E G. 32-128 | Nunn, J. 83-92-110-134 | Pauley, J. 32-162 |
| Mullins, W. F. 42 | Neel, Hiram A. 1 | Nunn, M.B. 98 | Pauley, J. P.,Jr. 14 |
| Muncy, A. J. 16 | Neel, J.34-43-73-119-120-137 | Nunn, R. L. 142 | Pauley, J.W.E. 85 |
| Muncy, C.P. 61 | Neel, J. 64-128-150-150-152 | Nunn. Wm. T. 66-123 | Pauley, R. 85 |
| Muncy, F. E. 47 | Neel, N. C. 22 | Odell, S. G. 106 | Pauley, Wm. J. 6 |
| Muncy, G. 42-148 | Neel, P. P. 12 | Ogle, T. W. 140 | Pauley, W. E. 143 |
| Muncy, H. J. 44 | Neel. R 47-50-135-142 | Olesey?, Geo. 40 | Pawley, I. G. 46 |
| Muncy, J. 25-28 | Neel. S. 97-127 | Oney, T.E. 118 | Peaco, E. 161 |
| Muncy, Minor 140 | Neel, T 15-24-36 | Orey, John 157 | Peak, J. 32-104 |
| Muncy, Wm A 13 | Neel, W. 37-96-110 116-137 | Ory, R. G. 148 | Pearson, J. H. 11 |
| Muncy, Wm. H. 6 | | Osborne, Ben C. 78 | Peck, J.M. 115 |
| Munsey, B. 124 | Neese, T. 112-144 | Overbay, A.H. 91 | Peck, M. R. 145 |
| Munsey, D.H. 117 | Nelson, I. 120 | Overstreet, J. H 30 | Peery, A.E. 58 |
| Munsey, E.M. 94 | Nelson, J. L. 110 | Overstreet, S. C. 12 | Peery, E. W. 73 |
| Munsey, Jesse N. 79 | Nelson, Rob't 39 | Owen, D.S. 116 | Peery, G.H. 102 |
| Munsey, J.P. 71-150 | Nestor, I. 148 | Oxley, Doc. 117 | Peery, H. E 67 |
| Munsey, K. G. 70 | Nestor, J.M. 119 | Oxley, W.R. 99 | Peery, Rufus 26 |
| Munsey, R.E. 84 | Nestor, V. G. 139 | Page, Amos 73 | Peery, S. E. 143 |
| Munsey, T. J. 72 | Newberry, A. 49-116 | Page, Grif. 38 | Peery, W. E. 42 |
| Munsey, W.H .89-102 | Newberry, D. B. 65 | Painter, G. D. 27 | Pegram, John H. 1 |
| Murcer, J.W. 16 | Newberry, E.H. 146 | Painter, J.C. 85 | Pendleton, W. R. 72 |
| Murrell, H. A. 134 | Newberry, J. A. 114 | Painter, S. G. 131 | Penley, B.H. 83 |
| Musser, L. D. 152 | Newberry, L. M. 42 | Painter, W. 21-87 | Penley, F.J. 101 |
| Mustard, C. 55-79-143 | Newberry, R. S. 135 | Painter, Z.L. 142 | Penley, S. 88 |
| Mustard, E.D. 97 | Newberry, Sam'l 56 | Parcell, T. D. 70 | Penley, W. 104-111-125 |
| Mustard, G. H. 148 | Newberry, T.W. 85 | Parker, B. F. 47 | |
| Mustard, J. H.,Jr. 27 | Newberry, W. 24-79-102-105-143 | Parsel, C. L. 40 | Perdue, J. 128-164 |
| Mustard, J. 15-117 | | Parsley, C. W. 164 | Perkey, T. B. 158 |
| Mustard, J. R. 64 | Newman, K. 98 | Parsell, A. 118-138 | Perkey, Wm. A. 23 |
| Mustard, N. C. 62 | Newman, W.A. 151 | Parsell, E. C. 58 | Perkins, B. F. 38 |
| Mustard, R. B. 67 | Nicewander, A. 148 | Patterson, J. 85-155 | Perkins, Geo. W. 61 |
| Mustard, S. 93 | Nicewander, M. 151 | Patterson, S. 76-119 | Perkins, H.W. 103 |
| Mustard, T.W. 117 | Nisewander, E.L 68 | Patterson, W.E. 53 | Perkins, J. A. 43 |
| Mustard, Wm. G. 8 | Nisewander, G. 16-39 | Pattison, W. 52-79 | Perry, J.G. 20 |
| Mustard, Wm. R. 28 | Nicewander, H. 28-81 | Patton, A. 93 | Poff, Sam 159 |
| Myers, E. 129 | Nisewander, H.W. 54 | Patton, C.R. 135 | Polk, E.C. 97 |
| Myers, John 48 | Nisewander, J. H. 45 | Patton, J. 69-113-127 | Porter, Wm. F. 66 |
| Myers, J. F. 30 | Nisewander, R. 9-24 | Patton, M. 82 | Powers, H. C. 55 |
| Myers, Wm. G. 57 | Nisewander, S. 110 | Patton, Robert 12 | Powers, J. 47-146 |
| Neal, B.A. 127 | | Patton, Sam. 48 | Powers, T. 113 |
| Neece, A. 75-140 | | | Prescott, J. H. 154 |
| Neece, B. 90 | | | |

Prescott, L. L.    153
Preston, Henry    73
Preston, W.    88
Preston, J. T.    15
Price, A.W.    116
Price, C. B.    19
Price, H. D.    26
Price, J. C.    126
Price, M.    162
Pruett, C.B.    105
Pruett, H.    35-52-54-98-162
Pruett, Isaac F.    4
Pruett, J.    3-42-70
Pruett, K.L.    96
Pruett, Otto    137
Pruett, P. D.    49
Pruett, S.    76-102
Pruett, W.    42-82-96-108
Pugh, Rob't J.    34-88
Purkey, A.W.    65
Purkey, Wm. A.    3
Purkey, P. W.    59
Queen, L. D.    109
Radford, K.    133
Radford, M. S.    158
Radford, W.    160
Ragland, J.C.    113
Ramsey, C.    91
Ramsey, Floyd    134
Ramsey, G.    85
Ramsey, H.    85
Ramsey, J.    33-93
Ramsey, L.    126
Ramsey, Otho    141
Ramsey, R. G.    59-72
Ramsey, W. C.    9-72-155
Ratliff, H.    129
Ratliff, J.    3-66-112-128
Reed, J.    84
Reedy, J. A.    83
Repass, A.    110 -151
Repass, C.    151
Repass, E. G.    130
Repass, F. M.    67
Repass, G. R.    133
Repass, H. T.    63
Repass, J.    10-104-

153
Repass, L.D.    62
Repass, M.D.    96
Repass, R.    66-132-157
Repass, S. A.    35
Repass, Sam. L.    57-105
Repass, W. R.    17
Repass, Zeyn    146
Reveley, R.J.    125
Rhudy, J.    69-138
Rice, P.    20
Richardson, A.    107
Richardson,C.N.    144
Richardson, G.E.    150
Richardson, H.    88
Richardson, J.    40 -88
Richardson, S.S.    147
Richardson, W.    115-124
Rider, G. F.    27
Rider, H.    106-113
Rider, John T.    17-125
Rider, S.    124
Rider, Wm.    17
Riffey, W. E.    161
Ritter, D.A.    95
Ritter, E.    93
Ritter, D. S.    73
Roach, Jno P.    13
Roberson, C.    52-78
Roberts, G.W.    85
Robertson, K. H.    133-162
Robertson, J.K.    110
Robinett, A.    96-139
Robinett, C.    33-103
Robinett, Dan'l    18
Robinett, F.    18-19
Robinett, G.    25-89
Robinett, H.    108-117
Robinett, Jas. S.    13
Robinett, Jas. W.    50
Robinett, M.    7-126
Robinett, R.    42-58-93
Robinett, S. B.    79
Robinett, S. S.    9
Robinett, Wilbern    1
Robinett, Wm. A.    8
Robinson, James    61

Robinson, T.    86
Robinson, R.W.    125
Robinson, W. L.    55
Rogers, G.W.    84
Roland, C. W.    65
Roland, M.    101
Roope, J. C.    158
Rorak, B.    165
Rose, A.    127
Rose, E.    104
Rose, Thos. W.    76
Rosenbaum, M. L.    60
Ross, F.    109
Ruble, D.    111
Ruble, H.    111
Ruble, R.    107
Rucker, C. L.    151
Rudder, C. M.    8-28-136
Rudder, J.    157
Rummion, J. D.    24
Russell, M. F.    137
Saddler, E. H.    148
Saddle, Henry    60
Saddler, H. G.    116
Sands, E.    124
Sanger, T.L.    53
Sarver, C.M.    26-29-55-140
Sarver, Giles    163
Sarver, E.W.    115
Sarver, F. H.    143
Sarver, J.    49-51-70
Sarver, L.N.    148
Sarver, S. E.    37-57
Sarver, W.    66-141
Saunders, H.    137
Saunders, R. P.    140
Saunders, W.    102-121
Scott, C.    53-118-142
Scott, Eldred L.    23
Scott, J    92
Scott, L.B.    99
Scott, T. F.    58
Sea, J.R.    91
Sexton, Obediah    76
Sexton, Rich F.    4
Shanklin, H.    132
Shannon, A.S.    120
Shannon, H. W.    44
Sharitz, C. W.    36

Sharitz, E.A.    26
Shelton, T. K.    155
Shappard, H.    42
Sheppard, J. M.    29-64
Shewey, Howard    28
Shewey, J. P.    141
Shewey, Walter    3
Shields, And.    74
Shields, R.    99
Short, Henry    28
Shrader, E.    94
Shrader, D.    91
Shrader, Isaac N.    19
Shrader, J.    8-56-111-121-147
Shrader, L.    91
Shrader, S. G.    36-73
Shrader, T.    14-100
Shrader, W.    86-118
Shufflebarger, A.    54
Shufflebarger, D.    135
Shufflebarger, H.    66
Shufflebarger, J.    41-155
Shufflebarger,T.    73
Shupe, Roy    162
Sluss, C.W.    111
Sifford, Gord.    40
Shutt, B. M.    163
Sifford, J.G.    105
Simpson, A.D.    81
Six, H.    124
Smith, A.    131
Smith, G.    74-99-146
Smith, J.    48-100-126-137-146
Smith, Marshall    9
Smith, Obadiah    8
Smith, S.    14-105
Smith, W.W.    84
Snead, Row. W.    23
Snead, B. F.    78
Snead, Chas. F.    69
Sneed, C. F.    9
Snodgrass, C. W.    69
Snow, W. E.    163
Songer, J. W.    155
Songer, W.A.    116
Spangler, C. C.    34
Spangler, D. G.    148

Spangler, J. 9-90-153

Spangler, L. B. 114

Spangler, M. 145

Spangler, T.J.B. 21

Spangler, W. 22-129

Sparks, R.L. 83

Spence, A.A. 126

Spiller, H. 91

Spiller, W. 82

Stacy, E. 163

Stafford, B.P. 69

Stafford, G. 87-138-138

Stafford, J. 22-115

Stafford, J. W. 64

Stafford, R. M. 43

Stafford, W. 36-105

Stalmaker, R. B. 143

Stanley, C. 123

Stanley, Floyd 131

Starks, C.J.M. 86

Starling, Ben. F. 64

Starling, D.107-108-154-145

Starling, F. 44-131

Starling, G.W. 32

Starling, G.,Jr. 115

Starling, J. 9-78-101

Starling, M.129-130

Starling, T.J. 29

StClair, W. 124

Steel, Eli 3

Steel, E. W. 37

Steel, George 2

Steel, H. 1-22-112

Steel, Samuel 12

Steel, W. 60-114

Stephens, J. 104-164

Stephens, L. 96

Stephens, S. 13-123

Stevens, J. 117

Stitt, C.J. 106

Stimson, James 34

Stimson, L. T. 28

Stimson, O. G. 35

Stimson, S. A. 22

Stimson, S. 15-16

Stinson, C. 102

Stinson, G. R. 155

Stinson, H. 42

Stinson, John 23

Stinson, W.N. 95

Stitt, W.T. 100

Stockner, N.P. 163

Stone, J. W. 155

Stowers, A. 1-40-75-97-103-123

Stowers, B. 83-160-161

Stowers, C. 56-62-105-139-166

Stowers, D. 101-114-127-163

Stowers, E. 7-12-26-89-138-159

Stowers, F. 15-79

Stowers, G. 3-10-89-97-103-162

Stowers, H. 15-90-119-147

Stowers, Jack 11

Stowers, Jas. H. 27

Stowers, J. 53-105

Stowers, John 5-29-53-56-75-135

Stowers, M. J. 38

Stowers, R. D. 159

Stowers, S. F. 38-84

Stowers, T. 121

Stowers, W. 133-147

Stowers, Wm. 2-14-31-87-126

Strock, J. 18-24-138

Strong, B. 106

Stuart, Alex. 63

Stuart, Edd 161

Stuart, S. M. 25

Stuart, W. B. 51

Stump, Jos. B 2

Stump, L. F. 150

Sublett, Jno. H. 55

Sublett, J. T. 48

Suiter, A. T. 14

Suiter, C. B. 72

Suiter, F. J. 23-47

Suiter, H. W. 104-141

Suiter, Jno. F. 63-64

Suiter, W. A. 77

Surratt, J. 25-34

Suthers, W.H. 22

Sutphin, C. E. 146

Sutton, B.R. 45

Switzer, C. 50

Tabor, A. 127

Tabor, C.W. 97

Tabor, F. G. 80-166

Tabor, J. 21-122

Talbert, J.P. 48

Tade, C. J. 139

Taylor, C.H. 36

Taylor, Enoch 146

Taylor, Green 63

Taylor, J. 6-19-117-128

Taylor, W. 16-134

Terry, B. 97

Terry, C.W. 51

Terry, Rob. J. 67

Terry, S.P. 22

Terry, Wm. S. 70

Testament, E. 149

Thomas, B. R. 138

Thomas, C. 28-134-144-157

Thomas, G. 32

Thomas, I.B. 157

Thomas, J. 143-165

Thomas, L. 88-100

Thomas, R. G. 29-120

Thomas, W.H. 100

Thomasson, W.G 30

Thompson, A. 57-115

Thompson, B. 29-57-152

Thompson, C. 53-58

Thompson, D. 7-87-158

Thompson, E.P. 125

Thompson, G. 2-26-108-132-152

Thompson, H. 2-16-20-32-57-131

Thompson, I.K. 127

Thompson, J. 4-5-11-12-34-35

Thompson, Jas.13-53-68-159

Thompson, Jno.54-80-94-106-123-134

Thompson, K. 144

Thompson, L. 46-138

Thompson, M. 44-82

Thompson, P.J. 165

Thompson, O.M 129

Thompson, R. 10-30

Thompson, S. C. 139

Thompson, T. 62

Thompson, W. 5-53-65

Thorn, J.H. 51

Tibbs, A. A. 19

Tibbs, G.S. 31

Tibbs, H. T. 5

Tibbs, J. 10-16-53-57-101-104

Tibbs, M. C. 109

Tibbs, P.A. 33

Tibbs, R.L. 45

Tibbs, S. 35-82-125-142

Tibbs, T. 81-166

Tibbs, W. 134

Tickle, B. 68-147

Tickle, D.L. 50

Tickle, G. 62-89

Tickle, G. H. 32-45

Tickle, H. B. 3

Tickle, L 59-149

Tickle, J. 11-57-149

Tickle, K. 126

Tickle, L.H. 114

Tickle, M.B. 86

Tickle, Peter C. 50

Tickle, R. 94

Tickle, S. 91

Tickle, W. 108-156

Tieche, A.W. 46

Tilson, W.H. 52

Tolbert, C. 60-130-134-153

Tolbert, D. 100

Tolbert, E. 117

Tolbert, J. 122-131

Tolbert, S.H. 39

Tolbert, W. 6-50-155

Townley, C. 153

Townley, M.S.I. 87

Townley, J.W. 20

Townley, T. 141-146

Townley, W. F. 152

Townsend, J.H. 113

Tracy, W. J. 135

9

# INDEX - Females

2

Starks, E. A. 54
Starks, S. J. 34
Starling, B.J. 81
Starling, Dora 76
Starling, E. 113-150-153
Starling, J. 100
Starling, M. 86-96-133-161
Starling, R. J. 102
Steel, G.A. 95
Steel, L. 122
Steel, Rebeaka 56
Steele, Clarissa 1
Steele, M. 1-1
Stephens, M. 157
Stimson, Ada 113
Stimpson, L. 41
Stimson, S. L. 29
Stinson, A. 113-134
Stinson, E. B. 148
Stinson, J. L. 107
Stinson, A. E. 134
Stinson, E. 148
Stinson, L. L. 133
Stinson, M. 29-139
Stinson, R. E. 133
Stone, H. 128
Stone, M. N. 150
Stowers, A.21-47-59-75-86-94-118
Stowers, Bet. 77
Stowers, C. 26-147-164
Stowers, D.M. 65
Stowers, E. 18-30-38-58-71
Stowers, F. 93
Stowers, G. 43-43-72
Stowers, H. A. 36
Stowers, I. 111-113
Stowers, K. M. 152
Stowers, L. 42-69-75-91-134
Stowers, M.2-3-6-23-38-54-72-78-88
Stowers, N.13-53-99-127-162
Stowers, Rach. 29
Stowers, S. 7-7-64-78-88--96-103-137

Straley, N. S. 47-53
Strock, K. 93
Strock, Q. B. 102
Stuart, C. 25-105
Stuart, J. G. 147
Stuart, M. 12-15-116
Stump, B. N. 155-161
Sturdivant, Annie 76
Sublett, B. 110
Sublett, E. 124
Sublett, F. N. 38
Sublett, I. 81
Sublett, M. 27- 45-47
Suiter, Angeline 76
Suiter, Elvina 14
Suiter, Julia 28
Suiter, L. M. 30
Suiter, M. 64-97-117
Suiter, Mira J. 8
Suiter, Rach. M. 63
Suiter, V.G. 33
Surrett, Rosa 32
Surratt, S.A.E. 15
Sutphin, C. 84
Sutphin, L. M. 144
Syra, Letitia E. 79
Tabor, B. W. 157
Tabor, Fan. E. 76
Tabor, G. D. 166
Tabor, H. M. 166
Tabor, M. 72-80-85
Tabor, N. 144
Tabor, R. H. 143
Tade, Ger. A. 73
Talbot, Ollie C. 55
Taylor, E.
Taylor, M. 125
Taylor, Nannie 79
Taylor, S. E. 6
Taylor, V. C. 66
Terry, Ann E. 52
Terry, B. H. 136
Terry, F. 149
Terry, L. E. 14
Terry, Mary J. 21
Terry, N. E. 30
Thomas, A. 90
Thomas, C. S. 144
Thomas, Hannah 63
Thomas, H. V. 6
Thomas, M.L. 42

Thomas, N. 128
Thomas, Jennie 59
Thomas, W. 155
Thompson, A. 5-153-155
Thompson, B.2-60-69-143
Thompson, C. 126-138-140-159
Thompson, D. 3-111
Thompson, E. 13-99-139
Thompson, F.B. 142
Thompson, I. V. 30
Thompson, J. 108-127-136
Thompson, L. 10-12-68-131-140-148
Thompson, M. 8-15-17-40-60-62-66-108-148
Thompson, N. 28-43-46-51-69-81-92
Thompson, O. 40-62
Thompson, P. 158
Thompson, R. 71-145
Thompson, S. 38-42-70-100-135-156
Thompson, V.A. 34-117
Thorn, Eliza. 69
Thorn, Lula M. 65
Thorn, M. 13-69
Thornton, J. A. 24
Thornton, M. 28-140
Thornton, V.P. 53
Tibbs, Alberty 59
Tibbs, E. 55-82-87-151
Tibbs, M. 33-76-77-125-165
Tibbs, N. 68-74
Tibbs, O. 83
Tibbs, P. 106
Tibbs, R. J. 152
Tibbs, S. E. 5
Tibbs, Unia L. 16
Tibbs, V.C. 84
Tieche, L. 120
Tickle, A.H. 126
Tickle, C. M. 72

Tickle, D. 24-106
Tickle, E.N. 27-63
Tickle, Eliz. 25-26
Tickle, Ella 71
Tickle, G. 152
Tickle, H. E. 52
Tickle, Hester A. 17
Tickle, I. A. 45
Tickle, L.M. 151
Tickle, J. 78-89
Tickle, M. 29-120
Tickle, M. E 44
Tickle, M. 53-120-151
Tickle, Mar. L. 76
Tickle, N.G. 127
Tickle, R. H. 163
Tickle, Sarah E. 31
Tickle, S. C. 49
Tickle, V.C. 21
Tieche, L. M. 120
Tilson, H. 84-121
Tilson, L.M. 42
Tilson, M. J. 51
Tilson, Mary V. 21
Tilson, R. 79-151
Tinkey, Viola 140
Tobler, Tena E. 24
Tolbert, J. A 26
Tolbert, M.E. 139
Tolbert, Virgie 136
Totten, R.E. 85
Towe, L.M. 131
Townley, H. V. 160
Townley, L. 124
Townley, R.M. 143
Tracy, L. 88
Trinkle, G. T. 140
Tuggle, A.O. 95
Turley, E. 113
Turley, L. D. 132
Turley, Mar. E. 26
Turley, P. 121
Turner, A. 101
Tynes, Edmenia 70
Tynes, L.B. 101
Umbarger, A. 111-146
Umbarger, B. 146
Umbarger, C. 37-82
Umbarger, D.E. 83

9

www.ingramcontent.com/pod-product-compliance
Lightning Source LLC
Chambersburg PA
CBHW080423270326
41929CB00018B/3132

* 9 7 8 0 7 8 8 4 7 7 7 6 8 *